MW00986568

The Old Farmer's Almanac

Calculated on a new and improved plan for the year of our Lord

1999

Being 3rd after LEAP YEAR and (until July 4)
223rd year of American Independence

FITTED FOR BOSTON AND THE NEW ENGLAND STATES, WITH SPECIAL CORRECTIONS AND CALCULATIONS TO ANSWER FOR ALL THE UNITED STATES.

Containing, besides the large number of Astronomical Calculations and the Farmer's Calendar for every month in the year, a variety of

NEW, USEFUL, AND ENTERTAINING MATTER.

ESTABLISHED IN 1792

by Robert B. Thomas

I wish that life should not be cheap, but sacred.
I wish the days to be as centuries, loaded, fragrant.

– RALPH WALDO EMERSON

COVER T.M. REGISTERED IN U.S. PATENT OFFICE

ISSN 0078-4516

LIBRARY OF CONGRESS CARD NO. 56-29681

Address all editorial correspondence to

THE OLD FARMER'S ALMANAC, DUBLIN, NH 03444

CONTENTS

The Old Farmer's Almanac • 1999

Weather

Features

page 10

page 96

page 186

page 108

(continued on page 4)

CONTENTS

(continued from page 2)

page 88

page 192

Charts, Tables, and Departments

How this 207-year-old Almanac became "old" on its 40th birthday . . .

It's perfectly understandable that so many people erroneously refer to this publication as "The Farmer's Almanac." After all, that was its original title when it first appeared in bookstores and on peddlers' wagons in the fall of 1792. It joined hundreds of other so-called "farmer's almanacs" being published during the latter years of the 18th century, when George Washington was serving his two terms as president. In fact, there were so many "farmer's almanacs" that the term came to mean a certain style of late-18th-century periodical published exclusively here in North America, as opposed to the "philomath" almanacs of England.

To say a periodical was a farmer's almanac, therefore, was to say it was American, was published annually, and featured astronomical calculations for each day of the year as well as planting tables, history, animal husbandry, recipes (for health cures and cookery), and an odd assortment of verses, aphorisms, and other elements. Oh, yes — most included, as did ours, long-range weather forecasts.

In the early American household, farmer's almanacs served the role that magazines, radio, and television do today — a major source of information and entertainment. A single shelf could hold the average household "library" in those days: perhaps an herbal (detailing the useful qualities of plants), a primer, a family Bible, and a farmer's almanac. Most people then had a direct connection to farming — were born on a farm, lived on a farm, had relatives who were farmers, or were themselves farmers. George Washington, for instance, qualified in all those categories.

By the year 1832, when Andrew Jackson was president, our particular farmer's almanac was the only survivor of all those that had been around during the late 18th century. New ones, of course, were still starting up each year, but most were short-lived. Ours, the one you are now holding in your hands, continued not only to survive but to prosper.

Thus it was that 1832 was a special year in the history of this farmer's almanac. It had survived for 40 years. And its founder, Robert B. Thomas, of Sterling, Massachusetts (whose name we continue to include on our cover and title page), decided to make it even more special — by changing its name. He added the adjective *Old,* not to describe *Farmer* but to indicate that his almanac was a survivor, an original. So instead of *The Farmer's Almanac,* his almanac became *The Old Farmer's Almanac.*

Thomas made no mention of the change in his "To Patrons" page that year, and we'd surmise there were probably three reasons. First of all, by this time his almanac was *already* the oldest continuously published periodical in North America, a distinction it has held ever since. Second, perhaps he wanted to do something significant for his publication's 40th anniversary. Finally, there's no doubt he wanted to differentiate *his* so-called farmer's almanac from all the fly-by-night competitors that went by the same name. That reasoning would apply today.

Oddly enough, after including *Old* in the title from 1832 through 1835, Thomas suddenly dropped it again on the ten subsequent editions remaining in his 54-year tenure as editor. Maybe the competition subsided during his last years and he didn't feel it was necessary. All we know is that it wasn't until the 1848 edition, two years after his death, that the word *Old* returned and became a permanent part of the title.

(continued on page 8)

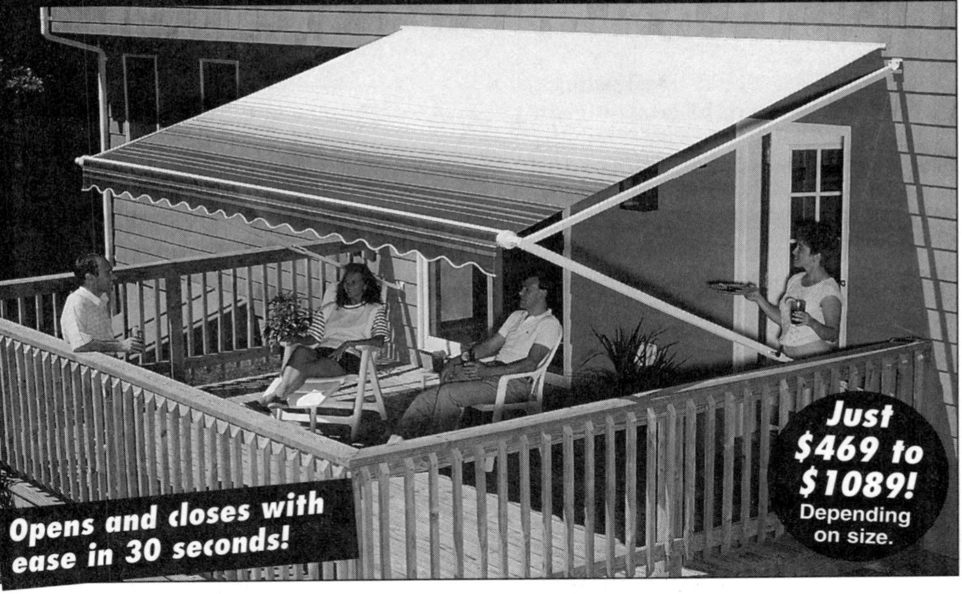

Still, 1832 was the first year we were referred to as *The Old Farmer's Almanac* — and to think that we were first considered "old" at the young age of 40! Who could have imagined then that we would continue on through the Civil War years; into the Gilded Age; past World War I, the Great Depression, and World War II; and through the recent decades — and now, with this 1999 edition, be poised to enter the fourth century in which we've existed? Maybe even more remarkable is that today we're being read by more people (nine million readers last year) than ever.

Maybe the secret of our longevity has been that, in some ways, we've never been "old." If you don't count the recurrence of time correction tables, reference charts, and the like, everything published in *The Old Farmer's Almanac* has always been spanking new, up-to-date, and of *current* interest to our readers, including, of course, this year.

Now, in case anyone is wondering, we have no plans to change our title again. *The Old Farmer's Almanac* is who we are, now and forever . . . although, if pressed, perhaps in another 207 years, like Thomas did in 1832, *maybe* we'd consider adding yet another word to our title — like *Very*. OK?

J.D.H., June 1998

However, it is by our works and not our words that we would be judged. These, we hope, will sustain us in the humble though proud station we have so long held in the name of

Your obedient servant,

Robt. B. Thomas.

The 1999 Edition of

THE OLD FARMER'S ALMANAC

Established in 1792 and published every year thereafter

Robert B. Thomas (1766-1846)
FOUNDER

EDITORIAL, ADVERTISING, AND PUBLISHING OFFICES
P.O. Box 520, Dublin, NH 03444
Phone: 603-563-8111 • Fax: 603-563-8252
Web site: www.almanac.com

YANKEE PUBLISHING INC., MAIN ST., DUBLIN, NH 03444
Joseph B. Meagher, *President;* Judson D. Hale Sr., *Senior Vice President;* Brian Piani, *Vice President* and *Chief Financial Officer;* Jody Bugbee, John Pierce, Joe Timko, and Sherin Wight, *Vice Presidents.*

Printed in U.S.A.

Tastes and Trends for 1999

BY JAMIE KAGELEIRY

Hot Collectibles

How to Predict What's In

■ "Collectibles," states collector Harry Rinker, "lag five to ten years behind oldies radio." Rinker says that oldies stations that used to play '50s and '60s music are now focusing on the '70s.

For now, the psychedelic **1960s** have it. Here's what to look for: '60s magazines, especially *TV Guide,* or *LIFE* with the Beatles or Marilyn Monroe on the cover. Also hot: posters from the '60s and tableware, especially plates and glassware.

Hold on to '70s clothing, TV and movie memorabilia, and toys.

Other standouts: **records from the 1940s** (not Bing Crosby) with photographs on the covers, and sheet music with photographs of celebrities.

And from the **Roaring '20s,** the hot collectible is the **cocktail shaker,** introduced during Prohibition. Watch for vintage chrome shakers shaped like skyscrapers, zeppelins, roosters, and golf bags.

"Tobaccianna" sounds like an opera but refers to smoking implements now seen as art objects. Antique pipes and humidors have doubled in value in the last ten years. Museum-grade antique meerschaum pipes go for $2,000 to $10,000.

Collector Cars (according to *Hemmings Motor News*):

- **1960-1970 Volvo 122: Good for 200,000 miles and nicely styled.**
- **1948-1951 Willys Jeepster: "This sportster is America's last phaeton."**
- **1963-1965 Ford Falcon Futura/Falcon Sprint convertible: "Mustang on the cheap."**
- **1966 Ford Thunderbird convertible: Ford's last convertible T-bird.**

Anything Titanic: We're betting this wave of collecting will continue at least through the New Year.

(continued)

Fashion

Colors

■ A couple of years ago, *Vogue* said brown was the new black. Looks like **gray** will be the new brown for winter and spring. **Blue** is showing up, too — baby blue, misty blue, indigo, and periwinkle. You'll see lots of navy in men's clothing, too.

Styles

■ The shift this year in design is toward the **classics** — straightforward, sophisticated designs. The word for **skirts** this winter is **long,** knee-length or just below, with many to the ankle. **Pleated** skirts will be especially popular. Watch for this "uniform": knee- or ankle-length skirt (often a knit, even cashmere) topped by a gray cashmere sweater or "twin set." **Cashmere,** always a splurge, will be showing up in pants, dresses, and even evening gowns (that would be a *big* splurge). Accompanying the longer skirts will be long vests, scarves, and coats.

Pants, for men and women, will be wide-legged and comfy. For fun, there will be some styles from the **1940s,** a glamorous look (women's hats with "personality," men's roomy suits) from a time when fashion was dominated by Hollywood, because Paris design was silenced by the war. Also, it's a style that looks good on people **swing dancing** and **drinking martinis,** two rages expected to enjoy good shelf lives.

In **running shoes,** watch for the retro gray New Balance shoe, plus Life-saver colors in other brands. **Chunky heels** for women still look good with most fashions. Stilettos are out.

Good News for 1999

No Generation War Here

■ A 1998 poll found that 51 percent of teenagers believe they get along with their parents "very well," and 46 percent said "fairly well." Eighty-nine percent of teens have to tell their parents where they're going when they go out. When asked whom they admire most, 44 percent of girls and 18 percent of boys named their mother (26 percent of boys and 8 percent of girls named Dad).

IQ Scores Are Up

■ Half the children taking the Stanford-Binet Intelligence Test in 1932 scored above 100, and half scored below. For children taking the same test today, half would score above 120, and half would score below. Explanations? Guesses include better nutrition, urbanization, smaller families, and — horrors! — even the increased agility of children's minds due to TV and video games.

A Walk a Day . . .

■ A major study has found that for people in their 60s, 70s, and 80s, walking just two miles a day, even at a leisurely pace, cuts the risk of death almost in half.

Giving Blood Is Good for You

■ A cardiologist at Kansas University

(continued)

Medical Center has found that men who donate blood at least once in three years are 30 percent less likely to develop heart disease than nondonors. One explanation: Periodic loss of blood reduces iron levels in the blood (good for the heart); it could be, too, that blood donors are healthier to start with.

Froggy Painkiller

■ Thank goodness for *Epibpedobates tricolor,* a poisonous Ecuadorean frog. A new painkiller extracted from its skin has all the benefits of morphine but none of the side effects (. . . except for the occasional croak).

More Blueberries, Please

■ Blueberries came out on top among common fruits and vegetables in antioxidant power (the ability to combat cell-damaging free radicals), reports the *UC Berkeley Wellness Letter*. Blueberries are rich in ellagic acid, shown to have potent anticancer effects in lab animals.

What to Watch Out For in 1999

Bungee Cords

■ Just when you thought it was safe to jump off a tower using a bungee cord, along comes this distressing news: Bungee cords, researchers warn, can snap you in the eye and cause serious wounds, increasing your risk of glaucoma.

Yelling

■ It's bad for you. Some otolaryngologists (nose and throat doctors) did a study on 42 drill instructors in an intensive training program. They found that in five days, the yellers had significant damage: swelling of the vocal cords and redness, with permanent damage after long-term abuse. So, KEEP IT DOWN!

Mountain Air

■ This seems crazy — isn't mountain air what cured Heidi? Researchers at Boston's Brigham and Women's Hospital have found that on days when air pollution is relatively high, hikers on Mount Washington end up with worse lung function than when they start out. Truth is, it's not the mountain air that's so bad, it's the city air rising to greet it.

Sleep Deprivation

■ In the past century, we have reduced our average sleep time by 20 percent, according to the National Sleep Foundation. When all time clues are removed, people sleep for 10.3 hours per day, the same as monkeys. But the average American, propelled awake by an alarm clock, sleeps only seven. Lack of sleep causes numerous car accidents and countless episodes of crabbiness.

Eating In and Eating Out

What's In

■ **"New World" fare.** This cuisine features ingredients such as coconuts, yucca, shrimp, mangoes, citrus fruits, almonds, kumquats, and coffee. It focuses on Caribbean cooking but is also used to describe any exotic/tropical blend of tastes, such as Vietnamese soft spring rolls with paw-paw slaw and peanut dipping sauce.

(c o n t i n u e d)

Speaking of tropical, it's now official: **The hotter the climate, the spicier the food.** Researchers compared India with Norway and found that in India, garlic, onions, and hot peppers are found in more than 70 percent of the recipes, and in Norway (land of lutefisk and lefse), barely any of those ingredients are used. The reasons? Hot spices inhibit 75 to 100 percent of the food-spoilage bacteria against which they were tested, bacteria that are far more prevalent in hot regions. Also, hot spices cool people down by making them sweat.

The Fickle Finger of Fat

■ Taste buds win, no-fat foods lose. In 1999, more food producers will throw up their hands and throw *in* a little more fat to make "guilt-free" crackers and cookies more palatable and to keep sales from slumping. Look for more "reduced fat" labels and fewer "low fat" and "fat free" claims. Consumers say they'd rather eat a little less of something that tastes good than lots of the "sugary straw" on the grocery shelves.

The Cost of Eating

■ The average adult will work 40 days this year to earn enough to pay the household food bill (better than the 129 days to pay taxes, though). Only 23 cents of every dollar spent on food finds its way into farmers' and growers' pockets.

It's Just Offal in the UK

■ The newest dining craze in England is the consumption of offal, or innards. Some menu selections that are meeting with praise: pig's-head salad (includes cheek, ears, and tongue on a mix of greens); roast bone-marrow and parsley salad; and chitterlings (pig's intestines) and kale.

Communal Dining

■ Watch for group seating in restaurants, where you sit next to strangers at a big long table. Communal tables rose to popularity during the French Revolution, where they were considered the great equalizers. In New York, strangers sitting next to each other have even been spotted trading plates for tastes.

On the Home Front

■ **Comfort is in,** and what better place to get comfortable than in a reclining chair? **Recliner** sales have been excellent of late, reports La-Z-Boy, the world's biggest producer. In a sign of the times, La-Z-Boy has introduced the "Summit" series of chairs, which include a heat massage motor, cup holder, built-in speaker phone, and extra jack for a modem. A digital answering machine is optional. And it even reclines! Fully loaded, it goes for just under $1,000.

Well-upholstered furniture will include **bouclé,** touted as "the next chenille."

(continued)

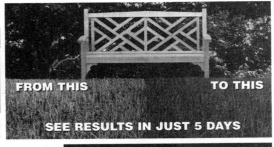

Vintage prints from the 1940s are being reissued. Also popular: leather club chairs, seen as "a sexier lounge-culture alternative to the lounger, especially for baby boomers who are aging," according to one furniture executive.

In the decorating world, green has faded and **blue is big,** especially powder blue (but not too pastel) for upholstery and painted walls. **Citrus colors,** especially toned-down oranges and yellows, will also be popular.

Watch for **double-duty furniture:** Murphy beds, once a symbol of being down-at-the-heels, have made a stylish comeback, with one high-end model in rosewood, complete with a wet bar (for $18,000). Other convertible furniture: beds that drop from the ceiling, and coffee tables that rise up to become dinner tables.

Lighting will take on greater importance as decor: Look for more **paper shades,** which give off a soft, warm glow.

FYI: San Francisco is once again the **most expensive housing** market in the country, for repeat and first-time buyers. The median home price is almost $290,000 and the average home price is $326,000. Orlando, Florida, has the lowest median home price, at $103,000; and Houston has the lowest average home price, at $116,900.

Pet News

Hypoallergenic cats?

■ Cat owners who are allergic to their pets but love them too much to give them up now have a new line of defense: **Wash the cat.** Airborne allergens from cats' sebaceous glands can be reduced by as much as 91 percent by a weekly shampoo. There's only one drawback to this simple cure: Most cats absolutely hate being washed.

Birdcage Syndrome

■ Birds in traditional square or round birdcages are at risk for getting **carpal tunnel syndrome** from walking the too-regular borders of their little domains. Glen Walter, of the Boston industrial design shop called (Eleven), has come to the rescue, designing cages with undulating borders. And for the **dog and the dog walker of the house,** (Eleven) has come up with a leash with a built-in flashlight.

Pupsterity

■ You have a dog you love. He's getting on in years. You'd like to have one of his puppies to keep, but you can't handle 101 dalmatians just now. No need to despair: Bank that dog's sperm. Canine sperm banks are all the rage. The service runs about $300; ask your local vet for a reference.

In Your Next Life (woof)

■ A survey of pet owners revealed that 76 percent feel guilty when they leave their pets home alone, and 61 percent include their pets in holiday plans. If they could choose to be a pet themselves, 57 percent of those surveyed would be a dog; 33 percent would be a cat.

(continued)

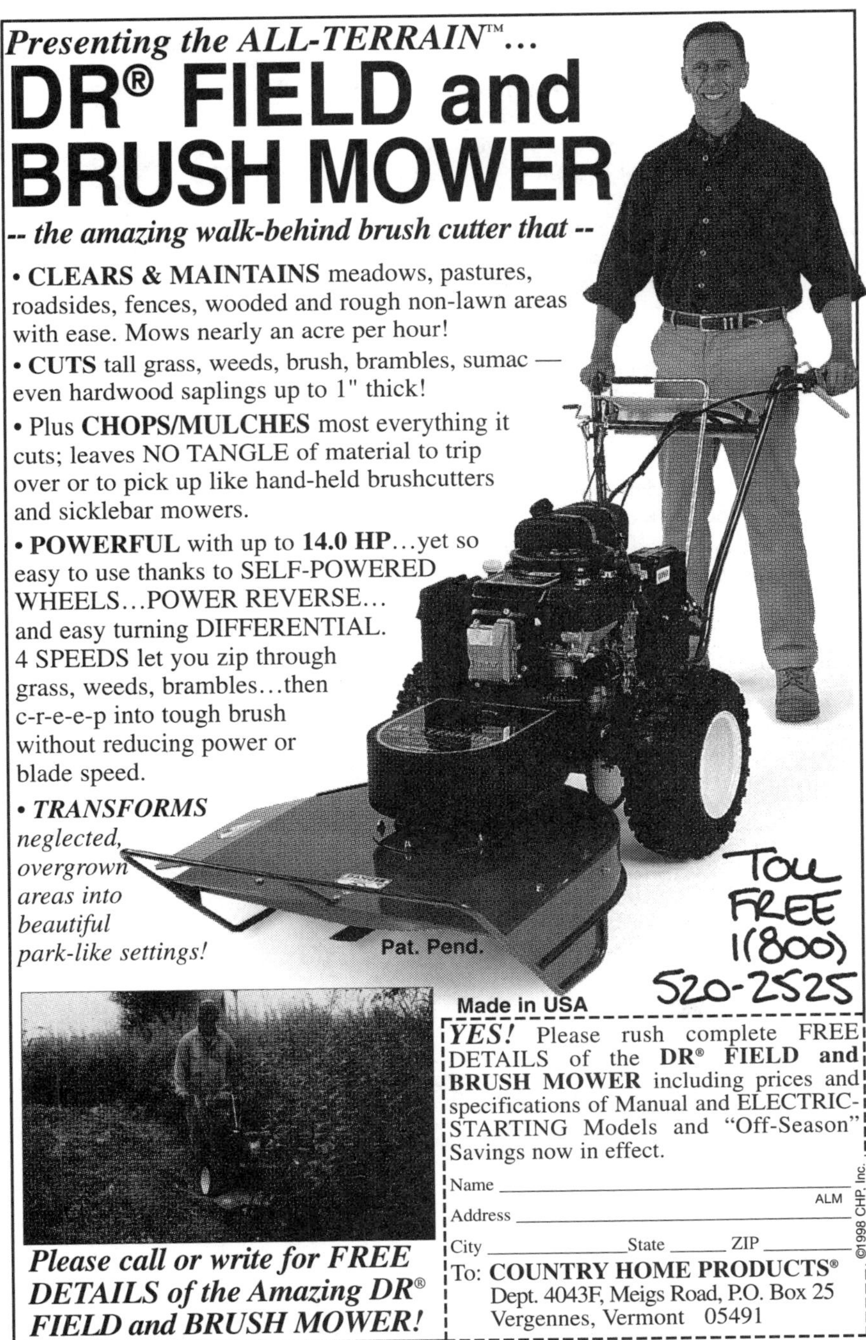

Presenting the ALL-TERRAIN™...
DR® FIELD and BRUSH MOWER
-- the amazing walk-behind brush cutter that --
• CLEARS & MAINTAINS meadows, pastures, roadsides, fences, wooded and rough non-lawn areas with ease. Mows nearly an acre per hour!
• CUTS tall grass, weeds, brush, brambles, sumac — even hardwood saplings up to 1" thick!
• Plus CHOPS/MULCHES most everything it cuts; leaves NO TANGLE of material to trip over or to pick up like hand-held brushcutters and sicklebar mowers.
• POWERFUL with up to 14.0 HP...yet so easy to use thanks to SELF-POWERED WHEELS...POWER REVERSE... and easy turning DIFFERENTIAL. 4 SPEEDS let you zip through grass, weeds, brambles...then c-r-e-e-p into tough brush without reducing power or blade speed.
• TRANSFORMS neglected, overgrown areas into beautiful park-like settings!
Pat. Pend.
TOLL FREE 1(800) 520-2525
Made in USA
Please call or write for FREE DETAILS of the Amazing DR® FIELD and BRUSH MOWER!
YES! Please rush complete FREE DETAILS of the DR® FIELD and BRUSH MOWER including prices and specifications of Manual and ELECTRIC-STARTING Models and "Off-Season" Savings now in effect.
Name
ALM
Address
City State ZIP
To: COUNTRY HOME PRODUCTS®
Dept. 4043F, Meigs Road, P.O. Box 25
Vergennes, Vermont 05491
©1998 CHP, Inc.

The State of Romance in 1999

The Numbers Don't Lie

■ The more education you have, the less often you have **sex,** according to a study in *American Demographics* magazine. High school graduates average 58 sexual contacts a year; college grads have sex 56 times a year; and those with graduate degrees have time for only 50 encounters annually. Other tidbits from that study:

- **Those who work more than 60 hours a week are 10 percent *more* sexually active than those working shorter hours.**
- **Only 5 percent of adults are sexually active at least three times a week.**
- **Married couples average about one sexual encounter a week.**
- **Jazz enthusiasts are 30 percent more sexually active than the average person.**

One of These Days, Alice . . .

■ Ralph Cramden knew it all along. After threatening to send Alice to the Moon, he ultimately always did what it takes to keep a marriage happy: **Let the wife get her way.** Researchers at the University of Washington studied 130 newlywed couples for six years. The marriages that worked all had one thing in common. According to John Gottman, one of the study's authors: "We found that only those newlywed men who are accepting of influence from their wives . . . end up in happy, stable marriages." The men, he says, who "fail to listen to their wives' complaints, greeting them with stonewalling, contempt, and belligerence, are doomed from the beginning."

The most-effective women used a gentle, **good-humored approach** in expressing their opinions.

The Differences Between Men and Women in 1999

Pillow Talk

■ DuPont Co. has recently done research on how people relate to their pillows. Women are more apt to **plump** their pillows to make them more comfortable, and men are more likely to **fold** them. Women are more likely to take their pillows along when they travel. Some of both genders admitted to being emotionally attached to their pillows.

Liquidity

■ Men are more full of it than women — of water, that is. A man's body is 60 to 65 percent water; women have only 50 to 60 percent. Men are probably more watery than women because they generally have more muscle mass.

Fear of Flying

■ According to a poll conducted by Marist College's Institute for Public Opinion, 34 percent of women said they were afraid to fly, but only 14 percent of men felt that way (or admitted to it).

The Cost of a Good Haircut

■ You've long noticed the price discrepancy in services for men and women: Men pay $1 a shirt

(continued)

for laundering, women pay $3. Haircuts for men are traditionally about half the cost of haircuts for women. Now, in New York City and a growing number of other places, laws forbid these gender-based discrepancies. So, will men pay more or will women pay less?

Flipping the Lid

■ A perpetual battle in the war of the sexes involves leaving the toilet seat up (or down). Technology has finally provided a solution to prevent surprise at night and to serve as a reminder: A night-light contraption attaches to the bowl and glows red if the seat is up, green if it's down. At $20, it sounds as if it's worth the price. For more information, call 800-686-1722.

High and Low Tech

■ Look for **one machine that does it all:** a handheld personal computer that does word processing, sends and receives E-mail, takes (and sends) pictures, and records voice messages. Your office can fit in your back pocket!

No PIN to Remember

■ Banks are testing ATMs that **scan a client's iris** instead of asking for a password. Other body parts are also able to be scanned: face, fingertips, and even voices are being tested.

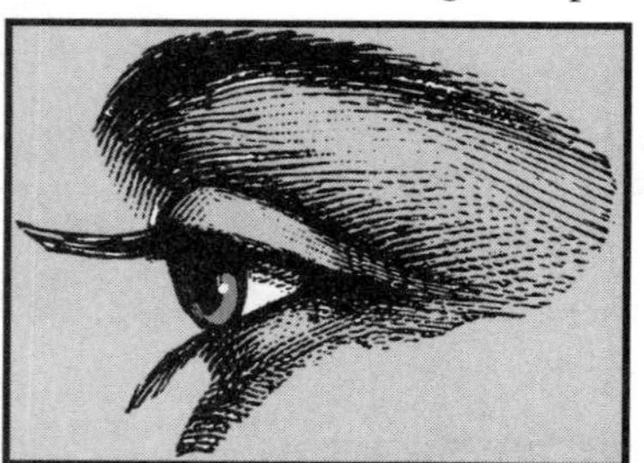

Green Dry-Cleaning

■ A revolutionary **dry-cleaning machine** that uses harmless liquid carbon dioxide and detergent, rather than water and hazardous chemicals, to clean clothes will be on the market before the turn of the year. A fine "green" way to get clothes clean!

Digital vs. Analog

■ According to a survey conducted by Timex, more than two-thirds of all watches purchased each year have an analog face. Consumers may agree with the retired physicist who says he wears an analog watch because **time travels in circles** and an analog watch gives him a truer sense of the passage of time.

Super Flashlight

■ An inventor at Georgia Tech has come up with a flashlight that can "see" through a concrete wall. A beam of microwaves penetrates the wall (it doesn't work on metal) and bounces back information about the slightest movement. Although it sounds perfect for friendly games of hide-and-seek, its best use, we guess, will be by police departments.

The Y2K Problem

■ The last word (or two) on the **Year 2000 Problem:** So much has been written about this major computer glitch that there's now an easy acronym: **Y2K.** And while experts around the world are scrambling to fix the Y2K problem, we hope someone is thinking about a point raised by Michael A. Coffino in a letter to *The New York Times* last spring: Start thinking now about the **Year 9999 Problem.** "Computer users in the year 10000 will probably be upset to learn that the only people who understand the code needed to fix the decamillennial bug have been dead for 8,000 years."

(continued)

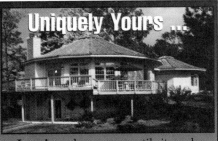

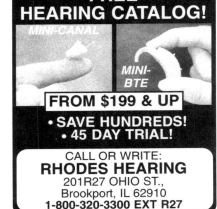

Invention Logic

■ **Words of wisdom on inventing** from octogenarian inventor **Jacob Rabinow,** holder of 230 U.S. patents and 1998 recipient of a Lifetime Achievement Award from the Lemelson-M.I.T. Awards Program: "The inventor has to remember things that seemingly have nothing to do with each other and then put them together in a way that is totally surprising. All creative work is done in this way. And this is the essence of invention."

Agricultural News

■ The outlook for North American farms in the **21st century** is optimistic. Expect **expanded farm exports** due to foreign population and income growth and more-liberal trade policies.

■ The number of **small farms** and large farms is growing. Farmers owning medium-sized farms are finding they must choose: Expand to maintain family income and competition, or shrink enough to hold a full-time job off the farm.

■ Look for **crop by-products** such as wheat and potato starch, rapeseed oil, and flax fiber to be used in the production of paint and the manufacture of lubricants and oil.

■ Farmers can equip their **cows with small magnets** inside the animals' second stomachs to protect them from sharp metal objects they might accidentally consume. The magnets are inserted with a special gun used for giving pills. Ask your local large-animal vet for details.

Demographica

■ In the 1950s, the "total fertility rate" in the world (the average number of children born per woman, per lifetime) was 5. Today that number is 2.8 and sinking fast. When the **fertility rate** drops, the median age of society climbs. In 1990, 6 percent of the world's population was over 65; by 2050, 15 to 19 percent will be over 65, prompting what demographer Ben Wattenberg has called a "grayby boom."

■ The average American plans to **retire by age 62** and live to be 84.

■ Sixty-six percent of Americans plan to spend more money on **travel** when they retire.

■ Manhattan has the country's largest concentration of **people living alone** — 48 percent.

■ Only 5.2 percent of elderly people live in nursing homes. Nearly 90 percent of people ages 65 through 74 report **no disability** whatsoever; even after the age of 85, 40 percent are fully functional.

(c o n t i n u e d)

How to Live to Be 100

■ The Rhodopi people of Bulgaria have the world's largest percentage of centenarians: 50 for every 100,000 people, compared with 39 per 100,000 in Azerbaijan, and 19 per 100,000 in the United States. Here are some explanations for the Bulgarians' longevity, in their own words, as reported in a recent *Boston Globe* article:

"I've studied them, and they have one thing in common. None of them wears a watch."

– Dr. Argir Kirkov Hadzhichristov, Bulgarian physician who has studied the group of centenarians

"I don't like to stay in one place too long. I walk a lot. I never use any medication. I work for myself, do my own dishes and my own mending."

– Slava Todorova Ardakova, 99, Rajkovo, Bulgaria

"You just have to learn how to say the hell with it — the hell with everything."

– Kuzman Kostandinov Varadilov, 94, downing a shot of rakia, a strong homemade brandy

"I take care of myself."

– Maria Chongarova, 103, who sleeps on a small, firm bed covered by a homemade blanket, and uses a wood stove to heat her food. She eats a diet of goat and sheep cheese, homemade bread, olives, beans, fruits and vegetables, and grilled meat, and drinks rakia. (Several of the centenarians smoke.)

"We take natural food, work with the land and with the animals. I get up with the Sun. I have a clock, but I can't read it."

– Minka Asenova Bandeva, 92

"God knows HIS job, and he will give me whatever he pleases."

– Shina Anastasova Iancheva, 94, who shares her home with five generations of her family in Oplacvachka

And from one American centenarian:

"I don't worry about anything. Worry never solved any problem . . . My advice is to go into something and stay with it until you like it. You can't like it until you obtain expertise in that work. And once you are an expert, it's a pleasure."

– Milton Garland, 102, Waynesboro, Pennsylvania. Milton is America's oldest known worker, having been employed by the same Pennsylvania engineering firm since 1920.

The Mood

■ Consumer confidence and success have been driving some trends: baby boomers are paying off **credit cards** — now more than 40 percent of card holders pay their full balance each month, compared with 29 percent in 1990. People are more practical about money. On the other hand, for some, luxury is back: **Boat sales** are booming.

■ But keeping up with the Joneses in the last years of the millennium doesn't mean just what it used to. These days, one of the ultimate status symbols is achieving a **simpler life:** being able to ditch the stockbroker career to go teach.

■ It's striking to note that in a single year, the number of respondents saying that "a lot of money" signifies **success** has fallen from one-third to one-quarter of those answering. Between 63 and 83 percent answered instead that such things as "being

(continued)

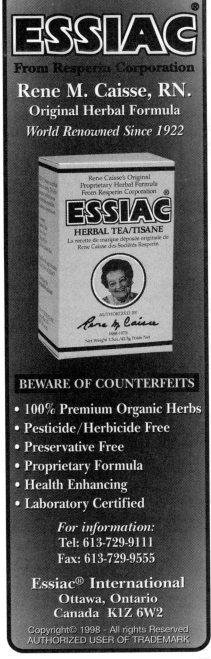

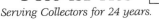

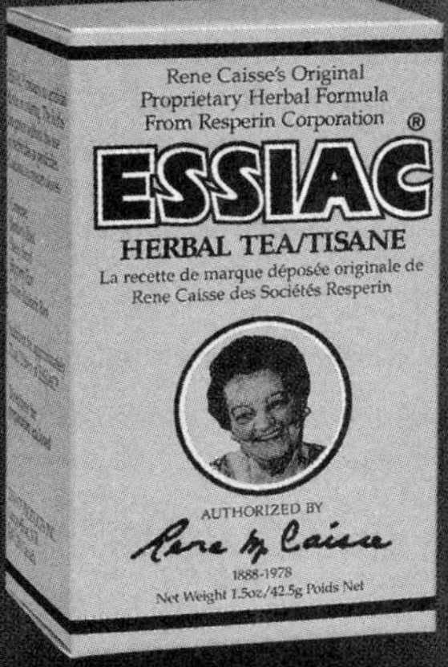

satisfied with your life" or "having a good marriage" or "having successful children" is what success means to them.

■ **Family time** is becoming a priority, and in a striking change in the last two decades, dads are really stepping up to the plate in two-earner families. More emphasis than ever is on **children.** In 1977, dads spent an average of 1.8 hours with their children on each workday and 5.2 hours on nonworkdays. By last year, men were putting in 2.3 hours on workdays and 6.4 hours on nonworkdays. Working women have stayed constant on workdays but put in more time with kids on nonworkdays (from 7.3 hours in 1977 to 8.3 hours in 1997). Parents are getting that extra time not from working fewer hours (the opposite is true) but from spending less time on their own pursuits.

■ It's a funny little thing, but the demand for **old-fashioned public clocks** is suddenly booming (orders are up 70 percent at one producer). "People are trying to get back a **sense of community,**" the *Wall Street Journal* wrote, quoting a Boston architect, "and a town center and clock towers do that." Another reason may be the sudden interest in **time passing,** with the coming turn of the century and the millennium. Attention to the philosophical side of life is strong, with many people expressing longings and concern about **spiritual matters.**

Weirdness

■ According to the *Fortean Times* of London, worldwide weirdness was up a full 4 percent in the last year, the biggest jump since 1993. Increases were seen in most categories, including visits by aliens, instances of spontaneous human combustion, falls from the sky, and sightings of water monsters (due largely to a big jump in "Nessie" sightings). Also up were hoaxes and panics, ineptitude and stupidity, and cults and conspiracies. Dare we suggest the hand of El Niño?

So Long, Farewell, Adios

Sayonara, Living Room

■ In 1997, one of every three new homes was built without a living room. Watch for this trend to continue — in a recent survey by the National Home Building Association, 40 percent of home buyers said they'd buy a house without a living room. This could be contributing to the La-Z-Boy craze: With the rise in popularity of "great rooms," or media or family rooms, watch for more "relaxed," less-formal furniture.

Butchering

■ The craft of butchering is now largely a thing of the past. In the old days, a real butcher served an apprenticeship of many years, learning the subtle but exquisite differences in meats and how best to cut them. In rural areas, butchers often raised, slaughtered, and processed the meat they sold. Most butchers cut steaks, roasts, and chops from hanging carcasses and could easily spot any flawed or unhealthy-looking flesh. These artisans are being replaced by supermarket meat workers, who often don't even know the difference between sirloin and top round. "Outside of the old-timers, it's a dying art," says Scott Rzesa, a director at the fine food store D'Agostino's in New York City. □□

The Oldest (Surviving) Photograph of the Moon:

Samuel D. Humphrey's 1849 Lunar Daguerreotype

One hundred fifty years ago, on the night of September 1, 1849, the nearly full Moon appeared over the town of Canandaigua, New York. At 10:30 P.M., Samuel D. Humphrey slid a highly polished, silver-plated copper sheet measuring 2¾x3¼ inches into his camera, which was pointed at the Moon. He then exposed the light-sensitive plate to the shining Moon nine times, varying the length of exposure from two minutes to one-half second. After developing the plate with mercury vapor, Humphrey sent his daguerreotype to Harvard College.

Louis Daguerre, the Frenchman who explained the secret of the world's first photographic technique in 1839, had daguerreotyped a faint image of the Moon, but the plate was soon lost in a fire. John W. Draper of New York City is credited with making the first clear daguerreotype of the Moon in March 1840, but this also was destroyed in a fire at the lyceum to which he had presented the plate.

By 1851, the Harvard College Observatory was producing detailed, world-renowned daguerreotypes of the Moon, doubtless inspired by Humphrey, whose 1849 daguerreotype is now considered by many to be the earliest extant photograph of the Moon.

– by Randy Miller

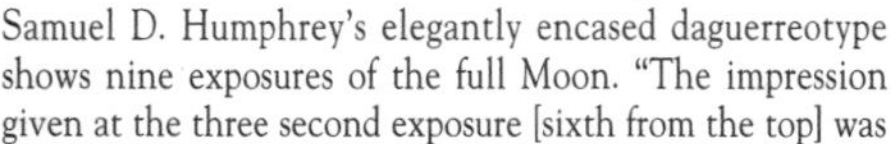

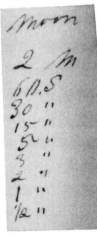

Samuel D. Humphrey's elegantly encased daguerreotype shows nine exposures of the full Moon. "The impression given at the three second exposure [sixth from the top] was the most strongly marked and possessed a free development in light and shadow," Humphrey wrote in his *Daguerreian Journal*, November 1, 1850.

– photo: Harvard College Observatory

How to Use This Almanac

Anywhere in the U.S.A.

Annually, for the interest and pleasure of our readers, *The Old Farmer's Almanac* provides a variety of astronomical data calculated for the upcoming year. It covers a wide range of phenomena — the rising and setting times of the Sun and the Moon; the declination of the Sun; the astronomical age and placement of the Moon and its monthly phases; selected times for observing the visible planets; solar and lunar eclipses; the dates and times of meteor showers; the transit times of the bright stars; and a monthly summary of astronomical highlights.

The Left-Hand Calendar Pages

(Pages 60-86)

Much of the data is contained in the Left-Hand Calendar Pages (pages 60-86). For the enlightenment of our readers, part of a sample page is reproduced below, with the individual entries explained on the next page.

☞ **Please note** that all the times given in this edition of the Almanac are calculated for **Boston, Massachusetts.** Key Letters accompany much of the data and are provided so that readers can correct the Boston times to those of their own localities. Examples given at right clarify this procedure. (Times throughout the Almanac are given in Eastern Standard Time [EST], except from 2:00 A.M., April 4, until 2:00 A.M., October 31, when Eastern Daylight Time [EDT] is given.)

Sample Left-Hand Calendar Page
(from November 1998 — page 60)

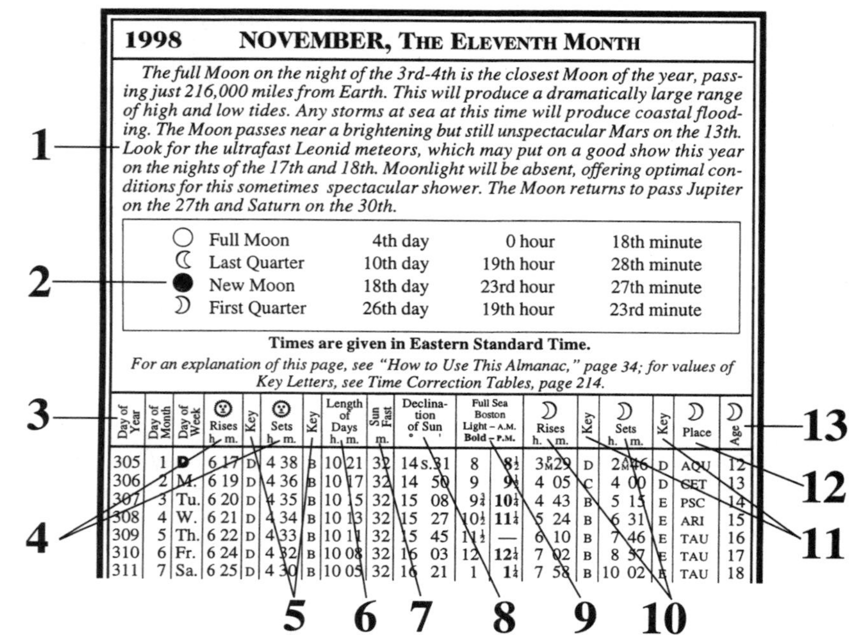

1998 NOVEMBER, The Eleventh Month

The full Moon on the night of the 3rd-4th is the closest Moon of the year, passing just 216,000 miles from Earth. This will produce a dramatically large range of high and low tides. Any storms at sea at this time will produce coastal flooding. The Moon passes near a brightening but still unspectacular Mars on the 13th. Look for the ultrafast Leonid meteors, which may put on a good show this year on the nights of the 17th and 18th. Moonlight will be absent, offering optimal conditions for this sometimes spectacular shower. The Moon returns to pass Jupiter on the 27th and Saturn on the 30th.

○	Full Moon	4th day	0 hour	18th minute
☾	Last Quarter	10th day	19th hour	28th minute
●	New Moon	18th day	23rd hour	27th minute
☽	First Quarter	26th day	19th hour	23rd minute

Times are given in Eastern Standard Time.

For an explanation of this page, see "How to Use This Almanac," page 34; for values of Key Letters, see Time Correction Tables, page 214.

Day of Year	Day of Month	Day of Week	☉ Rises h. m.	Key	☉ Sets h. m.	Key	Length of Days h. m.	Sun Fast m.	Declination of Sun ° '	Full Sea Boston Light – A.M.	Bold – P.M.	☽ Rises h. m.	Key	☽ Sets h. m.	Key	☽ Place	☽ Age
305	1	D	6 17	D	4 38	B	10 21	32	14 s.31	8	**8½**	3 P.M. 29	D	2 A.M. 46	D	AQU	12
306	2	M.	6 19	D	4 36	B	10 17	32	14 50	9	**9¼**	4 05	C	4 00	D	CET	13
307	3	Tu.	6 20	D	4 35	B	10 15	32	15 08	9¾	**10¼**	4 43	B	5 15	E	PSC	14
308	4	W.	6 21	D	4 34	B	10 13	32	15 27	10½	**11¼**	5 24	B	6 31	E	ARI	15
309	5	Th.	6 22	D	4 33	B	10 11	32	15 45	11½	—	6 10	B	7 46	E	TAU	16
310	6	Fr.	6 24	D	4 32	B	10 08	32	16 03	12	**12¼**	7 02	B	8 57	E	TAU	17
311	7	Sa.	6 25	D	4 30	B	10 05	32	16 21	1	**1¼**	7 58	B	10 02	E	TAU	18

1. The text heading the calendar page is a summary of the sky sightings for the month. These astronomical highlights appear on each month's calendar page.

2. This box gives the days and times of the Moon's phases for the month. (For more details, see Glossary, page 42.)

3. Each calendar page lists the days of the year, month, and week, using the traditional ecclesiastical designation for Sunday, called the Dominical Letter — D for 1998, C for 1999. (For further explanation, see Glossary, page 42.)

4. These two columns list the sunrise and sunset times (EST or EDT) for Boston for each day of the month.

5. The letters in these two Key Letter columns are designed to correct to other localities the sunrise/sunset times given for Boston. Note that each sunrise/sunset time has a Key Letter. The values (i.e., the number of minutes) assigned to these Key Letters are given in the **Time Correction Tables** on page 214. Simply find your city, or the city nearest you, in the tables, and locate the value in the appropriate Key Letter column. Add or subtract those minutes to the sunrise or sunset time given for Boston. (Because of the complexities of calculation for different locations, times may not be precise to the minute.)

Example:

To find the time of sunrise in Austin, Texas, on November 1, 1998:

Sunrise, Boston, with Key Letter D (p. 34)	6:17 A.M., EST
Value of Key Letter D for Austin (p. 214)	+29 minutes
Sunrise, Austin	6:46 A.M., CST

Use the same procedure to determine the time of sunset.

6. The Length of Days column denotes how long the Sun will be above the horizon in Boston for each day of the month. To determine the length of any given day in your locality, follow the procedure outlined in #5 to determine the sunrise and sunset times for your city. Then add 12 hours to the time of sunset and subtract the time of sunrise, and you will have the length of day.

Example:

Sunset, Albany, New York, Nov. 1	4:48
Add 12 hours	+ 12:00
	16:48
Subtract sunrise, Albany, Nov. 1	– 6:28
Length of day, Albany, Nov. 1 (10 hr., 20 min.)	10:20

7. The Sun Fast column is designed to change sundial time into clock time in Boston. A sundial reads natural, or Sun, time, which is neither Standard nor Daylight time except by coincidence. Simply subtract the minutes given in the Sun Fast column to get Boston clock time, and use Key Letter C in the Time Correction Tables (page 214) to correct the time for your city.

Example:

To change sundial time into clock time in Boston, Massachusetts, or Casper, Wyoming, on November 1, 1998:

Sundial reading, Nov. 1 (Boston or Casper)	12:00 noon
Subtract Sun Fast (p. 34)	– 32 minutes
Clock time, Boston	11:28 A.M., EST
Use Key C for Casper (p. 215)	+ 20 minutes
Clock time, Casper	11:48 A.M., MST

8. This column denotes the declination (i.e., the angular distance from the celestial equator) of the Sun in degrees and minutes, at noon, EST or EDT.

9. The times of daily high tides in Boston are recorded in lightface for A.M. and **boldface** for P.M. The "8" under Full Sea Boston on November 1 means that the first high tide will be at 8:00 A.M. (The height in feet of some of the high tides is shown on the Right-Hand Calendar Pages.) Where a dash is shown under Full Sea, it indicates that the time of high water occurs on or after midnight and so is recorded on the next day. Tide corrections for some localities can be found in the **Tide Correction Tables** on page 210.

10. These two columns list the moonrise and moonset times (EST or EDT) for Boston for each day of the month. (Dashes indicate that moonrise or moonset occurs on or after midnight and so is recorded on the next day.)

11. The letters in these two Key Letter columns are designed to correct to other localities the moonrise/moonset times given for Boston. The same procedure as explained in #5 for calculating sunrise/sunset is used *except* for an additional correction factor based on longitude (see table below). For the longitude of your city, consult the **Time Correction Tables** on page 214.

Longitude of city	Correction minutes
58°- 76°	0
77°- 89°	+1
90°-102°	+2
103°-115°	+3
116°-127°	+4
128°-141°	+5
142°-155°	+6

Example:

To determine the time of moonrise in Memphis, Tennessee, on November 1, 1998:

Moonrise, Boston, with Key Letter D (p. 34)	3:29 P.M., EST
Value of Key Letter D for Memphis (p. 216)	+ 5 minutes
Correction for Memphis longitude 90° 3'	+ 2 minutes
Moonrise, Memphis	3:36 P.M., CST

Use the same procedure to determine the time of moonset.

12. The Moon's place denoted in this column is its *astronomical,* or *actual,* placement in the heavens. (This should not be confused with the Moon's *astrological* place in the zodiac, as explained on page 168.) **All calculations in this Almanac, except for the astrological information on pages 164-168, are based on astronomy, not astrology.**

In addition to the 12 constellations of the astronomical zodiac, five other abbreviations may appear in this column: Auriga (AUR), a northern constellation between Perseus and Gemini; Cetus (CET), which lies south of the zodiac, just south of Pisces and Aries; Ophiuchus (OPH), a constellation primarily north of the zodiac but with a small corner between Scorpius and Sagittarius; Orion (ORI), a constellation whose northern limit first reaches the zodiac between Taurus and Gemini; and Sextans (SEX), which lies south of the zodiac except for a corner that just touches it near Leo.

13. The last column lists the Moon's age, which is the number of days since the previous new Moon. (The average length of the lunar month is 29.53 days.)

Further astronomical data can be found on page 48, which lists the eclipses and the principal meteor showers for 1999, as well as the dates of the full Moon over a five-year period.

The Visible Planets (pages 46-47) lists selected rising and setting times in 1999 for observing Venus, Mars, Jupiter, Saturn, and Mercury; page 50 carries the transit times of the bright stars for 1999. Both feature Key Letters, designed to convert the Boston times given to those of other localities (see #5 on previous page and #11 above).

The Twilight Zone on page 212 includes a chart that lets you calculate the length of twilight and the times of dawn and dark in your area.

The Right-Hand Calendar Pages

(Pages 61-87)

These pages are a combination of astronomical data; specific dates in mainly the Anglican church calendar, inclusion of which has always been traditional in American and English almanacs (though we also include some other religious dates); tide heights at Boston (the Left-Hand Calendar Pages include the daily times of high tides; the corrections for your locality are on page 210); quotations; anniversary dates; appropriate seasonal activities; and a rhyming version of the weather forecasts for New England. (Detailed forecasts for the entire country are presented on pages 120-149.)

The following list classifies some of the entries from the Right-Hand Calendar Pages, with a sample (the first part of November 1998) of a calendar page explained on the next page. Also, in keeping with the Almanac's tradition, the Chronological Cycles and Eras for 1999 are listed.

Movable Feasts and Fasts for 1999

Septuagesima Sunday	Jan. 31
Shrove Tuesday	Feb. 16
Ash Wednesday	Feb. 17
Palm Sunday	Mar. 28
Good Friday	Apr. 2
Easter Day	Apr. 4
Rogation Sunday	May 9
Ascension Day	May 13
Whitsunday-Pentecost	May 23
Trinity Sunday	May 30
Corpus Christi	June 3
1st Sunday in Advent	Nov. 28

The Seasons of 1998-1999

Fall 1998	Sept. 23, 1:37 A.M., EDT
Winter 1998	Dec. 21, 8:56 P.M., EST
Spring 1999	Mar. 20, 8:46 P.M., EST
Summer 1999	June 21, 3:49 P.M., EDT
Fall 1999	Sept. 23, 7:31 A.M., EDT
Winter 1999	Dec. 22, 2:44 A.M., EST

Chronological Cycles for 1999

Dominical Letter	C
Epact	13
Golden Number (Lunar Cycle)	5
Roman Indiction	7
Solar Cycle	20
Year of Julian Period	6712

Era	**Year**	**Begins**
Byzantine	7508	Sept. 14
Jewish (A.M.)*	5760	Sept. 10
Chinese (Lunar) (Hare)	4697	Feb. 16
Roman (A.U.C.)	2752	Jan. 14
Nabonassar	2748	Apr. 24
Japanese	2659	Jan. 1
Grecian (Seleucidae)	2311	Sept. 14 (or Oct. 14)
Indian (Saka)	1921	Mar. 22
Diocletian	1716	Sept. 12
Islamic (Hegira)*	1420	Apr. 16

**Year begins at sunset.*

Determination of Earthquakes

☞ Note the dates, on right-hand pages 61-87, when the Moon (☾) "rides high" or "runs low." The date of the high begins the most likely five-day period of earthquakes in the Northern Hemisphere; the date of the low indicates a similar five-day period in the Southern Hemisphere. You will also find on these pages a notation for Moon on the Equator (☾ on Eq.) twice each month. These times indicate a two-day earthquake period in both hemispheres.

Names and Characters of the Principal Planets and Aspects

☞ Every now and again on the Right-Hand Calendar Pages, you will see symbols conjoined in groups to tell you what is happening in the heavens. For example, ☌♄☾ opposite November 3, 1998 (see below), means that on that date, Saturn ♄ and the Moon ☾ are in conjunction ☌ or apparently near each other.

Here are the symbols used . . .

☉	Sun	⛢	Uranus
○ ● ☾	Moon	♆	Neptune
☿	Mercury	♇	Pluto
♀	Venus	☌	Conjunction, or in the same degree
⊕	Earth	☊	Ascending Node
♂	Mars	☋	Descending Node
♃	Jupiter	☍	Opposition, or 180 degrees
♄	Saturn		

Earth at Aphelion and Perihelion 1999

☞ Earth will be at perihelion on January 3, 1999, when it will be 91,400,005 miles from the Sun. Earth will be at aphelion on July 6, 1999, when it will be 94,512,258 miles from the Sun.

Sample Right-Hand Calendar Page

(from November 1998 — page 61)

Day of the month.

Day of the week.

Weather rhyme. (For detailed regional forecasts, see pages 120-149.)

The Dominical Letter for 1998 was D because the first Sunday of the year fell on the fourth day of January. The letter for 1999 is C.

Conjunction, or closest approach, of Saturn and the Moon.

23rd Sunday after Pentecost. (Sundays and special holy days generally appear in this typeface.)

St. Leo the Great was elected Bishop of Rome in A.D. 440. By interceding with Attila, he prevented the city's massacre by invading Huns. (Certain religious feasts and civil holidays appear in this typeface.)

The Moon is on the celestial equator.

First high tide at Boston is 9.7 feet; second high tide is 9.4 feet.

D. M.	D. W.	Dates, Feasts, Fasts, Aspects, Tide Heights	Weather ↓
1	**D**	22nd S. af. P. • All Saints • ☾ on Eq. • {10.6 10.8	*In*
2	M.	All Souls • *Flowers in bloom late in autumn indicate a bad winter.* • {11.3 11.1	*the*
3	Tu.	☌♄☾ • ☾ at perig. • Election Day •	*mountains,*
4	W.	**Full Beaver** ○ • Tomb of King Tut discovered, 1922 • Tides {12.4 11.5 •	*the*
5	Th.	Eight teams joined together to form the American Football League, 1959 • {12.5 — •	*first*
6	Fr.	Adolph Sax born, 1814 • *Music is the poetry of the air.* • Tides {11.3 12.4 •	*snow*
7	Sa.	New Jersey became first state to allow girls to play little league baseball, 1973 • {11.0 12.1 •	*is*
8	**D**	23rd S. af. P. • ☾ rides high • {10.6 11.5 •	*falling;*
9	M.	First issue of *The Atlantic Monthly* hit the newsstands, 1857 • {10.1 10.8 •	*geese*
10	Tu.	St. Leo the Great • The *Edmund Fitzgerald* sank, 1975 • {9.7 10.2	*are*
11	W.	St. Martin • Veterans Day • ☾ at ☊ • ☿ Gr. Elong (23° E.) •	
12	Th.	*If All Saints brings out winter, St. Martin brings out Indian summer.* • {9.3 9.4 •	*heading*
13	Fr.	☌♂☾ • ♃ stat. • *You never know your luck.* •	*south.*
14	Sa.	☾ on Eq. • Dow Jones closed above 1,000 mark, first time in 76 years, 1972 •	*We*
15	**D**	24th S. af. P. • Georgia O'Keefe born, 1887 • {9.7 9.4	*pause*
16	M.	6 inches snow, Tucson, Ariz., 1958 • Suez Canal opened, 1869 • {9.9 9.4 •	*at*
17	Tu.	St. Hugh of Lincoln • ☾ at apo. • August Mobius born, 1790 •	*our*
18	W.	St. Hilda • New ● • Tides {10.2 9.4 •	*feast*

For a more complete explanation of terms used throughout the Almanac, see Glossary, page 42.

Holidays and Observances, 1999

A selected list of commemorative days, with federal holidays denoted by *.

Jan. 1 New Year's Day*
Jan. 18 Martin Luther King Jr.'s Birthday *(observed)**
Feb. 2 Groundhog Day; Guadalupe-Hidalgo Treaty Day *(N.Mex.)*
Feb. 12 Abraham Lincoln's Birthday
Feb. 14 Valentine's Day
Feb. 15 Presidents Day*; Susan B. Anthony's Birthday *(Fla., Wis.)*
Feb. 16 Mardi Gras *(Baldwin & Mobile Counties, Ala.; La.)*
Feb. 22 George Washington's Birthday
Mar. 2 Town Meeting Day *(Vt.)*; Texas Independence Day
Mar. 15 Andrew Jackson Day *(Tenn.)*
Mar. 17 St. Patrick's Day; Evacuation Day *(Suffolk Co., Mass.)*
Apr. 2 Pascua Florida Day
Apr. 13 Thomas Jefferson's Birthday
Apr. 19 Patriots Day *(Maine, Mass.)*
Apr. 30 National Arbor Day
May 1 May Day
May 7 Truman Day *(Mo.)*
May 9 Mother's Day
May 15 Armed Forces Day
May 24 Victoria Day *(Canada)*
May 31 Memorial Day *(observed)**
June 1 Statehood Day *(Tenn.)*
June 5 World Environment Day
June 11 King Kamehameha I Day *(Hawaii)*
June 14 Flag Day
June 17 Bunker Hill Day *(Suffolk Co., Mass.)*
June 19 Juneteenth *(Fla., Okla., Tex.)*
June 20 Father's Day
June 21 West Virginia Day
July 1 Canada Day
July 4 Independence Day*
July 23 Pioneer Day *(Utah)*
Aug. 2 Colorado Day
Aug. 9 Victory Day *(R.I.)*
Aug. 16 Bennington Battle Day *(Vt.)*
Aug. 26 Women's Equality Day
Sept. 6 Labor Day*
Sept. 9 Admission Day *(Calif.)*
Oct. 9 Leif Eriksson Day
Oct. 11 Columbus Day *(observed)**; Thanksgiving Day *(Canada)*; Native Americans Day *(S.Dak.)*
Oct. 18 Alaska Day
Oct. 31 Halloween
Nov. 1 Nevada Day
Nov. 2 Election Day
Nov. 4 Will Rogers Day *(Okla.)*
Nov. 11 Veterans Day*
Nov. 19 Discovery Day *(Puerto Rico)*
Nov. 25 Thanksgiving Day*
Nov. 26 Acadian Day *(La.)*
Dec. 10 Wyoming Day
Dec. 25 Christmas Day*
Dec. 26 Boxing Day *(Canada)*

RELIGIOUS OBSERVANCES

Epiphany .... **Jan. 6**
Ash Wednesday .... **Feb. 17**
Palm Sunday .... **Mar. 28**
First day of Passover .... **Apr. 1**
Good Friday .... **Apr. 2**
Easter Day .... **Apr. 4**
Orthodox Easter .... **Apr. 11**
Islamic New Year .... **Apr. 17**
Whitsunday-Pentecost .... **May 23**
Rosh Hashanah .... **Sept. 11**
Yom Kippur .... **Sept. 20**
First day of Chanukah .... **Dec. 4**
First day of Ramadan .... **Dec. 9**
Christmas Day .... **Dec. 25**

How the Almanac Weather Forecasts Are Made

We derive our weather forecasts from a secret formula devised by the founder of this Almanac in 1792, enhanced by the most modern scientific calculations based on solar activity and current meteorological data. We believe that nothing in the universe occurs haphazardly but that there is a cause-and-effect pattern to all phenomena, thus making long-range weather forecasts possible. However, neither we nor anyone else has as yet gained sufficient insight into the mysteries of the universe to predict weather with anything resembling total accuracy.

Glossary

Aph. – Aphelion: The point in a planet's orbit that is farthest from the Sun.

Apo. – Apogee: The point in the Moon's orbit that is farthest from Earth.

Celestial Equator: The circle on the celestial sphere that is halfway between the celestial poles. It can be thought of as the plane of Earth's equator projected out onto the sphere.

Celestial Sphere: An imaginary sphere projected into space, with an observer on Earth as its center. It represents the entire sky. All celestial bodies other than Earth are imagined as being on its inside surface; it is used for describing their positions and motions.

Conj. – Conjunction: The apparent closest approach to each other of two celestial bodies. **Inf. – Inferior:** A conjunction in which the planet is between the Sun and Earth. **Sup. – Superior:** A conjunction in which the Sun is between the planet and Earth.

Declination: The angular distance of a celestial body measured perpendicularly north or south of the celestial equator — analogous to latitude on Earth. The Almanac gives the Sun's declination at noon EST or EDT.

Dominical Letter: The letter used to denote the Sundays in the ecclesiastical calendar in a particular year, determined by the date on which the first Sunday of that year falls. If Jan. 1 is a Sunday, the letter is A; if Jan. 2 is a Sunday, the letter is B; and so on to G. In a leap year, the letter applies through February and then takes the preceding letter.

Eclipse, Lunar: The Moon, at full phase, enters the shadow of Earth. **Total:** The Moon passes completely into the umbra (central dark part) of Earth's shadow. **Partial:** Only part of the Moon passes through the umbra. **Penumbral:** The Moon passes through only the penumbra (an area of partial darkness that surrounds the umbra).

Eclipse, Solar: The Moon passes between Earth and the Sun, and all three bodies are aligned in the same plane. **Annular:** The Moon appears silhouetted against the Sun, with a ring of sunlight showing around it.

Epact: A number from 1 to 30 that indicates the Moon's age at the instant Jan. 1 begins at the meridian of Greenwich, England; used for the ecclesiastical calendar.

Eq. – Equator: A great circle of Earth that is equidistant from the two poles.

Equinox, Autumnal: The Sun appears to cross the celestial equator from north to south. **Vernal:** The Sun appears to cross the celestial equator from south to north.

Era, Chronological: A system of reckoning time by numbering the years from an important occurrence or a particular point in time.

Evening Star: A planet that is above the western horizon at sunset and less than 180 degrees east of the Sun in right ascension.

Golden Number: A number in the 19-year cycle of the Moon, so called because of its importance in determining Easter. (The Moon repeats its phases approximately every 19 solar years.) To find the Golden Number of any year, add 1 to that year and divide the result by 19. The remainder is the Golden Number. When there is no remainder, the Golden Number is 19.

Gr. El. – Greatest Elongation: The greatest apparent angular distance of a planet from the Sun as seen from Earth.

Julian Period: A period of 7,980 years, beginning at 4713 B.C. and providing a chronological basis for the study of ancient history. Its system of astronomical dating, devised by 16th-century scholar Joseph Scaliger and named in honor of his father, Julius, allows the difference between two dates to be calculated more easily than with conventional civil calendars. To find the Julian year, add 4,713 to any year.

Moon Age: The number of days since the previous new Moon.

Moon on Equator: The Moon is on the celestial equator.

Moon Phases: Four particular states in the Moon's appearance, based on its position at each quarter of its complete cycle around Earth. **First Quarter:** The right half of the Moon is illuminated. **Full:** The Sun and the Moon are in opposition; the entire disk of the Moon is illuminated as viewed from Earth. **Last Quarter:** The left half of the Moon is illuminated. **New:** The Sun and the Moon are in conjunction; the entire disk of the Moon is darkened as viewed from Earth.

Moon Place, Astronomical: The actual position of the Moon within the constellations on the celestial sphere. **Astrological:** The position of the Moon within the astrological zodiac

(continued on page 44)

Best Fishing Days, 1999

(and other fishing lore from the files of *The Old Farmer's Almanac*)

Probably the best fishing times are when the ocean tides are restless before their turn and in the first hour of ebbing. All fish in all waters — salt and fresh — feed most heavily at those times.

The best temperatures for fish species vary widely, of course, and are chiefly important if you are going to have your own fishpond. The best temperatures for brook trout are 45° to 65° F. Brown and rainbow trout are more tolerant of higher temperatures. Smallmouth black bass do best in cool water. Horned pout take what they find.

Most of us go fishing when we can get time off, not because it is the best time. But there *are* best times:

■ One hour before and one hour after high tides, and one hour before and one hour after low tides. (The times of high tides are given on pages 60-86 and corrected for your locality on pages 210-211. Inland, the times for high tides correspond with the times the Moon is due south. Low tides are halfway between high tides.)

■ During "the morning rise" — after sunup for a spell — and "the evening rise" — just before sundown and the hour or so after.

■ When the water is still or rippled, rather than during a wind.

■ When there is a hatch of flies — caddis flies or mayflies, commonly. (The fisherman will have to match the hatching flies with *his* fly — or go fishless.)

■ When the breeze is from a westerly quarter rather than from the north or east.

■ When the barometer is steady or on the rise. (But, of course, even in a three-day driving northeaster, the fish aren't going to give up feeding. Their hunger clock keeps right on working, and the smart fisherman will find something they want.)

■ Starting on the day the Moon is new and continuing through the day it is full.

Moon Between New & Full, 1999

Jan. 1	**Apr. 16-30**	**Sept. 9-25**
Jan. 17-31	**May 15-30**	**Oct. 9-24**
Feb. 16-Mar. 2	**June 13-28**	**Nov. 7-23**
Mar. 17-31	**July 12-28**	**Dec. 7-22**
	Aug. 11-26	

Glossary *(continued)*

according to calculations made over 2,000 years ago. Because of precession of the equinoxes and other factors, this is not the Moon's actual position in the sky.

Moon Rides High/Runs Low: The Moon is highest above or farthest below the celestial equator.

Moonrise/Moonset: The Moon's rising above and descending below the horizon.

Morning Star: A planet that is above the eastern horizon at sunrise and less than 180 degrees west of the Sun in right ascension.

Node: Either of the two points on opposite sides of the celestial sphere where the Moon's orbit intersects the ecliptic.

Occn. – Occultation: The eclipse of a star or planet by the Moon or another planet.

Opposition: The Moon or a planet appears on the opposite side of the sky from the Sun (elongation 180 degrees).

Perig. – Perigee: The point in the Moon's orbit that is closest to Earth.

Perih. – Perihelion: The point in a planet's orbit that is closest to the Sun.

R.A. – Right Ascension: The coordinate on the celestial sphere for measuring the east/west positions of celestial bodies; analogous to longitude on Earth.

Roman Indiction: A number in a 15-year cycle, established Jan. 1, A.D. 313, as a fiscal term. Add 3 to any given year in the Christian era and divide by 15; the remainder is the Roman Indiction. When there is no remainder, the Roman Indiction is 15.

Solar Cycle: A period of 28 years, at the end of which the days of the month return to the same days of the week.

Solstice, Summer: The Sun is at its maximum (23.5°) north of the celestial equator. **Winter:** The Sun is at its maximum (23.5°) south of the celestial equator.

Stat. – Stationary: Halted apparent movement of a planet against the background of the stars just before it comes to opposition.

Sun Fast/Slow: The adjustment needed to reconcile sundial time to standard clock time. This adjustment factor is given in the Left-Hand Calendar Pages 60-86.

Sunrise/Sunset: The visible rising and setting of the Sun's upper limb across the unobstructed horizon of an observer whose eyes are 15 feet above ground level.

Twilight: The period of time between full darkness and sunrise and also between sunset and full darkness.

The Visible Planets, 1999

The times (EST/EDT) of the visible rising and setting of the planets Venus, Mars, Jupiter, and Saturn on the 1st, 11th, and 21st of each month are given below. The approximate times of their visible rising and setting on other days can be found with sufficient accuracy by interpolation. For an explanation of Key Letters (used in adjusting the times given here for Boston to the times in your town), see page 35 and pages 214-218. Key Letters appear as capital letters beside the times. (For definitions of morning and evening stars, see pages 42-44.)

VENUS enjoys a superb year. The dazzling planet emerges from behind the Sun in January and rises steadily higher in the western sky at dusk. Brightening, the evening star reaches greatest prominence in May before descending and finally vanishing in mid-July. It reemerges as a morning star in September and remains brilliant through year's end, reaching its predawn best in October. Venus is in conjunction with Jupiter on February 23, with Saturn on March 20, and with Mercury on August 26.

Boldface — P.M. Lightface — A.M.

Date		Time	Key	Date		Time	Key
Jan. 1	set	**5:31**	A	July 1	set	**10:45**	D
Jan. 11	"	**5:56**	A	July 11	"	**10:15**	D
Jan. 21	"	**6:22**	B	July 21	"	**9:38**	D
Feb. 1	"	**6:50**	B	Aug. 1	"	**8:45**	C
Feb. 11	"	**7:16**	B	Aug. 11 ...	"	**7:48**	C
Feb. 21	"	**7:41**	C	Aug. 21 ...	"	**6:49**	C
Mar. 1	"	**8:00**	C	Sept. 1	rise	4:57	B
Mar. 11 ...	"	**8:24**	D	Sept. 11 ...	"	4:06	B
Mar. 21 ...	"	**8:48**	D	Sept. 21 ...	"	3:32	B
Apr. 1	"	**9:16**	D	Oct. 1	"	3:14	B
Apr. 11	"	**10:40**	E	Oct. 11	"	3:07	B
Apr. 21	"	**11:02**	E	Oct. 21	"	3:09	B
May 1	"	**11:20**	E	Nov. 1	"	2:18	B
May 11 ...	"	**11:32**	E	Nov. 11 ...	"	2:31	C
May 21 ...	"	**11:38**	E	Nov. 21 ...	"	2:46	C
June 1	"	**11:35**	E	Dec. 1	"	3:04	D
June 11 ...	"	**11:25**	E	Dec. 11 ...	"	3:24	D
June 21 ...	set	**11:09**	D	Dec. 21 ...	"	3:45	D
				Dec. 31 ...	rise	4:07	D

MARS stands opposite the Sun on April 24, nearing its closest approach to Earth of the decade. At a distance of 53.8 million miles, it shines at an impressive magnitude -1.7 in Virgo. This performance comes just as the other naked-eye planets also put on exceptional apparitions. In April and May, the red planet rises at dusk and remains visible all night long. Fading thereafter, it remains visible for the rest of the year. Mars marches through Libra and Scorpius in the summer, finishing the year in Capricornus.

Boldface — P.M. Lightface — A.M.

Date		Time	Key	Date		Time	Key
Jan. 1	rise	12:30	C	July 1	set	1:12	B
Jan. 11	"	12:15	D	July 11	"	12:37	A
Jan. 21	rise	**11:57**	D	July 21	"	12:08	A
Feb. 1	"	**11:36**	D	Aug. 1	set	**11:38**	A
Feb. 11	"	**11:15**	D	Aug. 11 ...	"	**11:13**	A
Feb. 21	"	**10:50**	D	Aug. 21 ...	"	**10:49**	A
Mar. 1	"	**10:27**	D	Sept. 1	"	**10:27**	A
Mar. 11 ...	"	**9:54**	D	Sept. 11 ...	"	**10:08**	A
Mar. 21 ...	"	**9:16**	D	Sept. 21 ...	"	**9:53**	A
Apr. 1	"	**8:27**	D	Oct. 1	"	**9:40**	A
Apr. 11	"	**8:35**	D	Oct. 11	"	**9:30**	A
Apr. 21	"	**7:40**	D	Oct. 21	"	**9:22**	A
May 1	set	5:30	B	Nov. 1	"	**8:17**	A
May 11 ...	"	4:40	B	Nov. 11 ...	"	**8:15**	A
May 21 ...	"	3:53	B	Nov. 21 ...	"	**8:14**	A
June 1	"	3:05	B	Dec. 1	"	**8:14**	A
June 11 ...	"	2:24	B	Dec. 11 ...	"	**8:15**	A
June 21 ...	set	1:47	B	Dec. 21 ...	"	**8:17**	B
				Dec. 31 ...	set	**8:18**	B

JUPITER can be seen in the southwest before sunset the first few months of the year and in the east before sunrise as early as June, but it is in the fall that it puts on its finest performance. It reaches opposition on October 23, when it comes to its closest point to Earth of the decade. It shines at a brilliant magnitude -2.9 among the dim stars of Pisces, rising at sunset and standing high in the south a little after midnight. Jupiter is in conjunction with Venus on February 23 and with Mercury on May 1.

Boldface — P.M. Lightface — A.M.

Jan. 1	**set**	**10:19**	B	July 1	rise	1:22	B
Jan. 11	"	**9:48**	B	July 11	"	12:46	B
Jan. 21	"	**9:18**	C	July 21	"	12:10	B
Feb. 1......	"	**8:46**	C	Aug. 1	**rise**	**11:29**	B
Feb. 11....	"	**8:17**	C	Aug. 11 ...	"	**10:52**	B
Feb. 21....	"	**7:49**	C	Aug. 21 ...	"	**10:13**	B
Mar. 1	"	**7:27**	C	Sept. 1.....	"	**9:30**	B
Mar. 11 ...	"	**7:00**	C	Sept. 11...	"	**8:50**	B
Mar. 21 ...	"	**6:33**	C	Sept. 21...	"	**8:09**	B
Apr. 1......	"	**6:03**	C	Oct. 1	"	**7:23**	B
Apr. 11....	rise	6:00	B	Oct. 11	"	**6:41**	B
Apr. 21....	"	5:26	B	Oct. 21	"	**5:58**	B
May 1	"	4:52	B	Nov. 1.....	set	5:31	D
May 11 ...	"	4:18	B	Nov. 11...	"	4:45	D
May 21 ...	"	3:44	B	Nov. 21...	"	4:00	D
June 1	"	3:06	B	Dec. 1	"	3:17	D
June 11 ...	"	2:32	B	Dec. 11 ...	"	2:35	D
June 21 ...	rise	1:57	B	Dec. 21 ...	"	1:55	D
				Dec. 31 ...	set	1:17	D

SATURN has a fine year. The ringed world lingers in the evening sky in the southwest for the first few months, then vanishes behind the Sun to emerge in June as a morning star in the east before sunrise. Rising two hours earlier each month, Saturn reaches opposition on November 6, when it rises at sunset and is highest at midnight. This year the rings are tilted favorably, causing Saturn to achieve its greatest brightness since 1977. Saturn is in conjunction with Venus on March 20 and with Mercury on May 13.

Boldface — P.M. Lightface — A.M.

Jan. 1	set	1:18	D	July 1	rise	2:03	B
Jan. 11	"	12:39	D	July 11	"	1:26	B
Jan. 21	"	12:01	D	July 21	"	12:49	B
Feb. 1......	**set**	**11:18**	D	Aug. 1.....	"	12:08	B
Feb. 11....	"	**10:42**	D	Aug. 11...	**rise**	**11:30**	B
Feb. 21....	"	**10:07**	D	Aug. 21 ...	"	**10:51**	B
Mar. 1	"	**9:39**	D	Sept. 1.....	"	**10:08**	B
Mar. 11 ...	"	**9:05**	D	Sept. 11...	"	**9:29**	B
Mar. 21 ...	"	**8:32**	D	Sept. 21...	"	**8:49**	B
Apr. 1......	"	**7:55**	D	Oct. 1	"	**8:04**	B
Apr. 11....	"	**8:22**	D	Oct. 11	"	**7:23**	B
Apr. 21....	"	**7:49**	D	Oct. 21	"	**6:42**	B
May 1	"	**7:17**	D	Nov. 1.....	"	**4:57**	B
May 11 ...	rise	5:08	B	Nov. 11...	set	6:03	D
May 21 ...	"	4:32	B	Nov. 21...	"	5:20	D
June 1	"	3:52	B	Dec. 1	"	4:37	D
June 11 ...	"	3:16	B	Dec. 11 ...	"	3:55	D
June 21 ...	rise	2:39	B	Dec. 21 ...	"	3:13	D
				Dec. 31 ...	set	2:32	D

MERCURY plays a cat-and-mouse game with the Sun, darting in and out of the solar glare several times in 1999. A medium-bright star low in evening's twilight during the last week of February and the first week of March, it stands to the right of brilliant Jupiter. Its second evening apparition occurs between June 8 and July 4. As a morning star, low in the east just before sunrise, it is best seen from August 9 to 19, and from November 25 to December 10.

DO NOT CONFUSE 1) Venus with Jupiter from February 22 to 24, when they nearly merge into a single dazzling entity. They share the same creamy-white color, but Venus is always brighter. 2) Jupiter with Mercury in the evening twilight from March 3 to 12. Mercury is to the right and fainter than giant Jupiter. 3) Mars with Virgo's brightest star, Spica, during the last week of May. Mars is orange and brighter; Spica is blue-white. 4) Mars with Uranus on December 14. Visible only through binoculars, Uranus is green and much fainter.

Eclipses for 1999

There will be four eclipses in 1999, two of the Sun and two of the Moon. **Solar eclipses are visible only in certain areas. Lunar eclipses are technically visible from the entire night side of Earth, but during a penumbral eclipse, the dimming of the Moon's illumination is so slight as to be scarcely noticeable.**

1. Penumbral eclipse of the Moon, January 31. The beginning phase will be visible in Hawaii, the western United States, and western Canada. The end will be visible in Alaska except for the southeastern part. The Moon enters penumbra at 6:05 A.M., PST. The Moon leaves penumbra at 10:30 A.M., PST.

2. Annular eclipse of the Sun, February 15-16. This eclipse will not be visible in the United States or Canada.

3. Partial eclipse of the Moon, July 28. The beginning of the umbral phase will be visible in Hawaii and North America except for the northeastern part. The end will be visible in Hawaii and extreme western North America. The Moon enters penumbra at 4:56 A.M., EDT (1:56 A.M., PDT), and umbra at 6:22 A.M., EDT (3:22 A.M., PDT). The middle of the eclipse occurs at 7:34 A.M., EDT (4:34 A.M., PDT). The Moon leaves umbra at 8:46 A.M., EDT (5:46 A.M., PDT), and penumbra at 10:11 A.M., EDT (7:11 A.M., PDT).

4. Total eclipse of the Sun, August 11. Only the partial phase will be visible in North America, and this only from the northeastern United States and eastern Canada. There the Sun will rise partially eclipsed. The eclipse will end between 6:15 and 6:45 A.M., EDT, depending on your location within the area where the eclipse is visible.

Full-Moon Dates

	1999	2000	2001	2002	2003
Jan.	1 & 31	20	9	28	18
Feb.	—	19	8	27	16
Mar.	2 & 31	19	9	28	18
Apr.	30	18	7	26	16
May	30	18	7	26	15
June	28	16	5	24	14
July	28	16	5	24	13
Aug.	26	15	4	22	12
Sept.	25	13	2	21	10
Oct.	24	13	2	21	10
Nov.	23	11	1 & 30	19	8
Dec.	22	11	30	19	8

Principal Meteor Showers

Shower	Best Hour (EST/EDT)	Point of Origin	Date of Maximum*	Approx. Peak Rate (/hr.)**	Associated Comet
Quadrantid	5 A.M.	N	Jan. 4	80	—
Lyrid	5 A.M.	S	Apr. 21	12	Thatcher
Eta Aquarid	5 A.M.	SE	May 4	20	Halley
Delta Aquarid	3 A.M.	S	July 30	10	—
Perseid	5 A.M.	NE	Aug. 11-13	75	Swift-Tuttle
Draconid	10 P.M.	NW	Oct. 9	10	Giacobini-Zinner
Orionid	5 A.M.	S	Oct. 22	25	Halley
Taurid	Midnight	S	Nov. 9	6	Encke
Leonid	5 A.M.	S	Nov. 18	20	Tempel-Tuttle
Andromedid	10 P.M.	S	Nov. 25-27	5	Biela
Geminid	2 A.M.	NE	Dec. 14	65	—
Ursid	5 A.M.	N	Dec. 22	12	Tuttle

* **Date of actual maximum occurrence may vary by one or two days in either direction.**

** **The number of sporadic meteors seen per hour on clear nights is about six. The visibility of showers depends on how bright the Moon is on the night of the shower.**

Bright Stars, 1999

The upper table shows the time (EST or EDT) that each star transits the meridian at Boston (i.e., lies directly above the horizon's south point there) and its altitude above that point at transit on the dates shown. The time of transit on any other date differs from that of the nearest date listed by approximately four minutes for each day. To find the local time of the star's transit for a location other than Boston, correct the time at Boston by the value of Key Letter C for that location. (See footnote.)

Star	Constellation	Magnitude	Jan. 1	Mar. 1	May 1	July 1	Sept. 1	Nov. 1	Altitude (degrees)
			Time of Transit (EST/EDT) Boldface — P.M. Lightface — A.M.						
Altair	Aquila	0.8	**12:50**	8:59	5:59	1:59	**9:51**	**4:51**	56.3
Deneb	Cygnus	1.3	**1:41**	9:49	6:50	2:50	**10:42**	**5:42**	92.8
Fomalhaut	Psc. Aus.	1.2	**3:56**	**12:04**	9:04	5:04	1:01	**7:57**	17.8
Algol	Perseus	2.2	**8:07**	**4:15**	**1:15**	9:15	5:11	12:11	88.5
Aldebaran	Taurus	0.9	**9:34**	**5:42**	**2:42**	10:42	6:39	1:39	64.1
Rigel	Orion	0.1	**10:12**	**6:20**	**3:20**	11:21	7:17	2:17	39.4
Capella	Auriga	0.1	**10:14**	**6:22**	**3:22**	11:22	7:19	2:19	93.6
Bellatrix	Orion	1.6	**10:23**	**6:31**	**3:31**	11:31	7:28	2:28	54.0
Betelgeuse	Orion	var. 0.4	**10:53**	**7:01**	**4:01**	**12:01**	7:58	2:58	55.0
Sirius	Can. Maj.	–1.4	**11:43**	**7:51**	**4:51**	**12:51**	8:47	3:47	31.0
Procyon	Can. Min.	0.4	12:40	**8:45**	**5:45**	**1:45**	9:41	4:41	52.9
Pollux	Gemini	1.2	12:46	**8:51**	**5:51**	**1:51**	9:47	4:47	75.7
Regulus	Leo	1.4	3:09	**11:14**	**8:14**	**4:14**	**12:10**	7:10	59.7
Spica	Virgo	var. 1.0	6:26	2:34	**11:30**	**7:30**	**3:26**	10:27	36.6
Arcturus	Bootes	–0.1	7:17	3:25	12:21	**8:21**	**4:17**	11:17	66.9
Antares	Scorpius	var. 0.9	9:29	5:37	2:38	**10:34**	**6:30**	**1:30**	21.3
Vega	Lyra	0.0	11:37	7:45	4:45	12:41	**8:37**	**3:38**	86.4

Risings and Settings

To find the times of the star's rising and setting at Boston on any date, apply the interval shown to the time of the star's transit on that date. Subtract the interval for the star's rising; add it for its setting. To find the times for a location other than Boston, correct the times at Boston by the value of the Key Letter shown. (See footnote.) The directions in which the star rises and sets, shown for Boston, are generally useful throughout the United States. Deneb, Algol, Capella, and Vega are circumpolar stars — this means that they do not appear to rise or set but stay above the horizon.

Star	Interval hr. min.	Rising Key	Rising Dir.	Setting Key	Setting Dir.
Altair	6:36	B	EbN	E	WbN
Fomalhaut	3:59	E	SE	D	SW
Aldebaran	7:06	B	ENE	D	WNW
Rigel	5:33	D	EbS	B	WbS
Bellatrix	6:27	B	EbN	D	WbN
Betelgeuse	6:31	B	EbN	D	WbN
Sirius	5:00	D	ESE	B	WSW
Procyon	6:23	B	EbN	D	WbN
Pollux	8:01	A	NE	E	NW
Regulus	6:49	B	EbN	D	WbN
Spica	5:23	D	EbS	B	WbS
Arcturus	7:19	A	ENE	E	WNW
Antares	4:17	E	SEbE	A	SWbW

NOTE: The values of Key Letters are given in the Time Correction Tables (pages 214-218).

by Bob Berman

The Year of the Shooting

Just as an earthquake can be anything from an imperceptible tremor to a city-destroying visitation from hell, meteors can vary from barely visible did-I-imagine-that? streaks to exploding fireworks that leave onlookers gasping in awe. There's some sort of curious chemistry between the human spirit and "shooting stars," those fiery chunks that have fallen off asteroids or comets.

Away from city lights, five or six meteors appear every hour. Some are lazy intruders that sneak up on Earth from behind and enter our atmosphere at only ten miles per second; others are sizzling, 100-times-faster-than-a-bullet kamikazes that plow into us headfirst. The latter can arrive at speeds up to 44 miles per second — fast enough to burn up high in the atmosphere and vanish into dust in an eye blink. Some meteors leave behind lingering, glowing trails that slowly fade after several seconds, like Cheshire-cat smiles. Others emit sparkling fragments, like cheap matches made in Burma.

View of the Leonid meteor shower as seen at Niagara Falls on the night of November 12-13, 1833.

All meteors are smaller than you might think. A typical shooting star is only the size of an apple seed! If the stony chunk weighs more than two ounces, it is more brilliant than any star and casts shadows as it slices across the heavens. It's then termed a *fireball,* like the one seen over the northeastern United States on November 17, 1997. If it explodes violently into flaming fragments, it's called a *bolide*.

Most shooting stars appear during "showers," when Earth collides with millions of particles that have fallen off comets. Since we return to the same part of our orbit on the same day each year (with a one- to two-day variation each century), those intersection points recur reliably. They give us such famous meteor showers as the Perseid, a faithful summer-vacation companion every August 11 and 12; the Geminid on December 14, less likely to be observed in most

Stars

1999 offers prime viewing of meteors — seed-size frozen particles that blaze trails of light across the night sky. The Leonids in November promise an especially spectacular show.

of the Northern Hemisphere due to wintry weather; and the Leonid, a November shower with a tremendous variation in richness. In other words, you can see the most meteors during the last half of each year.

Unfortunately, conditions for meteor viewing have lately been less than favorable. That's because 1998's full Moons brightened the sky for two of the three best showers, allowing only a few superbright specimens to poke through the milkiness.

All this changes in 1999. The Moon will be totally absent during the August 11 and 12 dates of the magical Perseid; this year, the shower coincides with the new Moon. For the Geminid on December 14, the Moon will be present before midnight, but its phase will be only a crescent, with less than 1⁄15 the brilliance of a full Moon.

It's the Leonid shower on the night of November 17-18, 1999, that is attracting all the special interest. The Moon, just past its first quarter phase, will set by 1:00 A.M., leaving the remainder of the night pitch-black. For what, exactly? That's the question of the year.

The Leonids have been gaining in intensity for the last several Novembers — exactly what astronomers have expected, because the shower's parent comet, Tempel-Tuttle, has been steadily approaching us. Every 33.2 years, this comet, the machinery behind the Leonids, passes nearby as it swoops through the inner solar system, and we're now in the thick of things: Its closest passage to the Sun occurred February 28, 1998.

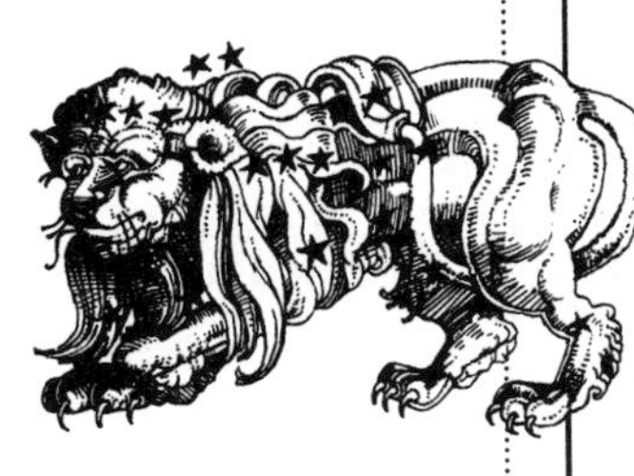

In 1966, the last time Tempel-Tuttle streaked by, it brought an amazing meteor "storm," during which 100 shooting stars were seen each second from the American Southwest. It is the possibility of such a mind-boggling, Armageddon-like intensity that has astronomers so excited. Because the ultrafast shooting stars seem, by a trick of perspective, to radiate from a single spot in the head of the constellation Leo the Lion, the effect is of a nonstop sparkler erupting violently from an invisible hole in the heavens.

Nobody knows if such a meteor storm will actually occur this time around. It didn't in 1933, but it definitely boggled the minds of millions of unprepared citizens in 1799, 1833, 1866, and again, to a lesser degree, in 1900. Also, the most intense fireworks persist for only an hour or two, so just a small section of Earth will be aimed in the right direction at the right time.

But it could be over your house, and would you want to be sleeping, only to kick yourself the next day when you hear about it on the news? Even those who don't get the storm will still see a nice shower — maybe as many meteors as one per minute, which would rival the show put on by the Perseid and Geminid.

Meteor watching requires no equipment. In fact, you don't even *want* a telescope because you don't want to restrict your view of the sky. For any of the three showers, choose a spot away from trees and other obstructions, and away from lights, too, if you can manage it. For the summer Perseid, spread a blanket or use a lawn chair to prevent neck cramp. Bring a companion: This is the perfect cheap date.

Keep your eyes glued skyward. Perseids and Leonids are very fast and come and go in a second or less. Meteors love to sneak across the sky when you aren't looking. You can face any direction, although northeast is slightly favored for the Perseids and Geminids. And don't worry about getting hit. These shower-type meteors are mostly stony ice balls that don't survive their passage through the atmosphere.

And if, from your location, it's cloudy for all three showers — a gloomy but conceivable possibility — remember that every clear night offers a stray shooting star every 10 or 12 minutes, on average. After this special year has passed, we still remain passengers on a world whose endless collisions with smaller objects light up all the nights of our lives. □□

Editor's note: See page 48 for a listing of the principal meteor showers seen each year from Earth.

The Astonishing Lunar Illumination

OF DECEMBER 22, 1999

Mark your calendar for the final full Moon of the millennium — a last hurrah of unusual brightness. *by Randy Miller*

Since 1793, when *The Old Farmer's Almanac* began tracking heavenly events and seasonal changes, the Moon has been full on the first day of winter just nine times. This year, 1999, marks the first time it has happened since 1980. But we have to go back 133 years, to 1866, to match this year's rare gathering of winter solstice, full Moon, *and* lunar perigee (the point in the Moon's orbit that is closest to Earth).

On December 22, 1999, the date of its nearest approach to us, the full Moon will appear measurably larger (about 14 percent) than it does when it's at apogee (the point in its elliptical orbit that is farthest from Earth). Rising just after sunset, gliding across the sky at about one full-Moon's width per hour, this Moon will be close by, high up, and shining at its most brilliant. Since Earth is several million miles closer to the Sun in winter, sunlight striking the Moon is 7 percent stronger. (Perihelion, our closest approach to the Sun, occurs just 12 days later, on January 3, 2000.)

The rarity of a solstitial full Moon — the average interval is about 19 years — reinforces the Moon's role as a beacon playing on human history. Although our research could not find a correlation between this lunar event and significant historical happenings on similar dates in the past*, the combination of astronomical forces will certainly affect the tides on December 22.

As astronomer Bob Berman explains, "Not only is the Moon at perigee, but it is also the *closest* one of the year, since the Moon's orbit keeps deforming, and it will be at its most eccentric then. During this time of proxigean tides [unusually high tides due to the Moon's phase and proximity to Earth], coastal flooding could occur if there is one more little extra effect, such as a storm at sea, on-shore winds, or low barometric pressure. The situation is primed for damage."

If the solstice night of December 22 is calm and cloudless, with the full Moon beaming down on a blanket of snow, it will be irresistibly attractive, and electrical illumination — even your car's headlights — may seem superfluous. Let's hope for clear weather.

---

* We *did* find that on the night of December 21, 1866, the Lakota Sioux staged a devastating retaliatory ambush of soldiers in the Wyoming Territory — perhaps planning the attack for that bright night, whose lunar confluence was identical to this year's.

Full Moon Occurrences on Solstice and Equinox Dates

1793-2020

Winter

Year	Date	Perigee/Apogee
1809	12/21	apogee, 22nd
1828	12/21	
1866	12/21	perigee, 21st
1885	12/21	perigee, 22nd
1904	12/22	
1942	12/22	apogee, 23rd
1961	12/21	
1980	12/21	
1999	12/22	perigee, 22nd
2010	12/21	

Spring

Year	Date
1829	3/20
1867	3/20
1924	3/20
1943	3/21
1981	3/20
2019	3/20

Summer

Year	Date	Perigee/Apogee
1796	6/20	apogee, 19th
1834	6/21	
1853	6/21	
1910	6/22	
1929	6/21	
1948	6/21	
1986	6/21	perigee, 21st
2016	6/20	

Autumn

Year	Date	Perigee/Apogee
1809	9/23	
1820	9/22	perigee, 21st
1839	9/23	perigee, 24th
1877	9/22	
1915	9/23	
1991	9/23	

Compiled from The Old Farmer's Almanac *and* Astronomical Tables of the Sun, Moon, and Planets, *by Jean Meeus (Willmann-Bell, 1995). The dates are for the Eastern Standard Time zone; Daylight Saving Time has been taken into account for the war years of 1917 and 1942-1945, and from April 1, 1967, onward. Also, dates for lunar perigee and apogee have been included where these fall on or near the full Moon.*

Seasons of the Year

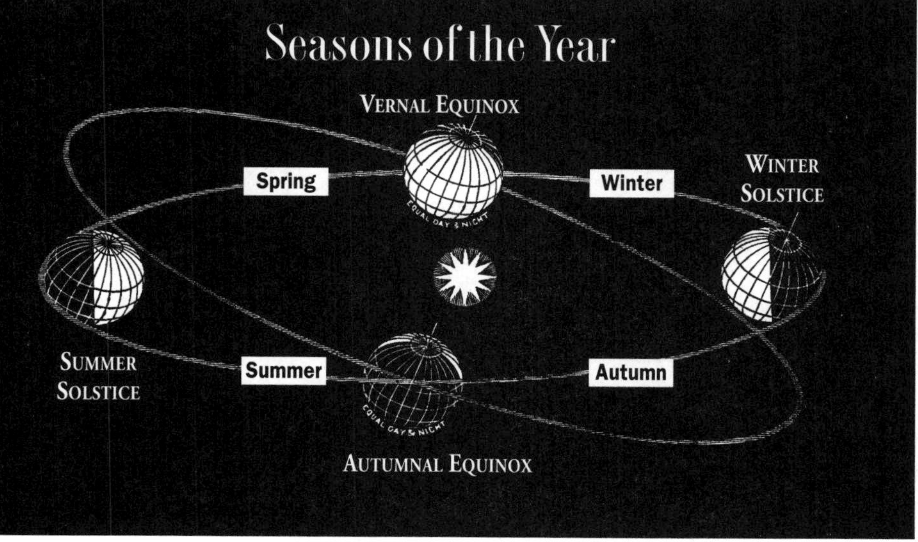

Where the Sun Rises and Sets

By using the table below and a compass, you can determine accurately where on the horizon the Sun will rise or set on a given day. The top half of the table is for those days of the year, between the vernal and autumnal equinoxes, when the Sun rises north of east and sets north of west. March 21 through June 21 are listed in the left column, June 21 through September 22 appear in the right column. Similarly arranged, the bottom half of the table shows the other half of the year, when the Sun rises south of east and sets south of west. Here's how it works. Say you live in Gary, Indiana, and need to know where the Sun will rise or set on October 10. Use the Time Correction Tables (pages 214-218) to determine the latitude of your city or the listed city nearest to you. Gary is at 41° latitude. Find the 40° latitude column and you see that on October 10 the Sun rises 8° south of east and sets 8° south of west. Of course, you can determine figures for other latitudes and days not actually shown in the table by using extrapolation.

Latitude Date	0°	10°	20°	30°	40°	50°	60°	Latitude Date
Mar. 21	0°	0°	0°	0°	0°	0°	0°	Sept. 22
Mar. 31	4° N	4° N	4° N	4° N	5° N	6° N	8° N	Sept. 14
Apr. 10	8° N	8° N	8° N	9° N	10° N	12° N	15° N	Sept. 4
Apr. 20	11° N	12° N	12° N	13° N	15° N	18° N	23° N	Aug. 24
May 1	15° N	16° N	16° N	17° N	20° N	23° N	31° N	Aug. 14
May 10	17°N	18° N	19° N	20° N	23° N	28° N	37° N	Aug. 4
May 20	20° N	21° N	21° N	23° N	26° N	32° N	43° N	July 25
June 1	22° N	22° N	23° N	26° N	29° N	36° N	48° N	July 13
June 10	23° N	24° N	24° N	27° N	31° N	37° N	51° N	July 4
June 21	23½° N	25° N	25° N	27° N	31° N	38° N	53° N	June 21
Sept. 22	0°	0°	0°	0°	0°	0°	0°	Mar. 21
Oct. 1	3° S	3° S	3° S	3° S	4° S	5° S	6° S	Mar. 14
Oct. 10	6° S	7° S	7° S	7° S	8° S	10° S	13° S	Mar. 5
Oct. 20	10° S	11° S	11° S	12° S	13° S	16° S	20° S	Feb. 23
Nov. 1	15° S	15° S	15° S	16° S	18° S	22° S	29° S	Feb. 12
Nov. 10	17° S	18° S	18° S	20° S	22° S	27° S	36° S	Feb. 2
Nov. 20	20° S	21° S	21° S	23° S	26° S	31° S	42° S	Jan. 23
Dec. 1	22° S	23° S	23° S	25° S	29° S	35° S	48° S	Jan. 13
Dec. 10	23° S	24° S	24° S	27° S	30° S	37° S	51° S	Jan. 4
Dec. 21	23½° S	25° S	25° S	27° S	31° S	38° S	53° S	Dec. 21

1998 NOVEMBER, THE ELEVENTH MONTH

The full Moon on the night of the 3rd-4th is the closest Moon of the year, passing just 216,000 miles from Earth. This will produce a dramatically large range of high and low tides. Any storms at sea at this time will produce coastal flooding. The Moon passes near a brightening but still unspectacular Mars on the 13th. Look for the ultrafast Leonid meteors, which may put on a good show this year on the nights of the 17th and 18th. Moonlight will be absent, offering optimal conditions for this sometimes spectacular shower. The Moon returns to pass Jupiter on the 27th and Saturn on the 30th.

○	Full Moon	4th day	0 hour	18th minute
☾	Last Quarter	10th day	19th hour	28th minute
●	New Moon	18th day	23rd hour	27th minute
☽	First Quarter	26th day	19th hour	23rd minute

Times are given in Eastern Standard Time.

For an explanation of this page, see "How to Use This Almanac," page 34; for values of Key Letters, see Time Correction Tables, page 214.

Day of Year	Day of Month	Day of Week	☉ Rises h. m.	Key	☉ Sets h. m.	Key	Length of Days h. m.	Sun Fast m.	Declination of Sun ° '	Full Sea Boston Light – A.M.	**Bold – P.M.**	☽ Rises h. m.	Key	☽ Sets h. m.	Key	☽ Place	☽ Age
305	1	**D**	6 17	D	4 38	B	10 21	32	14s.31	8	**8½**	3 P.M. 29	D	2 A.M. 46	D	AQU	12
306	2	M.	6 19	D	4 36	B	10 17	32	14 50	9	**9½**	4 05	C	4 00	D	CET	13
307	3	Tu.	6 20	D	4 35	B	10 15	32	15 08	9¾	**10¼**	4 43	B	5 15	E	PSC	14
308	4	W.	6 21	D	4 34	B	10 13	32	15 27	10½	**11¼**	5 24	B	6 31	E	ARI	15
309	5	Th.	6 22	D	4 33	B	10 11	32	15 45	11½	—	6 10	B	7 46	E	TAU	16
310	6	Fr.	6 24	D	4 32	B	10 08	32	16 03	12	**12¼**	7 02	B	8 57	E	TAU	17
311	7	Sa.	6 25	D	4 30	B	10 05	32	16 21	1	**1¼**	7 58	B	10 02	E	TAU	18
312	8	**D**	6 26	D	4 29	A	10 03	32	16 39	1¾	**2**	8 58	B	10 59	E	GEM	19
313	9	M.	6 27	D	4 28	A	10 01	32	16 56	2¾	**3**	10 00	B	11 A.M. 48	E	GEM	20
314	10	Tu.	6 29	D	4 27	A	9 58	32	17 13	3¾	**4**	11 P.M. 01	C	12 P.M. 30	E	CAN	21
315	11	W.	6 30	D	4 26	A	9 56	32	17 29	4¾	**5¼**	— —	–	1 06	D	LEO	22
316	12	Th.	6 31	D	4 25	A	9 54	32	17 46	6	**6¼**	12 A.M. 02	C	1 38	D	LEO	23
317	13	Fr.	6 32	D	4 24	A	9 52	31	18 02	7	**7¼**	1 02	C	2 07	D	LEO	24
318	14	Sa.	6 34	D	4 23	A	9 49	31	18 17	7¾	**8**	2 00	D	2 34	D	VIR	25
319	15	**D**	6 35	D	4 22	A	9 47	31	18 33	8½	**9**	2 58	D	3 02	C	VIR	26
320	16	M.	6 36	D	4 21	A	9 45	31	18 47	9¼	**9¾**	3 55	D	3 29	C	VIR	27
321	17	Tu.	6 37	D	4 21	A	9 44	31	19 02	9¾	**10¼**	4 52	E	3 58	B	VIR	28
322	18	W.	6 39	D	4 20	A	9 41	31	19 16	10½	**11**	5 49	E	4 30	B	LIB	0
323	19	Th.	6 40	D	4 19	A	9 39	30	19 30	11	**11½**	6 46	E	5 04	B	LIB	1
324	20	Fr.	6 41	D	4 18	A	9 37	30	19 44	11¾	—	7 42	E	5 43	B	OPH	2
325	21	Sa.	6 42	D	4 18	A	9 36	30	19 58	12¼	**12¼**	8 37	E	6 28	B	OPH	3
326	22	**D**	6 43	D	4 17	A	9 34	30	20 11	1	**1**	9 29	E	7 17	B	SAG	4
327	23	M.	6 45	D	4 16	A	9 31	29	20 23	1½	**1¾**	10 17	E	8 12	B	SAG	5
328	24	Tu.	6 46	D	4 16	A	9 30	29	20 36	2¼	**2½**	11 01	E	9 11	B	SAG	6
329	25	W.	6 47	D	4 15	A	9 28	29	20 47	3	**3¼**	11 A.M. 41	E	10 13	C	CAP	7
330	26	Th.	6 48	D	4 15	A	9 27	29	20 59	4	**4¼**	12 P.M. 18	D	11 P.M. 19	C	CAP	8
331	27	Fr.	6 49	E	4 14	A	9 25	28	21 10	4¾	**5¼**	12 52	D	— —	–	AQU	9
332	28	Sa.	6 50	E	4 14	A	9 24	28	21 21	5¾	**6¼**	1 26	D	12 A.M. 26	D	AQU	10
333	29	**D**	6 51	E	4 13	A	9 22	28	21 31	6¾	**7¼**	2 00	C	1 36	D	PSC	11
334	30	M.	6 53	E	4 13	A	9 20	27	21s.41	7¾	**8**	2 P.M. 35	C	2 A.M. 49	D	PSC	12

NOVEMBER hath 30 days. 1998

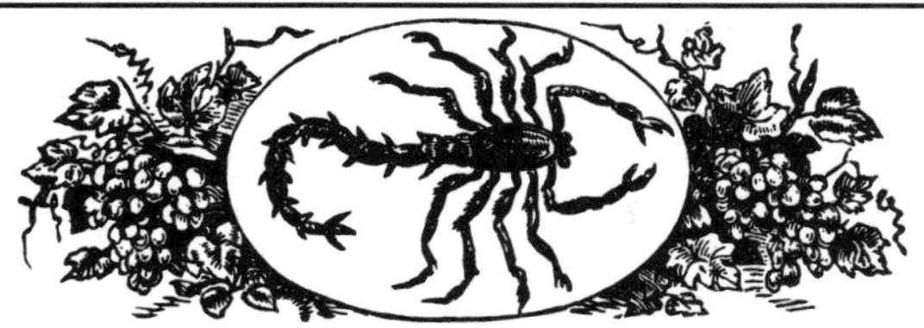

Now is the time for the burning of the leaves.
They go to the fire; the nostril pricks with smoke
Wandering slowly into a weeping mist.
Brittle and blotched, ragged and rotten sheaves!
– Laurence Binyon

D. M.	D. W.	Dates, Feasts, Fasts, Aspects, Tide Heights	*Weather* ↓
1	D	**22nd S. af. P.** • **All Saints** • ☾ on Eq. • {10.6/10.8	*In*
2	M.	**All Souls** • *Flowers in bloom late in autumn indicate a bad winter.* • {11.3/11.1	*the*
3	Tu.	☌ ♄ ☾ • ☾ at perig. • Election Day •	*mountains,*
4	W.	**Full Beaver** ○ • Tomb of King Tut discovered, 1922 • Tides {12.4/11.5 •	*the*
5	Th.	Eight teams joined together to form the American Football League, 1959 • {12.5/— •	*first*
6	Fr.	Adolph Sax born, 1814 • *Music is the poetry of the air.* • Tides {11.3/12.4 •	*snow*
7	Sa.	New Jersey became first state to allow girls to play little league baseball, 1973 • {11.0/12.1 •	*is*
8	D	**23rd S. af. P.** • ☾ rides high • {10.6/11.5 •	*falling;*
9	M.	First issue of *The Atlantic Monthly* hit the newsstands, 1857 • {10.1/10.8 •	*geese*
10	Tu.	**St. Leo the Great** • The *Edmund Fitzgerald* sank, 1975 • {9.7/10.2	*are*
11	W.	**St. Martin** • **Veterans Day** • ☾ at ☊ • ☿ Gr. Elong (23° E.) •	
12	Th.	*If All Saints brings out winter, St. Martin brings out Indian summer.* • {9.3/9.4 •	*heading*
13	Fr.	☌ ♂ ☾ • ♃ stat. • *You never know your luck.* •	*south.*
14	Sa.	☾ on Eq. • Dow Jones closed above 1,000 mark, first time in 76 years, 1972 •	*We*
15	D	**24th S. af. P.** • Georgia O'Keefe born, 1887 • {9.7/9.4	*pause*
16	M.	6 inches snow, Tucson, Ariz., 1958 • Suez Canal opened, 1869 • {9.9/9.4 •	*at*
17	Tu.	**St. Hugh of Lincoln** • ☾ at apo. • August Mobius born, 1790 •	*our*
18	W.	**St. Hilda** • **New** ● • Tides {10.2/9.4 •	*feast*
19	Th.	Lincoln delivered his short speech at Gettysburg, Pa., 1863 • Tommy Dorsey born, 1905 •	*to*
20	Fr.	☌ ☿ ☾ • Edwin Powell Hubble born, 1889 • {10.3/— •	*hear*
21	Sa.	☿ stat. • *As November 21, so the winter.* • Tides {9.3/10.2 •	*their*
22	D	**25th S. af. P.** • ☾ runs low • Tides {9.2/10.1 •	*loud*
23	M.	**St. Clement** • First jukebox installed, San Francisco, Calif., 1889 •	*calling,*
24	Tu.	☌ ♆ ☾ • ☌ ♅ ☾ • Scott Joplin born, 1868 • Tides {9.0/9.8 •	*a*
25	W.	*Loyalty to a petrified opinion never yet broke a chain or freed a human soul.* •	*forkful*
26	Th.	**Thanksgiving** • ☾ at ☋ • Tommy Dorsey died, 1956 • {9.1/9.7 •	*of*
27	Fr.	☌ ♃ ☾ • Bat Masterson born, 1853 • Tides {9.3/9.7 •	*turkey*
28	Sa.	First skywriting, "Hello USA," written over New York City, 1922 •	*halfway*
29	D	**1st S. in Advent** • ☾ on Eq. • {10.3/10.1 •	*to our*
30	M.	**St. Andrew** • ☌ ♇ ☉ • ☌ ♄ ☾ • {10.9/10.4	*mouth.*

I don't make jokes — I just watch the government and report the facts. – Will Rogers

Farmer's Calendar

A big blow last night: winds up to 40 miles per hour, the report this morning says. All night, the wind galloped and shouted about the house with a racket like world war. Soldiers recall that going into battle you least expect the noise. The sound of battle, they write, is more than the sounds of the particular things that must make it up: guns, cries, machinery, violent motion. Battle has a strange noise of its own, greater than all these.

So it is with a high wind. You can analyze its noise only so far. You can hear the trees being bent, the wind boiling around the corners of the house. You can hear doors banging, windows rattling, the banshee wail of a loose piece of roofing metal. But over all is a wild orchestral roar — the sound of the wind itself.

The worst of it is, you can't sleep. There is something in a strong wind by night that gets under the lid of your brain, just as it does with your window shutters, and makes rest impossible. I can sleep in snow and rain and even in the perpetual emergency that is night in a great city. But let the wind blow hard, and I find I can do nothing but lie there and listen to it. It's not all suffering, though. Windborne sleeplessness, for one thing, is good medicine against self-congratulation. Over and over again, you think of every stupid thing you have ever done, said, believed, and wanted. That's bad. Then you think of every stupid thing you have *not* done, said, and so on. That's far worse. In the end, if you can, you do best to give yourself up to the gale. Tomorrow morning, the world will look like Fifth Avenue after the parade has passed.

1998 DECEMBER, THE TWELFTH MONTH

Look for Mercury in the east before dawn from the 11th to the 26th. This innermost planet floats below the crescent Moon on the 16th and above it the next morning. Jupiter, currently the night's most brilliant "star," and bright Saturn well to its left are now both high in the sky at nightfall and well placed throughout the night. The Moon keeps Jupiter company on the 24th and passes Saturn on the 27th. The winter solstice occurs on the 21st, at 8:56 P.M., EST. While members of the mass media correctly announce this as the shortest day, the earliest sunset occurred two weeks earlier, and afternoon daylight is already growing longer.

○	Full Moon	3rd day	10th hour	19th minute
☾	Last Quarter	10th day	12th hour	53rd minute
●	New Moon	18th day	17th hour	42nd minute
☽	First Quarter	26th day	5th hour	46th minute

Times are given in Eastern Standard Time.

For an explanation of this page, see "How to Use This Almanac," page 34; for values of Key Letters, see Time Correction Tables, page 214.

Day of Year	Day of Month	Day of Week	☉ Rises h. m.	Key	☉ Sets h. m.	Key	Length of Days h. m.	Sun Fast m.	Declination of Sun ° '	Full Sea Boston Light – A.M.	**Bold – P.M.**	☽ Rises h. m.	Key	☽ Sets h. m.	Key	☽ Place	☽ Age
335	1	Tu.	6 54	E	4 13	A	9 19	27	21s.50	8½	**9**	3 P.M. 13	C	4 A.M. 03	E	CET	13
336	2	W.	6 55	E	4 12	A	9 17	26	21 59	9½	**10**	3 56	B	5 17	E	ARI	14
337	3	Th.	6 56	E	4 12	A	9 16	26	22 08	10¼	**11**	4 45	B	6 31	E	TAU	15
338	4	Fr.	6 57	E	4 12	A	9 15	26	22 16	11	**11¾**	5 39	B	7 41	E	TAU	16
339	5	Sa.	6 58	E	4 12	A	9 14	25	22 23	**12**	—	6 39	B	8 44	E	GEM	17
340	6	**D**	6 59	E	4 12	A	9 13	25	22 30	12¾	**12¾**	7 42	B	9 39	E	GEM	18
341	7	M.	7 00	E	4 12	A	9 12	24	22 37	1½	**1¾**	8 46	C	10 26	E	CAN	19
342	8	Tu.	7 01	E	4 11	A	9 10	24	22 44	2½	**2¾**	9 50	C	11 05	E	CAN	20
343	9	W.	7 01	E	4 11	A	9 10	24	22 50	3¼	**3½**	10 51	C	11 A.M. 40	D	LEO	21
344	10	Th.	7 02	E	4 12	A	9 10	23	22 56	4¼	**4½**	11 P.M. 51	C	12 P.M. 10	D	LEO	22
345	11	Fr.	7 03	E	4 12	A	9 09	23	23 00	5¼	**5½**	— —	–	12 38	D	VIR	23
346	12	Sa.	7 04	E	4 12	A	9 08	22	23 05	6¼	**6½**	12 A.M. 49	D	1 06	C	VIR	24
347	13	**D**	7 05	E	4 12	A	9 07	22	23 09	7	**7½**	1 47	D	1 33	C	VIR	25
348	14	M.	7 06	E	4 12	A	9 06	21	23 13	7¾	**8¼**	2 44	E	2 01	C	VIR	26
349	15	Tu.	7 06	E	4 12	A	9 06	21	23 16	8½	**9**	3 41	E	2 31	B	LIB	27
350	16	W.	7 07	E	4 13	A	9 06	20	23 19	9¼	**9¾**	4 39	E	3 04	B	LIB	28
351	17	Th.	7 08	E	4 13	A	9 05	20	23 21	10	**10½**	5 36	E	3 42	B	SCO	29
352	18	Fr.	7 08	E	4 13	A	9 05	19	23 23	10¾	**11¼**	6 31	E	4 25	B	OPH	0
353	19	Sa.	7 09	E	4 14	A	9 05	19	23 24	11¼	**11¾**	7 25	E	5 13	B	SAG	1
354	20	**D**	7 09	E	4 14	A	9 05	18	23 25	**12**	—	8 15	E	6 06	B	SAG	2
355	21	M.	7 10	E	4 15	A	9 05	18	23 25	12½	**12½**	9 01	E	7 04	B	SAG	3
356	22	Tu.	7 10	E	4 15	A	9 05	17	23 25	1¼	**1¼**	9 43	E	8 06	B	CAP	4
357	23	W.	7 11	E	4 16	A	9 05	17	23 25	2	**2**	10 21	D	9 10	C	CAP	5
358	24	Th.	7 11	E	4 16	A	9 05	16	23 24	2¾	**2¾**	10 56	D	10 17	C	AQU	6
359	25	Fr.	7 12	E	4 17	A	9 05	16	23 23	3½	**3¾**	11 A.M. 29	D	11 P.M. 24	C	AQU	7
360	26	Sa.	7 12	E	4 17	A	9 05	15	23 21	4½	**4¾**	12 P.M. 01	D	— —	–	PSC	8
361	27	**D**	7 12	E	4 18	A	9 06	15	23 18	5¼	**5¾**	12 34	C	12 A.M. 33	D	CET	9
362	28	M.	7 13	E	4 19	A	9 06	14	23 15	6¼	**6¾**	1 09	C	1 43	E	PSC	10
363	29	Tu.	7 13	E	4 20	A	9 07	14	23 12	7¼	**7¾**	1 48	B	2 55	E	ARI	11
364	30	W.	7 13	E	4 20	A	9 07	13	23 09	8¼	**8¾**	2 32	B	4 07	E	TAU	12
365	31	Th.	7 13	E	4 21	A	9 08	13	23s.04	9	**9¾**	3 P.M. 22	B	5 A.M. 18	E	TAU	13

DECEMBER hath 31 days. 1998

Give human nature reverence for the sake
Of One who bore it, making it divine
With the ineffable tenderness of God.
– *John Greenleaf Whittier*

D. M.	D. W.	Dates, Feasts, Fasts, Aspects, Tide Heights	Weather ↓
1	Tu.	☿ in inf. ☌ • First "Christmas Club," Carlisle, Pa., 1909 • {11.5 10.7	*Bright*
2	W.	☾ at perig. • Barney Clark received first artificial heart, 1982 • {12.0 10.9 •	*and*
3	Th.	**Full Cold** ○ • Oberlin College, first true co-ed college, opened, 1833 • {12.3 10.9	*bitter*
4	Fr.	*A Streetcar Named Desire* opened in New York City, 1947 • {12.4 10.9 •	*before*
5	Sa.	☾ rides high • Prohibition ended with ratification of the 21st Amendment, 1933 •	*the*
6	**D**	**2nd S. in Advent** • Dave Brubeck born, 1920 • {10.7 11.9 •	*cold*
7	M.	**St. Nicholas** • Pearl Harbor attacked, 1941 • Larry Bird born, 1956 •	*eases.*
8	Tu.	☾ at ☊ • *The history of the world is but the biography of great men.* • {10.0 10.7	*Snow*
9	W.	U.S. Golf Association legalized steel-shaft golf clubs, 1926 • {9.7 10.0 •	*flurries*
10	Th.	70° F, New York City, 1946 • Emily Dickinson born, 1830 • {9.4 9.5	*blow*
11	Fr.	☿ stat. • U.S. soldiers camped in Arizona attacked by wild longhorn bulls, 1846 •	*in*
12	Sa.	☾ on Eq. • ☌ ♂ ☾ • George Grant patented the golf tee, 1899 • {9.2 8.8	*on*
13	**D**	**3rd S. in Advent** • Tides {9.3 8.8 •	*boreal*
14	M.	**St. Lucy** • **First day of Chanukah** • ☾ at apo. •	*breezes.*
15	Tu.	Bill of Rights ratified, 1791 • *They have rights who dare maintain them.* • {9.7 8.9 •	*The*
16	W.	☌ ☿ ☾ • Ember Day • Boston Tea Party, 1773 • {9.9 9.0 •	*Sun*
17	Th.	Orville and Wilbur Wright made first successful airplane flights at Kitty Hawk, N.C., 1903 • {10.1 9.1	*is*
18	Fr.	**New** ● • Ember Day • Thirteenth Amendment ratified, 1865 • {10.3 9.1	*so*
19	Sa.	☿ Gr. Elong (22° W.) • Ember Day • Halcyon Days • {10.3 9.2 •	*weak*
20	**D**	**4th S. in Advent** • ☾ runs low • Tides {— 10.4	*even*
21	M.	**St. Thomas** • **Winter Solstice** • ☌ ♆ ☾ • {9.2 10.4 •	*charity*
22	Tu.	☌ ♅ ☾ • Beware the Pogonip. • Connie Mack born, 1862 •	*freezes.*
23	W.	☾ at ☋ • Federal Reserve System created, 1913 • {9.4 10.2 •	*But*
24	Th.	"Silent Night, Holy Night" composed, 1818 • Tides {9.5 10.1 •	*remember*
25	Fr.	**Christmas Day** • ☌ ♃ ☾ • Tides {9.6 9.9 •	*the*
26	Sa.	**St. Stephen** • ☾ on Eq. • **Boxing Day (Canada)** • {9.8 9.7 •	*star,*
27	**D**	**1st S. af. Ch.** • ☌ ♄ ☾ • Tides {10.1 9.7 •	*and*
28	M.	**St. John** • **Holy Innocents** • *Dare to be wise.* • {10.5 9.7 •	*the*
29	Tu.	Gas lighting was installed at the White House, 1848 • Texas statehood, 1848 •	*stable,*
30	W.	♄ stat. • ☾ at perig. • Rudyard Kipling born, 1865 • {11.3 10.0 •	*and*
31	Th.	*Each day the world is born anew For him who takes it rightly.* – Lowell • {11.7 10.2 •	*Jesus.*

Farmer's Calendar

Five miles down the road is a little, one-horse ski area that caters to locals: beginners, families, school groups. It's not a resort. You can ski, and you can eat a hamburger: no condominiums, no shopping, no fine dining. A nice place. Early in December, before the real winter storms begin, they roll out their snowmaking guns. I like to watch them in action.

On the first clear nights to get sharply cold, the snow guns appear. They look like large, ungainly water birds: storks or pelicans lined up at intervals on the ski trails that climb the hill. The snow guns are, I guess, essentially powerful sprayers, lawn sprinklers on steroids. They spray a fine stream of water 50 to 60 feet into the dry, cold air, where it freezes and falls back to the ground as snow in brilliant, shimmering parabolas. Under the night lights, snowmaking looks like a fireworks show: the glorious Fourth strayed into the wrong season. At my ski area, they run the snow guns all night long, and in the morning, they're ready for business.

It's the damnedest thing, too, when you think about it. Snow, at first, would seem to be a brute fact, the simple, inescapable condition of winter in the North. You love it or you hate it. But no: It's not snow that matters, it's where the snow is. If nature doesn't furnish snow where we want it, we'll figure out a way to put it there, even if doing so means we have to spend millions to make our own. At the same time, 100 feet away, we're spending more millions to *remove* snow from other places, like roads and parking lots. What better image for the mind of man: so smart, so dumb?

1999 JANUARY, THE FIRST MONTH

This spectacular sky-year begins auspiciously with a full Moon on January 1, which happens only a few times per century. Earth is closest to the Sun (perihelion) on the 3rd, at a distance of 91,400,005 miles. Venus slowly emerges from behind the Sun, appearing low in the southwest at dusk. The evening star is in conjunction with green Uranus on the 13th, an event visible with the aid of binoculars. For more-observable gatherings, watch the Moon skim very near to brilliant Jupiter on the evening of the 21st and pass near bright Saturn late on the 23rd, shortly before conjunction.

○	Full Moon	1st day	21st hour	49th minute
☾	Last Quarter	9th day	9th hour	22nd minute
●	New Moon	17th day	10th hour	46th minute
☽	First Quarter	24th day	14th hour	15th minute
○	Full Moon	31st day	11th hour	6th minute

Times are given in Eastern Standard Time.

For an explanation of this page, see "How to Use This Almanac," page 34; for values of Key Letters, see Time Correction Tables, page 214.

Day of Year	Day of Month	Day of Week	☉ Rises h. m.	Key	☉ Sets h. m.	Key	Length of Days h. m.	Sun Fast m.	Declination of Sun ° '	Full Sea Boston Light – A.M.	**Bold – P.M.**	☽ Rises h. m.	Key	☽ Sets h. m.	Key	☽ Place	☽ Age
1	1	Fr.	7 13	E	4 22	A	9 09	12	22s.59	10	**10¾**	4 P.M. 19	B	6 A.M. 24	E	ORI	14
2	2	Sa.	7 14	E	4 23	A	9 09	12	22 54	10¾	**11½**	5 21	B	7 23	E	GEM	15
3	3	**C**	7 14	E	4 24	A	9 10	12	22 48	11¾	—	6 25	B	8 15	E	CAN	16
4	4	M.	7 14	E	4 25	A	9 11	11	22 42	12½	**12½**	7 31	C	8 59	E	CAN	17
5	5	Tu.	7 14	E	4 26	A	9 12	11	22 36	1¼	**1½**	8 35	C	9 37	D	LEO	18
6	6	W.	7 13	E	4 27	A	9 14	10	22 29	2	**2¼**	9 37	D	10 10	D	LEO	19
7	7	Th.	7 13	E	4 28	A	9 15	10	22 22	2¾	**3**	10 37	D	10 40	D	LEO	20
8	8	Fr.	7 13	E	4 29	A	9 16	9	22 14	3¾	**4**	11 P.M. 36	D	11 08	D	VIR	21
9	9	Sa.	7 13	E	4 30	A	9 17	9	22 05	4½	**5**	— —	–	11 A.M. 35	C	VIR	22
10	10	**C**	7 13	E	4 31	A	9 18	8	21 56	5½	**5¾**	12 A.M. 34	D	12 P.M. 03	C	VIR	23
11	11	M.	7 12	E	4 32	A	9 20	8	21 47	6¼	**6¾**	1 31	E	12 32	B	LIB	24
12	12	Tu.	7 12	E	4 33	A	9 21	8	21 37	7¼	**7¾**	2 28	E	1 04	B	LIB	25
13	13	W.	7 12	E	4 34	A	9 22	7	21 27	8	**8½**	3 25	E	1 39	B	SCO	26
14	14	Th.	7 11	E	4 35	A	9 24	7	21 17	8¾	**9¼**	4 22	E	2 20	B	OPH	27
15	15	Fr.	7 11	E	4 36	A	9 25	7	21 06	9½	**10**	5 17	E	3 06	B	SAG	28
16	16	Sa.	7 11	E	4 38	A	9 27	6	20 55	10¼	**10¾**	6 09	E	3 58	B	SAG	29
17	17	**C**	7 10	E	4 39	A	9 29	6	20 43	10¾	**11½**	6 57	E	4 55	B	SAG	0
18	18	M.	7 09	E	4 40	A	9 31	5	20 31	11½	—	7 42	E	5 57	B	CAP	1
19	19	Tu.	7 09	E	4 41	A	9 32	5	20 19	12¼	**12¼**	8 22	E	7 02	C	CAP	2
20	20	W.	7 08	E	4 42	A	9 34	5	20 06	12¾	**1**	8 58	D	8 08	C	AQU	3
21	21	Th.	7 08	E	4 44	A	9 36	5	19 53	1½	**1¾**	9 32	D	9 16	D	AQU	4
22	22	Fr.	7 07	E	4 45	A	9 38	4	19 39	2¼	**2½**	10 05	D	10 25	D	PSC	5
23	23	Sa.	7 06	D	4 46	A	9 40	4	19 26	3	**3½**	10 37	C	11 P.M. 34	D	CET	6
24	24	**C**	7 05	D	4 47	A	9 42	4	19 11	4	**4½**	11 11	C	— —	–	PSC	7
25	25	M.	7 05	D	4 49	A	9 44	3	18 57	5	**5½**	11 A.M. 47	B	12 A.M. 43	E	CET	8
26	26	Tu.	7 04	D	4 50	A	9 46	3	18 42	5¾	**6½**	12 P.M. 28	B	1 53	E	TAU	9
27	27	W.	7 03	D	4 51	A	9 48	3	18 26	7	**7½**	1 13	B	3 02	E	TAU	10
28	28	Th.	7 02	D	4 53	A	9 51	3	18 10	8	**8½**	2 05	B	4 08	E	TAU	11
29	29	Fr.	7 01	D	4 54	A	9 53	3	17 54	9	**9½**	3 03	B	5 09	E	GEM	12
30	30	Sa.	7 00	D	4 55	A	9 55	2	17 38	9¾	**10½**	4 06	B	6 03	E	GEM	13
31	31	**C**	6 59	D	4 57	A	9 58	2	17s.21	10¾	**11¼**	5 P.M. 11	B	6 A.M. 51	E	CAN	14

JANUARY hath 31 days. 1999

Saint Agnes' Eve — Ah, bitter chill it was!
The owl, for all his feathers, was a-cold;
The hare limped trembling through the frozen grass,
And silent was the flock in woolly fold.
– John Keats

D. M.	D. W.	Dates, Feasts, Fasts, Aspects, Tide Heights	*Weather* ↓
1	Fr.	New Year's Day • **Circumcision** • Full Wolf ○ •	*Just*
2	Sa.	☾ rides high • Alice B. Sanger, first female White House stenographer, reported for work, 1890	*a*
3	**C**	**2nd S. af. Ch.** • ⊕ at perihelion • {11.8 / —	*dusting,*
4	M.	St. Elizabeth Seton • ☾ at ☊ • Tides {10.3 / 11.5 •	*then*
5	Tu.	☌ ♀ ♆ • Twelfth Night • King Camp Gillette born, 1855 •	*we're*
6	W.	**Epiphany** • Teddy Roosevelt died, 1919 • {9.8 / 10.4	*powdered!*
7	Th.	St. Distaff's Day • Marian Anderson first black singer to perform at Met, 1955 •	*Warmy,*
8	Fr.	☾ on Eq. • First viewing of "Mona Lisa" in the U.S., Washington, D.C., 1963 •	*but*
9	Sa.	☌ ♂ ☾ • Mississippi seceded from the Union, 1861 • {9.2 / 8.8 •	*mighty*
10	**C**	**1st S. af. Ep.** • Buffalo Bill Cody died, 1917 •	*stormy —*
11	M.	☾ at apo. • Plough Monday • John A. Macdonald, first Canadian prime minister, born, 1815	*has*
12	Tu.	*Blowing is not playing the flute; you must make use of your fingers.* • {9.2 / 8.3 •	*someone*
13	W.	St. Hilary • ☌ ♀ ♅ • Alfred Fuller, founder of the Fuller Brush Co., born, 1885	*got*
14	Th.	Propitious day for birth of women. • *One is not born a genius, one becomes a genius.* • {9.6 / 8.6	*a*
15	Fr.	A donkey was first used to symbolize the Democratic Party in a political cartoon, 1870 • {9.9 / 8.8	*life*
16	Sa.	☾ runs low • Poet Robert Service born, 1874 • Dizzy Dean born, 1911 • {10.2 / 9.0	*raft*
17	**C**	**2nd S. af. Ep.** • New ● • Benjamin Franklin born, 1706 •	
18	M.	Martin Luther King Jr.'s Birthday • A. A. Milne born, 1882 •	*for*
19	Tu.	☾ at ☋ • ☌ ♀ ☾ • Edgar Allan Poe born, 1809 • {9.5 / 10.8 •	*me?*
20	W.	St. Fabian • Favorable day for birth of men. • George Burns born, 1896 •	*What's*
21	Th.	St. Agnes • ☌ ♃ ☾ • President Carter pardoned draft evaders, 1977 •	*a*
22	Fr.	St. Vincent • ☾ on Eq. • ☌ ♆ ☉ • Tides {10.1 / 10.5	*nice*
23	Sa.	Elizabeth Blackwell became first woman in U.S. to receive M.D. degree, 1849 • {10.2 / 10.1 •	*week*
24	**C**	**3rd S. af. Ep.** • ☌ ♄ ☾ • Edith Wharton born, 1862 •	*like*
25	M.	Conversion of Paul • *The finger of God never leaves identical fingerprints.* •	*you*
26	Tu.	Sts. Timothy & Titus • ☾ at perig. • Tides {10.5 / 9.3	*doing*
27	W.	Severe 3-day freeze began in Florida; 11 million boxes of citrus damaged, 1940 • {10.6 / 9.3 •	*in a*
28	Th.	St. Thomas Aquinas • Artur Rubinstein born, 1887 •	*month*
29	Fr.	☾ rides high • Ice cream cone-rolling machine patented, 1924 • W. C. Fields born, 1880 •	*like*
30	Sa.	Maryland became last of the 13 original states to adopt the Articles of Confederation, 1781 •	*this?*
31	**C**	**Septuagesima** • Full Old ○ • Penumbral Eclipse ☾ • {11.3 / 10.0	

Farmer's Calendar

Somewhere I have read that wood ashes are good for flowering trees and shrubs. I hope it's true, for if it's not, the flowering trees and shrubs on this place may be in trouble. That's because wood ashes are not scarce here. Money, talent, and good sense are frequently in short supply. Wood ashes we've got.

Mainly they come from a big iron stove in the kitchen, which runs most of every day from about November through April. I shovel out the ashes every third or fourth day and collect them in a copper scuttle. Four of these scuttles, I'm guessing, amount to a bushel basket. You begin to see that by midwinter there arises a need for something to do with the ashes. When we're lucky enough to get a bad ice storm, I put ashes down on the walk to make it less slippery. This works all right, but we don't have enough bad ice storms to use up all our ashes, something I find I can't wholeheartedly regret. Our pioneer forebears, I understand, made soap out of wood ashes. But I am not a pioneer; I buy my soap at the soap store.

Imagine my relief on finding that wood ashes boost the shrubbery. Their benefit has to do with potassium, I think, but who cares? It's a break for me. We have around this house four lilacs, six rosebushes, and a little cherry tree. By the end of January (provided the ice storms have held off), they are up to their knees in ashes. By spring they will look like survivors of the eruption of Mount St. Helens. "Please!" the roses, lilacs, and cherry will say. "Enough! No more potassium!"

1999 FEBRUARY, THE SECOND MONTH

Venus now ascends further out of the Sun's glare during evening twilight. This is the scene of the year's most spectacular conjunction and one of the best of the decade: From February 22 to 24, dazzling Venus and brilliant Jupiter, after the Moon the sky's two brightest objects, nearly "touch." Mercury, bright but not brilliant, dangles below them. (If you see anything beneath the Jupiter-Venus duo, you've found this elusive, innermost planet, since no bright stars are in that vicinity.) The crescent Moon passes near Venus on the 17th and Jupiter on the 18th. Meanwhile, Orion reaches its yearly pinnacle, conspicuous in the southern sky. Its belt stars point leftward to Sirius, the heaven's brightest star. The Dog Star is a binary system; the human eye actually sees the combined light of two close-together stars, Sirius and its white-dwarf companion.

☾	Last Quarter	8th day	6th hour	58th minute
●	New Moon	16th day	1st hour	39th minute
☽	First Quarter	22nd day	21st hour	43rd minute

Times are given in Eastern Standard Time.

For an explanation of this page, see "How to Use This Almanac," page 34; for values of Key Letters, see Time Correction Tables, page 214.

Day of Year	Day of Month	Day of Week	☼ Rises h. m.	Key	☼ Sets h. m.	Key	Length of Days h. m.	Sun Fast m.	Declination of Sun ° '	Full Sea Boston Light – A.M.	Bold – P.M.	☽ Rises h. m.	Key	☽ Sets h. m.	Key	☽ Place	☽ Age
32	1	M.	6 58	D	4 58	A	10 00	2	17 s.04	11½	—	6 P.M. 16	C	7 A.M. 31	E	LEO	15
33	2	Tu.	6 57	D	4 59	A	10 02	2	16 47	12	**12¼**	7 20	C	8 07	D	LEO	16
34	3	W.	6 56	D	5 00	A	10 04	2	16 30	12¾	**1**	8 22	D	8 39	D	LEO	17
35	4	Th.	6 55	D	5 02	A	10 07	2	16 12	1½	**1¾**	9 22	D	9 08	D	VIR	18
36	5	Fr.	6 54	D	5 03	A	10 09	2	15 54	2¼	**2½**	10 21	D	9 36	C	VIR	19
37	6	Sa.	6 53	D	5 04	A	10 11	2	15 36	3	**3¼**	11 P.M. 19	D	10 04	C	VIR	20
38	7	**C**	6 52	D	5 06	A	10 14	2	15 17	3¾	**4¼**	— —	–	10 32	B	VIR	21
39	8	M.	6 50	D	5 07	B	10 17	1	14 58	4½	**5**	12 A.M. 16	E	11 03	B	LIB	22
40	9	Tu.	6 49	D	5 08	B	10 19	1	14 39	5½	**6**	1 13	E	11 A.M. 37	B	LIB	23
41	10	W.	6 48	D	5 10	B	10 22	1	14 19	6¼	**7**	2 10	E	12 P.M. 14	B	OPH	24
42	11	Th.	6 47	D	5 11	B	10 24	1	14 00	7¼	**8**	3 05	E	12 57	B	OPH	25
43	12	Fr.	6 45	D	5 12	B	10 27	1	13 40	8	**8¾**	3 58	E	1 46	B	SAG	26
44	13	Sa.	6 44	D	5 13	B	10 29	1	13 20	9	**9½**	4 48	E	2 41	B	SAG	27
45	14	**C**	6 43	D	5 15	B	10 32	1	13 00	9¾	**10¼**	5 35	E	3 42	B	CAP	28
46	15	M.	6 41	D	5 16	B	10 35	1	12 39	10½	**11**	6 17	E	4 46	C	CAP	29
47	16	Tu.	6 40	D	5 17	B	10 37	1	12 19	11¼	**11¾**	6 56	E	5 54	C	CAP	0
48	17	W.	6 38	D	5 19	B	10 41	2	11 58	11¾	—	7 32	D	7 03	D	AQU	1
49	18	Th.	6 37	D	5 20	B	10 43	2	11 37	12¼	**12½**	8 06	D	8 13	D	AQU	2
50	19	Fr.	6 36	D	5 21	B	10 45	2	11 15	1	**1½**	8 39	D	9 24	D	CET	3
51	20	Sa.	6 34	D	5 22	B	10 48	2	10 54	1¾	**2¼**	9 13	C	10 35	E	PSC	4
52	21	**C**	6 33	D	5 24	B	10 51	2	10 32	2¾	**3¼**	9 49	B	11 P.M. 45	E	CET	5
53	22	M.	6 31	D	5 25	B	10 54	2	10 10	3½	**4**	10 28	B	— —	–	ARI	6
54	23	Tu.	6 30	D	5 26	B	10 56	2	9 48	4½	**5¼**	11 A.M. 11	B	12 A.M. 54	E	TAU	7
55	24	W.	6 28	D	5 27	B	10 59	2	9 26	5½	**6¼**	12 P.M. 00	B	2 00	E	TAU	8
56	25	Th.	6 27	D	5 29	B	11 02	2	9 04	6½	**7½**	12 55	B	3 01	E	ORI	9
57	26	Fr.	6 25	D	5 30	B	11 05	3	8 42	7¾	**8½**	1 54	B	3 57	E	GEM	10
58	27	Sa.	6 23	D	5 31	B	11 08	3	8 19	8¾	**9½**	2 57	B	4 45	E	CAN	11
59	28	**C**	6 22	D	5 32	B	11 10	3	7 s.56	9¾	**10¼**	4 P.M. 01	C	5 A.M. 28	E	CAN	12

FEBRUARY hath 28 days. 1999

On the wind in February
Snowflakes float still,
Half inclined to turn to rain,
Nipping, dripping, chill.
– *Christina G. Rossetti*

D. M.	D. W.	Dates, Feasts, Fasts, Aspects, Tide Heights	*Weather* ↓
1	M.	St. Brigid • ☾ at ☊ • ☌ ♅ ☉ • Tides {11.3 —	*Lakes*
2	Tu.	**Candlemas** • Groundhog Day • -28° F, Hartford, Conn., 1789 •	*turn*
3	W.	Buddy Holly, Ritchie Valens, and "The Big Bopper" killed in a plane crash, 1959 • Tides {10.0 10.7	*to*
4	Th.	☾ on Eq. • ☿ in sup. ☌ • Charles Lindbergh born, 1902 •	*flakes;*
5	Fr.	St. Agatha • Mandatory inspection at U.S. airports, 1972 • Tides {9.7 9.7	*waders*
6	Sa.	☌ ♂ ☾ • *No one ever told a story well standing up or fasting.* • {9.5 9.2 •	*may*
7	C	**Sexagesima** • Main group of Dead Sea Scrolls discovered, 1947 •	*be*
8	M.	☾ at apo. • Boy Scouts of America incorporated, 1910 • Tides {9.0 8.3 •	*what*
9	Tu.	A record-breaking 73 million people watched the Beatles' first appearance on *The Ed Sullivan Show,* 1964 •	*it*
10	W.	Alanson Crane patented first fire extinguisher, 1863 • Leontyne Price born, 1927 • {8.9 8.0	*takes*
11	Th.	Yalta Conference ended, 1945 • Thomas Alva Edison born, 1847 • {9.1 8.1 •	*to*
12	Fr.	☾ runs low • Abraham Lincoln born, 1809 • Charles Darwin born, 1809 •	*bring*
13	Sa.	*Love does not consist in gazing at each other but in looking together in the same direction.* • {9.7 8.8	*your*
14	C	**Quinquagesima** • **Valentine's Day** • ☌ ♆ ☾ • {10.1 9.2	
15	M.	Presidents Day • ☾ at ☋ • Galileo born, 1564 •	*Valentine*
16	Tu.	Shrove Tuesday • **New** ● • Eclipse ☉ • {10.9 10.1 •	*a*
17	W.	**Ash Wednesday** • Winter's back breaks. • {11.1 — •	*gift,*
18	Th.	☌ ♀ ☾ • ☌ ♃ ☾ • Louis Comfort Tiffany born, 1848	*unless*
19	Fr.	☾ on Eq. • *Time and words can't be recalled, even if it was only yesterday.* • {10.7 11.0	*your*
20	Sa.	☾ at perig. • ☌ ♄ ☾ • Walter Winchell died, 1972 •	*darlin'*
21	C	**1st S. in Lent** • Charles Scribner born, 1821 • {10.9 10.3 •	*lives*
22	M.	**Pure Monday** • George Washington born, 1732 • Tides {10.7 9.8 •	*far in-*
23	Tu.	☌ ♀ ♃ • Siege of the Alamo began, 1836 • George F. Handel born, 1685	*land,*
24	W.	St. Matthias • Ember Day • The Voice of America radio network began broadcasting, 1942	*if*
25	Th.	☾ rides high • Record-breaking 91.6° F, Los Angeles, 1921 • {10.3 9.0 •	*you get*
26	Fr.	Ember Day • Six people killed by a bomb at the World Trade Center, New York City, 1993 •	*my*
27	Sa.	Ember Day • Singer Marian Anderson born, 1897 • Tides {10.5 9.5	*drift.*
28	C	**2nd S. in Lent** • **Sunday of Orthodoxy** • ☾ at ☊	

Dancing is wonderful training for girls; it's the first way you learn to guess what a man is going to do before he does it.

– Christopher Morley

Farmer's Calendar

Several years ago, on a bright winter morning when the temperature hadn't yet made it much above zero, I looked out the window at the bird feeder, then looked again. There was a ringer out there, fraternizing with the chickadees and titmice. It was a little thing from off that page in the bird book where they all look like sparrows who have been dipped for a shorter or longer time in raspberry juice. Half a dozen species around there were a good deal alike, but this one was easy to spot with its bright-red skullcap. It was a redpoll, a bit of a rarity for these parts, and a bird that always gives me a lift when it appears, not because of its superior beauty or remarkable behavior but because of its itinerary.

The redpoll is one of those birds that live for the most part in the latitudes of Hudson Bay and find their way to northern New England as winter migrants. Redpolls turn up here every few years, and they're good for morale just because they evidently regard Vermont as a place to go to get away from the winter. Think about that. For these birds, Florida is right here; this is the Caribbean. When the robins and bluebirds have fled to the real Florida, the redpolls arrive among us to spread their blankets on the beaches and under the palms of southern Vermont. They think that four feet of snow and fifteen below amounts to a tropic, a place of indolent refuge. Now, if reflecting on that isn't worth at least twenty degrees on your thermometer, then it may be time for you to consider wintering in Miami with the more delicate species.

1999 MARCH, THE THIRD MONTH

Venus, becoming still higher and brighter, hosts a series of eye-catching encounters in the western sky a half hour after sunset. On the 3rd, it's just above Jupiter, with little Mercury a bit lower. From the 17th to the 20th, Saturn sits just to the right of Venus, looking anemic in comparison with the dazzling planet. Mercury remains easily visible for those with unobstructed western horizons during the first week of this month. From the 3rd to the 12th, it floats just to the right of brilliant Jupiter. The vernal equinox occurs at 8:46 P.M., EST, on the 20th.

○	Full Moon	2nd day	1st hour	58th minute
☾	Last Quarter	10th day	3rd hour	40th minute
●	New Moon	17th day	13th hour	48th minute
☽	First Quarter	24th day	5th hour	18th minute
○	Full Moon	31st day	17th hour	49th minute

Times are given in Eastern Standard Time.

For an explanation of this page, see "How to Use This Almanac," page 34; for values of Key Letters, see Time Correction Tables, page 214.

Day of Year	Day of Month	Day of Week	☉ Rises h. m.	Key	☉ Sets h. m.	Key	Length of Days h. m.	Sun Fast m.	Declination of Sun ° '	Full Sea Boston Light – A.M.	**Bold – P.M.**	☽ Rises h. m.	Key	☽ Sets h. m.	Key	☽ Place	☽ Age
60	1	M.	6 20	D	5 34	B	11 14	3	7 s.34	10½	**11**	5 P.M. 04	C	6 A.M. 05	D	LEO	13
61	2	Tu.	6 19	D	5 35	B	11 16	3	7 11	11¼	**11¾**	6 07	D	6 37	D	LEO	14
62	3	W.	6 17	D	5 36	B	11 19	3	6 48	**12**	—	7 08	D	7 08	D	VIR	15
63	4	Th.	6 15	D	5 37	B	11 22	4	6 25	12¼	**12¾**	8 08	D	7 36	C	VIR	16
64	5	Fr.	6 14	D	5 38	B	11 24	4	6 01	1	**1¼**	9 07	D	8 04	C	VIR	17
65	6	Sa.	6 12	D	5 40	B	11 28	4	5 38	1¾	**2**	10 05	E	8 32	C	VIR	18
66	7	**C**	6 10	D	5 41	B	11 31	4	5 15	2¼	**2¾**	11 02	E	9 02	B	LIB	19
67	8	M.	6 09	D	5 42	B	11 33	5	4 52	3	**3½**	11 P.M. 59	E	9 34	B	LIB	20
68	9	Tu.	6 07	D	5 43	B	11 36	5	4 29	3¾	**4½**	— —	–	10 10	B	SCO	21
69	10	W.	6 05	D	5 44	B	11 39	5	4 05	4¾	**5¼**	12 A.M. 54	E	10 50	B	OPH	22
70	11	Th.	6 04	D	5 46	B	11 42	5	3 42	5½	**6¼**	1 48	E	11 A.M. 36	B	SAG	23
71	12	Fr.	6 02	C	5 47	B	11 45	6	3 17	6½	**7¼**	2 38	E	12 P.M. 27	B	SAG	24
72	13	Sa.	6 00	C	5 48	B	11 48	6	2 54	7½	**8**	3 26	E	1 24	B	SAG	25
73	14	**C**	5 59	C	5 49	B	11 50	6	2 31	8¼	**9**	4 09	E	2 26	C	CAP	26
74	15	M.	5 57	C	5 50	B	11 53	6	2 07	9¼	**9¾**	4 50	E	3 33	C	CAP	27
75	16	Tu.	5 55	C	5 51	B	11 56	7	1 43	10	**10½**	5 27	D	4 42	D	AQU	28
76	17	W.	5 53	C	5 53	B	12 00	7	1 20	10¾	**11¼**	6 02	D	5 53	D	AQU	0
77	18	Th.	5 52	C	5 54	B	12 02	7	0 56	11½	—	6 36	D	7 06	D	PSC	1
78	19	Fr.	5 50	C	5 55	B	12 05	8	0 32	12	**12¼**	7 11	C	8 19	E	PSC	2
79	20	Sa.	5 48	C	5 56	C	12 08	8	0 s.08	12¾	**1**	7 47	B	9 33	E	CET	3
80	21	**C**	5 46	C	5 57	C	12 11	8	0 n.15	1½	**2**	8 26	B	10 44	E	ARI	4
81	22	M.	5 45	C	5 58	C	12 13	8	0 39	2¼	**2¾**	9 09	B	11 P.M. 53	E	TAU	5
82	23	Tu.	5 43	C	5 59	C	12 16	9	1 02	3¼	**3¾**	9 57	B	— —	–	TAU	6
83	24	W.	5 41	C	6 01	C	12 20	9	1 26	4¼	**5**	10 50	B	12 A.M. 57	E	ORI	7
84	25	Th.	5 40	C	6 02	C	12 22	9	1 50	5¼	**6**	11 A.M. 48	B	1 54	E	GEM	8
85	26	Fr.	5 38	C	6 03	C	12 25	10	2 13	6¼	**7¼**	12 P.M. 49	B	2 44	E	CAN	9
86	27	Sa.	5 36	C	6 04	C	12 28	10	2 36	7½	**8¼**	1 52	C	3 28	E	CAN	10
87	28	**C**	5 34	C	6 05	C	12 31	10	3 00	8½	**9¼**	2 55	C	4 05	E	LEO	11
88	29	M.	5 33	C	6 06	C	12 33	11	3 23	9½	**10**	3 57	C	4 39	D	LEO	12
89	30	Tu.	5 31	C	6 07	C	12 36	11	3 47	10¼	**10¾**	4 58	D	5 09	D	LEO	13
90	31	W.	5 29	C	6 09	C	12 40	11	4 n.10	11	**11¼**	5 P.M. 58	D	5 A.M. 38	D	VIR	14

MARCH hath 31 days. 1999

And time remembered is grief forgotten,
And frosts are slain and flowers begotten,
And in green underwood and cover
Blossom by blossom the spring begins.
– Algernon Charles Swinburne

D. M.	D. W.	Dates, Feasts, Fasts, Aspects, Tide Heights	*Weather* ↓
1	M.	**St. David** • Pennsylvania became first state to abolish slavery, 1780 • Tides {10.8 / 10.0	*In*
2	Tu.	**St. Chad** • **Full Crust** ○ • First issue of *Time* on newsstands, 1923 •	*like a*
3	W.	☿ Gr. Elong. (18° E.) • Congress voted to install gas lighting in the Capitol, 1847 •	*lamb —*
4	Th.	☾ on Eq. • Old Inauguration Day • Jane Goodall born, 1934 • {10.1 / 10.4	*bam!*
5	Fr.	-5° F, St. Louis, Mo., 1960 • 72° F, New York City, 1880 • Tides {10.1 / 10.1	*Brief*
6	Sa.	☌ ♂ ☾ • Fall of the Alamo, 1836 • Michelangelo born, 1475 • {9.9 / 9.6	*relief,*
7	**C**	**3rd S. in Lent** • Alexander Graham Bell patented telephone, 1876 •	*then*
8	M.	☾ at apo. • *A man in the wrong may more easily be convinced than one half right.* •	*good*
9	Tu.	☿ stat. • Charles Graham received first patent for artificial teeth, 1822 • {9.2 / 8.3 •	*grief!*
10	W.	U.S. government issued its first paper money, 1862 • Harriet Tubman died, 1913 •	*Snows,*
11	Th.	Johnny Appleseed died, 1845 • Spanish flu epidemic hit the U.S., 1918 • {8.9 / 8.0	*blows,*
12	Fr.	**St. Gregory** • ☾ runs low • FDR broadcast his first "Fireside Chat," 1933 •	*frozen*
13	Sa.	☌ ♆ ☾ • First appearance of "Uncle Sam" in a political cartoon, 1852 • {9.2 / 8.5	*toes.*
14	**C**	**4th S. in Lent** • ☌ ♅ ☾ • ♇ stat. • {9.7 / 9.0	*March*
15	M.	☾ at ☋ • Beware the Ides of March. • First blood bank, Chicago, Ill., 1937 •	*will*
16	Tu.	*With most people, unbelief in one thing is founded upon blind belief in another.* • {10.7 / 10.2 •	*starch*
17	W.	**St. Patrick** • **New** ● • Rudolf Nureyev born, 1938 •	*you —*
18	Th.	☾ on Eq. • ♂ stat. • ☌ ♃ ☾ • Tides {11.4 / — •	*so*
19	Fr.	**St. Joseph** • ☿ in inf. ☌ • ☾ at perig. • ☌ ♀ ☾ • ☌ ♄ ☾	
20	Sa.	☌ ♀ ♄ • **Vernal Equinox** • Mister Rogers born, 1928 • {11.5 / 11.3	*it goes.*
21	**C**	**5th S. in Lent** • Tides {11.6 / 10.9 •	*Astronomers*
22	M.	First women's collegiate basketball game, Smith College, Northampton, Mass., 1893 • {11.4 / 10.4 •	*may*
23	Tu.	Joan Crawford born, 1908 • John Pennel set indoor pole vault record, 16 feet 3 inches, 1963 •	*say*
24	W.	Elvis Presley reported to his local draft board, 1958 • Tides {10.7 / 9.3 •	*it's*
25	Th.	**Annunciation** • ☾ rides high • Aretha Franklin born, 1942 •	*spring,*
26	Fr.	Menachem Begin and Anwar Sadat signed peace treaty, 1979 • Tides {10.0 / 9.1 •	*but*
27	Sa.	☾ at ☊ • Sarah Vaughan born, 1924 • Gloria Swanson born, 1899 •	*winter's*
28	**C**	**Palm Sunday** • Dwight D. Eisenhower died, 1969 •	*having*
29	M.	*There is no disputing a proverb, a fool, and the truth.* • Pearl Bailey born, 1918 • {10.2 / 9.8 •	*one*
30	Tu.	Larry Bird scored 53 points against Indiana — the most ever by a Celtic during a regular season game, 1983	*last*
31	W.	☾ on Eq. • **Full Worm** ○ • Gordie Howe born, 1928 • {10.3 / 10.2 •	*fling!*

Farmer's Calendar

The City of Boston, I have been told, doesn't much exert itself in winter to clear its streets of snow, not because of incapacity or neglect but from philosophy. In Boston, they reason that the snow will melt all by itself sooner or later; why bother to plow it, then? So it seems we can add one more item to the surprisingly long list of things that have a variety somehow associated with this old city: Boston ferns, Boston rockers, Boston cream pie — and *Boston snow,* defined as snow that nobody quite gets around to doing anything about.

I live 125 miles north and west of Boston. We have Boston snow up here, too, as it happens, but not as much. There, I guess, all snow is Boston snow; wherever it falls, whenever, in whatever quantities, they ignore it. Hereabouts, whether or not a storm consists of Boston snow depends mainly on the date. How many times have you shoveled yourself out so far this winter? How sick are you of snow — not merely snow itself but snow as an *idea*?

Up here, by March, the answers to those two questions, in many years, are Nine or ten, and Very sick, thanks. So it is that each year on St. Patrick's Day, I adjust my attitude toward snow. I take the Boston view. Usually there is significant, shovelable snow to come. I let it lie. I wade through it. I don't see it. I know it will take its leave by and by. And I hide the snow shovel at the very back of the cellar, behind the boxes and the old magazines, inaccessible. In the season of Boston snow, I'm for having a Boston snow shovel.

1999 APRIL, THE FOURTH MONTH

This is the month for Mars. The red planet, which is actually pumpkin-colored, reaches its best opposition of the decade on the 24th. By month's end, Mars comes closest to Earth since 1990, outshining all the night's stars including the Dog Star, Sirius. At 53.8 million miles and at magnitude -1.7, it is unmistakable as it dominates the eastern sky at nightfall. The Moon and Mars conjunct on the 3rd and again on the 29th. A challenge for telescope or binocular owners is the view of the waning crescent Moon and Uranus in the eastern predawn sky on the 11th. Daylight Saving Time begins at 2:00 A.M. on the 4th.

☾	Last Quarter	8th day	22nd hour	51st minute
●	New Moon	16th day	0 hour	22nd minute
☽	First Quarter	22nd day	15th hour	1st minute
○	Full Moon	30th day	10th hour	55th minute

After 2:00 A.M. on April 4, Eastern Daylight Time (EDT) is given.

For an explanation of this page, see "How to Use This Almanac," page 34; for values of Key Letters, see Time Correction Tables, page 214.

Day of Year	Day of Month	Day of Week	☉ Rises h. m.	Key	☉ Sets h. m.	Key	Length of Days h. m.	Sun Fast m.	Declination of Sun ° '	Full Sea Boston Light – A.M.	**Bold – P.M.**	☽ Rises h. m.	Key	☽ Sets h. m.	Key	☽ Place	☽ Age
91	1	Th.	5 27	B	6 10	C	12 43	11	4N.33	11½	—	6 PM 57	D	6 AM 05	C	VIR	15
92	2	Fr.	5 26	B	6 11	C	12 45	12	4 56	12	**12¼**	7 55	E	6 33	C	VIR	16
93	3	Sa.	5 24	B	6 12	C	12 48	12	5 19	12½	**1**	8 53	E	7 02	B	LIB	17
94	4	**C**	6 22	B	7 13	C	12 51	12	5 42	1	**2½**	10 50	E	8 33	B	LIB	18
95	5	M.	6 21	B	7 14	D	12 53	13	6 05	2¾	**3¼**	11 PM 46	E	9 07	B	SCO	19
96	6	Tu.	6 19	B	7 15	D	12 56	13	6 28	3½	**4**	— —	–	9 45	B	OPH	20
97	7	W.	6 17	B	7 16	D	12 59	13	6 50	4¼	**4¾**	12 AM 40	E	10 28	B	SAG	21
98	8	Th.	6 15	B	7 18	D	13 03	14	7 13	5	**5¾**	1 31	E	11 AM 16	B	SAG	22
99	9	Fr.	6 14	B	7 19	D	13 05	14	7 35	6	**6½**	2 19	E	12 PM 10	B	SAG	23
100	10	Sa.	6 12	B	7 20	D	13 08	14	7 57	6¾	**7½**	3 03	E	1 09	B	CAP	24
101	11	**C**	6 10	B	7 21	D	13 11	14	8 19	7¾	**8½**	3 44	E	2 12	C	CAP	25
102	12	M.	6 09	B	7 22	D	13 13	15	8 41	8¾	**9¼**	4 21	E	3 19	C	AQU	26
103	13	Tu.	6 07	B	7 23	D	13 16	15	9 03	9½	**10**	4 57	D	4 28	D	AQU	27
104	14	W.	6 06	B	7 24	D	13 18	15	9 25	10½	**11**	5 31	D	5 40	D	AQU	28
105	15	Th.	6 04	B	7 25	D	13 21	15	9 46	11¼	**11¾**	6 05	C	6 55	D	CET	29
106	16	Fr.	6 02	B	7 27	D	13 25	16	10 07	**12**	—	6 40	C	8 10	E	PSC	0
107	17	Sa.	6 01	B	7 28	D	13 27	16	10 29	12½	**1**	7 19	B	9 25	E	ARI	1
108	18	**C**	5 59	B	7 29	D	13 30	16	10 50	1¼	**1¾**	8 01	B	10 38	E	TAU	2
109	19	M.	5 58	B	7 30	D	13 32	16	11 10	2	**2¾**	8 49	B	11 PM 47	E	TAU	3
110	20	Tu.	5 56	B	7 31	D	13 35	16	11 31	3	**3¾**	9 42	B	— —	–	TAU	4
111	21	W.	5 54	B	7 32	D	13 38	17	11 52	4	**4½**	10 40	B	12 AM 49	E	GEM	5
112	22	Th.	5 53	B	7 33	D	13 40	17	12 12	5	**5¾**	11 AM 42	B	1 43	E	GEM	6
113	23	Fr.	5 51	B	7 34	D	13 43	17	12 33	6	**6¾**	12 PM 45	B	2 29	E	CAN	7
114	24	Sa.	5 50	B	7 36	D	13 46	17	12 52	7	**7¾**	1 48	C	3 08	E	LEO	8
115	25	**C**	5 48	B	7 37	D	13 49	17	13 12	8¼	**9**	2 50	C	3 42	D	LEO	9
116	26	M.	5 47	B	7 38	D	13 51	18	13 31	9¼	**9¾**	3 51	C	4 13	D	LEO	10
117	27	Tu.	5 46	B	7 39	D	13 53	18	13 50	10	**10½**	4 51	D	4 42	C	VIR	11
118	28	W.	5 44	B	7 40	D	13 56	18	14 09	10¾	**11¼**	5 50	D	5 09	C	VIR	12
119	29	Th.	5 43	B	7 41	D	13 58	18	14 28	11½	**11¾**	6 48	E	5 36	C	VIR	13
120	30	Fr.	5 41	B	7 42	D	14 01	18	14N.46	**12¼**	—	7 PM 46	E	6 AM 04	C	VIR	14

APRIL hath 30 days. 1999

April is here!
Blithest season of all the year;
The little brook laughs as it leaps away;
The lambs are out on the hills at play.
– Eben E. Rexford

D. M.	D. W.	Dates, Feasts, Fasts, Aspects, Tide Heights	*Weather* ↓
1	Th.	**First day of Passover** • **All Fools** • ☌ ♃ ☉ • ☿ stat. •	
2	Fr.	**Good Friday** • First White House Easter-egg roll, 1877 •	*Fools*
3	Sa.	☌ ♂ ☾ • Washington Irving born, 1783 • Tides {10.2 9.8 •	*slush*
4	C	**Easter** • **Daylight Saving Time begins, 2:00 A.M.** • ☾ at apo. • {10.1 9.5	*in*
5	M.	Daniel F. Bakeman, last surviving soldier of the Revolutionary War, died at age 109, 1869 • {9.9 9.2	*with*
6	Tu.	André Previn born, 1929 • Blue herons return to Vinalhaven, Maine • Tides {9.7 8.8 •	*rain*
7	W.	*It is comparison that makes men happy or miserable.* • Billie Holiday born, 1915 • {9.4 8.5 •	*and*
8	Th.	☾ runs low • First international major-league baseball game, Montreal Expos vs. N.Y. Mets, 1969	*snow;*
9	Fr.	Golf Hall of Fame created, 1941 • Dust storm, Texas, 1956 • Tides {9.0 8.2 •	*mud-*
10	Sa.	Occn. ♆ ☾ • ASPCA chartered, 1866 • {9.1 8.5 •	*puddley,*
11	C	**1st S. af. Easter** • **Orthodox Easter** • ☾ at ☋ •	
12	M.	First U.S. truancy law enacted in New York City, 1853 • Tides {9.7 9.5 •	*then*
13	Tu.	Thomas Jefferson born, 1743 • Jefferson Memorial dedicated, 1943 •	*things*
14	W.	☾ on Eq. • ☌ ☿ ☾ • Space shuttle *Columbia* completed first mission, 1981	*turn*
15	Th.	*The thing generally raised on city land is taxes.* • Thomas Hart Benton born, 1889 •	*ugly.*
16	Fr.	New ● • ☿ Gr. Elong. (28° W.) • Tides {11.4 — •	*Memorize*
17	Sa.	☾ at perig. • Diet of Worms excommunicated Martin Luther, 1521 •	*these*
18	C	**2nd S. af. Easter** • ☌ ♀ ☾ • {12.2 11.3 •	*sunny*
19	M.	Oklahoma City bombing, 1995 • U.S. abandoned the gold standard, 1933 • {12.1 10.9 •	*skies.*
20	Tu.	*Let it rain in April and May for me, And all the rest of the year for thee.* • {11.8 10.4 •	*It might*
21	W.	**St. Anselm** • ☾ rides high • Gen. Sam Houston led Texans to victory, 1836 •	*be*
22	Th.	Congress authorized use of motto "In God We Trust" on U.S. money, 1864 • {10.7 9.5	*weeks*
23	Fr.	**St. George** • ☾ at ☊ • Otto Preminger died, 1986 • {10.2 9.3	*before*
24	Sa.	♂ at ☍ • Robert B. Thomas born, 1766 • Tides {9.9 9.3	*a reprise.*
25	C	**3rd S. af. Easter** • First use of guillotine, 1792	*Drearier:*
26	M.	**St. Mark** • Independent Order of Odd Fellows established, 1819 • {9.7 9.7 •	*Yard*
27	Tu.	☾ on Eq. • ☌ ♄ ☉ • Expo '67 opened in Montreal, Canada, 1967 •	*looks*
28	W.	*The worth of a thing is best known by the want of it.* • Lionel Barrymore born, 1878 •	*like*
29	Th.	**St. Catherine** • ☌ ♂ ☾ • Jerry Seinfeld born, 1954 • {9.8 10.2	*Lake*
30	Fr.	**Full Pink** ○ • Casey Jones died in the crash of the Cannonball Express, 1900	*Superior.*

What is the difference between a taxidermist and a tax collector? The taxidermist takes only your skin. – Mark Twain

Farmer's Calendar

Long before the garden begins to produce — indeed, before it has been planted — it achieves its first, and in a way its best, perfection, a condition from which its subsequent career, however fruitful, can be only a decline. I'm talking about the perfection of a plan as it is put into practice but before it meets experience. Where I live, that moment comes, say, two thirds of the way through April, when you plant the peas and radishes and lay out the rows for the rest of the garden.

It's there, in the laying out of the rows, that in April you can make your garden a success of a kind impossible in later months. I split new stakes and get a ball of new twine to mark the rows. I take a 20-foot tape up to the garden so I can keep the rows honest. Putting them in by eyeball would be good enough for the plants, but it wouldn't be good enough for the mind, and it's the mind I'm gardening for. I make sure the twine is taut, the lines straight, and the corners square. The spirit who presides over the garden today is not Demeter but Euclid.

I think I take these pains in the garden before it really is a garden because doing so is a kind of magic to make me a better gardener than I am. With my perfect lines and my tape measure, I'm trying to fool myself. It doesn't work. I know that in six weeks, the garden will be a mess; in ten, it will be a jungle. But for right now, it looks pretty sharp, doesn't it? Pretty trig? Today the garden looks for all the world as though somebody around here knew what he was doing.

1999 MAY, THE FIFTH MONTH

This month belongs to Venus. Although the blazing evening star will continue to brighten further through June, it has now reached its highest point in the sky, allowing it to shine for several hours after sunset. When darkness falls, the cloud-shrouded world stands a hundred times brighter than any star and will inevitably prompt numerous UFO reports. Because of their different angles of orbit this season, the Moon and Venus will have few close conjunctions; however, the two pass near each other on the 18th. Mars, still brilliant but fading rapidly, passes impressively close to Virgo's brightest star, blue-white Spica, the last week of May.

☾	Last Quarter	8th day	13th hour	28th minute
●	New Moon	15th day	8th hour	5th minute
☽	First Quarter	22nd day	1st hour	34th minute
○	Full Moon	30th day	2nd hour	40th minute

Times are given in Eastern Daylight Time.

For an explanation of this page, see "How to Use This Almanac," page 34; for values of Key Letters, see Time Correction Tables, page 214.

Day of Year	Day of Month	Day of Week	☼ Rises h. m.	Key	☼ Sets h. m.	Key	Length of Days h. m.	Sun Fast m.	Declination of Sun ° '	Full Sea Boston Light – A.M.	**Bold – P.M.**	☽ Rises h. m.	Key	☽ Sets h. m.	Key	☽ Place	☽ Age
121	1	Sa.	5 40	B	7 43	D	14 03	18	15N.05	12½	**12¾**	8 P.M. 44	E	6 A.M. 34	B	LIB	15
122	2	**C**	5 39	B	7 44	D	14 05	19	15 23	1	**1½**	9 40	E	7 07	B	LIB	16
123	3	M.	5 37	B	7 46	D	14 09	19	15 41	1½	**2¼**	10 35	E	7 43	B	OPH	17
124	4	Tu.	5 36	A	7 47	D	14 11	19	15 58	2¼	**2¾**	11 P.M. 27	E	8 24	B	OPH	18
125	5	W.	5 35	A	7 48	D	14 13	19	16 16	3	**3½**	— —	–	9 10	B	SAG	19
126	6	Th.	5 33	A	7 49	D	14 16	19	16 33	3¾	**4¼**	12 A.M. 16	E	10 01	B	SAG	20
127	7	Fr.	5 32	A	7 50	D	14 18	19	16 49	4½	**5¼**	1 01	E	10 57	B	SAG	21
128	8	Sa.	5 31	A	7 51	D	14 20	19	17 06	5¼	**6**	1 42	E	11 A.M. 57	B	CAP	22
129	9	**C**	5 30	A	7 52	D	14 22	19	17 22	6¼	**7**	2 19	E	1 P.M. 01	C	CAP	23
130	10	M.	5 29	A	7 53	D	14 24	19	17 37	7¼	**7¾**	2 54	D	2 07	C	AQU	24
131	11	Tu.	5 27	A	7 54	D	14 27	19	17 53	8	**8¾**	3 27	D	3 16	D	AQU	25
132	12	W.	5 26	A	7 55	D	14 29	19	18 08	9	**9½**	4 00	D	4 28	D	PSC	26
133	13	Th.	5 25	A	7 56	D	14 31	19	18 23	10	**10¼**	4 34	C	5 42	D	PSC	27
134	14	Fr.	5 24	A	7 57	D	14 33	19	18 37	10¾	**11¼**	5 10	C	6 58	E	CET	28
135	15	Sa.	5 23	A	7 59	E	14 36	19	18 52	11¾	—	5 50	B	8 14	E	ARI	0
136	16	**C**	5 22	A	8 00	E	14 38	19	19 06	12	**12¾**	6 36	B	9 27	E	TAU	1
137	17	M.	5 21	A	8 01	E	14 40	19	19 20	1	**1½**	7 27	B	10 35	E	TAU	2
138	18	Tu.	5 20	A	8 02	E	14 42	19	19 33	1¾	**2½**	8 25	B	11 P.M. 35	E	GEM	3
139	19	W.	5 19	A	8 03	E	14 44	19	19 46	2¾	**3½**	9 28	B	— —	–	GEM	4
140	20	Th.	5 18	A	8 04	E	14 46	19	19 59	3½	**4¼**	10 33	B	12 A.M. 26	E	CAN	5
141	21	Fr.	5 18	A	8 05	E	14 47	19	20 11	4½	**5¼**	11 A.M. 38	C	1 09	E	LEO	6
142	22	Sa.	5 17	A	8 06	E	14 49	19	20 23	5½	**6½**	12 P.M. 42	C	1 45	E	LEO	7
143	23	**C**	5 16	A	8 06	E	14 50	19	20 34	6¾	**7½**	1 44	D	2 17	D	LEO	8
144	24	M.	5 15	A	8 07	E	14 52	19	20 46	7¾	**8¼**	2 44	D	2 46	D	VIR	9
145	25	Tu.	5 14	A	8 08	E	14 54	19	20 57	8¾	**9¼**	3 44	D	3 14	C	VIR	10
146	26	W.	5 14	A	8 09	E	14 55	19	21 07	9½	**10**	4 42	D	3 41	C	VIR	11
147	27	Th.	5 13	A	8 10	E	14 57	19	21 18	10½	**10¾**	5 40	E	4 08	B	VIR	12
148	28	Fr.	5 12	A	8 11	E	14 59	18	21 28	11¼	**11¼**	6 37	E	4 37	B	LIB	13
149	29	Sa.	5 12	A	8 12	E	15 00	18	21 37	11¾	—	7 35	E	5 08	B	LIB	14
150	30	**C**	5 11	A	8 12	E	15 01	18	21 46	12	**12½**	8 30	E	5 43	B	OPH	15
151	31	M.	5 11	A	8 13	E	15 02	18	21N.55	12½	**1**	9 P.M. 24	E	6 A.M. 23	B	OPH	16

MAY hath 31 days. 1999

New flowery scents strewed everywhere,
New sunshine poured in largesse fair,
"We shall be happy now," we say.
A voice just trembles through the air,
And whispers, "May." – *Sarah C. Woolsey*

D. M.	D. W.	Dates, Feasts, Fasts, Aspects, Tide Heights	*Weather* ↓
1	Sa.	Sts. Philip & James • May Day • ☌ ☿ ♃ • ♂ closest approach •	
2	C	4th S. af. Easter • ☾ at apo. • {10.3 9.5 •	*Daffo-*
3	M.	Invention of the Cross • National Public Radio began broadcasting, 1971 •	*dilicious.*
4	Tu.	Columbus discovered Jamaica, 1494 • Al Capone jailed for tax evasion, 1932 •	*Signs*
5	W.	☾ runs low • First recorded U.S. train robbery, North Bend, Ohio, 1865 • {9.9 8.9 •	*are*
6	Th.	♆ stat. • Willie Mays born, 1931 • Sigmund Freud born, 1856 •	*auspicious.*
7	Fr.	☌ ♆ ☾ • *The hardest tumble a man can make is to fall over his own bluff.* •	*Not*
8	Sa.	Julian of Norwich • ☾ at ☋ • ☌ ⛢ ☾ • {9.3 8.7 •	*so*
9	C	Rogation S. • First of the Nazi book burnings occurred, 1933 • {9.4 9.0	*hot,*
10	M.	Golden spike driven, Promontory Point, Utah, 1869 • Tides {9.5 9.5	*but*
11	Tu.	Three • Great Dust Bowl Storm darkened skies from Oklahoma to Atlantic coast, 1934 •	*who's*
12	W.	☾ on Eq. • Chilly • Farley Mowat born, 1921 • {10.2 10.8	*complaining?*
13	Th.	Ascension • Saints • ☌ ♃ ☾ • ☌ ☿ ♄ •	*At*
14	Fr.	Lewis and Clark set out from St. Louis, Mo., bound for the Pacific coast, 1804 • {10.9 12.0 •	*least*
15	Sa.	New ● • ☾ at perig. • Amid much fanfare, nylon stockings went on sale, 1940 •	*it's*
16	C	1st S. af. Asc. • First Academy Awards presented, 1929 • {12.4 11.2	*not*
17	M.	First running of the Kentucky Derby, 1875 • *First catch your hare, then cook it.* •	*raining!*
18	Tu.	☾ rides high • ☌ ♀ ☾ • Margot Fonteyn born, 1919 • {12.3 10.8	*Wet —*
19	W.	St. Dunstan • Famous "Dark Day" in New England, 1780 • Tides {11.9 10.4	*don't*
20	Th.	Orthodox Ascension • ☾ at ☊ • Dolley Madison born, 1768 •	*put*
21	Fr.	Shavuot • Sister Maria Innocentia Hummel born, 1909 • Tides {10.7 9.7 •	*away*
22	Sa.	⛢ stat. • *Wise men talk because they have something to say; fools, because they have to say something.*	*those*
23	C	Whit S. • Pentecost • Tides {9.7 9.5 •	*slickers*
24	M.	Victoria Day (Canada) • Bob Dylan born, 1941 • Frank Oz born, 1944 • {9.4 9.6 •	*yet.*
25	Tu.	St. Bede • ☾ on Eq. • ☿ in sup. ☌ • {9.3 9.7 •	*Here's*
26	W.	St. Augustine of Canterbury • ☌ ♂ ☾ • Ember Day •	*the*
27	Th.	First running of the Preakness, 1873 • Great St. Louis Tornado, 1896 • Tides {9.2 10.0	*buzz:*
28	Fr.	Ember Day • Amnesty International founded, 1961 • Tides {9.3 10.2	*Summer*
29	Sa.	☾ at apo. • Ember Day • *Fools need advice most, but wise men only are the better for it.* •	*is,*
30	C	Trinity • Orthodox Pentecost • Full Flower ○ • ♇ at ☍	
31	M.	Visit. of Mary • Memorial Day • {10.3 9.2 •	*winter was.*

Farmer's Calendar

If you go outdoors much in the north in May, you soon discover that bug repellent doesn't work on the blackflies. Those whining, swarming, sometimes biting little insects make springtime in the woodlands a prize that, so long awaited, can be hard to enjoy. However well you baste yourself with whatever offensive stuff, the blackflies will still buzz about you by the hundreds. They fly into your eyes, your nose, your ears. You inhale them and have to spit them out. To meet this kind of assault takes more than perfume.

Hence the blackfly veil, a net that fits loosely over your head and neck. The one I have is made of a netting so fine that it seems to float before my eyes just on the edge of invisibility, a dark haze. A good blackfly veil can drive you almost as crazy as the blackflies themselves.

The veil works, though. It's about the only thing that does. And so it is that during blackfly season, ordinarily familiar woodlands, meadows, gardens, and yards become like the lost cities of Islam, and their inhabitants become devotees, exotic and unknowable. Originally, I read, the veil prescribed for Muslim women was as much for protection as for modesty. "Tell thy wives and thy daughters ... to draw their veils close around them when they go abroad," instructs the Koran, ". . . that they may be recognized and not annoyed." *And not annoyed.* That's what everybody wants. But the blackflies, perhaps, have gone the Prophet one better, as hereabouts men and women both are seen to be subject to the Hill Country purdah.

1999 JUNE, THE SIXTH MONTH

Saturn and Jupiter, moving closer together, return from behind the Sun this month. Observers will be able to preview the ringed world in the eastern predawn sky on the 11th when it hovers over the thin crescent Moon, with brilliant Jupiter above and to the right. On the evening of the16th, incredibly luminous Venus and the Moon meet in the west, with little Mercury floating halfway between them and the point of sunset. That sizzling planet remains easy to spot just above the horizon for the rest of the month. The solstice occurs on the 21st, at 3:49 P.M., EDT, bringing the beginning of summer.

☾	Last Quarter	7th day	0 hour	20th minute
●	New Moon	13th day	15th hour	3rd minute
☽	First Quarter	20th day	14th hour	13th minute
○	Full Moon	28th day	17th hour	37th minute

Times are given in Eastern Daylight Time.

For an explanation of this page, see "How to Use This Almanac," page 34; for values of Key Letters, see Time Correction Tables, page 214.

Day of Year	Day of Month	Day of Week	☉ Rises h. m.	Key	☉ Sets h. m.	Key	Length of Days h. m.	Sun Fast m.	Declination of Sun ° '	Full Sea Boston Light – A.M.	**Bold – P.M.**	☽ Rises h. m.	Key	☽ Sets h. m.	Key	☽ Place	☽ Age
152	1	Tu.	5 10	A	8 14	E	15 04	18	22N.03	1¼	**1¾**	10 P.M. 14	E	7 A.M. 07	B	SAG	17
153	2	W.	5 10	A	8 15	E	15 05	18	22 11	1¾	**2½**	11 00	E	7 56	B	SAG	18
154	3	Th.	5 09	A	8 15	E	15 06	18	22 18	2½	**3¼**	11 P.M. 42	E	8 50	B	SAG	19
155	4	Fr.	5 09	A	8 16	E	15 07	17	22 25	3¼	**3¾**	— —	–	9 49	B	CAP	20
156	5	Sa.	5 08	A	8 17	E	15 09	17	22 32	4	**4¾**	12 A.M. 20	D	10 50	C	CAP	21
157	6	**C**	5 08	A	8 18	E	15 10	17	22 39	4¾	**5½**	12 55	D	11 A.M. 54	C	AQU	22
158	7	M.	5 08	A	8 18	E	15 10	17	22 45	5¾	**6¼**	1 28	D	1 P.M. 00	D	AQU	23
159	8	Tu.	5 08	A	8 19	E	15 11	17	22 50	6¾	**7¼**	1 59	D	2 08	D	PSC	24
160	9	W.	5 07	A	8 19	E	15 12	17	22 55	7½	**8**	2 31	D	3 19	D	CET	25
161	10	Th.	5 07	A	8 20	E	15 13	16	23 00	8½	**9**	3 05	C	4 31	E	PSC	26
162	11	Fr.	5 07	A	8 21	E	15 14	16	23 04	9½	**10**	3 41	B	5 46	E	ARI	27
163	12	Sa.	5 07	A	8 21	E	15 14	16	23 08	10½	**10¾**	4 23	B	7 01	E	TAU	28
164	13	**C**	5 07	A	8 22	E	15 15	16	23 12	11½	**11¾**	5 11	B	8 13	E	TAU	0
165	14	M.	5 07	A	8 22	E	15 15	16	23 16	**12¼**	—	6 06	B	9 18	E	ORI	1
166	15	Tu.	5 07	A	8 23	E	15 16	15	23 18	12½	**1¼**	7 08	B	10 15	E	GEM	2
167	16	W.	5 07	A	8 23	E	15 16	15	23 20	1½	**2¼**	8 14	B	11 03	E	CAN	3
168	17	Th.	5 07	A	8 23	E	15 16	15	23 22	2¼	**3**	9 22	B	11 P.M. 44	E	CAN	4
169	18	Fr.	5 07	A	8 24	E	15 17	15	23 24	3¼	**4**	10 28	C	— —	–	LEO	5
170	19	Sa.	5 07	A	8 24	E	15 17	14	23 25	4¼	**5**	11 A.M. 33	C	12 A.M. 19	D	LEO	6
171	20	**C**	5 07	A	8 24	E	15 17	14	23 25	5¼	**5¾**	12 P.M. 35	D	12 50	D	VIR	7
172	21	M.	5 07	A	8 25	E	15 18	14	23 25	6¼	**6¾**	1 35	D	1 18	C	VIR	8
173	22	Tu.	5 08	A	8 25	E	15 17	14	23 25	7¼	**7¾**	2 35	D	1 45	C	VIR	9
174	23	W.	5 08	A	8 25	E	15 17	14	23 25	8	**8½**	3 33	D	2 12	C	VIR	10
175	24	Th.	5 08	A	8 25	E	15 17	13	23 24	9	**9¼**	4 31	E	2 40	B	LIB	11
176	25	Fr.	5 08	A	8 25	E	15 17	13	23 23	9¾	**10**	5 28	E	3 11	B	LIB	12
177	26	Sa.	5 09	A	8 25	E	15 16	13	23 21	10¾	**10¾**	6 24	E	3 44	B	SCO	13
178	27	**C**	5 09	A	8 25	E	15 16	13	23 18	11¼	**11½**	7 19	E	4 22	B	OPH	14
179	28	M.	5 10	A	8 25	E	15 15	13	23 16	**12**	—	8 11	E	5 04	B	SAG	15
180	29	Tu.	5 10	A	8 25	E	15 15	12	23 13	12	**12¾**	8 59	E	5 52	B	SAG	16
181	30	W.	5 10	A	8 25	E	15 15	12	23N.09	12¾	**1¼**	9 P.M. 43	E	6 A.M. 45	B	SAG	17

JUNE hath 30 days. 1999

Mine is the Month of Roses; yes and mine
The Month of Marriages! All pleasant sights
And scents, the fragrance of the blossoming vine,
The foliage of the valleys and the heights.
– Henry Wadsworth Longfellow

D. M.	D. W.	Dates, Feasts, Fasts, Aspects, Tide Heights	*Weather* ↓
1	Tu.	**St. Justin** • Snow fell in Cleveland, Ohio, and Buffalo and Rochester, N.Y., 1843	*Beaming*
2	W.	☾ runs low • All U.S.-born Indians were granted full citizenship, 1924 • {10.2 / 9.1	*then*
3	Th.	**Corpus Christi** • ☌ ♆ ☾ • Tides {10.1 / 9.0	*steaming*
4	Fr.	☾ at ☋ • ☌ ♅ ☾ • Tiananmen Square Massacre, 1989 • {9.9 / 9.0	*with*
5	Sa.	**St. Boniface** • ♂ stat. • Tides {9.8 / 9.1 •	*lightning*
6	C	**2nd S. af. P.** • **Orthodox All Saints** •	*gleaming.*
7	M.	*Many ideas grow better when transplanted into another mind than in the one where they sprung up.* •	*It's*
8	Tu.	☾ on Eq. • Ad for commercially made ice cream appeared in *New York Gazette,* 1786	*too nice*
9	W.	☌ ♃ ☾ • Donald Duck made his first film appearance, 1934 • {9.8 / 10.6 •	*for*
10	Th.	☌ ♄ ☾ • President Nixon removed 21-year embargo on trade with China, 1971	*classes,*
11	Fr.	**St. Barnabas** • ♀ Gr. Elong. (45° E.) • Tides {10.3 / 11.7	*complain*
12	Sa.	☾ at perig. • National Baseball Hall of Fame dedicated, Cooperstown, N.Y., 1939 •	*lads*
13	C	**3rd S. af. P.** • New ● • Tides {10.7 / 12.4 •	*and*
14	M.	**St. Basil** • Stars and Stripes adopted as the official flag, 1777 •	*lasses.*
15	Tu.	☾ rides high • ☌ ☿ ☾ • Mario Cuomo born, 1932 • {12.4 / 10.8 •	*Grads*
16	W.	☌ ♀ ☾ • New York Giants hosted first Ladies' Day baseball game, 1883 • {12.2 / 10.6	*get*
17	Th.	☾ at ☊ • Term "G.I. Joe" appeared for first time in comic strip *Yank,* 1942	*roasted*
18	Fr.	Dr. Sally Ride became first American woman in space, 1983 • Tides {11.3 / 10.1 •	*while*
19	Sa.	First running of the Belmont Stakes, 1867 • Guy Lombardo born, 1902 •	*they're*
20	C	**4th S. af. P.** • Congress adopted the Great Seal of U.S., 1782	*toasted.*
21	M.	**Summer Solstice** • ☾ on Eq. • Tides {9.5 / 9.6 •	*Commencement*
22	Tu.	☌ ♂ ☾ • *Marriage is the greatest educational institution on Earth.* •	*speeches*
23	W.	**Midsummer Eve** • William Penn signed peace treaty with Indians, 1683 • {8.9 / 9.6 •	*tend*
24	Th.	**Nativ. John the Baptist** • Henry Ward Beecher born, 1813 •	*toward*
25	Fr.	☾ at apo. • Gov. John Winthrop introduced the table fork to colonial America, 1630	*flowery,*
26	Sa.	*A growing Moon and a flowing tide are lucky times to be married in.* • {8.8 / 10.0 •	*except*
27	C	**5th S. af. P.** • Illinois passed first seat belt law, 1955 • {8.9 / 10.1 •	*when*
28	M.	**St. Irenaeus** • **Full Strawberry** ○ • ☿ Gr. Elong. (26° E.) •	*skies*
29	Tu.	**Sts. Peter & Paul** • ☾ runs low • Harmon Killebrew born, 1936 •	*are*
30	W.	☌ ♆ ☾ • U.S. Pure Food and Drug Act passed, 1906 • {10.3 / 9.2	*showery.*

The fixity of a habit is generally in direct proportion to its absurdity. – Marcel Proust

Farmer's Calendar

High up (*very* high) on the slopes of the Green Mountains of Vermont, there grows a nondescript wild plant, *Otiosus futilis,* called in English good-for-nothing or uselesswort and in Canadian French *herbe qui fait rien.* It's a small, scraggly, low plant, and its flower lacks any particular charm. But despite its unprepossessing character, *O. futilis* is much sought after by horticulturists for this reason: It is the only native North American plant *not* known to have medicinal value.

Perhaps nobody knows exactly how many species of plants are native to our continent; one authority offers the number 16,108 for the United States alone. That seems like a lot of different plants, but more remarkable than our flora's size is its supposed usefulness. If you believe folklore, herbal lore, Indian lore, and modern writers on natural medicines, there is no plant so idle that it can't fix up some part of your anatomy. There are plants that work on your liver, your heart, your lungs, your joints. There are plants that put you to sleep, that keep you awake, that help you digest, that help you give birth — and on and on.

Does it all seem too good? Indeed, shouldn't the commonly accepted notion that practically every plant has the power to come to man's aid begin to inspire skepticism? Can't there be one plant that doesn't *do* anything but just sits there? Yes: *O. futilis.* It won't brighten your eye or make your hair grow. But in the clamor of an oversold herbalism, it will help keep you sane. Maybe it's not so useless after all.

1999 JULY, THE SEVENTH MONTH

Despite the warm weather, Earth is farthest from the Sun (aphelion) on the 6th, at 94,512,258 miles. Venus, now at its most brilliant but lower than it was in May, has the season's closest, most eye-catching conjunction with the crescent Moon on the 15th. Forming a triangle with the brilliant duo is Leo's blue star, Regulus, which hovers nearest to Venus from the 9th to the 13th. Steadily braced binoculars show that Venus, as if to imitate the Moon, is now a striking crescent. On the 28th, the Moon undergoes a partial eclipse; the umbral phase starts at 6:22 A.M., EDT, which is after sunrise on the East Coast but still nighttime for observers further west.

☾	Last Quarter	6th day	7th hour	57th minute
●	New Moon	12th day	22nd hour	24th minute
☽	First Quarter	20th day	5th hour	0 minute
○	Full Moon	28th day	7th hour	25th minute

Times are given in Eastern Daylight Time.

For an explanation of this page, see "How to Use This Almanac," page 34; for values of Key Letters, see Time Correction Tables, page 214.

Day of Year	Day of Month	Day of Week	☼ Rises h. m.	Key	☼ Sets h. m.	Key	Length of Days h. m.	Sun Fast m.	Declination of Sun ° '	Full Sea Boston Light – A.M.	**Bold – P.M.**	☽ Rises h. m.	Key	☽ Sets h. m.	Key	☽ Place	☽ Age
182	1	Th.	5 11	A	8 25	E	15 14	12	23N.06	1½	**2**	10 PM 22	E	7 AM 43	B	CAP	18
183	2	Fr.	5 11	A	8 25	E	15 14	12	23 02	2	**2¾**	10 58	D	8 43	B	CAP	19
184	3	Sa.	5 12	A	8 25	E	15 13	12	22 57	2¾	**3½**	11 PM 31	D	9 46	C	AQU	20
185	4	**C**	5 13	A	8 25	E	15 12	11	22 52	3½	**4¼**	— —	–	10 51	C	AQU	21
186	5	M.	5 13	A	8 24	E	15 11	11	22 46	4¼	**5**	12 AM 03	D	11 AM 57	D	AQU	22
187	6	Tu.	5 14	A	8 24	E	15 10	11	22 40	5¼	**5¾**	12 33	C	1 PM 05	D	CET	23
188	7	W.	5 14	A	8 23	E	15 09	11	22 34	6¼	**6¾**	1 05	C	2 14	E	PSC	24
189	8	Th.	5 15	A	8 23	E	15 08	11	22 28	7¼	**7¾**	1 39	C	3 26	E	CET	25
190	9	Fr.	5 16	A	8 23	E	15 07	11	22 21	8¼	**8½**	2 16	B	4 38	E	TAU	26
191	10	Sa.	5 17	A	8 22	E	15 05	10	22 13	9¼	**9½**	3 00	B	5 50	E	TAU	27
192	11	**C**	5 17	A	8 22	E	15 05	10	22 05	10¼	**10½**	3 50	B	6 58	E	TAU	28
193	12	M.	5 18	A	8 21	E	15 03	10	21 57	11¼	**11½**	4 48	B	7 59	E	GEM	0
194	13	Tu.	5 19	A	8 21	E	15 02	10	21 49	**12**	—	5 52	B	8 52	E	GEM	1
195	14	W.	5 20	A	8 20	E	15 00	10	21 40	12¼	**1**	7 00	B	9 37	E	CAN	2
196	15	Th.	5 20	A	8 19	E	14 59	10	21 30	1¼	**1¾**	8 08	C	10 16	E	LEO	3
197	16	Fr.	5 21	A	8 19	E	14 58	10	21 20	2	**2¾**	9 16	C	10 49	D	LEO	4
198	17	Sa.	5 22	A	8 18	E	14 56	10	21 10	3	**3½**	10 21	C	11 19	D	LEO	5
199	18	**C**	5 23	A	8 17	E	14 54	9	21 00	3¾	**4¼**	11 AM 23	D	11 PM 47	D	VIR	6
200	19	M.	5 24	A	8 17	E	14 53	9	20 50	4¾	**5¼**	12 PM 24	D	— —	–	VIR	7
201	20	Tu.	5 25	A	8 16	E	14 51	9	20 39	5½	**6**	1 23	E	12 AM 15	C	VIR	8
202	21	W.	5 26	A	8 15	E	14 49	9	20 27	6½	**7**	2 22	E	12 43	C	LIB	9
203	22	Th.	5 27	A	8 14	E	14 47	9	20 15	7½	**7¾**	3 19	E	1 12	B	LIB	10
204	23	Fr.	5 27	A	8 13	E	14 46	9	20 03	8¼	**8¾**	4 16	E	1 44	B	SCO	11
205	24	Sa.	5 28	A	8 12	E	14 44	9	19 51	9¼	**9½**	5 11	E	2 20	B	OPH	12
206	25	**C**	5 29	A	8 11	E	14 42	9	19 38	10	**10¼**	6 05	E	3 01	B	OPH	13
207	26	M.	5 30	A	8 11	D	14 41	9	19 25	10¾	**11**	6 55	E	3 47	B	SAG	14
208	27	Tu.	5 31	A	8 10	D	14 39	9	19 12	11½	**11¾**	7 41	E	4 38	B	SAG	15
209	28	W.	5 32	A	8 08	D	14 36	9	18 58	**12¼**	—	8 22	E	5 35	B	CAP	16
210	29	Th.	5 33	A	8 07	D	14 34	9	18 44	12¼	**1**	9 00	E	6 35	B	CAP	17
211	30	Fr.	5 34	A	8 06	D	14 32	9	18 30	1	**1½**	9 34	D	7 38	C	AQU	18
212	31	Sa.	5 35	A	8 05	D	14 30	9	18N.15	1¾	**2¼**	10 PM 06	D	8 AM 43	C	AQU	19

JULY hath 31 days. 1999

A moon-flooded prairie; a dreaming
Of brown-fisted farmers; a gleaming
Of fireflies eddying nigh —
And that is July!
– James N. Matthews

D. M.	D. W.	Dates, Feasts, Fasts, Aspects, Tide Heights	*Weather* ↓
1	Th.	**Canada Day** • ☾ at ☋ • ☌ ♅ ☾ • Tides {10.3 / 9.2	*Fire-*
2	Fr.	Amelia Earhart disappeared over the Pacific, 1937 • Tides {10.3 / 9.3 •	*works*
3	Sa.	Dog Days begin. • Israelis rescued 103 hostages at Entebbe airport, Uganda, 1976 •	*fizzle*
4	**C**	**6th S. af. P.** • **Independence Day** • {10.1 / 9.6 •	*in*
5	M.	Hailstorm in Rapid City, S.D., killed 16 horses, injured many others, 1891 • {10.0 / 9.8	*drizzle.*
6	Tu.	☾ on Eq. • ⊕ at aphelion • Tides {9.9 / 10.1 •	*Have a*
7	W.	☌ ♃ ☾ • First comic book published, Hudson, N.Y., 1802 •	*cookout,*
8	Th.	☌ ♄ ☾ • First reading of Declaration of Independence, 1776 • {9.7 / 10.8	*then*
9	Fr.	President Zachary Taylor died in office after serving only 1 year, 4 months, 1850 •	*Look Out!*
10	Sa.	Marcel Proust born, 1871 • Arthur Ashe born, 1943 • {9.9 / 11.6	*Temperatures*
11	**C**	**7th S. af. P.** • ☾ at perig. • ☿ stat. •	*couldn't*
12	M.	☾ rides high • **New** ● • Henry David Thoreau born, 1817 • {10.3 / 12.1	*get*
13	Tu.	*Meeting interesting people depends less on where you go than who you are.* • {10.5 / —	*much*
14	W.	☾ at ☊ • ☌ ☿ ☾ • ♀ Gr. Bril. • Bastille Day • {12.1 / 10.5 •	
15	Th.	**St. Swithin** • ☌ ♀ ☾ • Rembrandt born, 1606 •	*higher;*
16	Fr.	Buchenwald concentration camp opened, 1937 • First atomic bomb test explosion, 1945	*out*
17	Sa.	Disneyland opened in Anaheim, Calif., 1955 • Cornscateous air is everywhere. • {11.0 / 10.2 •	*of*
18	**C**	**8th S. af. P.** • ☾ on Eq. • Nelson Mandela born, 1918 •	*the*
19	M.	First Women's Rights Convention held at Seneca Falls, N.Y., 1848 • {9.8 / 9.7 •	*frying*
20	Tu.	☌ ♂ ☾ • Riot Act took effect in England, 1715 • Tides {9.3 / 9.5 •	*pan,*
21	W.	*Don't go through life with catchers' mitts on both hands — you need to be able to throw something back.*	*into*
22	Th.	**St. Mary Magdalene** • John Dillinger killed, 1934 • {8.6 / 9.4 •	*the fire.*
23	Fr.	☾ at apo. • Fluoride in drinking water found to reduce tooth decay, 1956 •	*Rainy*
24	Sa.	Antoine de la Mothe Cadillac landed at the site of Detroit, 1701 •	*respite —*
25	**C**	**9th S. af. P.** • Mussolini ousted and arrested, 1943 • {8.6 / 9.8 •	*hot*
26	M.	**St. James** • **St. Ann** • ☾ runs low • ♆ at ☍ • ☿ in inf. ☌	
27	Tu.	♀ stat. • H. J. Heinz Co. incorporated, 1900 • Tides {9.0 / 10.3 •	*and*
28	W.	☾ at ☋ • Occn. ♆ ☾ • **Full Thunder** ○ • Eclipse ☾ •	
29	Th.	**Sts. Mary & Martha** • Occn. ♅ ☾ • {10.4 / 9.4 •	*humid,*
30	Fr.	*Regrets over yesterday and fear of tomorrow are twin thieves that rob us of the moment.* •	*boomers*
31	Sa.	David Scott and James Irwin rode the Lunar Roving Vehicle on the Moon, 1971 •	*rumored.*

Farmer's Calendar

Except on picnics and in their kitchens, most people evidently like ants. We feel a friendship for them that is unlike our response to any other insect. No insect has had better press from poets and authors, including our very best and biggest. Why? What is it about ants?

Not their looks. Many of the animals we most enjoy are animals that somehow look like people: frogs, geese, bears. Ants don't look like anything but ants. Others of our favorite animals don't look like us so much but seem to have the same kind of minds we have: dogs and cats, horses, dolphins. But nobody ever made friends with an ant. They hardly exist as individuals. That, perhaps, is our clue: We mostly experience ants in numbers, operating collectively. It is as a community that ants, severally almost invisible, make their appeal to us.

But only so far. "The ants are a people not strong, yet they prepare their meat in the summer," says the Proverb. Laborious, thorough, and completely willing to submerge the individual in and for the mass, ants succeed, and we like them just because we understand their individual insignificance and recognize their collective power. But we are seldom willing to work as hard or — especially — to sink our own pride as low. And so our affection for the ant is complex and includes a measure of superiority, the kind of negative admiration we may feel for those who possess virtues we acknowledge but are in no hurry to imitate.

1999 AUGUST, THE EIGHTH MONTH

The Moon passes Jupiter on the morning of the 4th before totally covering the Sun on the 11th. Visibility in North America, however, is limited to the northeastern United States and eastern Canada, where the Sun will rise partially eclipsed. After midnight on the 11th and 12th, the Perseid meteor shower reaches a peak of nearly a meteor a minute under ideal moonless skies. Starting on the 9th, Mercury returns to the eastern predawn sky until the 19th. On the 20th, Venus passes between Earth and the Sun, as it does every 19 months. While it is now at its closest approach to Earth, Venus is lost in the solar glare.

☾	Last Quarter	4th day	13th hour	27th minute
●	New Moon	11th day	7th hour	8th minute
☽	First Quarter	18th day	21st hour	47th minute
○	Full Moon	26th day	19th hour	48th minute

Times are given in Eastern Daylight Time.

For an explanation of this page, see "How to Use This Almanac," page 34; for values of Key Letters, see Time Correction Tables, page 214.

Day of Year	Day of Month	Day of Week	☉ Rises h. m.	Key	☉ Sets h. m.	Key	Length of Days h. m.	Sun Fast m.	Declination of Sun ° '	Full Sea Boston Light – A.M.	Bold – P.M.	☽ Rises h. m.	Key	☽ Sets h. m.	Key	☽ Place	☽ Age
213	1	**C**	5 36	A	8 04	D	14 28	9	18N.00	2½	**3**	10 P.M. 37	D	9 A.M. 49	D	AQU	20
214	2	M.	5 37	A	8 03	D	14 26	9	17 44	3¼	**3¾**	11 08	C	10 A.M. 57	D	CET	21
215	3	Tu.	5 38	A	8 02	D	14 24	9	17 29	4	**4½**	11 P.M. 40	C	12 P.M. 05	D	PSC	22
216	4	W.	5 39	A	8 01	D	14 22	9	17 13	5	**5¼**	— —	–	1 14	E	CET	23
217	5	Th.	5 40	A	7 59	D	14 19	10	16 57	5¾	**6¼**	12 A.M. 16	B	2 25	E	ARI	24
218	6	Fr.	5 41	A	7 58	D	14 17	10	16 40	7	**7¼**	12 56	B	3 35	E	TAU	25
219	7	Sa.	5 42	A	7 57	D	14 15	10	16 24	8	**8¼**	1 41	B	4 42	E	TAU	26
220	8	**C**	5 44	A	7 55	D	14 11	10	16 07	9	**9¼**	2 34	B	5 45	E	ORI	27
221	9	M.	5 45	A	7 54	D	14 09	10	15 50	10	**10¼**	3 34	B	6 41	E	GEM	28
222	10	Tu.	5 46	A	7 53	D	14 07	10	15 32	11	**11¼**	4 39	B	7 29	E	CAN	29
223	11	W.	5 47	A	7 51	D	14 04	10	15 15	11¾	—	5 47	C	8 10	E	CAN	0
224	12	Th.	5 48	A	7 50	D	14 02	10	14 57	12	**12¾**	6 56	C	8 46	D	LEO	1
225	13	Fr.	5 49	A	7 49	D	14 00	11	14 39	1	**1½**	8 03	C	9 18	D	LEO	2
226	14	Sa.	5 50	A	7 47	D	13 57	11	14 20	1¾	**2¼**	9 07	D	9 47	D	VIR	3
227	15	**C**	5 51	B	7 46	D	13 55	11	14 02	2½	**3**	10 10	D	10 15	C	VIR	4
228	16	M.	5 52	B	7 44	D	13 52	11	13 43	3¼	**3¾**	11 A.M. 11	D	10 43	C	VIR	5
229	17	Tu.	5 53	B	7 43	D	13 50	11	13 24	4	**4½**	12 P.M. 10	E	11 12	B	VIR	6
230	18	W.	5 54	B	7 41	D	13 47	12	13 04	5	**5¼**	1 09	E	11 P.M. 43	B	LIB	7
231	19	Th.	5 55	B	7 40	D	13 45	12	12 45	5¾	**6¼**	2 06	E	— —	–	LIB	8
232	20	Fr.	5 56	B	7 38	D	13 42	12	12 25	6¾	**7**	3 02	E	12 A.M. 18	B	OPH	9
233	21	Sa.	5 57	B	7 37	D	13 40	12	12 05	7¾	**8**	3 56	E	12 56	B	OPH	10
234	22	**C**	5 58	B	7 35	D	13 37	12	11 45	8¾	**8¾**	4 47	E	1 40	B	SAG	11
235	23	M.	5 59	B	7 34	D	13 35	13	11 25	9½	**9¾**	5 35	E	2 29	B	SAG	12
236	24	Tu.	6 00	B	7 32	D	13 32	13	11 05	10¼	**10½**	6 18	E	3 24	B	SAG	13
237	25	W.	6 02	B	7 30	D	13 28	13	10 44	11	**11¼**	6 58	E	4 23	B	CAP	14
238	26	Th.	6 03	B	7 29	D	13 26	14	10 24	11¾	**11¾**	7 34	D	5 26	B	CAP	15
239	27	Fr.	6 04	B	7 27	D	13 23	14	10 03	**12¼**	—	8 07	D	6 32	C	AQU	16
240	28	Sa.	6 05	B	7 26	D	13 21	14	9 42	12½	**1**	8 39	D	7 39	D	AQU	17
241	29	**C**	6 06	B	7 24	D	13 18	14	9 20	1¼	**1¾**	9 10	D	8 47	D	PSC	18
242	30	M.	6 07	B	7 22	D	13 15	15	8 59	2	**2½**	9 43	C	9 56	D	PSC	19
243	31	Tu.	6 08	B	7 21	D	13 13	15	8N.37	2¾	**3¼**	10 P.M. 17	C	11 A.M. 06	E	CET	20

AUGUST hath 31 days. 1999

High noon in August! over all the land
The very air is palpitant with heat;
While stretching far, the fields of ripening wheat
Unrippled lie as plains of yellow sand!
– Henry S. Cornwell

D. M.	D. W.	Dates, Feasts, Fasts, Aspects, Tide Heights	Weather ↓
1	C	10th S. af. P. • Lammas Day • {10.6 10.0 •	*Blazing*
2	M.	☾ on Eq. • President Warren G. Harding died in office, 1923 • {10.4 10.2 •	*days,*
3	Tu.	☌ ♃ ☾ • Maggie Kuhn, founder of Gray Panthers, born, 1905 •	*amazing*
4	W.	☌ ♄ ☾ • 108° F, Spokane, Wash., 1961 • {10.0 10.5 •	*nights —*
5	Th.	☿ stat. • Cornerstone laid for Statue of Liberty pedestal, 1884 • {9.7 10.6 •	*hey,*
6	Fr.	Transfiguration • Atomic bomb dropped on Hiroshima, 1945 • {9.5 10.8	*Ben*
7	Sa.	Name of Jesus • ♅ at ☍ • ☾ at perig. •	*Franklin!*
8	C	11th S. af. P. • Matthew Henson, explorer, born 1866 • {9.6 11.2 •	*Go*
9	M.	St. Dominic • ☾ rides high • Occn. ☿ ☾ • {9.8 11.5 •	*fly*
10	Tu.	St. Laurence • ☾ at ☊ • Smithsonian Institution founded, 1846	*a kite!*
11	W.	St. Clare • New ● • Eclipse ☉ • Dog Days end. •	*The*
12	Th.	First issue of *Sports Illustrated* published, 1954 • Tides {11.6 10.4 •	*rain*
13	Fr.	*The worse luck now, the better another time.* • Florence Nightingale died, 1910 • {11.4 10.5	*in*
14	Sa.	☿ Gr. Elong. (19° W.) • President Truman announced Japanese surrender, 1945 •	*Maine*
15	C	12th S. af. P. • Assumption • ☾ on Eq. • {10.7 10.2 •	*is*
16	M.	Gold discovered in northern Canada, set off the Klondike Gold Rush, 1896 • {10.2 9.9	*plainly*
17	Tu.	Cat Nights begin. • U.S. government headquarters moved to Philadelphia, 1790 • {9.6 9.7 •	*on*
18	W.	☌ ♂ ☾ • *Most people resist change, yet it's the only thing that brings progress.* •	*the*
19	Th.	☾ at apo. • Gail Borden patented condensed milk, 1856 • {8.7 9.2 •	*wane —*
20	Fr.	♀ in inf. ☌ • *The Mikado* opened in New York City, 1885 •	*campers*
21	Sa.	♇ stat. • Arthur Eldred became first Eagle Scout, 1912 • Tides {8.2 9.2 •	*must*
22	C	13th S. af. P. • Ray Bradbury born, 1920 • {8.3 9.4 •	*refrain*
23	M.	☾ runs low • Sacco and Vanzetti executed, 1927 • Gene Kelly born, 1912 •	*from*
24	Tu.	St. Bartholomew • ☌ ♆ ☾ • Cal Ripkin Jr. born, 1960 •	*flame.*
25	W.	☾ at ☋ • ♃ stat. • ☌ ♅ ☾ • Tides {9.2 10.3 •	*Cool*
26	Th.	☌ ☿ ♀ • Full Sturgeon ○ • Tides {9.6 10.6 •	*off*
27	Fr.	*The trouble with using experience as a guide is that the final exam often comes first and then the lesson.*	*with a*
28	Sa.	St. Augustine of Hippo • Tides {10.8 10.3 •	*ceiling*
29	C	14th S. af. P. • ☾ on Eq. • {10.9 10.6 •	*drummer:*
30	M.	♄ stat. • *Bigger is not necessarily better, and going faster is not necessarily progress.*	*Exit*
31	Tu.	☌ ♃ ☾ • Maria Montessori born, 1870 • Tides {10.7 10.9	*summer.*

Farmer's Calendar

Anyone who finds himself lying on the ground beside his vegetable patch using a pair of desk shears to cut the grass and weeds that grow along the fence may suspect that he has been too long a gardener. How did it come to this?

I did without a garden fence for some time, but eventually the deer found the limit of my generosity. I didn't mind sharing the garden with them, but I insisted that my share be somewhat larger than theirs, as a rule, not smaller. The deer never grasped that. I've had a fence for five years now. It's the usual thing: wooden posts with chicken wire stapled on. It works; the deer stay out.

The trouble with a fence, of course, is that you can't mow underneath it to get the weeds that have grown up close beside and within the structure of the fence. The power rotary mower leaves a belt of flourishing weeds on both sides of the wire. I got a sickle, and that worked better but never well. I kept hanging the sickle up on the fence wire.

I tried the shears as a kind of joke at first. But I soon found they worked, really, pretty well. By lying down right beside the fence, I could get the shears under the wire and clip the weeds easily. The work was going on very steadily — perhaps a bit slowly — when a member of my family suggested I use nail scissors for a cleaner, more detailed look.

It is an important moment when you are awakened from the daft dream that your life has become. I now own a Weed Whacker and keep the shears only for show.

1999 SEPTEMBER, THE NINTH MONTH

This month, Venus, in its faster orbit around the Sun, pulls ahead of Earth and races upward just before sunrise. Each week, it climbs higher in the east as bright morning twilight begins, and looks its best as an impressive crescent through small telescopes or steadily braced binoculars. The Moon will be near Venus on the 7th, near Mars on the 16th in the evening sky, near Jupiter on the morning of the 27th, and near Saturn on the morning of the 28th. The autumnal equinox occurs on the 23rd at 7:31 A.M., EDT. Meanwhile, night now falls so much earlier each evening that the autumn constellations seem frozen in place at each successive dusk.

☾	Last Quarter	2nd day	18th hour	17th minute
●	New Moon	9th day	18th hour	2nd minute
☽	First Quarter	17th day	16th hour	6th minute
○	Full Moon	25th day	6th hour	51st minute

Times are given in Eastern Daylight Time.

For an explanation of this page, see "How to Use This Almanac," page 34; for values of Key Letters, see Time Correction Tables, page 214.

Day of Year	Day of Month	Day of Week	☼ Rises h. m.	Key	☼ Sets h. m.	Key	Length of Days h. m.	Sun Fast m.	Declination of Sun ° '	Full Sea Boston Light – A.M.	Bold – P.M.	☽ Rises h. m.	Key	☽ Sets h. m.	Key	☽ Place	☽ Age
244	1	W.	6 09	B	7 19	D	13 10	15	8 N.16	3¾	**4**	10 P.M. 55	B	12 P.M. 16	E	ARI	21
245	2	Th.	6 10	B	7 17	D	13 07	16	7 54	4½	**5**	11 P.M. 39	B	1 26	E	TAU	22
246	3	Fr.	6 11	B	7 15	D	13 04	16	7 32	5½	**6**	— —	–	2 33	E	TAU	23
247	4	Sa.	6 12	B	7 14	D	13 02	16	7 10	6¾	**7**	12 A.M. 28	B	3 36	E	ORI	24
248	5	**C**	6 13	B	7 12	D	12 59	17	6 47	7¾	**8**	1 24	B	4 33	E	GEM	25
249	6	M.	6 14	B	7 10	D	12 56	17	6 25	8¾	**9**	2 26	B	5 23	E	GEM	26
250	7	Tu.	6 15	B	7 09	D	12 54	17	6 03	9¾	**10**	3 32	B	6 06	E	CAN	27
251	8	W.	6 16	B	7 07	D	12 51	18	5 40	10¾	**11**	4 39	B	6 43	D	LEO	28
252	9	Th.	6 17	B	7 05	C	12 48	18	5 17	11½	**11¾**	5 45	C	7 16	D	LEO	0
253	10	Fr.	6 18	B	7 03	C	12 45	18	4 55	**12¼**	—	6 51	D	7 46	D	LEO	1
254	11	Sa.	6 19	B	7 02	C	12 43	19	4 32	12½	**1**	7 55	D	8 15	C	VIR	2
255	12	**C**	6 21	B	7 00	C	12 39	19	4 09	1¼	**1¾**	8 57	D	8 43	C	VIR	3
256	13	M.	6 22	B	6 58	C	12 36	19	3 46	2	**2¼**	9 57	E	9 12	B	VIR	4
257	14	Tu.	6 23	B	6 56	C	12 33	20	3 23	2¾	**3**	10 57	E	9 42	B	LIB	5
258	15	W.	6 24	B	6 55	C	12 31	20	3 00	3½	**3¾**	11 A.M. 55	E	10 15	B	LIB	6
259	16	Th.	6 25	B	6 53	C	12 28	20	2 37	4¼	**4½**	12 P.M. 52	E	10 51	B	SCO	7
260	17	Fr.	6 26	B	6 51	C	12 25	21	2 14	5¼	**5½**	1 47	E	11 P.M. 33	B	OPH	8
261	18	Sa.	6 27	B	6 49	C	12 22	21	1 51	6	**6¼**	2 39	E	— —	–	SAG	9
262	19	**C**	6 28	B	6 47	C	12 19	22	1 27	7	**7¼**	3 27	E	12 A.M. 19	B	SAG	10
263	20	M.	6 29	C	6 46	C	12 17	22	1 04	8	**8¼**	4 12	E	1 11	B	SAG	11
264	21	Tu.	6 30	C	6 44	C	12 14	22	0 41	8¾	**9**	4 53	E	2 08	B	CAP	12
265	22	W.	6 31	C	6 42	C	12 11	23	0 N.17	9¾	**10**	5 30	E	3 09	B	CAP	13
266	23	Th.	6 32	C	6 40	C	12 08	23	0 S.05	10½	**10¾**	6 05	D	4 14	C	AQU	14
267	24	Fr.	6 33	C	6 39	C	12 06	23	0 28	11	**11½**	6 37	D	5 21	D	AQU	15
268	25	Sa.	6 34	C	6 37	C	12 03	24	0 52	11¾	—	7 09	D	6 30	D	PSC	16
269	26	**C**	6 35	C	6 35	C	12 00	24	1 15	12¼	**12½**	7 42	C	7 41	D	CET	17
270	27	M.	6 36	C	6 33	C	11 57	24	1 39	1	**1¼**	8 16	C	8 53	E	PSC	18
271	28	Tu.	6 38	C	6 32	B	11 54	25	2 02	1¾	**2**	8 54	B	10 05	E	ARI	19
272	29	W.	6 39	C	6 30	B	11 51	25	2 25	2½	**2¾**	9 36	B	11 A.M. 17	E	TAU	20
273	30	Th.	6 40	C	6 28	B	11 48	25	2 S.48	3½	**3¾**	10 P.M. 24	B	12 P.M. 27	E	TAU	21

SEPTEMBER hath 30 days. 1999

There are flowers enough in the summertime,
More flowers than I can remember —
But none with the purple, gold, and red
That dyes the flowers of September!
– *Mary Howitt*

D. M.	D. W.	Dates, Feasts, Fasts, Aspects, Tide Heights	Weather ↓
1	W.	☌ ♄ ☾ • Provinces of Saskatchewan and Alberta established, 1905 • {10.4 10.9 •	*Beg*
2	Th.	☾ at perig. • U.S. Dept. of Treasury established, 1789 • Tides {10.0 10.8 •	*your*
3	Fr.	*It's impossible to truly teach without learning something yourself.* • {9.6 10.7 •	*pod-*
4	Sa.	10-year-old Barney Flaherty became first U.S. newsboy, 1833 • Henry Ford II born, 1917 •	*den,*
5	C	**15th S. af. P.** • ☾ rides high • Tides {9.4 10.7 •	*but*
6	M.	**Labor Day** • Marquis de Lafayette born, 1757 • Tides {9.5 10.8 •	*it's*
7	Tu.	☾ at ☊ • ☌ ♀ ☾ • First Miss America pageant held, 1921 •	*sod-*
8	W.	☿ in sup. ☌ • President Nixon pardoned, 1974 • Tides {10.1 11.1 •	*den.*
9	Th.	♀ stat. • **New** ● • Marilyn Bell swam across Lake Ontario, 1954 •	*Sun*
10	Fr.	*You learn the most from people who are learning themselves.* • Tides {10.5 — •	*dapples*
11	Sa.	**Rosh Hashanah** • ☾ on Eq. • D. H. Lawrence born, 1885 •	*apples.*
12	C	**16th S. af. P.** • Olympic gold-medalist Jesse Owens born, 1913 •	*It's*
13	M.	U.S. government took out its first loan, 1789 • John J. Pershing born, 1860 • {10.3 10.2 •	*wet*
14	Tu.	**Holy Cross** • Elizabeth Ann Seton canonized, 1975 • Tides {9.9 10.0 •	*and*
15	W.	Ember Day • Greenpeace founded, 1971 • Agatha Christie born, 1890 •	*swirly —*
16	Th.	☌ ♂ ☾ • ☾ at apo. • *Mayflower* set sail, 1620 • {8.9 9.4 •	*frost*
17	Fr.	Ember Day • Hank Williams Sr. born, 1923 • NFL formed, 1920 •	*comes*
18	Sa.	Ember Day • Joe Kittinger completed first solo transatlantic balloon crossing, 1984 •	*early.*
19	C	**17th S. af. P.** • ☾ runs low • Tides {8.2 9.1 •	*Summer*
20	M.	**Yom Kippur** • Occn. ♆ ☾ • Upton Sinclair born, 1878 •	*rallies,*
21	Tu.	**St. Matthew** • ☾ at ☋ • ☌ ♅ ☾ • Tides {8.6 9.6 •	*but*
22	W.	*How you do your work is a portrait of yourself.* • Nathan Hale executed, 1776 • {9.1 10.0 •	*soon*
23	Th.	**Autumnal Equinox** • Lou Brock stole his record-breaking 935th base, 1979 •	*retreats,*
24	Fr.	Babe Ruth played his last game with the New York Yankees, 1934 • Jim Henson born, 1936 •	*and*
25	Sa.	**Succoth** • ☾ on Eq. • **Full Harvest** ○ • {10.7 —	*gardeners*
26	C	**18th S. af. P.** • ♀ Gr. Bril. • John Coltrane born, 1926 •	*cover*
27	M.	☌ ♃ ☾ • 60-hour storm dumped 21.3 inches of snow at Denver Airport, 1936 •	*their*
28	Tu.	☌ ♄ ☾ • ☾ at perig. • Ed Sullivan born, 1902 • {11.1 11.5 •	*veggies*
29	W.	**St. Michael** • First of 7 deaths from poison-contaminated Tylenol, 1982 • {10.8 11.5	*with*
30	Th.	**St. Jerome** • Gershwin's *Porgy and Bess* premiered in Boston, 1935 • {10.4 11.2	*sheets.*

I honestly believe it is better to know nothing than to know what ain't so. – Josh Billings

Farmer's Calendar

It's generally in September, beginning when the nights turn consistently chilly and continuing right through and on past the first little freezes, that the asters bloom. They are the year's last flower show. The last and one of the most complex, for asters, unspectacular as they are, are flowers that resist science and are therefore particularly dear, though exasperating.

Asters are a kind of daisy. *Gray's Botany* lists 68 species in eastern North America. Nobody knows for sure how many species of asters there are, however, because, as *Gray's* puts it, asters include "the most complicated and difficult section in our flora, the specific lines . . . often obscured by hybridization." Combining and recombining the same genetic material among these many ostensible species makes for species whose defining edges are seldom fixed and certain.

In my area, among the first asters you notice are the ones having purple or violet flowers with yellow centers. Later come the asters with scores of tiny white flowers. These last seem to bloom well past the time of the first frost. When they've gone by, the show is over. I think the asters I have described are *Aster novae-angliae,* and *A. vimineus.* Don't hold me to it, though, please. If science can't pin asters down, I won't pretend to. Perhaps the flux of heredity and definition among asters is a reminder that every species is a work in progress. It's true for asters more conspicuously, but no more certainly, than it is for ourselves.

1999 OCTOBER, THE TENTH MONTH

During October's final week, Venus achieves its greatest separation from the Sun and stands highest above the eastern horizon as morning twilight begins. Although it remains a conspicuous morning star through year's end, it will slowly descend and fade after this month's dazzling apex. On the 23rd, Jupiter reaches opposition, at its closest and most brilliant of the year and of the decade. At magnitude -2.9, it's a dazzling standout among the dim stars of Pisces. It rises at sunset and is highest around midnight. Daylight Saving Time ends at 2:00 A.M. on the 31st.

☾	Last Quarter	2nd day	0 hour	2nd minute
●	New Moon	9th day	7th hour	34th minute
☽	First Quarter	17th day	11th hour	0 minute
○	Full Moon	24th day	17th hour	2nd minute
☾	Last Quarter	31st day	7th hour	4th minute

After 2:00 A.M. on October 31, Eastern Standard Time (EST) is given.

For an explanation of this page, see "How to Use This Almanac," page 34; for values of Key Letters, see Time Correction Tables, page 214.

Day of Year	Day of Month	Day of Week	☼ Rises h. m.	Key	☼ Sets h. m.	Key	Length of Days h. m.	Sun Fast m.	Declination of Sun ° '	Full Sea Boston Light – A.M.	Bold – P.M.	☽ Rises h. m.	Key	☽ Sets h. m.	Key	☽ Place	☽ Age
274	1	Fr.	6 41	C	6 26	B	11 45	26	3 s.12	4¼	**4¾**	11 P.M. 19	B	1 P.M. 32	E	TAU	22
275	2	Sa.	6 42	C	6 25	B	11 43	26	3 35	5½	**5¾**	— —	–	2 30	E	GEM	23
276	3	**C**	6 43	C	6 23	B	11 40	26	3 58	6½	**6¾**	12 A.M. 19	B	3 21	E	GEM	24
277	4	M.	6 44	C	6 21	B	11 37	27	4 21	7½	**8**	1 22	B	4 05	E	CAN	25
278	5	Tu.	6 45	C	6 19	B	11 34	27	4 45	8¾	**9**	2 28	B	4 43	E	LEO	26
279	6	W.	6 46	C	6 18	B	11 32	27	5 08	9½	**10**	3 34	C	5 17	D	LEO	27
280	7	Th.	6 47	C	6 16	B	11 29	28	5 31	10½	**10¾**	4 38	C	5 47	D	LEO	28
281	8	Fr.	6 49	C	6 14	B	11 25	28	5 53	11¼	**11½**	5 42	D	6 16	D	VIR	29
282	9	Sa.	6 50	C	6 13	B	11 23	28	6 16	**12**	—	6 44	D	6 43	C	VIR	0
283	10	**C**	6 51	C	6 11	B	11 20	28	6 39	12¼	**12½**	7 46	D	7 12	B	VIR	1
284	11	M.	6 52	C	6 09	B	11 17	29	7 02	1	**1¼**	8 46	E	7 41	B	LIB	2
285	12	Tu.	6 53	C	6 08	B	11 15	29	7 24	1½	**1¾**	9 45	E	8 13	B	LIB	3
286	13	W.	6 54	C	6 06	B	11 12	29	7 47	2¼	**2½**	10 43	E	8 48	B	SCO	4
287	14	Th.	6 55	D	6 04	B	11 09	29	8 09	3	**3¼**	11 A.M. 38	E	9 27	B	OPH	5
288	15	Fr.	6 57	D	6 03	B	11 06	30	8 31	3¾	**4**	12 P.M. 31	E	10 11	B	OPH	6
289	16	Sa.	6 58	D	6 01	B	11 03	30	8 53	4½	**4¾**	1 21	E	11 00	B	SAG	7
290	17	**C**	6 59	D	6 00	B	11 01	30	9 15	5½	**5¾**	2 07	E	11 P.M. 54	B	SAG	8
291	18	M.	7 00	D	5 58	B	10 58	30	9 37	6½	**6½**	2 48	E	— —	–	CAP	9
292	19	Tu.	7 01	D	5 57	B	10 56	30	9 59	7¼	**7½**	3 26	E	12 A.M. 52	C	CAP	10
293	20	W.	7 02	D	5 55	B	10 53	31	10 20	8¼	**8½**	4 01	E	1 54	C	CAP	11
294	21	Th.	7 04	D	5 53	B	10 49	31	10 42	9	**9¼**	4 34	D	2 59	C	AQU	12
295	22	Fr.	7 05	D	5 52	B	10 47	31	11 03	9¾	**10**	5 06	D	4 07	D	AQU	13
296	23	Sa.	7 06	D	5 50	B	10 44	31	11 24	10½	**11**	5 38	C	5 18	D	CET	14
297	24	**C**	7 07	D	5 49	B	10 42	31	11 45	11¼	**11¾**	6 12	C	6 30	E	PSC	15
298	25	M.	7 08	D	5 48	B	10 40	31	12 06	**12**	—	6 48	C	7 44	E	CET	16
299	26	Tu.	7 10	D	5 46	B	10 36	32	12 27	12½	**12¾**	7 30	B	8 59	E	ARI	17
300	27	W.	7 11	D	5 45	B	10 34	32	12 47	1¼	**1½**	8 17	B	10 13	E	TAU	18
301	28	Th.	7 12	D	5 43	B	10 31	32	13 07	2¼	**2½**	9 11	B	11 A.M. 23	E	TAU	19
302	29	Fr.	7 13	D	5 42	B	10 29	32	13 27	3¼	**3¼**	10 11	B	12 P.M. 26	E	GEM	20
303	30	Sa.	7 15	D	5 41	B	10 26	32	13 47	4	**4¼**	11 14	B	1 20	E	GEM	21
304	31	**C**	6 16	D	4 39	B	10 23	32	14 s.07	4¼	**4½**	11 P.M. 20	B	1 P.M. 07	E	CAN	22

OCTOBER hath 31 days. 1999

Now by great marshes wrapt in mist,
Or past some river's mouth,
Throughout the long, still autumn day
Wild birds are flying south.
– *Wilfred Campbell*

D. M.	D. W.	Dates, Feasts, Fasts, Aspects, Tide Heights	*Weather* ↓
1	Fr.	St. Remigius • John Philip Sousa named director of U.S. Marine Corps Band, 1880 •	*Now*
2	Sa.	☾ rides high • First day of 767-day drought, Bagdad, Calif., 1912 • {9.6 10.6 •	*from*
3	C	19th S. af. P. • Watch for line storms — lash of St. Francis. •	*forth*
4	M.	St. Francis of Assisi • ☾ at ☊ • Tides {9.4 10.3 •	*the*
5	Tu.	☌♀☾ • 116° F in Sentinel, Ariz., 1917 • Tecumseh died, 1813 •	*northern*
6	W.	*On the mountains of truth you can never climb in vain.* • Tides {9.9 10.5 •	*hills,*
7	Th.	The musical *Cats* opened on Broadway, 1982 • Yo-Yo Ma born, 1955 •	*splendor*
8	Fr.	☾ on Eq. • The Great Fire of Chicago leveled 3½ square miles, 1871 • {10.4 10.5	*rolls*
9	Sa.	New ● • 4 inches of snow, Boston, 1703 • John Lennon born, 1940 • {10.5 —	*to*
10	C	20th S. af. P. • ☌☿☾ • {10.4 10.5 •	*southern*
11	M.	Columbus Day • **Thanksgiving Day (Canada)** • Tides {10.2 10.5 •	*coasts;*
12	Tu.	Barometer at 25.69 inches, Typhoon Tip, Philippines, 1979 • Robert E. Lee died, 1870 •	*now*
13	W.	♆ stat. • Margaret Thatcher born, 1925 • Molly Pitcher born, 1754 • {9.6 10.0	*the*
14	Th.	☾ at apo. • *Never ascribe to an opponent motives meaner than your own.*	*prophesying*
15	Fr.	☌♂☾ • John Kenneth Galbraith born, 1908 • {8.8 9.4 •	*chills,*
16	Sa.	☾ runs low • David Ben-Gurion born, 1886 • Eugene O'Neill born, 1888 •	*now*
17	C	21st S. af. P. • First issue of *National Geographic* magazine went on sale, 1888	*the*
18	M.	St. Luke • ☾ at ☋ • ☌♆☾ • {8.3 9.0 •	*thoughts*
19	Tu.	Occn. ♅☾ • St. Luke's Little Summer • Dow Jones fell 508 points, 1987 •	*of*
20	W.	Cork-centered baseball first used in World Series game, 1910 • Tides {8.9 9.5 •	*Indian*
21	Th.	Dizzy Gillespie born, 1917 • Vietnam War protestors stormed the Pentagon, 1967 •	*hosts.*
22	Fr.	*If you think you have influence, try ordering someone else's dog around.* • {10.1 10.4 •	*Now the*
23	Sa.	☾ on Eq. • ♅ stat. • ♃ at ☍ • {10.8 10.8	*pumpkins,*
24	C	22nd S. af. P. • **Full Hunter's** ○ • ☿ Gr. Elong. (24° E.)	*now*
25	M.	St. Crispin • ☌♄☾ • Pablo Picasso born, 1881 • {11.8 —	*the*
26	Tu.	☾ at perig. • 4 inches of snow, New York City, 1859 • {11.2 12.1 •	*squashes,*
27	W.	Fred Waller received patent for water skis, 1925 • Dylan Thomas born, 1914 •	*trick-or-*
28	Th.	Sts. Simon & Jude • Statue of Liberty dedicated, 1886 • {10.8 11.9 •	*treaters*
29	Fr.	☾ rides high • -33° F, Soda Butte, Wyo., 1917 • Tides {10.5 11.5 •	*in*
30	Sa.	♀ Gr. Elong. (46° W.) • *Rain in October means wind in December.* •	*galoshes.*
31	C	23rd S. af. P. • All Hallows Eve • ☾ at ☊ •	

Farmer's Calendar

"A crop is a crop," the poet says. He is writing about the fallen leaves that he puts out such effort to gather, load, and dispose of. It seems to him to be a lot of work for not much return, but *a crop is a crop.*

One way or another you have to put in your time with the year's dead leaves. You can rake them and burn them. You can rake them and cram them into bags. You can rake them into the gutter and let the authorities deal with them. You can buy or hire a machine and blow them into the next township. But sooner or later, if you are any good, you must grapple with them.

Here we come up against a grand principle of human existence, a principle that is essentially religious and derives from Original Sin. The law being that sinful mankind must labor for bread, we discover a kind of corollary to that law: The less nourishing the bread, the more the labor. Hence, there accumulates around every useless thing a task: dead leaves, grass clippings, old newspapers, tin cans, empty bottles, and a million other silly things that must be worked over and organized so as to be made to disappear. In a manner of speaking, we must add value to what has no value in order to be rid of it. On the deepest level, that makes no sense, and its absurdity is our clue to the universality of its application. Less benefit, more work is law given not on Earth but from Heaven, and so we had better like it. *A crop is a crop,* or, put another way: The bad news is these leaves are good for nothing. The good news is we've got lots of them.

1999 NOVEMBER, THE ELEVENTH MONTH

Saturn reaches opposition on the 6th. It is now brighter than it has been for two decades, shining at an impressive magnitude -0.2 among the skimpy stars of Aries. It now rises at sunset and is visible throughout the night. Starting at midnight on the night of the 17th-18th, the erratic Leonid meteor shower peaks and could put on an awesome display (see feature on page 52). The Moon stands near Jupiter on the 20th and near Saturn on the 21st. Mercury reappears low in the east before dawn on the 25th. Soon after nightfall on the 28th, Mars and Neptune are very close, affording telescope users an unusually good opportunity to locate the eighth planet.

●	New Moon	7th day	22nd hour	53rd minute
☽	First Quarter	16th day	4th hour	3rd minute
○	Full Moon	23rd day	2nd hour	4th minute
☾	Last Quarter	29th day	18th hour	18th minute

Times are given in Eastern Standard Time.

For an explanation of this page, see "How to Use This Almanac," page 34; for values of Key Letters, see Time Correction Tables, page 214.

Day of Year	Day of Month	Day of Week	☼ Rises h. m.	Key	☼ Sets h. m.	Key	Length of Days h. m.	Sun Fast m.	Declination of Sun ° '	Full Sea Boston Light – A.M.	**Bold – P.M.**	☽ Rises h. m.	Key	☽ Sets h. m.	Key	☽ Place	☽ Age
305	1	M.	6 17	D	4 38	B	10 21	32	14s.26	5¼	**5½**	— —	–	1 P.M. 46	E	LEO	23
306	2	Tu.	6 18	D	4 37	B	10 19	32	14 45	6¼	**6¾**	12 A.M. 26	C	2 21	D	LEO	24
307	3	W.	6 20	D	4 35	B	10 15	32	15 04	7½	**7¾**	1 31	C	2 51	D	LEO	25
308	4	Th.	6 21	D	4 34	B	10 13	32	15 22	8¼	**8¾**	2 34	D	3 19	D	VIR	26
309	5	Fr.	6 22	D	4 33	B	10 11	32	15 41	9	**9½**	3 36	D	3 47	C	VIR	27
310	6	Sa.	6 23	D	4 32	B	10 09	32	15 59	9¾	**10¼**	4 37	D	4 14	C	VIR	28
311	7	**C**	6 25	D	4 31	B	10 06	32	16 17	10½	**11**	5 37	E	4 42	B	VIR	0
312	8	M.	6 26	D	4 30	A	10 04	32	16 34	11	**11½**	6 36	E	5 13	B	LIB	1
313	9	Tu.	6 27	D	4 28	A	10 01	32	16 52	11¾	—	7 35	E	5 46	B	LIB	2
314	10	W.	6 28	D	4 27	A	9 59	32	17 09	12¼	**12¼**	8 31	E	6 24	B	OPH	3
315	11	Th.	6 30	D	4 26	A	9 56	32	17 26	12¾	**1**	9 26	E	7 06	B	OPH	4
316	12	Fr.	6 31	D	4 25	A	9 54	32	17 42	1½	**1¾**	10 17	E	7 52	B	SAG	5
317	13	Sa.	6 32	D	4 24	A	9 52	31	17 58	2¼	**2½**	11 04	E	8 44	B	SAG	6
318	14	**C**	6 33	D	4 23	A	9 50	31	18 14	3	**3¼**	11 A.M. 46	E	9 40	B	SAG	7
319	15	M.	6 35	D	4 23	A	9 48	31	18 29	4	**4**	12 P.M. 25	E	10 39	B	CAP	8
320	16	Tu.	6 36	D	4 22	A	9 46	31	18 44	4¾	**5**	1 00	D	11 P.M. 41	B	CAP	9
321	17	W.	6 37	D	4 21	A	9 44	31	18 59	5¾	**5¾**	1 32	D	— —	–	AQU	10
322	18	Th.	6 38	D	4 20	A	9 42	31	19 13	6½	**6¾**	2 03	D	12 A.M. 46	C	AQU	11
323	19	Fr.	6 39	D	4 19	A	9 40	30	19 27	7¼	**7¾**	2 34	D	1 53	D	PSC	12
324	20	Sa.	6 41	D	4 18	A	9 37	30	19 41	8¼	**8½**	3 06	C	3 03	D	CET	13
325	21	**C**	6 42	D	4 18	A	9 36	30	19 55	9	**9½**	3 40	C	4 16	E	PSC	14
326	22	M.	6 43	D	4 17	A	9 34	30	20 08	9¾	**10¼**	4 19	B	5 31	E	ARI	15
327	23	Tu.	6 44	D	4 16	A	9 32	29	20 20	10½	**11¼**	5 04	B	6 47	E	TAU	16
328	24	W.	6 45	D	4 16	A	9 31	29	20 33	11½	—	5 56	B	8 02	E	TAU	17
329	25	Th.	6 47	D	4 15	A	9 28	29	20 44	12	**12¼**	6 55	B	9 11	E	ORI	18
330	26	Fr.	6 48	D	4 15	A	9 27	29	20 56	1	**1¼**	8 00	B	10 12	E	GEM	19
331	27	Sa.	6 49	E	4 14	A	9 25	28	21 07	1¾	**2**	9 08	B	11 04	E	CAN	20
332	28	**C**	6 50	E	4 14	A	9 24	28	21 18	2¾	**3**	10 16	C	11 A.M. 47	E	CAN	21
333	29	M.	6 51	E	4 13	A	9 22	28	21 29	3¾	**4**	11 P.M. 23	C	12 P.M. 24	E	LEO	22
334	30	Tu.	6 52	E	4 13	A	9 21	27	21s.39	5	**5¼**	— —	–	12 P.M. 56	D	LEO	23

NOVEMBER hath 30 days. 1999

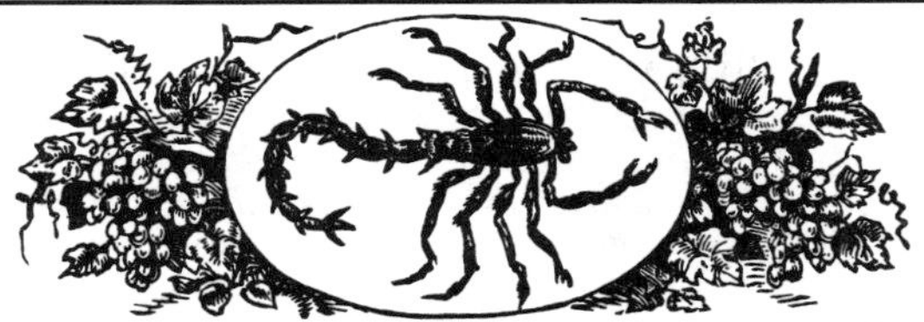

Tonight the winds began to rise
And roar from yonder dropping day:
The last red leaf is whirled away,
The rooks are blown about the skies.
– Alfred, Lord Tennyson

D. M.	D. W.	Dates, Feasts, Fasts, Aspects, Tide Heights	Weather ↓
1	M.	**All Saints** • First medical school for women opened, Boston, 1848 •	*Warm*
2	Tu.	**All Souls** • Election Day • Daniel Boone born, 1734 • {9.6 10.0	*enough*
3	W.	☌ ♀ ☾ • Detroit-Windsor auto tunnel opened, 1930 • Tides {9.8 9.9 •	*for*
4	Th.	Iranian militants seized U.S. Embassy in Teheran, 1979 • Will Rogers born, 1879 •	*outdoor*
5	Fr.	☾ on Eq. • ☿ stat. • Ida Tarbell born, 1857 • {10.2 9.9 •	*chores,*
6	Sa.	♄ at ☍ • 13 inches of snow, St. Louis, Mo., 1951 • Paderewski born, 1860 •	*now*
7	C	**24th S. af. P.** • New ● • Tides {10.5 9.8 •	*and*
8	M.	The Louvre opened to public for first time, 1793 • Bonnie Raitt born, 1949 •	*then*
9	Tu.	*Make the little decisions with your head and the big decisions with your heart.* • {10.4 —	*a blow.*
10	W.	**St. Leo the Great** • Martin Luther born, 1483 • {9.5 10.3 •	*Gather*
11	Th.	**St. Martin** • **Veterans Day** • ☾ at apo. • Tides {9.3 10.1 •	*in*
12	Fr.	NFL record: Detroit Lions fumbled 11 times, 1967 • Elizabeth Cady Stanton born, 1815	*those*
13	Sa.	☾ runs low • ☌ ♂ ☾ • Sadie Hawkins Day • {8.8 9.6 •	*winter*
14	C	**25th S. af. P.** • ☾ at ☋ • ☌ ♆ ☾ •	*stores,*
15	M.	☌ ⛢ ☾ • ☿ in inf. ☌ • ☿ transit over ☉ •	*soon*
16	Tu.	*The future joy makes the past and the present bearable.* • Tides {8.6 9.1 •	*enough*
17	W.	**St. Hugh of Lincoln** • American Theosophical Society founded, 1875 • {8.8 9.2	*the*
18	Th.	**St. Hilda** • Mickey Mouse appeared in his first film, *Steamboat Willie,* 1928 •	*snow.*
19	Fr.	☾ on Eq. • First life insurance policy issued to a woman, 1850 • Tides {9.8 9.8 •	*Stuff*
20	Sa.	☌ ♃ ☾ • Kenesaw Mountain Landis born, 1866 • {10.5 10.2 •	*the*
21	C	**26th S. af. P.** • ☌ ♄ ☾ • Tides {11.2 10.6	*turkey,*
22	M.	Hoagie Carmichael born, 1899 • Billie Jean King born, 1943 • {11.8 10.9 •	*say*
23	Tu.	**St. Clement** • Full Beaver ○ • ☾ at perig. • {12.2 11.0 •	*the*
24	W.	☿ stat. • Lee Harvey Oswald shot and killed, 1963 • {12.5 — •	*blessing,*
25	Th.	**Thanksgiving** • Andrew Carnegie born, 1835 • Upton Sinclair died, 1968 •	*pass*
26	Fr.	☾ rides high • Ford roadsters on sale for $260, 1925 • Tides {10.8 12.1 •	*the*
27	Sa.	☾ at ☊ • *It doesn't do any good to buy expensive tools if you can never find them.*	*sage*
28	C	**1st S. in Advent** • ☌ ♂ ♆ • Tides {10.2 11.0 •	*and*
29	M.	First Army-Navy football game, 1890 (Navy 24 - Army 0) • Tides {9.9 10.4 •	*onion*
30	Tu.	**St. Andrew** • -45° F, Pokegama Dam, Minn., 1896 •	*dressing.*

You can't depend on your eyes when your imagination is out of focus. – Mark Twain

Farmer's Calendar

Nobody is certain why children so love dinosaurs. Perhaps dinosaurs represent what children somehow believe, or wish, their parents were: large, strong, dumb, and conveniently extinct. However that may be, there's no doubt about the affinity of kids for the tyrannosaurs, triceratops, and the rest. If you want to get caught up on dinosaurs, ask a bright ten-year-old. But don't expect a quick lesson. There has been a good deal of activity in the dinosaur market in recent years. Dinosaurs aren't as easy as they were.

Once dinosaurs were safe and settled. You had the enormous, placid ones with long necks that went on all fours and ate plants. You had the scary, upright ones that ate the former. You had the dinosaurs that swam and the dinosaurs that flew. All were big, slow, and dull — and in those days that was about it.

Today things are more complicated. Now we have dinosaurs that were small and speedy, social, perhaps warm-blooded, and even intelligent in a wild, foxy way. As old fossils are reexamined and new ones are dug up, it develops that the more we know about dinosaurs, the more there is to know.

Why does science always do this to us? You would think that as the science of a field accumulated, it would eventually produce a simpler, more permanent understanding. In fact, the opposite happens: Increasing science makes a subject more complex, provisional, and undecided. That's good news for you if you write signs for museums, but it's frustrating for the rest of us.

1999 DECEMBER, THE TWELFTH MONTH

The Moon and Venus keep company on the 4th, while Mercury hovers between Venus and the eastern predawn horizon during the first week. The tiny planet floats to the upper right of the waning crescent Moon on the 6th. On the 12th, the first two hours after nightfall bring a very tight conjunction of the Moon, Mars, and Uranus in the southwest. Mars and Uranus are especially close on the 14th, a superb chance for binocular users to observe the seventh planet. The 22nd offers a rare combination of winter solstice (at 2:44 A.M., EST), full Moon, and lunar perigee, when the Moon reaches its closest approach of 1999, ending the year with a flourish.

●	New Moon	7th day	17th hour	32nd minute
☽	First Quarter	15th day	19th hour	50th minute
○	Full Moon	22nd day	12th hour	31st minute
☾	Last Quarter	29th day	9th hour	4th minute

Times are given in Eastern Standard Time.

For an explanation of this page, see "How to Use This Almanac," page 34; for values of Key Letters, see Time Correction Tables, page 214.

Day of Year	Day of Month	Day of Week	☉ Rises h. m.	Key	☉ Sets h. m.	Key	Length of Days h. m.	Sun Fast m.	Declination of Sun ° '	Full Sea Boston Light – A.M.	**Bold – P.M.**	☽ Rises h. m.	Key	☽ Sets h. m.	Key	☽ Place	☽ Age
335	1	W.	6 53	E	4 13	A	9 20	27	21s.48	6	**6¼**	12 A.M. 27	D	1 P.M. 25	D	VIR	24
336	2	Th.	6 54	E	4 12	A	9 18	27	21 57	7	**7¼**	1 29	D	1 52	C	VIR	25
337	3	Fr.	6 55	E	4 12	A	9 17	26	22 06	7¾	**8¼**	2 30	D	2 19	C	VIR	26
338	4	Sa.	6 56	E	4 12	A	9 16	26	22 14	8¾	**9**	3 30	E	2 46	C	VIR	27
339	5	**C**	6 57	E	4 12	A	9 15	25	22 21	9¼	**9¾**	4 29	E	3 15	B	LIB	28
340	6	M.	6 58	E	4 12	A	9 14	25	22 29	10	**10½**	5 28	E	3 47	B	LIB	29
341	7	Tu.	6 59	E	4 12	A	9 13	25	22 36	10¾	**11¼**	6 25	E	4 23	B	OPH	0
342	8	W.	7 00	E	4 11	A	9 11	24	22 42	11¼	**11¾**	7 21	E	5 03	B	OPH	1
343	9	Th.	7 01	E	4 11	A	9 10	24	22 49	**12**	—	8 13	E	5 48	B	SAG	2
344	10	Fr.	7 02	E	4 12	A	9 10	23	22 54	12½	**12½**	9 02	E	6 38	B	SAG	3
345	11	Sa.	7 03	E	4 12	A	9 09	23	22 59	1¼	**1¼**	9 46	E	7 33	B	SAG	4
346	12	**C**	7 04	E	4 12	A	9 08	22	23 04	1¾	**2**	10 26	E	8 30	B	CAP	5
347	13	M.	7 05	E	4 12	A	9 07	22	23 08	2½	**2¾**	11 01	E	9 30	C	CAP	6
348	14	Tu.	7 05	E	4 12	A	9 07	21	23 12	3¼	**3½**	11 A.M. 34	D	10 33	C	AQU	7
349	15	W.	7 06	E	4 12	A	9 06	21	23 16	4	**4¼**	12 P.M. 04	D	11 P.M. 37	C	AQU	8
350	16	Th.	7 07	E	4 13	A	9 06	20	23 19	5	**5¼**	12 33	D	— —	–	AQU	9
351	17	Fr.	7 08	E	4 13	A	9 05	20	23 21	5¾	**6¼**	1 03	C	12 A.M. 43	D	CET	10
352	18	Sa.	7 08	E	4 13	A	9 05	19	23 23	6¾	**7¼**	1 35	C	1 51	D	PSC	11
353	19	**C**	7 09	E	4 14	A	9 05	19	23 24	7½	**8**	2 10	B	3 03	E	CET	12
354	20	M.	7 09	E	4 14	A	9 05	18	23 25	8½	**9**	2 50	B	4 17	E	TAU	13
355	21	Tu.	7 10	E	4 14	A	9 04	18	23 25	9¼	**10**	3 38	B	5 32	E	TAU	14
356	22	W.	7 10	E	4 14	A	9 04	17	23 25	10¼	**10¾**	4 33	B	6 46	E	TAU	15
357	23	Th.	7 11	E	4 15	A	9 04	17	23 25	11	**11¾**	5 37	B	7 53	E	GEM	16
358	24	Fr.	7 11	E	4 16	A	9 05	16	23 25	**12**	—	6 46	B	8 51	E	GEM	17
359	25	Sa.	7 12	E	4 17	A	9 05	16	23 23	12¾	**12¾**	7 57	B	9 41	E	CAN	18
360	26	**C**	7 12	E	4 17	A	9 05	15	23 21	1½	**1¾**	9 07	C	10 22	E	LEO	19
361	27	M.	7 12	E	4 18	A	9 06	15	23 19	2½	**2¾**	10 15	C	10 57	D	LEO	20
362	28	Tu.	7 13	E	4 19	A	9 06	14	23 16	3½	**3¾**	11 P.M. 20	C	11 28	D	LEO	21
363	29	W.	7 13	E	4 19	A	9 06	14	23 13	4½	**4¾**	— —	–	11 A.M. 56	D	VIR	22
364	30	Th.	7 13	E	4 20	A	9 07	14	23 09	5¼	**5¾**	12 A.M. 22	D	12 P.M. 23	C	VIR	23
365	31	Fr.	7 13	E	4 21	A	9 08	13	23s.05	6¼	**6¾**	1 A.M. 23	D	12 P.M. 50	C	VIR	24

DECEMBER hath 31 days. 1999

We've had some pleasant rambles,
And merry Christmas gambols,
And roses with our brambles,
Adieu, old year, adieu!
– George Lunt

D. M.	D. W.	Dates, Feasts, Fasts, Aspects, Tide Heights	*Weather* ↓
1	W.	Rosa Parks refused to give up her bus seat, Montgomery, Ala., 1955 • Tides {9.7 9.6 •	*Pack*
2	Th.	☾ on Eq. • ☌ ♇ ☉ • ☿ Gr. Elong (20° W.) • Maria Callas born, 1923 •	*the*
3	Fr.	☌ ♀ ☾ • First successful human heart transplant, 1967 • Tides {9.9 9.3	*malls*
4	Sa.	**First day of Chanukah** • 70° F, Boston, Mass., 1982 • Tides {10.0 9.3	*with*
5	**C**	**2nd S. in Advent** • ☌ ☿ ☾ • {10.2 9.3 •	*hours*
6	M.	**St. Nicholas** • First issue of *Ladies' Home Journal* published, 1883 •	*of*
7	Tu.	**St. Ambrose** • **New** ● • Pearl Harbor attacked, 1941 • {10.3 9.2	*folly.*
8	W.	☾ at apo. • Reagan and Gorbachev signed the INF treaty, 1987 • {10.3 9.2 •	*Get*
9	Th.	*If December be changeable and mild, the whole winter will remain a child.* • {10.2 — •	*ready*
10	Fr.	☾ runs low • First Nobel Prizes awarded, 1901 • Alfred Nobel died, 1896 • {9.1 10.1	*for*
11	Sa.	☾ at ☋ • ☌ ♆ ☾ • King Edward VIII abdicated, 1936 • {9.0 10.0 •	*a*
12	**C**	**3rd S. in Advent** • ☌ ♂ ☾ • ☌ ♅ ☾ •	*storm,*
13	M.	**St. Lucy** • The "Mona Lisa," missing for 2 years, was recovered and returned to The Louvre, 1913 •	*by*
14	Tu.	☌ ♂ ♅ • Halycon Days • Nostradamus born, 1503 • {8.8 9.4 •	*golly!*
15	W.	Ember Day • *Gone with the Wind* premiered at Loew's Grand Theatre in Atlanta, Ga., 1939 •	*Even*
16	Th.	*From error to error, one discovers the entire truth.* • Tides {9.2 9.2 •	*Santa*
17	Fr.	☾ on Eq. • Ember Day • William Lyon Mackenzie King born, 1874 •	*loses*
18	Sa.	☌ ♃ ☾ • Ember Day • Divorce became legal in Italy, 1970 •	*focus*
19	**C**	**4th S. in Advent** • ☌ ♄ ☾ • Tides {10.7 9.9 •	*in*
20	M.	Bus boycott ended, Montgomery, Ala., 1956 • Sacagawea died, 1812 • {11.3 10.2 •	*pre-*
21	Tu.	**St. Thomas** • ♃ stat. • Beware the Pogonip. •	*millennial*
22	W.	**Winter Solstice** • ☾ at perig. • **Full Long Nights** ○ • {12.3 10.7	*hocus*
23	Th.	☾ rides high • Bell Labs announced the invention of the transistor, 1947 •	*pocus.*
24	Fr.	☾ at ☊ • Kit Carson born, 1809 • Howard Hughes born, 1905 • {12.4 —	*Snow*
25	Sa.	**Christmas Day** • *Peace on Earth, Goodwill to men.* •	*descends*
26	**C**	**1st S. af. Ch.** • **Boxing Day (Canada)** • Tides {10.5 11.5	*as the*
27	M.	**St. John** • **St. Stephen** • Marlene Dietrich born, 1901 •	*century*
28	Tu.	**Holy Innocents** • William Semple patented chewing gum, 1869 • {10.0 10.2	*ends:*
29	W.	☾ on Eq. • Massacre at Wounded Knee, S.D., 1890 • Tides {9.8 9.6 •	*Ready!*
30	Th.	First color TV sets on sale, 1953 • Simon Guggenheim born, 1867 • {9.6 9.1 •	*Set!*
31	Fr.	*Fill your life with experiences, not excuses.* • {9.5 8.8 •	*Oh-oh-oh!*

Farmer's Calendar

If you want to know what the future has in store in any field, you ask those especially concerned. Is your interest sports? Ask a player. Is it loan rates? Ask a banker. Is it elections? Ask someone who has to run for office. Skip the experts and find a witness whose own life will be affected by the course of events you're inquiring about; find someone on the ground, so to speak.

This principle, no more than common sense, is part of the reason people hang stubbornly onto folk weather lore in a scientific age in which that lore ought to be obsolete. Most of us, no doubt, get our weather forecasts from TV and radio — that is, from broadcasters who pass on the conclusions of meteorologists. We have confidence in these scientific forecasts for the best possible reason: We have found them to be generally accurate. Nevertheless, the prescientific indicators of weather — the acorns, groundhogs, woolly bear caterpillars, and so on — are not forgotten. Though they survive mainly as humor, they do survive.

Why don't we let the old weather signs go, at last, and put all our faith in meteorology? Because meteorology isn't on the ground. Those likable, attractive people on the TV, even the scientists whose findings they report, aren't concerned with the weather the way a deer mouse, say, is. If the former get it wrong, they may have to find a job in Sioux Falls. But for them, that's the worst thing that happens. The deer mouse has a different stake. If he underestimates the winter to come and fails to provide in his nest, he starves.

WHERE ORDINARY STUFF COMES FROM

The Uncommon History of Common Objects

The common objects of daily life in the 20th century — things like thermostats and telephones — are an almost invisible presence. They are always at hand but seldom considered, noticed but not seen, as if they were rocks left behind by a glacier, a fact of the landscape. But these common objects have a pedigree. They were born earlier in this century, many in the 1930s, in hopes of building a brighter tomorrow. Now these once-revolutionary designs have become familiar forms in our lives.

Henry Dreyfuss: His designs epitomized the 20th-century look.

– photo: Cooper-Hewitt, National Design Museum, Smithsonian Inst./Art Resource, N.Y. Photo by Tom Carroll, 1967

The P.O.T.

■ **Bell Telephone selected Henry** Dreyfuss to redesign the telephone in 1946. Although few Americans have ever heard of Dreyfuss, most have probably used one of his designs. In his 44-year career as an industrial designer, he shaped hundreds of products: the Big Ben alarm clock, the John Deere tractor, the Hoover vacuum cleaner, the Polaroid camera, the Singer sewing machine, and even the 20th Century Limited for the New York Central Railroad (for which he designed everything from the

by Howard Mansfield

dishes in the dining car to the gleaming locomotive itself).

Dreyfuss and his design team spent 3,000 hours and worked through many clay models of the telephone, simplifying the design, making it more comfortable to use and more durable. Bell wanted a sturdy

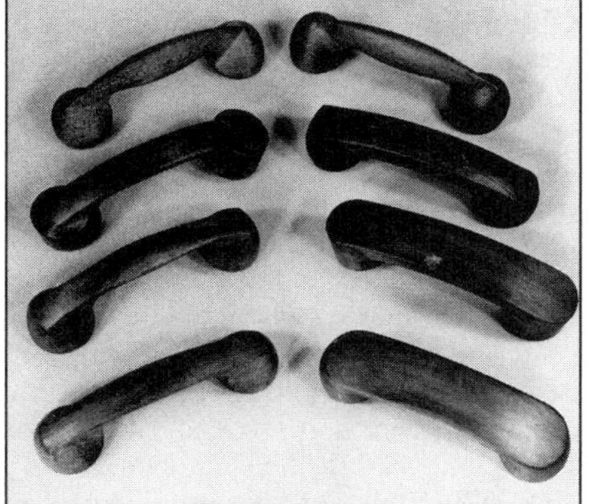

– from *Henry Dreyfuss, Industrial Designer: The Man in the Brown Suit* (1997)

Prototypes for the new handset created by Dreyfuss and his design team, 1946.

phone, because the company would own all of them and rent them to consumers.

The old handset on the 1930s Model 302 had a triangular cross section, difficult to cradle between the head and shoulder. Dreyfuss's office came up with the shape we know — "a lumpy rectangle." Dreyfuss disliked the new handset at first sight, slamming it down so hard that it broke the base of the model. He said it gave him "griptophobia." The design team was unperturbed, explaining that it was meant to be gripped and hung up firmly.

The Model 500 desk phone — in black only — was first produced in 1949. The letters and numbers were set outside the black dial wheel. Despite Dreyfuss's careful work, however, it took people longer to dial the new phone. A "human-engineering psychologist" said it was because people couldn't tell when the black dial had stopped spinning against the black background. White "aiming dots" were added, and Bell Telephone produced an astonishing 161 million telephones of this model.

Dreyfuss later designed the Princess and Trimline phones, but the Model 500 — the classic, black desktop rotary-dial telephone — was the staple of Ma Bell, scribbled on order forms by customer service representatives as P.O.T. — Plain Old Telephone.

The Round

Before the Honeywell "Round" thermostat, all thermostats were small boxes. It bothered Henry Dreyfuss that they always looked crooked on the wall. A couple of Honeywell engineers experimented with a round shape before World War II, but problems arose in making a workable curved thermometer. After the war, the project was revived. Dreyfuss, who liked to practice sketching perfect circles on cocktail napkins, discarded the idea of a curved thermometer and refined the design. In 1953, after more than $600,000 was spent in development, the "Round,"

– Honeywell Inc.

Model T-86, was introduced. Double-page ads in *Life* and *The Saturday Evening Post* showed a colorful parade of Rounds. The design was so distinctive that Honeywell trademarked the word *Round*. The most common version today, Model T-87, was updated in 1964 to accommodate air-conditioning. It may be the most ubiquitous household object in the world. Look for it on a wall near you.

Cold Fashion

In the early 1930s, the refrigerator still looked like its predecessor, the icebox: a box set up on legs, topped with a circular cooling unit called a "monitor top" because it resembled the turret on the famous Civil War gunboat. It was Dreyfuss and other industrial designers who created the box we have in our kitchens today.

For his client, General Electric, Dreyfuss designed a plain box, eschewing any of the popular streamlining touches of the 1930s: no "speedlines," no dressing up the refrigerator as a skyscraper. The 1934 "flattop," as Model CF-1-B16 was known, was a sober citizen of the modern kitchen.

Sears liked what it saw and asked Dreyfuss to redesign *its* refrigerator. With the GE contract in mind, he declined, suggesting a fellow designer, the flamboyant Raymond Loewy. Loewy's 1935 Coldspot was a sharp-looking product: Three parallel lines ran up the center. Inside, chrome ribbing continued the vertical theme. The Coldspot became a leading seller.

Sears followed Detroit's lead and began introducing annual model changes. Each year, Loewy brought forth a new, snazzier design: 1936 had a single chrome strip down the front and a round nameplate; 1937 eliminated the line down the center; 1938 had a V-shaped front, much like a car. (Loewy had also designed the front of the Hupmobile.) Each model change brought a jump in sales, but the basic box form has held for more than 60 years.

– Sears, Roebuck & Co.

The Sears 1935 Coldspot refrigerator, designed by Raymond Loewy, had a streamlined, vertical look.

The Proto Minivans

The car of the future, envisioned by designers of the 1930s, would be streamlined, with a roomy interior that allowed for flexible seating. Raymond Loewy and another industrial designer, Norman Bel Geddes, designed a number of teardrop-shaped cars and buses (and ships and airplanes), but none progressed beyond drawings and models.

Two designers got their future cars on the road. Buckminster Fuller excited New York City when he took H. G. Wells for a ride in his 1933 Dymaxion Car. This radical car could, he said, seat 11, get 22 miles to the gallon, and turn 90 or 180 degrees on its three wheels. "It steered with a third wheel on its tail, the way a fish or bird or boat or airplane must steer," said Fuller. "When I wanted to park in a space

Buckminster Fuller's 1933 Dymaxion Car seated 11 and could turn on a dime.

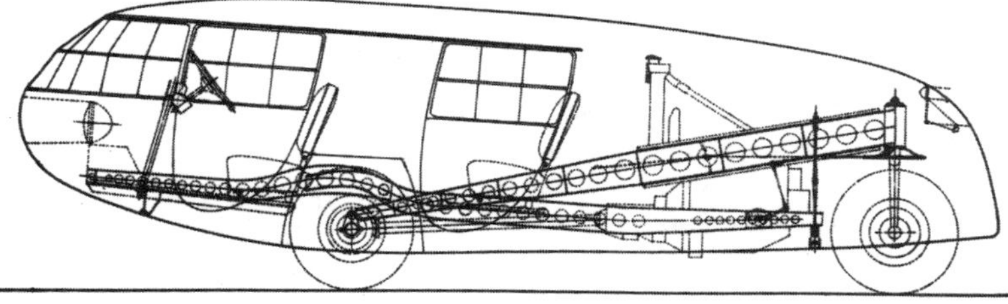

just the length of my car, I would simply bring my nose into the curb and throw my rear wheels sideways, and she went right in — flop — like that."

But Fuller's Dymaxion Car was in an accident in Chicago, just outside the 1933 Century of Progress Exposition, which led a British group to cancel its order for the next car, although the Dymaxion was not at fault. However, only three were ever built.

William Stout was an inventor who had pioneered the all-metal airplane in America. His 1935 Scarab Beetle car looked a little pudgy, but Stout claimed it was the same width and length as a 1935 Ford. Although he never tested it in a wind tunnel, he claimed that it was a good model of what he called "terranautics." The Beetle had a short hood, and the engine was in the rear. The passengers could sit on a six-foot-long couch or in two movable seats. It was never put into production.

The Scarab Beetle, the Dymaxion Car,

William Stout's 1935 Scarab Beetle anticipated the "soccer Mom" minivans of today.

– National Automotive History Collection

the teardrop-shaped cars of Bel Geddes and Loewy — all these dream cars disappeared by the start of World War II. Yet all are the eccentric ancestors of today's minivan.

(continued)

The Auto Temple

■ **Before Walter Dorwin Teague created the** sleek white Texaco gas station in 1937, filling-station design was a free-for-all. Gas was dispensed from stuccoed pueblos, steep-roofed English cottages, classical pavilions, Indian tepees, Oriental pagodas, and little shacks with a pump out front. To the public, many of these places were grease pits. Teague surveyed drivers to find out what they wanted: It was cleanliness. Station owners wanted an office with a clear view of the pumps.

Working with architect Robert Jordan Harper, Teague created a crisp Machine Age look. There were five variations, some specifically designed for corner lots. Type C was the most common: a rectangular building with two or more service bays and an office that projected out three feet. A canopy could be added to the front, with three green speed lines carried around the lip of the canopy and a large Texaco sign on the canopy roof that could be backlit at night. The stations were built of porcelain-enamel metal panels, brick, stucco, or wood.

The well-lit white cube run by the man who wore the star helped Texaco establish "an image of service, an image of cleanliness, an oasis for your car," says preservationist Charles Olson, who wrote his master's thesis on the Texaco station. It was "one of the first applications of corporate America placing its symbol on the landscape," Olson says. The form-giving design was quickly copied by Mobil and Gulf.

Aggressively marketing its products during the Great Depression, Texaco used the stations as vending machines. To increase sales, the men's room was placed inside, where motorists would have to walk past displays of goods. (The women's room had an outside entrance.) Lighting, it was shown, could increase nighttime sales by 25 percent.

Starting in 1938, Texaco began advertising "Texaco Registered Rest Rooms — Clean Across the Country." The "White Patrol," a fleet of 48 inspectors in white cars, visited stations in every state to make sure the uniformed owners were living up to a pledge they had signed to keep the rest rooms clean and fully equipped.

Teague's 1937 design served Texaco for almost 30 years. Some 10,000 stations were built before it was retired in 1964 for a domestic design with a mansard roof and fieldstone front. Teague once boasted that there were "plenty of good service stations . . . more beautiful than any number of banal temples and capitols."

• • • • • • • • • • • • • •

(continued on page 94)

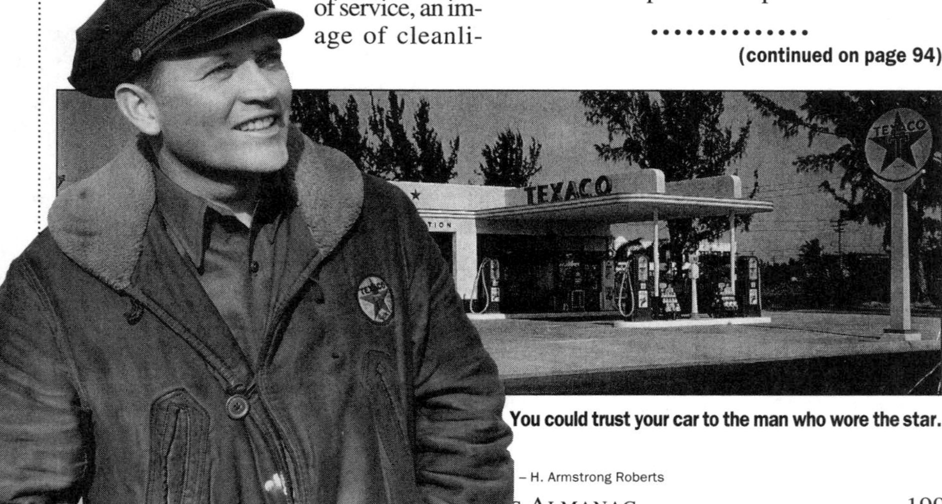

– Texaco Inc.

You could trust your car to the man who wore the star.

– H. Armstrong Roberts

Designing the Future

■ At the 1939 World's Fair in New York, "tomorrow" was on everyone's mind. And the leaders of tomorrow were the industrial designers, the ones who would work with engineers and scientists to build us out of the Great Depression. The future was just another product, like a toaster or a refrigerator. The fair featured a Town of Tomorrow, a Rocketport of the Future, a Dairy World of Tomorrow, a Soda Fountain of the Future, and going it all one better, a World of the Day After Tomorrow.

Perhaps most enchanting was the General Motors exhibit, Futurama. More than 5 million people saw it, at times waiting in lines that stretched for a mile. The exhibit designer, the inventive Norman Bel Geddes, had made his name designing kitchen appliances, cars, and trains, honing his flair for the dramatic by designing Broadway stage sets.

In Futurama, Bel Geddes worked up a sight for Depression-weary eyes: the world of 1960. Each visitor sat in an armchair that moved along a conveyor for a 16-minute flight over the world of tomorrow. Sitting down, the first thing the time traveler heard from a speaker in the back of the chair was, "Strange? Fantastic? Unbelievable? Remember, this is the world of 1960."

Then below, as if seen from a low-flying plane, the wonders unfolded. There was an America crossed by high-speed highways on which teardrop-shaped cars sped along at 100 miles per hour, past experimental orchards with each tree under its own glass sphere. In the city, tall curving towers ringed expanses of greenery. At the base of the towers, the highways met in massive intersections more than 20 lanes wide. No pedestrians were in sight. (This future was, after all, sponsored by General Motors.)

As the excursion ended, the chairs passed close by one intersection from the city of 1960, and the travelers heard: "In a moment, we will arrive on this very street intersection — to become part of this selfsame scene in the World of Tomorrow — in the wonder world of 1960 — 1939 is 20 years ago! *All eyes to the future!"* Sure enough, visitors now stood at a full-size street corner of the future. It may have been a letdown, though. In that future, the streets were thick with GM cars and trucks of 1939.

But no matter, the future would be well designed. And it has been, with handsome phones and thermostats, zippy refrigerators and cars — and happy consumers. It's a world of sleek and flashy objects that the industrial designers of the '30s and '40s barely dreamed of. □□

Bel Geddes *(above left)* and his 1939 Futurama *(above)* transported viewers to the sleek world of 1960.

– photos this page: Bel Geddes Collection, University of Texas, courtesy of the Estate of Norman Bel Geddes. Edith L. Bel Geddes, Executrix

Joe the Crow

AND OTHER TALES

The Crow unquestionably is a remarkably clever bird. This is clearly demonstrated in many ways by his conduct in his natural state, and has been borne out in the cases of many hundreds of tamed Crows, who have furnished endless amusement for their owners. Apparently such birds always display a thieving propensity, amounting to what would be considered kleptomania in human beings." So said Edward Howe Forbush, the famous ornithologist who died in 1929, leaving the three-volume *Birds of Massachusetts and Other New England States.*

Forbush was describing the common crow of New England, *Corvus brachyrhynchos* (short-billed crow), of the family Corvidae, cousin to the raven, jay, magpie, rook, jackdaw, and nutcracker — corvid, for short. With an average length between 17 and 21 inches, the crow is smaller than the raven (21 to 26½ inches) but larger than the bluejay (11 to 12½ inches). The fish crow (*C. ossifragus,* Latin for "bonebreaker") is slightly smaller than the common crow, but its reputation is worse, due to its fondness for raiding the nests of shorebirds. Across the country is *C. caurinus,* the northwestern crow.

To many researchers, corvids are considered the most intelligent and sociable of all the bird species. They form tight family bonds, spending months or even years with their parents. They'll bond with people, too, as keepers of pet crows (now illegal in many areas) will tell you.

– Sara Mintz Zwicker

Joe the Crow

Bud French and his family, of Nelson, New Hampshire, found themselves caretaking a nearly starved fledgling crow for a summer, after the weakened bird turned up in a culvert that the road crew was cleaning out. Luckily, Bud and his kids had a reserve supply of night crawlers for fishing, but pretty soon they'd excavated large areas of their lawn while digging for more worms to keep up with feedings. Eventually they supplemented the worms with moistened dog kibble and liquid baby vitamins.

The crow, initially housed in a dog crate, soon began to act like their Shelties, hopping in and out of doors and demanding to come inside with the dogs. One of the cats started leaving dead mice for Joe. Forbush had noted that the crow "knows a good thing when he sees it," and this was certainly true of Joe.

As the summer progressed, Bud and his wife, Kelly, began what he called a "tough-love program," trying to spur the bird to greater independence so that he could return to the wild. Joe the Crow clearly preferred to be inside, however, especially during thunderstorms. During one evening storm, he circled the house, shrieking and pressing his whole body against the windows and doors, insisting on being let in. Bud and his family held firm. Finally, Joe gave it up; but instead of roosting in a tree or in the barn, the crow found a neighbor working in his garage and boarded there for the night.

Joe followed Bud around town, flying beside his truck. "He'd leave a pebble on the windshield if he knew you, just to say he'd been there," Bud said. Once Joe brought home a dime and traded it for a nickel. (Bud and his kids figured maybe they were onto something, but Joe didn't repeat the trick.) Joe stole the girls' barrettes and hair scrunchies and pulled the price tags off items displayed outside the art gallery on the village green. He perched above the crowd at Old Home Day, just spying and "yelling" at people. He gained a reputation as a trickster and a scold, but the villagers humored him as a "character."

By the end of the summer, Joe the Crow had taken up with a gang of other crows, flying off with them at night and returning by day, especially if Bud was reclaiming a field nearby, picking rocks and turning up earthworms. The other

by Martha White

Collectively, we refer to a "charm" of goldfinches and a "convocation" of eagles, but when we speak of crows, we call them a "murder." As it turns out, stories have been told about this smart, sociable, thieving black bird since ancient days. Here are a few of them.

crows would remain in the treetops while Joe came down to pluck out the worms. Bud thinks Joe bonded with two crows — other juveniles probably — and by the end of October, Joe the Crow disappeared.

The French family had no doubts about the bird's intelligence. As a kid, Bud had raised a woodchuck named Chipper. Bud remembers both wild animals as smart but in different ways. "The crow was always thinking ahead and changing the game. The crow would outthink you."

Talking Turkey, or, uh, Crow

From the corvids' loud vocal habits come associations with banshee-like figures, scolds, and witches, as well as with magicians and sorcerers. Just as the owl's voice became much dreaded in the sickroom, so did the crow's call (or mere presence) come to be considered a presage of death. It's said that Cicero was forewarned of his death by the fluttering of ravens. Crows are called contentious, and in hieroglyphics the symbol of a crow stands for discord and strife.

Word has it that crows can be quite articulate, and you don't have to split their tongues, either. Forbush related accounts of wild crows who were heard calling the cows or the cat, or repeating other oft-heard phrases, such as "Hello Joe" or "Now you've done it" or "Ah go on." Bernd Heinrich, biologist and raven researcher at the University of Vermont (and author of *Ravens in Winter,* Summit Books, 1989), has similar stories about ravens. One bird, Heinrich told interviewers, could mimic the sounds at a nearby construction site: "3, 2, 1, kaboom!"

Regarding crow language, Cornell University ecological researcher Dr. Kevin McGowan describes the familiar pattern of short, repeated caws as "standard territorial language. It's saying, 'This is my spot, I'm here today, you'd better stay away.' But if there's a predator — a hawk or an owl — it's more drawn out, more guttural, more like 'Aargh!' Usually that brings other crows; first the family, then neighbors, then anyone in the vicinity."

Bad Omens?

For "knowing too much," we call the crow a trickster and a slanderer. The old Irish spirit Babd, a goddess of war, appeared as a hooded crow and was thought to incite armies, encouraging destruction and war-madness. Crows and ravens have been our witnesses to war because of their habit of following armies and feeding on the carnage. The same is true in areas of pestilence and famine, and consequently corvids have been accused of predicting death and spreading disease instead of merely following it. Lord Macaulay (1800-1859) described the Scottish belief in "the foresight of a raven," saying, "Of inspired birds ravens are accounted the most prophetical. . . ." Another war god, Odin, carried a raven on each shoulder, called Hugin and Munnin, or Mind and Memory.

Eats Like a Bird (a peck at a time)

It is true that, in their diets, crows are both scavengers and predators. The great tome *Birds of America* (T. Gilbert Pearson, editor, and Forbush one of its contributing editors), published in 1917, lists the pros and cons of the crow appetite: "The Crow is commonly regarded as a blackleg and a thief. . . . That he does pull up sprouting corn, destroy chickens, and rob the nests of young birds has been repeatedly proved. Nor are these all of his sins. He is known to eat frogs, toads, salamanders, and some small snakes, all harmless creatures that do some good by eating insects." On the other hand, the authors explain, the crow should be "credited" for the mice he consumes, as well as quantities of beetles, June bugs, grasshoppers, caterpillars, and cutworms.

Forbush and others delight in stories where gunners have decimated the crows in a given area, intending to protect pasture or newly planted corn, only to find that the land then falls prey to an onslaught of insects that ruin the grazing or eat the corn crop. As you might expect, crows prove a necessary part of the balance. (And Bud French says that, years ago, you planted tarred corn seed to deter crows.) We know of one rural Maine resident who feeds the crows his meat scraps, leaving the bones and leftovers atop a flat, wooden platform on a long, vertical pole, so that the crows can get them but the dogs and raccoons cannot. For this favor, he gets a great opportunity to observe crows.

How to Make a Crow Go

Not everyone wants to attract crows. When asked if there's any way to get rid of a crow, or a large roost of crows, in settings such as car dealerships or downtown malls, Kevin McGowan suggests disturbing their food source. First, observe whether the crows are coming in to feed in the daytime, possibly raiding urban dumpsters that spill over with French fries and the like. If that's the case, clean up the garbage.

Possibly, though, the crows are coming in to congregate and socialize before nightfall, or they may be coming in to roost for the night.

CROWS AND THE WEATHER

On the first of March,
The crows begin to
search;
By the first of April,
They're sitting still;
By the first of May,
They're all flown
away,
Coming greedy back
again,
With October's wind
and rain.

– English saying

(continued)

THE BLACKNESS OF CROWS

"Unfortunately for the Crow he has a bad reputation, and it must be admitted that there is some reason for the low regard in which he is held among men. First he is black, the color of evil; then, he knows too much; his judgment of the range of a gun is too nearly correct."

– Edward Howe Forbush

"Crows are black all the world over."

– Chinese proverb

"If a crow help us in, sirrah, we'll pluck a crow together."

– Shakespeare's Comedy of Errors

(In the Shakespeare quote, the first reference is to an iron crowbar; to "pluck a crow together" is to wage a loud argument or have a bone to pick with someone.)

The social roost, something like an evening bar scene, shifts periodically within a given area. You might broadcast a recording of crow alarm sounds, making the tapes yourself or buying them from farm-supply stores.

In urban areas, nighttime lighting attracts crows because it helps them see predators such as owls. You could turn out the lights or, McGowan suggests, wait until the crows are settled in, then make them think there's an owl in their midst. They're "plucky" about owls and hawks in the daytime, he says, and may attempt to mob them, but they're apt to change nighttime roosts if they don't feel safe.

When (and How) to Eat Crow

Worse than eating your hat, the term *eating crow* derives from an American Revolutionist's humiliation of an imprisoned British officer. Given that crows and ravens were known to feed on wartime casualties, the insult must have been hard to swallow.

Birds similar to crows have not been unknown in the kitchen, however. An old European tradition involved the shooting of black rooks. The young birds (or "simps") were cleaned and put into tough-crusted "standing pies" with hard-boiled eggs, slices of bacon, a piece of beefsteak, and a few herbs, much as pigeon pie might still be made in England.

Hannah Wolley, author of *The Compleat Servantmaid* (1685), described the proper kitchen terms for preparing various game birds. "In cutting up small birds, it is proper to thigh them — as in 'Thigh that Woodcock, thigh that Pigeon'; but as to others, say 'Mince that Plover, wing that Curlew, unjoint that Bittern, disfigure that Peacock, display that Crane, dismember that Heron.'" Hannah did not name the crow, raven, or rook, which probably means she didn't consider them kitchen-worthy, but we submit "murder those Crows" for anyone of a mind to put four-and-twenty into a pie. □□

A Brief History of Briefs

and Boxers, Drawers, and Breeches

Hang on to your trousers! Here's everything (or almost everything) you ever wanted to know about (gasp!) men's underwear.

by Victoria Doudera

Just what *did* the ancient Romans wear under their drafty togas? Roman men were known to wear a loincloth, or *subligaculum*. So did the ancient Egyptians, although it's hard to believe that King Tut needed *all* 145 linen loincloths that were buried with him in 1352 B.C. Men in the Middle Ages wore a long version of underwear, called *braies* or *breeches*, that tied at the waist. Because cotton — a staple of today's underwear fabrication — was not widely available in Europe until the 1660s, medieval nobles wore breeches made of fine linen, whereas the peasants made do with scratchy garments made from rougher stuff, usually wool.

Perhaps some peasants resented wearing uncomfortable underwear, but devout folk viewed it as a virtue. Like the hair shirts worn by monks as a religious discipline, to tolerate coarse underwear represented penitence and humility. As the wearing of underwear became

– illustrations this page: Corbis-Bettmann

more and more accepted, doing without breeches became a holy practice, too. Historical records assert that the most pious on the pilgrimages were often without shoes, shirts, and breeches.

By the close of the medieval period, wearing underwear — long, short, or somewhere in between — was the mark of a civilized man. A traveler to the Emerald Isle complained that Ireland's four kings "wore no breeches" and commissioned some to be made "of fine linen cloth" as a gift.

Starting in the 1500s, as tunics shortened to waist length, breeches became outerwear, and nobility adopted close-fitting, bias-cut silk or linen underwear called *trousers* or *strossers*. Peasants still wore breechclouts (i.e., loincloths).

Underwear of the day offered men (and women) not only warmth but also another type of protection: a barrier between valuable vestments and filthy skin. Frequent bathing was not a high priority among Europeans until the18th century. Instead, both sexes relied on perfumes to mask their body odors, and underclothes to protect their costly garments.

During the 1600s, male underwear came to be called *drawers,* due to the action it took to "draw" the garment — now fashionably tight — up the legs. Cotton was now widely available, although it was considered linen's social inferior. To dress smartly still meant linen, oftentimes lined with "China silk." Later in the century, the first drawers with buttons appeared.

When the Pilgrims came to New England on the *Mayflower* in 1620, at least a few of the men on board brought underwear. An inventory of the possessions of William Wright, for example, who died in Plymouth, Massachusetts, in 1633, lists among his worldly goods "two paire of boot brieches; an old paire of cotten drawers; and 3 paire of linnen drawers." His neighbor, the Elder William Palmer, was ahead of his time: Among his possessions are listed "two paire of drawers, red & greene."

Over 100 years later, Benjamin Franklin — not quite a trendsetter — wrote, ". . . during a hot Sunday in June 1750, I sat in my chamber with no other clothes on than a shirt and a pair of long linen drawers." By the late 18th century, an influential group of young, well-traveled Englishmen had greatly boosted the popularity of underwear. Nicknamed the Macaroni Club for their fondness for foreign foods, these dandies introduced an idea that had lapsed since the days of the Romans: personal cleanliness. Gentlemen of the day were advised to wear "no perfumes, but very fine linen, plenty of it" and to partake of "country washing." Thanks to the Macaronis, money spent on underwear increased. *(continued)*

***Starting in the 1500s, tunics shortened to waist length, and breeches became outerwear called* trousers.**

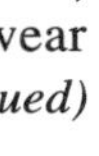

– illustrations this page: Corbis-Bettmann

The union suit covered the wearer from wrist to ankle, offering an undershirt and drawers in one piece.

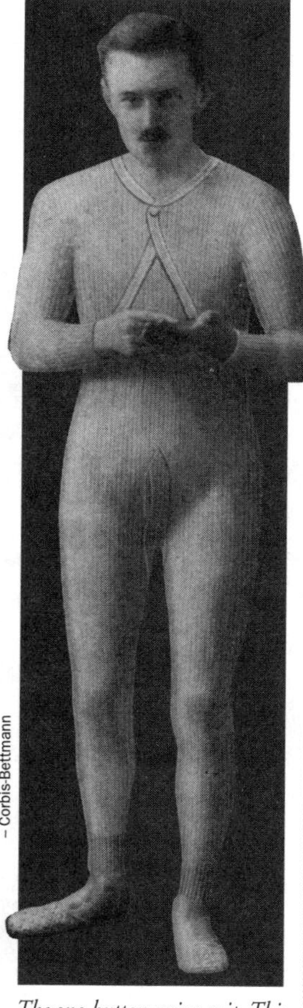
– Corbis-Bettmann

The one-button union suit. This version is by Fuld & Hatch Knitting Co., patented in June 1914.

Above right: *An ad for the versatile Kenosha Klosed Krotch demonstrated its assets.*

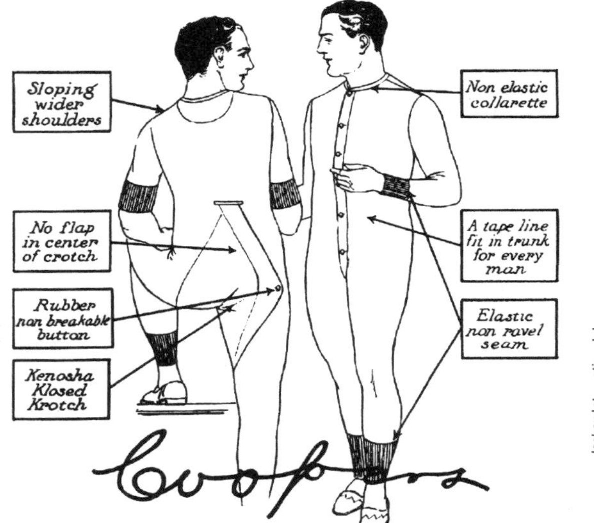

– Jockey International, Inc.

Drawers became shorter in keeping with the fashions of the times (the Macaronis also introduced "false calves" for more shapely male legs), but there were other styles as well: long, footed versions reminiscent of pajamas; high-waisted flannel underwear that laced up the front; and the long linen favorites some folks just couldn't part with.

The 19th century ushered in a period of extreme modesty, in which legs could only be called "limbs," a man's trousers were called "inexpressibles," and drawers, which gentlefolk preferred not even to *contemplate,* were referred to as "linens." Although cleanliness was now a virtue, the Victorian body was not permitted to see the light of day. Instead, it was covered by layer upon layer of handmade underclothes — all scrupulously clean.

The invention of the bicycle in 1839 led to short drawers of absorbent stockinette as well as "combination suits" of short pants and an attached vest. In the mid-1800s, the sewing machine was perfected, and men's underwear improved in fit. When the Civil War broke out in 1861, the northern soldiers wore snug, two-piece long underdrawers and vests made from southern cotton.

When Boston boxing champion John L. Sullivan wore long wool drawers as a boxing costume, these became known as *long johns*. They led to the creation, in 1892, of the first American advance in underwear for men: the popular *union suit*.

The union suit covered the wearer from wrist to ankle, offering an undershirt and drawers in one piece. Although this garment furnished warmth in the days before central heating, the union suit's design had a fundamental flaw. A trip to the outhouse meant totally disrobing — a chilly prospect in the winter. To stop the shivering, the Cooper Underwear Company of Kenosha, Wisconsin, introduced a unique garment in 1910. Called the *Kenosha Klosed Krotch,* it was a union suit featuring two pieces of fabric lapped over each other like an *X*. Men everywhere warmed to this invention, and the new suit was a huge success.

The entry of the United States into World War I in 1917 democratized underwear for men. Soldiers — regardless of rank — were issued comfortable woven shorts as part of their uniform. Perhaps because they were issued to military men in a box, the loose-fitting shorts were nicknamed *boxer shorts*.

When the war ended and soldiers returned to civilian life, they longed for the ease of their military "boxers." Sports and central heating were both becoming popular, and the old union suit was just too warm for many men. Underwear manufacturers like Cooper's responded, and sleeveless T-shirts and boxer shorts outfitted the men of the Roaring Twenties. Even taciturn President Calvin Coolidge voiced a preference for the new, more comfortable underwear.

Improved methods of dyeing fabric soon resulted in salmon pink, peach, and sky-blue boxers. The pastel hues appealed not only to men but to the ladies buying them or perhaps glimpsing them under romantic conditions. Suddenly, sex appeal — for centuries a function of women's lingerie — was a factor in men's underwear as well.

The year 1934 saw the birth of the men's *brief.* A senior vice president of the Cooper Underwear Company (famous for its unique union suit) chanced to see a postcard from the French Riviera showing a man in a bathing suit that ran from his waist

– Jockey International, Inc.

JOCKEY and JOCKEY Figure Design are trademarks of and used with permission of Jockey International, Inc.

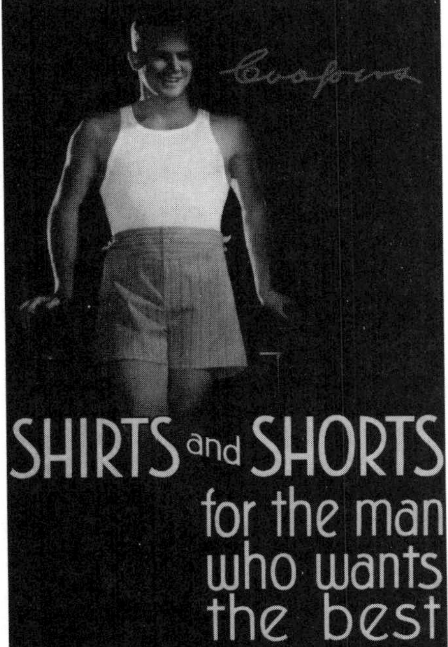

– Jockey International, Inc.

Left: *Comfy boxer shorts pleased guys in the 1920s.* Above: *Jockey's Skants, in a 1959 ad.*

– Corbis-Bettmann

– Corbis-Bettmann

Boxers began to take a backseat to the new briefs, although they were still favored by many traditionalists.

just to the upper thigh. The executive then envisioned underwear that would fulfill the same function as an athletic supporter, commonly called a *jockstrap*. When the design was completed, the garment was christened the *Jockey* brief. It debuted in Chicago in 1935, and although a blizzard had struck, shoppers flocked to Marshall Field & Co. in the Loop to buy the brief.

Not only was the design of this novel underwear revolutionary, but it was packaged and sold in an entirely new way. From the turn of this century, underclothes were sold in much the same way as shoes, with a salesman retrieving boxed merchandise from a storeroom. Men could not choose between or compare brands, and young women were often too embarrassed to ask for men's underwear. Coopers, Inc., as it was now called, thus invented the male torso mannequin to model the briefs and packaged the product in cellophane, arranged in displays on the floor so that customers could freely pick and choose.

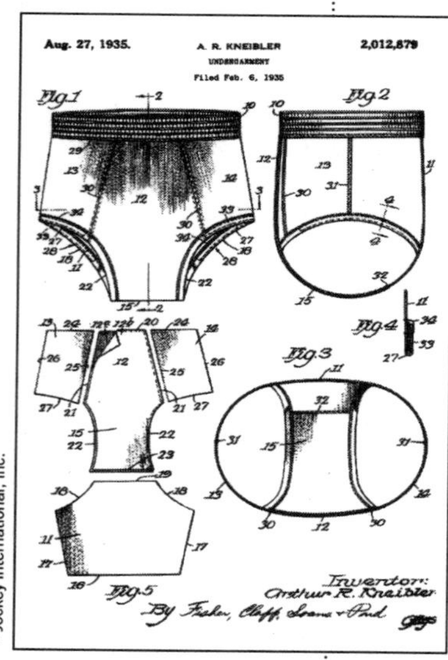

– Jockey International, Inc.

Patent drawings for the first-ever men's briefs, awarded to the Jockey brand on August 27, 1935.

After World War II, the era of fashion underwear began. The brief was manufactured in colorful French tricot, and innovations such as animal prints and Valentine hearts soon followed. The first tie-in with Hollywood and men's underwear took place in 1950, when a Jockey brief called Fancy Pants was marketed along with a movie of the same name starring Lucille Ball and Bob Hope.

Boxers began to take a backseat to the new briefs, although they were still favored by many traditionalists. Sailors even had their own term for their boxers and undershirts: *Skivvies.* An even briefer brief — bikini underwear, trademarked *Skants* — was introduced by Coopers, Inc., in 1959, but it was not until the 1970s that bikinis became popular. In 1972, the company that invented both the brief and the Kenosha Klosed Krotch became Jockey International, Inc. It is still a leading manufacturer of underwear today.

Briefs are now the most popular underwear style for men, but boxers have been making a comeback. John Cronce, corporate communications manager at Jockey, says, "It's a generational thing. As soon as Dad wears briefs, it's no longer cool, and kids start searching for something else to wear."

For hundreds of years, underwear — while perhaps not the star — has played an important supporting role in the rich history of clothing. What will the coming millennium reveal for men's underwear? It's a safe bet that manufacturers — and consumers — won't simply be resting on their laurels. □□

THE TOP 10 FEEL-GOOD HERBS

Natural remedies have enjoyed a resurgence of interest, and rightly so. The "feel-good" herbs are the latest rage, from the controversial yohimbe (touted as an aphrodisiac for men but potentially fatal in excess) to the popular ginkgo biloba (a circulation enhancer believed to aid memory and the libido). With all the hype and glory, it can be difficult to know what to believe. Luckily, in most cases, there are centuries of tradition and experience to guide us about the usefulness of these ancient herbs.

A User's Guide to the Top

CALENDULA. Creams and balms of this "pot marigold" *(Calendula officinalis)* are often effective as an antiseptic and anti-inflammatory agent for diaper rash, chapped hands and lips, and other minor skin irritations. Various commercial varieties are available. Your grandmother probably made her own salve, and you can do the same (see recipe on page 111). The purest forms use just the petals, but many include the entire flower head. Do not confuse this plant with the French marigold *(Tagetes patula),* often used as an insecticide.

ECHINACEA. Commonly known as purple coneflower, echinacea *(Echinacea purpurea* or *E. angustifolium)* is an herb used in teas, capsules, and tinctures to enhance immunity to colds and flu, and to fight kidney and mucous infections. Perhaps more than any other herbal remedy, echinacea has enjoyed a widespread new popularity, and its role is being studied in many immunity-related diseases. The root is the part generally used, although the flower can be used, as well. Echinacea is sometimes adulterated, so buy it from a reputable source or grow your own. Short-term use (up to 2 tablespoons of dried herb steeped in water and taken as often as three times a day) is generally advised; at higher doses, you risk nausea or dizziness. Some commercial teas combine goldenseal (see page 110) with echinacea, which may create uncertain dosage.

Calendula | *Feverfew*

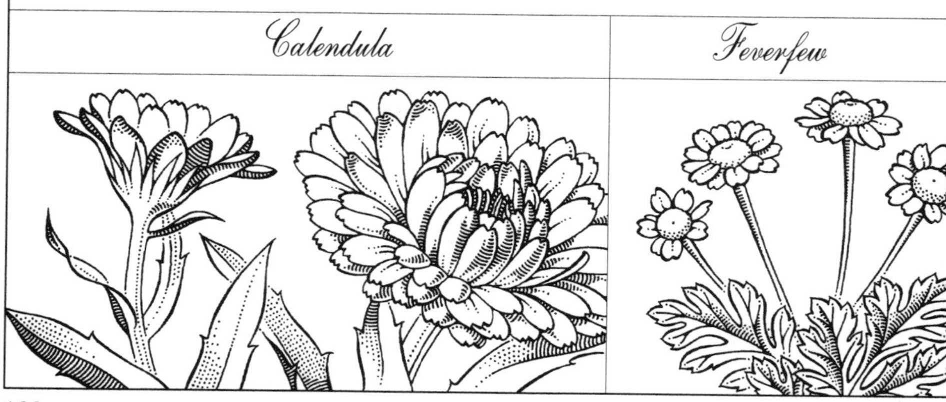

– illustrated by Sara Mintz Zwicker

"Newly improved!" . . . "Scientifically advanced!" . . .
"A revolutionary new herbal breakthrough!" . . .
Would you guess that these phrases advertise medicines that, in some cases, have been used for thousands of years? by Martha White

0 Herbs for Your Mind and Body

FEVERFEW. For brainpower and enhanced memory, feverfew *(Chrysanthemum parthenium* or *Tanacetum parthenium)* is a vasodilator that is considered to enhance blood circulation to the brain and, sometimes, relieve or prevent migraines. Midsummer daisy and featherfew are other, old names for this herb, but do not confuse it with feverwort. Traditional uses for feverfew are for menstrual cramps and indigestion, but not — as you might think — for fever. One leaf, up to three times a day, can be chewed (stop if mouth sores form) or used as a tea. Capsules are also available, but only good-quality sources contain the active ingredient, parthenolide. Avoid feverfew if you are pregnant or on blood thinners.

GINSENG. First, know your ginsengs. The root of the American ginseng *(Panax quinquefolius)* is considered a digestive aid. The Asiatic ginseng root *(Panax ginseng)* is supposed to provide a short-term aid for exhaustion, concentration, and resistance to stress; it also may help to regulate hormones, thus enhancing fertility. A third, the closely related Siberian ginseng *(Eleutherococcus senticosus),* is considered even more invigorating to the nerves. Pure sources

GINKGO BILOBA. The Chinese have been using ginkgo, from the *Ginkgo biloba* tree, also called the maidenhair tree, for thousands of years for conditions related to aging, such as headaches, hearing loss, and dizziness. More-recent German and French studies suggest that ginkgo leaves in a tea may help concentration, memory, and Alzheimer's symptoms. (Avoid the seeds, which can cause headaches or skin trouble.) For impotence, ginkgo leaves taken in tea once or twice a day is suggested because of its circulation-enhancing effect. "Vitality" and "libido" remedies often contain ginkgo.

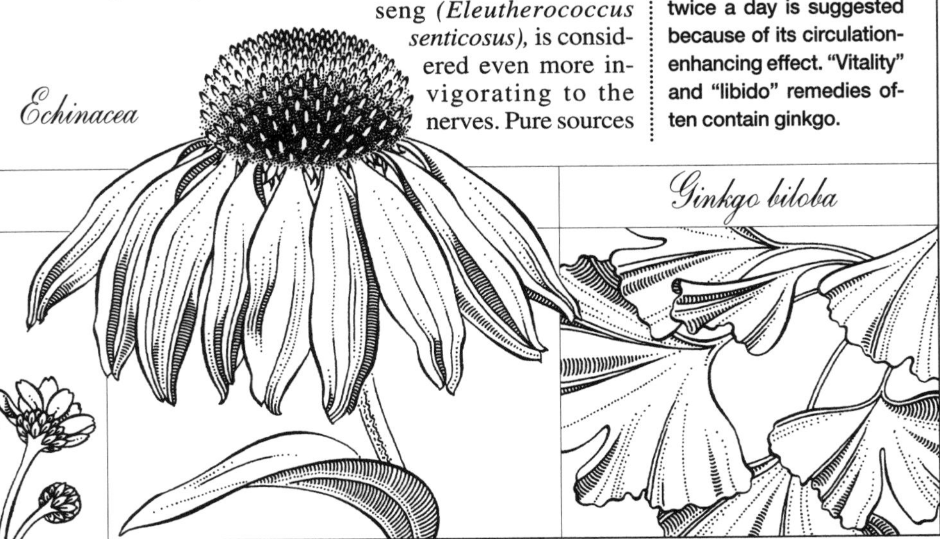

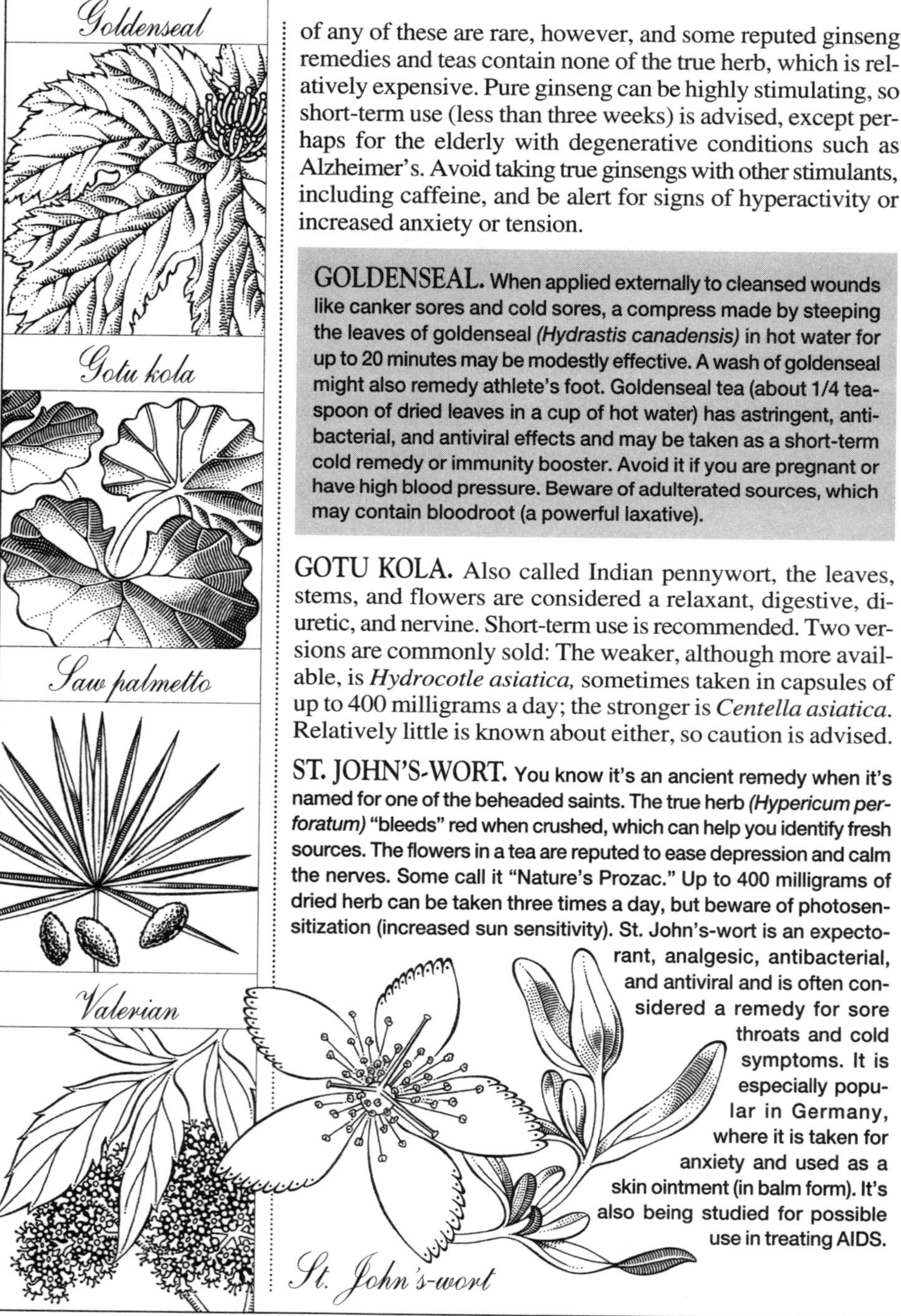

of any of these are rare, however, and some reputed ginseng remedies and teas contain none of the true herb, which is relatively expensive. Pure ginseng can be highly stimulating, so short-term use (less than three weeks) is advised, except perhaps for the elderly with degenerative conditions such as Alzheimer's. Avoid taking true ginsengs with other stimulants, including caffeine, and be alert for signs of hyperactivity or increased anxiety or tension.

GOLDENSEAL. When applied externally to cleansed wounds like canker sores and cold sores, a compress made by steeping the leaves of goldenseal *(Hydrastis canadensis)* in hot water for up to 20 minutes may be modestly effective. A wash of goldenseal might also remedy athlete's foot. Goldenseal tea (about 1/4 teaspoon of dried leaves in a cup of hot water) has astringent, antibacterial, and antiviral effects and may be taken as a short-term cold remedy or immunity booster. Avoid it if you are pregnant or have high blood pressure. Beware of adulterated sources, which may contain bloodroot (a powerful laxative).

GOTU KOLA. Also called Indian pennywort, the leaves, stems, and flowers are considered a relaxant, digestive, diuretic, and nervine. Short-term use is recommended. Two versions are commonly sold: The weaker, although more available, is *Hydrocotle asiatica,* sometimes taken in capsules of up to 400 milligrams a day; the stronger is *Centella asiatica*. Relatively little is known about either, so caution is advised.

ST. JOHN'S-WORT. You know it's an ancient remedy when it's named for one of the beheaded saints. The true herb *(Hypericum perforatum)* "bleeds" red when crushed, which can help you identify fresh sources. The flowers in a tea are reputed to ease depression and calm the nerves. Some call it "Nature's Prozac." Up to 400 milligrams of dried herb can be taken three times a day, but beware of photosensitization (increased sun sensitivity). St. John's-wort is an expectorant, analgesic, antibacterial, and antiviral and is often considered a remedy for sore throats and cold symptoms. It is especially popular in Germany, where it is taken for anxiety and used as a skin ointment (in balm form). It's also being studied for possible use in treating AIDS.

SAW PALMETTO. This is a popular remedy for benign prostate enlargement. To promote healthy prostate function and urinary flow, consider saw palmetto *(Serenoa serrulata* or *Sabal serrulata),* but continue your routine checkups, as well. Seek a reputable source for an oil-based extract of the berries; 320 milligrams per day in capsule form is suggested by some practitioners. It's a diuretic and urinary antiseptic. Be aware that saw palmetto use can influence blood tests in misleading ways and sometimes interferes with prescription drugs, so keep your doctor informed.

VALERIAN. **"Generally recognized as safe" by the U.S. Food and Drug Administration, valerian *(Valeriana officinalis)* can be taken in tea (made by steeping 1 to 4 grams of the fresh or dried root in hot water) or in the popular capsule form to ease insomnia and aid relaxation. Valerian is sometimes recommended for muscle cramps and spasms, as well. After smelling and tasting the tea (reminiscent of sweaty sneakers), many people find they prefer the capsules. Start slowly. Too much can cause vomiting, headaches, dizziness, and depression. Traditional remedies also recommend the smelly herb for rat-trap bait and for attracting cats!**

Calendula Salve

dried fresh calendula flowers
olive oil
beeswax
benzoin tincture

Chop the dried flowers and cover them with olive oil. Cover and soak for about two weeks. Strain through muslin, composting the plant parts, and add up to 4 parts beeswax to every 10 parts calendula oil. A few drops of benzoin tincture will help the salve keep well over time. Store in a covered container. Apply externally to sunburn, minor scrapes and bruises, and chapped lips.

RISKY HERBS. Seek expert advice before using any of the following herbal remedies:

Borage oil. Restricted in some countries; can damage liver

Calamus. Carcinogenic

Celandine. Restricted in some countries; poisonous in large doses

Chaparral. Can damage liver

Coltsfoot. Can damage liver

Comfrey. Can damage liver

Eucalyptus. Best used externally rather than ingested; oil is highly toxic

Germander (occasionally sold as skullcap). Sometimes sold in weight-control remedies; can damage liver

Jin Bu Huan. Can damage liver

Lemon balm. Linked with inhibiting thyroid hormones; avoid if you have Graves' disease or other thyroid difficulties

Licorice (the medicinal variety, not the candy, which rarely contains real licorice). Prolonged use can destroy electrolyte balance

Life root. Can damage liver

Lobelia (also called pukeweed). A controlled substance in some countries; can affect breathing

Ma huang (also called ephedra). Restricted in some countries; excess can damage nerves or cause stroke

Pokeweed. Toxic

Sassafras. Carcinogenic

Skullcap. (See germander)

Wintergreen oil. Toxic

Yohimbe. Can be fatal in excess

A Cautionary Note

Government regulations prevent herbal suppliers from making medical claims about herbs unless costly scientific tests substantiate the results. Consequently, labels may not offer much practical information and will often carry disclaimers, such as "these products are not intended to diagnose, treat, cure, or prevent any disease." To protect yourself, buy only from a reputable source and begin slowly. For utmost safety, consult a qualified health practitioner before proceeding on any course of internal remedies, especially if you are pregnant or nursing, have other conditions such as high blood pressure or diabetes, or are taking any prescription drugs. □□

Martha White is the author of *Traditional Home Remedies* (Time-Life Books, 1997), part of *The Old Farmer's Almanac* Home Library Series. To order, call 800-277-8844, or check your local bookstore.

MR. SMITH'S

MADDENING Mind-Manglers

Try your hand at these puzzles, compiled for *The Old Farmer's Almanac* by Raynor R. Smith Sr., mathematics teacher at Keene Middle School in Keene, New Hampshire.

Answers appear on page 182.

1 In the house of Mr. and Mrs. Strange is a strange room. In the strange room are 6 strange rugs; on each strange rug are 6 strange 6-legged tables; on each of the 6 strange 6-legged tables are 6 strange 6-legged creatures. How many legs are in the strange room of Mr. and Mrs. Strange if there are no humans in the room?

2 **Mr. Willoughby sells some land valued at $8,000 to Mrs. Hansen at a 10% loss. Mrs. Hansen sells the land back to Mr. Willoughby at a 10% gain. What is the result of the two transactions?**

3 A knife weighs as much as two spoons, three spoons weigh as much as a knife and a fork, and a plate weighs as much as a knife and a spoon. If a fork weighs 4 ounces, how much do the other items weigh?

4 **Waldo had a 12:30 P.M. appointment with his accountant, whose office was 72 miles from Waldo's house. If Waldo averaged 48 miles per hour for the trip and arrived 10 minutes late for his appointment, when did he leave his house?**

5 In a game of chance, Emily doubled her money and then spent $10. In a second game of chance, she tripled her money and then spent $12. If she left the casino with $60, how much money did she start with?

6 **Which of the digits 0 to 9 come next in this pattern? Why?**
8, 5, 4, 9, 1, 7, _, _, _, _

7 Which of these statements is/are true?
⅕ is the average of ¼ and ⅙.
⅓ exceeds ¼ by ⅓ of ¼.
⅓ of ¼ is greater than ¼ of ⅓.

8 **November 22 is the 22nd day of the 11th month. How many days in a year are multiples of their month number?**

9 The Beatles have a concert in 17 minutes and must cross over a bridge to get to the concert location. They must be there in exactly 17 minutes. It is night and they must carry a flashlight to see their way. They can't toss the flashlight across or leave it anywhere. No one may be left alone on the bridge without a flashlight. There are no tricks. Each Beatle travels at a different speed; when traveling in pairs, they must walk at the slower Beatle's pace. The bridge will not support more than two Beatles at a time. How do they get across in 17 minutes? Here are the speeds of the Beatles: Paul takes 1 minute to cross; John, 2 minutes; George, 5 minutes; and Ringo, 10 minutes.

10 **A new invention, Molly's Absolutely Special Harvester (MASH), can harvest 60% of a crop every time it is set out to cross a field. If MASH is set out on a potato field three times, what percent of the entire crop will be harvested after the third swipe?**

How to Find the Day of the Week for Any Given Date

To compute the day of the week for any given date as far back as the mid-18th century, proceed as follows:

Add the last two digits of the year to one-quarter of the last two digits (discard any remainder if it doesn't come out even), the given day, and the month key number from the box below. Divide the sum by 7; the number left over (the remainder) is the day of the week (1 is Sunday, 2 is Monday, and so on). If it comes out even, the day is Saturday. If you go back before 1900, add 2 to the sum before dividing; before 1800, add 4. Don't go back before 1753. From 2000 to 2099, subtract 1 from the sum before dividing.

	KEY
January	**1**
leap year	**0**
February	**4**
leap year	**3**
March	**4**
April	**0**
May	**2**
June	**5**
July	**0**
August	**3**
September	**6**
October	**1**
November	**4**
December	**6**

Example: **The Dayton Flood was on Tuesday, March 25, 1913.**

Last two digits of year:	13
One-quarter of these two digits:	3
Given day of month:	25
Key number for March:	4
Sum:	45

45/7=6, with a remainder of 3. The flood took place on Tuesday, the third day of the week.

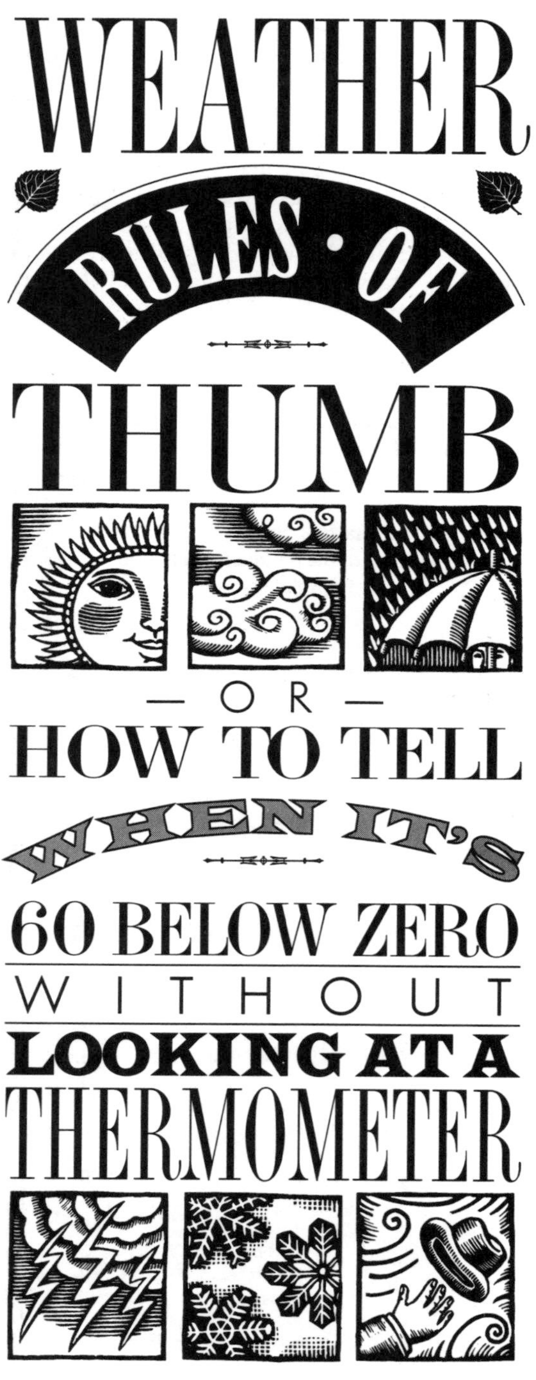

WEATHER
RULES · OF
THUMB
— OR —
HOW TO TELL
WHEN IT'S
60 BELOW ZERO
WITHOUT
LOOKING AT A
THERMOMETER

■ What is a weather rule of thumb? First, let's define what it is not.

A weather rule of thumb is not to be confused with *weather folklore,* which typically uses some sort of natural phenomenon to predict the weather. The tradition that there will be six more weeks of winter if the groundhog sees its shadow on February 2 is classic weather folklore, as is the belief that the severity of the coming winter can be foretold by the thickness of autumn's butternut hulls. Weather folklore, often focusing on the distant future, is far from infallible. (According to one scientific study, the groundhog's accuracy in predicting the arrival of spring — as observed over a period of 60 years — was a mere 28 percent.)

Nor is a weather rule of thumb the same thing as a *weather proverb,* which might be defined as a traditional weather saying — often in verse — that may contain a kernel of good, hard science. Consider the proverb "When dew is on the grass, rain will never come to pass." The two conditions necessary for the formation of dew — clear skies overnight and little or no wind — are good indicators of stable weather. Although the proverb may not explain why, the presence of heavy dew in the morning means that the weather is likely to remain good for at least 24 to 36 hours.

Weather rules of thumb focus on what might be called "nowcasting" — explaining or quantifying what the weather is doing at the present moment. (Some rules of thumb are useful forecasting tools as well.) Although there might seem to be little glory in looking at the present conditions, it's just plain satisfying to know when snow begins to squeak underfoot or how much an inch of rain weighs. The following list includes some favorite rules contributed by weather experts from across the country.

BY JON VARA

– illustrated by Beth Krommes

■ Take a cup of warm water outdoors and fling the contents into the air. If it freezes in midair and hits the ground with a sound like glass breaking, the temperature is somewhere between -60° and -70° F.

– Dave Anderson, National Weather Service observer, Barrow, Alaska

■ **During calm, clear weather, the dew point (the temperature at which dew appears) during the early evening — at about 6:00 or so — is an excellent predictor of what the overnight low is going to be. In other words, if the evening dew point is 32° F or below, gardeners should be prepared for a frost. This rule doesn't apply to very dry areas in the West, but it works well in most of the eastern and central states.**

– Dr. Dale Linvill, professor of agricultural meteorology, Clemson University, Clemson, South Carolina

■ If you're wondering whether an approaching thunderstorm is going to break overhead or blow over, pay attention to the air temperature and the wind. If you feel a chilly downdraft, abandon any idea that the storm will pass by. It's almost certain to be raining hard where you are within ten minutes.

– Chuck Ryerson, U.S. Army Cold Regions Research and Engineering Laboratory, Hanover, New Hampshire

(continued)

■ If a jet flying overhead doesn't leave a visible contrail, you can be pretty sure it won't rain the next day.

– Jeff Johnson, meteorologist with Northwest Weathernet, Inc., a private weather consulting service, Issaquah, Washington

■ To estimate the weight of accumulated snow on a roof, add 6 pounds per square foot for each 12 inches of snow that falls. Add another 6 pounds per square foot for each inch of rain that falls on top of old snow. (Most structures in the snowbelt are designed to withstand loads of 30 to 40 pounds per square foot.)

– Penn State Weather Communications Group, University Park, Pennsylvania

■ When Minnesota and Wisconsin, under a uniform air mass, are experiencing clear weather in March, and the ground is covered with snow, temperatures on the ground in the northern portions of both states are typically five degrees warmer than those in the south. That's because the dark-colored evergreen trees in the north absorb sunlight and re-radiate it as heat, while the bare snowy ground in southern areas reflects most of the sunlight.

– Don Moldenhauer, meteorologist with EarthWatch Communications, a weather graphics software company, Minneapolis, Minnesota

■ Packed snow begins to squeak underfoot at about 5° F. At 0° F, it squeaks with a distinct hollow sound.

– Mark Breen, meteorologist, The Fairbanks Museum, St. Johnsbury, Vermont

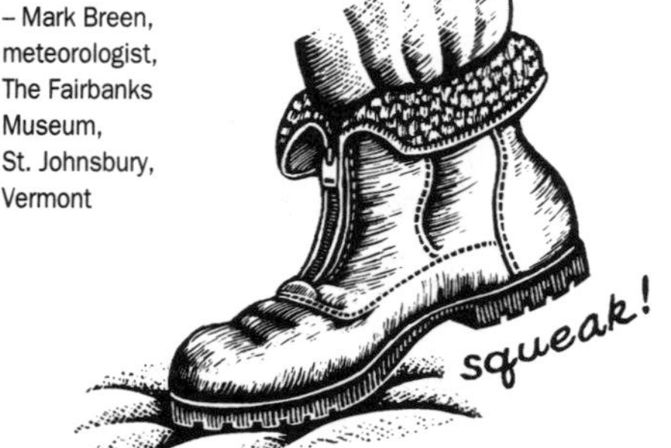

■ If it's snowing hard enough that you can't use your high beams while driving because the flakes in the air reflect the light back into your eyes, you can figure the snow is accumulating at a rate of about an inch per hour.

– Dr. Samuel Colbeck, U.S. Army Cold Regions Research and Engineering Laboratory, Hanover, New Hampshire

■ Walking a mile through six inches of snow takes as much effort as walking two miles on bare ground.

– Fred Gadomski, meteorologist, Pennsylvania State University, University Park, Pennsylvania

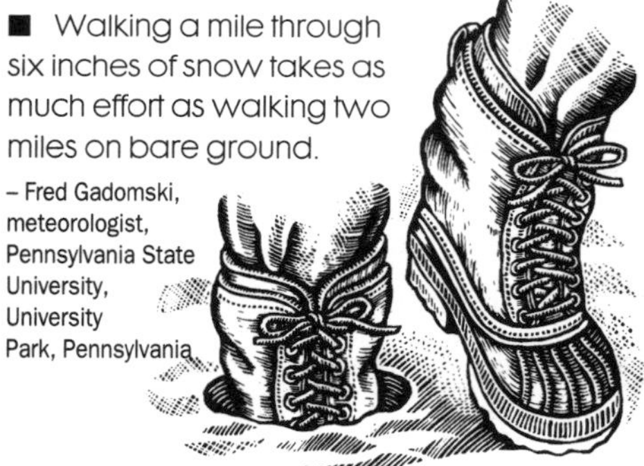

■ At middle latitudes in the northern hemisphere, winds circulate clockwise within high-pressure systems and counterclockwise within low-pressure systems. If the wind is at your back, a high would be on your right and a low would be on your left. This is known as Buys Ballot's Law, named for the Dutch meteorologist who first noted this weather rule in 1857.

– Terry Nathan, Ph.D., professor of atmospheric science, University of California, Davis

■ Watch for bugs when you're flying in a private plane. The higher you encounter flying insects, the smaller the chance of rain. During dry conditions, you might see them up as high as 3,000 feet. If you don't see any insects above 2,000 feet, you're probably looking at an increasing chance of rain.

– Ross Dixon, meteorologist with Weather Affirmations, a private weather consulting service, Oklahoma City, Oklahoma

■ Throughout the northern latitudes of the United States, for each 300-foot increase in elevation, snow will remain on the ground for another ten days during the spring.

– Steve Maleski, meteorologist, The Fairbanks Museum, St. Johnsbury, Vermont

■ **If a steady, moderate rain falls all day, you've probably picked up about an inch of rain. A brief, heavy thunderstorm will typically produce a quarter of an inch or so.**

– Mark Breen, meteorologist, The Fairbanks Museum, St. Johnsbury, Vermont

■ **Most large-scale weather systems at middle latitudes are about 600 miles across. Thus, when you are on an airplane traveling at 600 miles per hour, expect to see pronounced changes in the weather after only one hour of flying.**

– Terry Nathan, Ph.D., professor of atmospheric science, University of California, Davis

Temperature Conversion Formulas

Fahrenheit to Celsius

To convert temperatures in degrees Fahrenheit to Celsius, subtract 32 and multiply by .5556 (or 5/9).

Example: (50° F - 32) x .5556 = 10° C

Celsius to Fahrenheit

To convert temperatures in degrees Celsius to Fahrenheit, multiply by 1.8 (or 9/5) and add 32.

Example: 30° C x 1.8 + 32 = 86° F

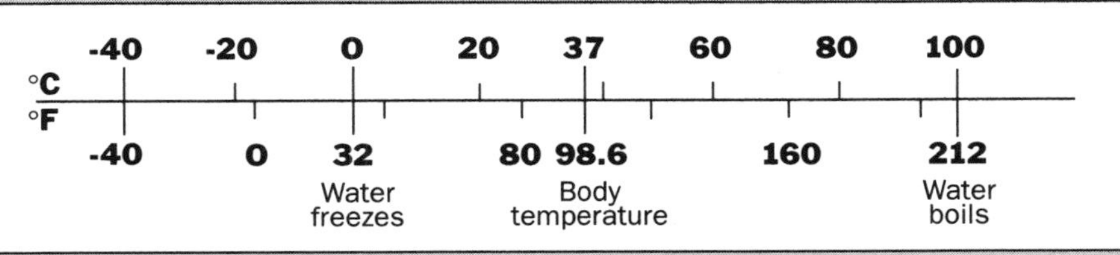

1" Water = How Much Snow?

	Water	Average Snow	Heavy, Wet Snow	Dry, Powdery Snow
Inches	1	10	4-5	15
Centimeters	2.5	25	10-13	38

How to Predict the Weather

Step into Gus Wickstrom's office in Tompkins, Saskatchewan. Gus, a man of Swedish descent who's lived in this prairie province all of his 60-plus years, is a weather forecaster. He can predict upcoming conditions for the next six months, yet his technology requires no fancy equipment, no high-tech razzle-dazzle. All Gus needs is a barn and a farmhand or two standing by . . . because he predicts the weather by looking at a pig spleen.

Every six months or so, Gus slaughters a pig, and in the frugal way of farm families, he finds a way to use everything but the squeal, as they say. Gus closely scrutinizes the spleen, using a method he learned from his father and Harold Pearson, a neighbor.

Here's a drawing of a spleen from a pig Gus slaughtered in January of 1998, and his predictions for the next six months.

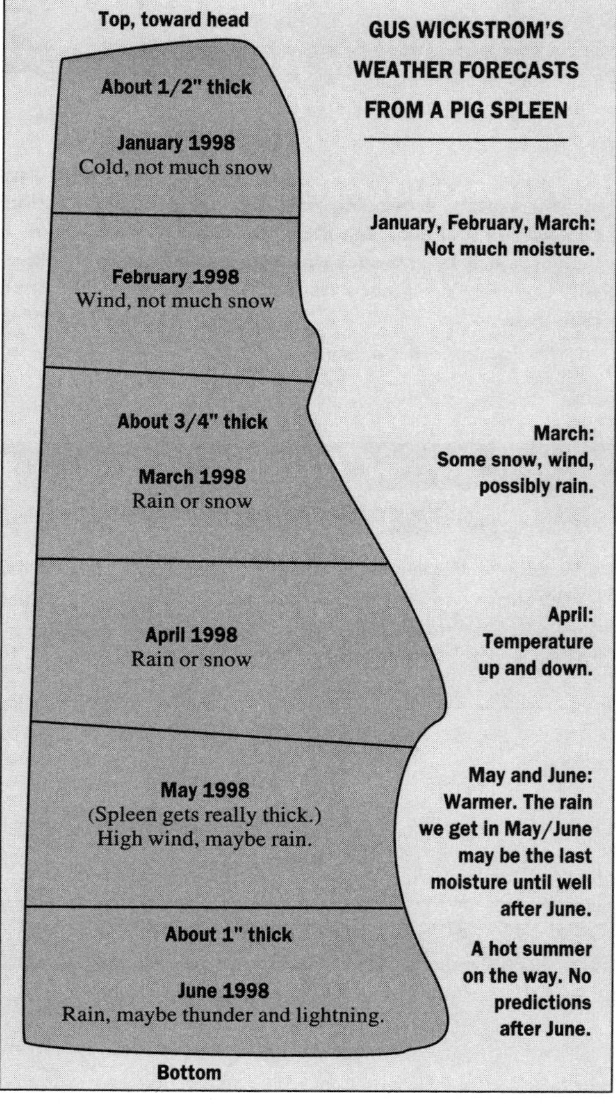

Using a Pig Spleen

You can call it folklore — but what do you call it when it works?

by Christina Cherneskey

GUS'S METHOD: Divide the spleen into six areas, each representing one month. The top of the spleen (closest to the pig's head) shows the current month. The bottom indicates the end of the upcoming six-month period. Where the spleen thickens, a change in the weather is indicated, usually pointing to a cold spell. Where there's a pronounced bulge, expect even more inclement weather. Gus can even read wind and rain into the variations in the spleen.

Seventy-two-year-old Joe King, in Wynyard, Saskatchewan, also learned pig-spleen weather predicting from *his* father. But Joe is adamant that the pig must be slaughtered in the fall or early winter; a spring spleen, says Joe, is not nearly as accurate. His method predicts only temperature, not precipitation. In the fall of 1997, Joe slaughtered his pig and pulled out a spleen that was even all the way through. This, he says, was one of the first indications that Saskatchewan would experience an even-tempered winter. Never mind that meteorologists were hysterical about the phenomenon called El Niño; or that onionskins and cornhusks were thick. Joe predicted a mild winter with just a few cold days, and his temperature predictions were right on the money.

I checked with a few animal scientists, whose reactions were of disbelief. After all, said the experts, a spleen is a vascular, ductless organ that stores blood, destroys worn-out red blood cells, forms lymphocytes, and so on. "A spleen," I was reminded, "is a useful organ that has bodily functions. It has nothing to do with predicting the weather."

I found myself defending this form of weather prophesying, even though I know it's folklore. I too have farming in my blood. So I went to the one person I knew would have the answer — *my* father. "I recall," Dad said, going back to his upbringing on a farm near Goodeve, Saskatchewan, "that our Polish neighbors also looked at the spleen of a pig to forecast the weather. And I know it's something the Ukrainian families did as well."

Aha, I thought to myself. It's not just Gus and Joe — it's in many cultures, probably more than I'll ever know. Those who believe in pig-spleen weather prognosticating have seen it work, and that's just the way it is. □□

General Weather Forecast 1998-1999

(For details, see the regional forecasts beginning on page 122.)

The coming winter will be much different than the past one, with colder-than-normal temperatures over much of the nation and above-normal snowfall in the Northeast and Northwest. The summer season will be more typical, with a fairly active hurricane season.

NOVEMBER THROUGH MARCH will be very cold overall in the northern Great Plains southward to northern Texas and westward to the Rocky Mountains. Cold temperatures will also predominate from the Middle Atlantic states to New England and the eastern Great Lakes, and in southern Florida. It will be warmer than normal from northern Florida to North Carolina and from southern Texas to southern California.

November will be cold in much of the country, especially from the northern Great Plains to the Pacific Northwest, with relatively warm temperatures in the Northeast and Southwest. The pattern will shift in December, with very cold weather the rule in the eastern two-thirds of the country and above-normal temperatures in the West. Another shift is expected in mid-January, as temperatures in the Great Lakes, Middle Atlantic states, and New England turn milder, while cold air pushes into the northern Rocky Mountains. Above-normal temperatures will continue in the Northeast and Great Lakes in February and expand to the Deep South and eastern Great Plains, while cold air becomes entrenched in the western part of the nation. March will be cold just about everywhere.

Precipitation will be above normal in the Pacific Northwest, the Rocky Mountains, much of California, New York, and New England. Below-normal precipitation is expected from Maryland to Florida, westward through the Ohio and Tennessee Valleys and Deep South, and into the central Great Plains, Texas, and the Desert Southwest.

Look for more **snowfall** than normal in New England, New York, and New Jersey, and in the northern Great Plains, Rocky Mountains, Pacific Northwest, and California mountains. Snowfall will be near to below normal in the Ohio Valley, Great Lakes, Middle Atlantic states, and central Great Plains.

APRIL AND MAY will see cooler-than-normal temperatures from the Middle Atlantic states northward to New England and westward through the northern and central Great Plains. The Pacific Northwest will be warmer than normal, with temperatures near to slightly below normal elsewhere.

Expect below-normal rainfall in New England, eastern New York, the northern and central Great Plains, the Desert Southwest, and the Pacific Northwest. Southern California and the area from Ohio to northern Illinois will be rainier than normal, with near-normal rainfall elsewhere.

JUNE THROUGH AUGUST will bring near-normal temperatures to much of the country. It will be hotter than normal in Texas, Oklahoma, and southern California, and cooler than normal from the Delmarva Peninsula to the Appalachians and north to the Finger Lakes of New York, in the Rocky Mountains, and in the Desert Southwest.

Rainfall will be above normal in the northern Great Plains, and below normal from the Carolinas to Florida and westward to Texas and Oklahoma, and in New England, New York, and the southern Great Lakes. Elsewhere, near-normal rainfall is expected. Above-normal hurricane and tropical-storm activity is expected, with the first half of September particularly active.

SEPTEMBER AND OCTOBER will be warmer than normal in the vast central part of the nation. Other areas will have near-normal temperatures. Watch for heavy rainfall in central and northern Florida, Georgia, South Carolina, and southeastern New England. It will be drier than normal from the Desert Southwest and Texas to the northern Great Plains. Elsewhere, rainfall will be close to normal.

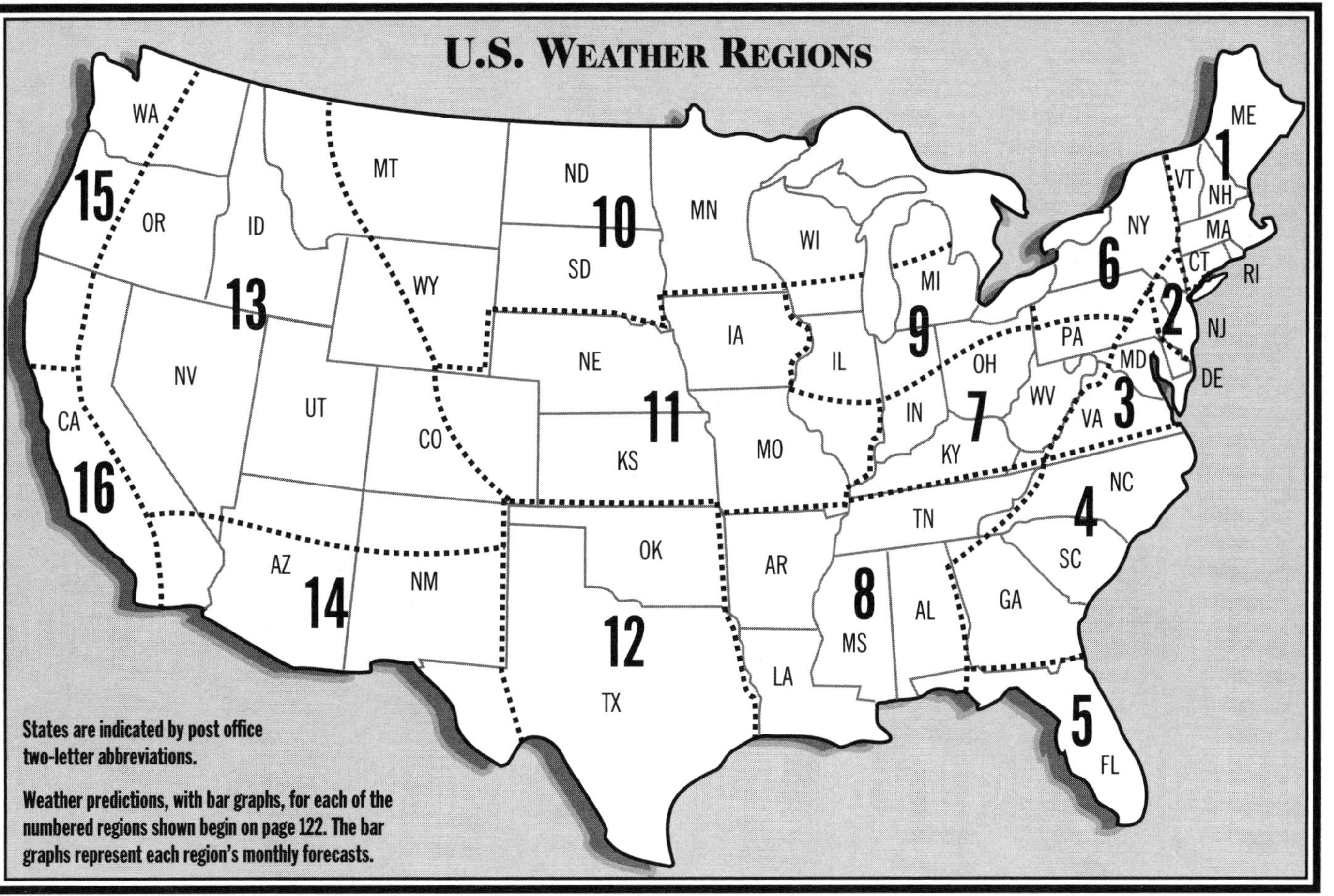
U.S. Weather Regions
WA
OR
CA
ID
NV
MT
WY
UT
AZ
CO
NM
ND
SD
NE
KS
OK
TX
MN
IA
MO
AR
LA
WI
IL
MI
IN
OH
KY
TN
MS
AL
GA
FL
SC
NC
VA
WV
PA
MD
DE
NJ
NY
CT
RI
MA
VT
NH
ME
1
2
3
4
5
6
7
8
9
10
11
12
13
14
15
16
States are indicated by post office two-letter abbreviations.
Weather predictions, with bar graphs, for each of the numbered regions shown begin on page 122. The bar graphs represent each region's monthly forecasts.

REGION

1 NEW ENGLAND

FORECAST

SUMMARY: The coming winter, overall, will be near normal in temperature — quite a bit colder than last winter, especially from mid-December into early January. The latter half of January and February will be relatively mild. Then just when you think you are out of the woods, March will roar in, bringing winter back. Although snowfall will be a bit below normal through February, heavy March snow will put us above normal for the season. Other heavy snow will occur in mid-November and early February in the interior, and in the second week of January along the coast.

April and May will be cooler and drier than normal. Temperatures from June through August will be cooler than normal overall. Pleasantly warm temperatures will be interrupted by heat waves in early and mid-June, early July, and mid-August. Rainfall during the summer season will be a little below normal.

A hurricane will bring heavy rain to the coast in the second week of September. Watch for an early frost in the North and the interior just before midmonth. A string of sunny days in mid-October will start cold and then turn warm, but as November approaches, another winter is on the way.

NOV. 1998: Temp. 44° (1° above avg.); precip. 6" (2" above avg.). 1-3 Sunny. 4-9 Heavy rain, cool. 10-13 Sunny, mild. 14-17 Rain, then warm. 18-22 Showers, mild. 23-25 Colder, snow. 26-30 Flurries north, sprinkles south.

DEC. 1998: Temp. 26° (5° below avg.); precip. 2.5" (1" below avg.). 1-5 Showers, then colder. 6-9 Snow and rain. 10-18 Sunny, cold. 19-25 Snow, then frigid. 26-31 Occasional snow, not as cold.

JAN. 1999: Temp. 27° (1° above avg.; 4° above avg. north); precip. 3" (1" below avg. west; 1" above avg. east). 1-6 Flurries, then cold. 7-11 Snowstorm, then milder. 12-21 Stormy, mild periods. 22-26 Sunny, mild. 27-31 Flurries, seasonable.

FEB. 1999: Temp. 30° (3° above avg.); precip. 4" (1" above avg.). 1-4 Rain, then snow. 5-11 Heavy rain coast, snow inland. 12-14 Windy and mild, coastal rain. 15-19 Rain, showers inland. 20-22 Rain, then snow. 23-28 Turning colder, mostly dry.

MAR. 1999: Temp. 33° (5° below avg.); precip. 5.5" (2" above avg.). 1-4 Mild, then snowstorm. 5-7 Mild, showers. 8-12 Northeaster, cold. 13-17 Mostly dry, chilly. 18-23 Rain, then wet snow. 24-27 Mild days, cold nights. 28-31 Cold and snowy, rain coast.

APR. 1999: Temp. 44° (5° below avg.); precip. 3" (0.5" below avg.). 1-7 Rain and snow, then mild. 8-10 Rain, then warm. 11-17 Cold rain, then sun. 18-20 Damp, misty. 21-26 Cool, showers. 27-30 Chilly, rain.

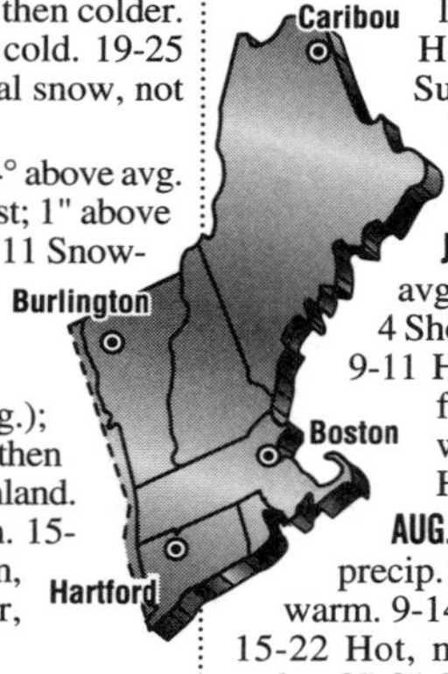

MAY 1999: Temp. 53° (4° below avg.); precip. 2.5" (1" below avg.). 1-6 Warm, then thunderstorms, cooler. 7-15 Cool, sunny, few showers. 16-17 Sunny, warm. 18-24 Showers, cool. 25-27 Sunny, warm. 28-31 Thunderstorms, then cooler.

JUNE 1999: Temp. 65° (avg.); precip. 2.5" (1" below avg.). 1-3 Sunny, cool. 4-8 Hot, then thunderstorms. 9-11 Sunny, warm. 12-15 Cool. 16-20 Heat wave, few thunderstorms. 21-25 Sunny, cool. 26-30 Hot, then showery.

JULY 1999: Temp. 69° (2° below avg.); precip. 4" (0.5" above avg.). 1-4 Showers, cool. 5-8 Hot, then cooler. 9-11 Heavy rain, chilly. 12-19 Warm, few thunderstorms. 20-24 Sunny, warm. 25-26 Rainy, cool. 27-31 Humid, few thunderstorms.

AUG. 1999: Temp. 69° (1° below avg.); precip. 2.5" (1" below avg.). 1-8 Sunny, warm. 9-14 Cool; then hot, thunderstorms. 15-22 Hot, mostly dry. 23-26 Heavy rain, cooler. 27-31 Sunny.

SEPT. 1999: Temp. 62° (1° below avg.); precip. 5" (2" above avg.). 1-6 Hot, then damp and cool. 7-9 Sunny, warm. 10-14 Heavy rain, frost north. 15-18 Warmer. 19-24 Chilly, heavy rain. 25-30 Chilly, rainy.

OCT. 1999: Temp. 53.5° (0.5° above avg.); precip. 2.5" (1" below avg.). 1-4 Rain south, then warm. 5-11 Rainy intervals. 12-17 Sunny, cold. 18-22 Indian summer-like. 23-26 Sunny, seasonable. 27-31 Rain, then colder.

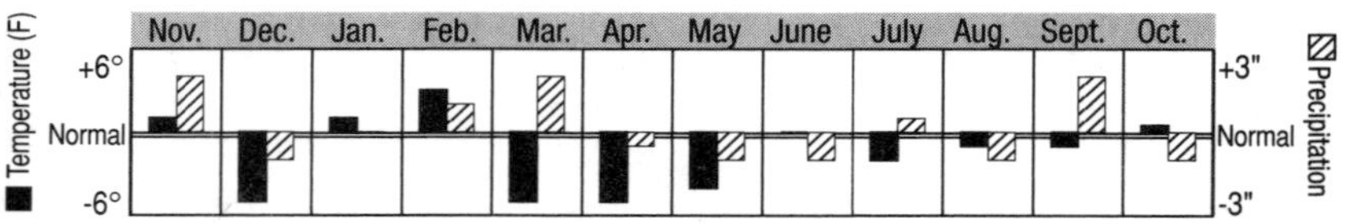

REGION **2**

GREATER NEW YORK–NEW JERSEY

FORECAST

SUMMARY: Temperatures overall this winter will be colder than normal, with above-normal snowfall. Expect several snowstorms, near Christmas, in mid-January, and in early and mid-March. The season will get off to a cold start, with well-below-normal temperatures in December and early January. The latter half of January and February will be relatively mild, but just as you start thinking spring, cold weather will return, and March will be the snowiest month of all.

Unusually chilly weather is expected in April and May, though not without some warmer periods. Expect warm spring temperatures in mid-April, early May, and mid-May. April and May will be drier than normal but with heavy rain possible around the middle of both months.

Overall, June through August will be cooler than normal, with near-normal rainfall. Hot spells are likely in June, early July, and mid-August. For the most part, rain will fall as showers and thunderstorms, but watch for a few days of nearly continuous rain in mid- to late August.

September will start warm and humid, then turn cooler as the month progresses. October will start and end with cool, damp weather but with many pleasant days in between.

NOV. 1998: Temp. 45° (avg.); precip. 4" (0.5" above avg.). 1-2 Sunny, warm. 3-6 Rain, then cooler. 7-10 Rainy, chilly. 11-15 Cool, showers. 16-20 Milder, then showers. 21-24 Colder. 25-30 Showers, cool.

DEC. 1998: Temp. 30° (5° below avg.); precip. 1.5" (2" below avg.). 1-4 Mild, then cold. 5-8 Chilly, few sprinkles. 9-11 Sunny, cold. 12-15 Sprinkles; flurries in suburbs. 16-22 Sunny, cold. 23-25 Flurries, then frigid. 26-29 Snow, then milder. 30-31 Cold.

JAN. 1999: Temp. 28.5° (0.5° below avg.); precip. 2" (1" below avg.). 1-7 Cold, few flurries. 8-12 Sunny, cold. 13-18 Rain; turning to snow north. 19-31 Clouds and sun, breezy, few flurries.

FEB. 1999: Temp. 34° (3° above avg.); precip. 5.5" (2" above avg.). 1-3 Rainy, milder. 4-5 Sunny, cold. 6-11 Rainy, mild. 12-19 Sunny intervals, mild. 20-23 Colder, snow then rain. 24-26 Sunny, cold. 27-28 Rainy, mild.

MAR. 1999: Temp. 36° (4° below avg.); precip. 5" (1.5" above avg.). 1-3 Mild, then rain to snow. 4-11 Cold; then rain, mild. 12-15 Mild. 16-19 Rainy, chilly. 20-23 Snow, possibly heavy. 24-31 Sunny, cold.

APR. 1999: Temp. 43° (7° below avg.); precip. 3" (0.5" below avg.). 1-3 Rain, cold. 4-8 Chilly. 9-12 Mild, then rain and cold. 13-18 Sunny intervals, seasonable. 19-22 Cool, rain. 23-30 Breezy, cool, dry.

MAY 1999: Temp. 57° (3° below avg.); precip. 2.5" (1.5" below avg.). 1-4 Warm, few showers. 5-9 Cool, sunny. 10-15 Chilly, rainy. 16-24 Hot; then cool, showers. 25-31 Cool, few showers.

JUNE 1999: Temp. 70° (avg.); precip. 3" (0.5" below avg.). 1-3 Warmer. 4-7 Hot; then thunderstorms, cool. 8-13 Cool, sunny intervals. 14-20 Sunny, hot, humid. 21-24 Cool. 25-30 Hot, humid, few thunderstorms.

JULY 1999: Temp. 73° (2° below avg.); precip. 5" (1" above avg.). 1-5 Thunderstorms, then cool. 6-9 Hot; then cool, rainy. 10-13 Warmer, showers. 14-21 Warm, humid. 22-25 Damp, cool. 26-31 Warm, humid, few thunderstorms.

AUG. 1999: Temp. 72° (1° below avg.); precip. 3" (1" below avg.). 1-8 Sunny, warm. 9-11 Cool, showery. 12-16 Hot, humid, hazy. 17-22 Thunderstorms, cooler; then hot. 23-26 Rainy, cool. 27-31 Sunny, seasonable.

SEPT. 1999: Temp. 65.5° (0.5° below avg.); precip. 3.5" (avg.). 1-11 Warm, humid; few showers. 12-17 Sunny, cool. 18-21 Rainy, mild. 22-25 Cool. 26-30 Seasonable, few showers.

OCT. 1999: Temp. 56° (1° above avg.); precip. 2.5" (0.5" below avg.). 1-3 Damp, cool. 4-9 Seasonable, sunny. 10-16 Showers, then cool. 17-21 Sunny, warm. 22-26 Mild. 27-31 Rain, cool.

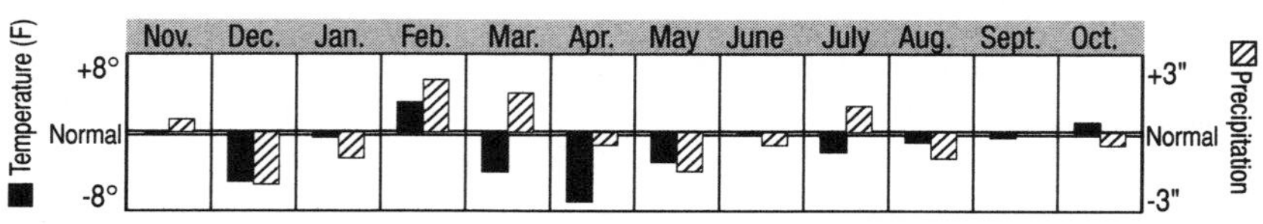

REGION

3 MIDDLE ATLANTIC COAST

FORECAST

SUMMARY: Overall, snowfall and temperature will be below normal in the coming winter season. November, December, and January will be drier than normal, with near-normal precipitation in February and March. The eastern part of the region will have little or no snow, while snowstorms will blanket the western part on several occasions. November, December, and January will be colder than normal, while February will be milder than normal. Cold weather in March will herald an unusually chilly spring. Coldest temperatures will occur in early December and from late December into early January.

April and May will be cooler than normal, with near-normal rainfall. The heaviest rain is expected in mid-April, with the season's first hot weather not until mid-May.

June, July, and August will be slightly cooler than normal overall, despite several hot spells. Rainfall will be near normal in June, with the heaviest rain early in the month. July will be wet, with heavy thunderstorms in the second week and toward month's end. Relatively dry weather will prevail in August, with few thunderstorms.

September and October will bring typical weather for that time of year. Rainfall will be a bit below normal in September. Watch for heavy rain at the start and end of October.

NOV. 1998: Temp. 48.5° (0.5° below avg.); precip. 2" (1" below avg.). 1-3 Warm, showers. 4-10 Cool, sunny. 11-13 Showers, then chilly. 14-18 Cold rain, then warmer. 19-23 Cold, some rain. 24-28 Sunny, seasonable. 29-30 Cold, chilly.

DEC. 1998: Temp. 35° (4° below avg.); precip. 1" (2" below avg.). 1-5 Turning colder. 6-9 Occasional rain, mild. 10-21 Sunny, cold. 22-24 Showers; flurries west. 25-29 Cold, then milder. 30-31 Cold.

JAN. 1999: Temp. 33° (1° below avg.); precip. 1.5" (1.5" below avg.). 1-3 Cold, flurries, showers. 4-10 Sunny, seasonable. 11-17 Rain east, snow west. 18-24 Showers, then flurries. 25-31 Cold, sunny.

FEB. 1999: Temp. 40° (3° above avg.); precip. 3.5" (0.5" above avg.). 1-3 Snow west, warming east. 4-10 Cold, rain, snow. 11-14 Sunny, mild. 15-22 Mild, some rain. 23-28 Cold; rain, snow west.

MAR. 1999: Temp. 44° (2° below avg.); precip. 3.5" (avg.). 1-8 Warm, few showers. 9-14 Mild; rain north. 15-23 Cold; rain, snow north and west. 24-31 Sunny, chilly.

APR. 1999: Temp. 50° (6° below avg.); precip. 3.5" (avg.). 1-3 Showers; flurries northwest. 4-10 Milder. 11-16 Heavy rain, chilly. 17-22 Showers, cool. 23-30 Cool, few showers.

MAY 1999: Temp. 63° (2° below avg.); precip. 3.5" (0.5" below avg.). 1-4 Warming. 5-9 Showers, cool. 10-16 Seasonal, dry. 17-25 Hot; then thunderstorms, cool. 26-31 Warm; then showers, cool.

JUNE 1999: Temp. 72° (2° below avg.); precip. 3.5" (avg.). 1-4 Rain, then warm. 5-8 Heavy rain, chilly. 9-15 Sunny, warming. 16-21 Hazy, hot, humid. 22-25 Showers, cooler. 26-30 Hot, thunderstorms.

JULY 1999: Temp. 77° (1° below avg.); precip. 7.5" (3" above avg.). 1-4 Thunderstorms, cooler. 5-7 Sunny, hot. 8-14 Heavy thunderstorms. 15-20 Warm. 21-31 Frequent thunderstorms, hot.

AUG. 1999: Temp. 74° (2° below avg.); precip. 2.5" (2" below avg.). 1-9 Hot, then cool, few showers. 10-17 Thunderstorms, then hot. 18-22 Sunny, seasonable. 23-27 Thunderstorms, cooler. 28-31 Sunny, seasonable.

SEPT. 1999: Temp. 70° (avg.); precip. 2.5" (1" below avg.). 1-5 Sunny, hot. 6-12 Showers, seasonable. 13-21 Sunny; cool, then hot. 22-30 Cooler, showers.

OCT. 1999: Temp. 59° (avg.); precip. 4" (1" above avg.). 1-4 Rainy, raw. 5-12 Warm, then showers. 13-20 Sunny days, cool nights. 21-31 Rainy periods.

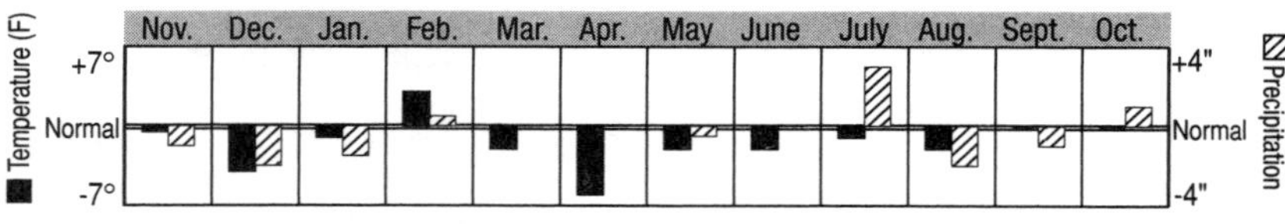

Advertisement

Honey, Garlic and Vinegar Better Than Prescription

(SPECIAL) We know from scholars that ancient civilizations relied on their healing power for a wide variety of ailments. In fact, honey was so prized by the Romans for its medicinal properties that it was used instead of gold to pay taxes. Egyptian doctors believed garlic was the ultimate cure-all. And vinegar is said to have been used for everything from arthritis to obesity for thousands of years.

Today doctors and researchers hail the healing abilities of honey, garlic and vinegar as much more than folklore. Hundreds of scientific studies have been conducted on this dream team of healers. The results are conclusive on their amazing power to prevent and cure many common health problems.

These studies prove that this trio from nature's pharmacy can help **reduce blood pressure, lower cholesterol, improve circulation, lower blood sugar levels and help fight cancer.** Scientific evidence also indicates that they can be of medicinal value in the treatment of: **arthritis, athlete's foot, bronchitis, burns, colds and flu, cold sores, constipation, cramps, diarrhea, eczema, earaches, fatigue, fungus, heart problems, muscle aches, prostatitis, rheumatism, ringworm, sinus congestion, sore throat, urinary infections, virus and yeast infections and more.**

A new book called *Honey, Garlic & Vinegar Home Remedies* is now available to the general public. It shows you exactly how to make hundreds of remedies using honey, garlic and vinegar separately and in unique combinations. Each preparation is carefully described along with the health condition for which it is formulated .

Learn how to prepare ointments, tonics, lotions, poultices, syrups and compresses in your own kitchen. Whip up a batch to treat:

- **ARTHRITIS:** Doctor reports that this remedy helps relieve the pain with no side effects
- **AGE SPOTS:** Watch them fade with this mixture
- **CORNS & CALLOUSES:** Get rid of them fast with this natural method
- **HEADACHE:** Enjoy fast relief without drugs
- **HEMORRHOIDS:** Don't suffer another day without this proven recipe
- **LEG CRAMPS:** Try this simple way to quick relief
- **MUSCLE ACHES:** Just mix up a batch of this and rub it on
- **STINGS & BITES:** Medical journals recommend this remedy to reduce pain and swelling fast
- **STOMACH PROBLEMS:** This remedy calms upset stomach and is noted in medical journals for ulcers
- **TOOTHACHE:** This remedy gives instant relief until you can get to the dentist
- **WEIGHT LOSS:** Secret remedy speeds fat burn and flushes stubborn fat from hiding places

Discover all these health tips and more. You'll find: ***Dozens of easy-to-make beauty preparations for hair and skin, including a wrinkle smoother that really works. *Loads of delicious recipes using these health-giving super foods. *Tons of money-saving cleaning compounds to keep your home, car and clothing sparkling.**

Right now, as part of a special introductory offer, you can receive a special press run of the book *Honey, Garlic & Vinegar Home Remedies* for only $8.95 plus $1.00 postage and handling. Your satisfaction is 100% guaranteed. You must be completely satisfied, or simply return it in 90 days for a full refund — no questions asked.

HERE'S HOW TO ORDER: Simply print your name and address and the word "Remedies" on a piece of paper and mail it along with a check or money order for only $9.95 to: THE LEADER CO., INC., Publishing Division, Dept. HG790, P.O. Box 8347, Canton, Ohio 44711. (Make checks payable to The Leader Co., Inc.) VISA or MasterCard send card number and expiration date. Act now. Orders are filled on a first-come, first-served basis.

REGION

4 PIEDMONT & SOUTHEAST COAST

FORECAST

SUMMARY: The period from November through March will be milder and drier than normal. November will see warm periods alternating with rain and chill. December and January will be dry, with colder-than-normal temperatures. February will bring well-above-normal rainfall and temperatures, then March will return to cool and dry weather. The best chances for snow are in late November and late January, with an ice storm hitting the interior at the start of the new year. The coldest temperatures will be in early and late December.

April will be cool, with near-normal rainfall; May will be much warmer, with less rain than normal. The first hot weather of the season will occur in mid-May.

June through August will be a bit warmer and drier than normal. June will start and end with hot weather. Look for a heat wave in early July, with hot, humid weather throughout the month, punctuated by scattered thunderstorms. The hottest temperatures will occur in mid-August, relieved by severe thunderstorms.

September will start and end hot. A hurricane or tropical storm will pose a threat toward month's end. October will offer lots of sunshine, warm days, and cool nights.

NOV. 1998: Temp. 55.5° (0.5° above avg.); precip. 3" (avg.). 1-3 Warm, then showers. 4-10 Sunny, seasonable. 11-14 Cool, rainy. 15-20 Warm, dry. 21-27 Seasonable, showers. 28-30 Cold, heavy rain.

DEC. 1998: Temp. 44° (2° below avg.); precip. 1" (3" below avg.). 1-5 Sunny, cold. 6-13 Few showers. 14-21 Sunny, cold. 22-24 Mild; then showers, cold. 25-31 Mild, then cold.

JAN. 1999: Temp. 42° (avg.); precip. 2" (2" below avg.). 1-4 Some rain; ice northwest. 5-19 Sunny, mild days. 20-23 Rainy, mild. 24-31 Cold, rainy episodes.

FEB. 1999: Temp. 50° (6° above avg.); precip. 6" (2" above avg.). 1-5 Mild; then rain, cool. 6-10 Heavy rain, mild. 11-15 Mild, then showers. 16-18 Sunny, warm. 19-24 Warm, some rain. 25-28 Sunny, cool.

MAR. 1999: Temp. 53° (1° below avg.); precip. 3.5" (1" below avg.). 1-8 Periods of rain, seasonable. 9-13 Showers, colder. 14-22 Rain north, pleasant south. 23-26 Sunny, chilly. 27-31 Sunny, seasonable.

APR. 1999: Temp. 59° (3° below avg.); precip. 3.5" (avg.). 1-3 Rain north. 4-10 Warm, few showers. 11-16 Cool, then rain. 17-21 Warming, then thunderstorms. 22-30 Sunny, cool.

MAY 1999: Temp. 72° (2° above avg.); precip. 3" (0.5" below avg.). 1-11 Warm, few thunderstorms. 12-19 Sun, cool; then hot. 20-27 Hot days, comfortable nights. 28-31 Thunderstorms, then cooling.

JUNE 1999: Temp. 76° (avg.); precip. 3.5" (0.5" below avg.). 1-6 Hot, few thunderstorms. 7-13 Sunny, cool; then hot. 14-19 Hot, hazy sun, few thunderstorms. 20-24 Cooler. 25-30 Hot, humid, a thunderstorm or two.

JULY 1999: Temp. 81° (1° above avg.); precip. 4.5" (avg.). 1-7 Heat wave. 8-15 Hot, few thunderstorms. 16-23 Few thunderstorms, seasonable. 24-31 Hazy sun, hot, humid.

AUG. 1999: Temp. 80° (2° above avg.); precip. 3" (1" below avg.). 1-7 Hot, humid, few thunderstorms. 8-21 Scorching sunshine. 22-27 Thunderstorms, then cooler. 28-31 Sunny, seasonable.

SEPT. 1999: Temp. 74° (avg.); precip. 4.5" (1" above avg.; 5" above south). 1-6 Hot, few thunderstorms. 7-11 Seasonable, few thunderstorms. 12-16 Sunny, cooler. 17-20 Sunny, hot. 21-26 Thunderstorms; then sunny, cooler. 27-30 Flooding rains.

OCT. 1999: Temp. 66° (2° above avg.); precip. 2.5" (0.5" below avg.). 1-7 Sunny, warm. 8-11 Few thunderstorms. 12-20 Sunny, comfortable. 21-27 Showers, seasonable. 28-31 Sunny, cooler.

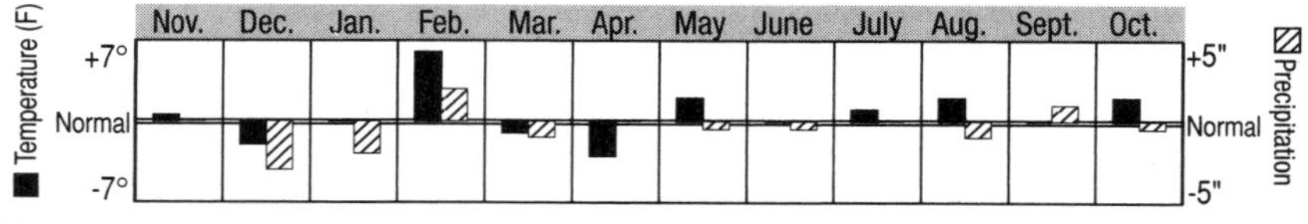

REGION 

FLORIDA

FORECAST

SUMMARY: Temperatures from November through March will average near normal, with below-normal rainfall. January will be the coldest month, with a freeze in central Florida at midmonth. February will be mild, especially in the north, where temperatures will average 8 degrees above normal. March will be cooler than normal. November through March will be drier than normal across Florida despite heavy local thunderstorms. Substantial rainfall will occur in mid-November, early December, and early and late January.

Despite heavy rains in mid- and late April and mid-May, spring precipitation will be below normal. Temperatures will be pleasant for the most part, with April a bit cooler than normal and May a bit warmer.

June will continue relatively dry, despite a few heavy thunderstorms. Rainfall will pick up in July, especially in the north, but August will be much drier than normal, with local drought developing. Temperatures from June through August will be close to normal.

September and October will bring near-normal temperatures, with well-above-normal rainfall in October. A hurricane is possible the second week of September, especially in the south.

NOV. 1998: Temp. 68° (avg.); precip. 1" (0.5" above avg. north; 2" below south). 1-2 Pleasant. 3-6 Showers, then cooler. 7-12 Sunny, cool. 13-15 Thunderstorms. 16-21 Sunny, warm. 22-28 Showers, then pleasant. 29-30 Thunderstorms.

DEC. 1998: Temp. 62° (1° below avg.); precip. 0.5" (2" below avg.). 1-5 Showers, cooler. 6-12 Mild, few showers. 13-20 Cool north, showers south. 21-31 Sunny, seasonable.

JAN. 1999: Temp. 58° (3° below avg.); precip. 2.5" (0.5" below avg.). 1-7 Rain, then cool. 8-19 Rain north; turning cold. 20-25 Showers, seasonable. 26-31 Rainy, warmer.

FEB. 1999: Temp. 68.5° (8° above avg. north; 3° above south); precip. 1" (2" below avg.). 1-4 Warm; showers south. 5-15 Showers, warm. 16-23 Cool, then warming. 24-28 Sunny, cool.

MAR. 1999: Temp. 66° (1° below avg.); precip. 1.5" (2" below avg.). 1-4 Warm, rain north. 5-13 Cool, showers; then warm. 14-21 Warm, few showers. 22-31 Sunny, cool.

APR. 1999: Temp. 70° (2° below avg.); precip. 3" (avg.; 1" above central). 1-12 Sunny, warm. 13-16 Cool, thunderstorms. 17-22 Warm, then thunderstorms. 23-28 Sunny, seasonable. 29-30 Rain, heavy north.

MAY 1999: Temp. 78° (2° above avg.); precip. 2.5" (1.5" below avg.). 1-6 Warm, few showers. 7-16 Warm, heavy local thunderstorms. 17-22 Sunny, hot. 23-31 Thunderstorms south, sunny and hot elsewhere.

JUNE 1999: Temp. 78° (2° below avg.); precip. 3.5" (1" below avg. north; 4" below south). 1-5 Warm, scattered showers. 6-11 Thunderstorms. 12-19 Sunny, seasonable. 20-23 Few thunderstorms. 24-30 Warm; thunderstorms north.

JULY 1999: Temp. 82° (1° above avg. north; 1° below south); precip. 7" (2" above avg. north; 2" below south). 1-6 Humid, few thunderstorms. 7-16 Seasonable. 17-20 Sunny, hot. 21-31 Hot, few thunderstorms.

AUG. 1999: Temp. 83° (1° above avg.); precip. 4" (3" below avg.). 1-9 Warm, few thunderstorms. 10-19 Hot, mostly dry. 20-31 Warm, few thunderstorms.

SEPT. 1999: Temp. 79° (1° below avg.); precip. 6" (1" below avg. north; 1" above south). 1-7 Hot, many thunderstorms. 8-12 Possible hurricane south. 13-18 Seasonable. 19-24 Warm, few thunderstorms. 25-30 Cooler, few thunderstorms.

OCT. 1999: Temp. 76° (1° above avg.); precip. 10" (7" above avg.; 1" above south). 1-5 Warm, showers. 6-11 Warm, few thunderstorms. 12-16 Dry. 17-22 Flooding rains north. 23-31 Few thunderstorms.

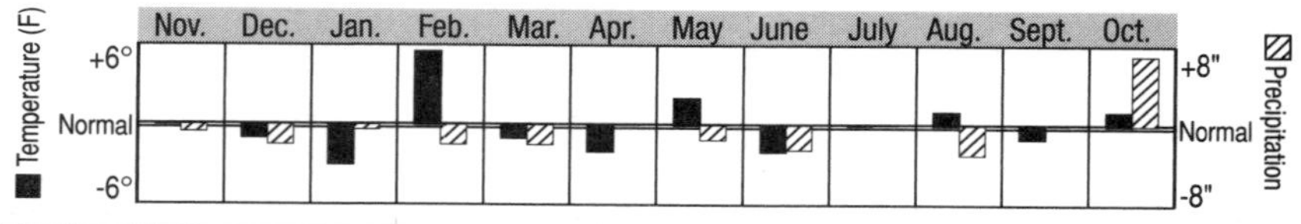

REGION

UPSTATE NEW YORK

FORECAST

SUMMARY: In contrast with last winter, November through March will be colder and snowier than normal, with the possibility of snowstorms in every month. The first snowstorm will occur before Thanksgiving, followed by a cold December with frequent lake snows. January will start cold, with a thaw in midmonth. Temperatures in February will be milder than normal, with big snowstorms to start and end the month. March will be much colder and snowier than normal, with storms at midmonth and a snow "dump" to close the month. The coldest temperatures will occur in mid- and late December.

Spring will be chilly, with temperatures in April and May about 5 degrees below normal. Precipitation will be near normal in the west and relatively dry in the east.

June through August will be slightly cooler and drier than normal. The hottest weather will be in mid-June and mid-August. July will be the rainiest month, with thunderstorms to start and end the month.

September will be wetter than normal, with frequent heavy rain. October will start mild but turn much colder, with a freeze around the middle of the month. This cold spell will be followed by Indian summer-like weather before showers and cool temperatures arrive.

NOV. 1998: Temp. 40° (1° above avg.); precip. 3.5" (1" above avg. east; 1" below west). 1-2 Sunny, warm. 3-5 Rain, cool. 6-9 Showers, then cold. 10-15 Rain, snow showers. 16-20 Mild, rain. 21-24 Snowstorm, cold. 25-30 Chilly; rain, snow.

DEC. 1998: Temp. 23° (4° below avg.); precip. 3" (1" above avg. west; 1" below east). 1-5 Cold, heavy lake snows. 6-9 Snow turning to rain. 10-22 Cold, flurries, lake snows. 23-27 Frigid; white Christmas. 28-31 Milder, then cold.

JAN. 1999: Temp. 22° (1° above avg.); precip. 1.5" (1" below avg.). 1-12 Cold, flurries, lake snows. 13-15 Mild, rain, snow. 16-22 Cold, flurries. 23-28 Cold, occasional snow. 29-31 Flurries.

FEB. 1999: Temp. 26° (3° above avg.); precip. 3.5" (1" above avg.). 1-3 Snowstorm. 4-9 Cold, some snow. 10-13 Snow to rain. 14-17 Rain; snow north. 18-20 Mild, then cold. 21-23 Snowstorm. 24-28 Very cold, flurries.

MAR. 1999: Temp. 28° (5° below avg.); precip. 5" (2" above avg.). 1-4 Flurries, cold. 5-8 Milder. 9-13 Rain, then snow. 14-17 Mild, then colder. 18-22 Heavy snow. 23-26 Very cold. 27-31 Mild, then snowstorm.

APR. 1999: Temp. 39° (6° below avg.); precip. 2" (1" below avg.). 1-5 Cold, flurries. 6-13 Showers, milder. 14-18 Sunny, seasonable. 19-30 Showers, colder.

MAY 1999: Temp. 51° (5° below avg.); precip. 3.5" (1" above avg. west; 1" below east). 1-4 Showers, warm. 5-14 Cool, showers. 15-19 Spring showers. 20-24 Cloudy, cool. 25-31 Rapid changes.

JUNE 1999: Temp. 64.5° (0.5° below avg.); precip. 2.5" (1" below avg.). 1-3 Sunny, warmer. 4-7 Thunderstorms, then cool. 8-13 Mainly dry, warmer. 14-20 Showers, then hot. 21-25 Thunderstorms, cooler. 26-30 Seasonable.

JULY 1999: Temp. 69° (2° below avg.); precip. 4" (0.5" above avg.). 1-3 Thunderstorms, cooler. 4-7 Sunny, warm. 8-11 Cool; rain east. 12-18 Rainy episodes. 19-24 Cool, then warmer. 25-31 Thunderstorms, warm.

AUG. 1999: Temp. 67° (1° below avg.); precip. 2" (2" below avg.). 1-7 Sunny, comfortable. 8-13 Warm, thunderstorms west. 14-19 Seasonable, few thunderstorms. 20-23 Hot, then thunderstorms. 24-31 Seasonable, dry.

SEPT. 1999: Temp. 60° (1° below avg.); precip. 6.5" (3" above avg.). 1-7 Rainy, warm. 8-11 Sunny, warm; then thunderstorms. 12-15 Cool. 16-20 Warmer, rain. 21-30 Rain, seasonable.

OCT. 1999: Temp. 53° (3° above avg.); precip. 1" (2" below avg.). 1-3 Sunny. 4-12 Mild, rainy spells. 13-17 Sunny days, cold nights. 18-22 Sunny, warm. 23-31 Cool, few showers.

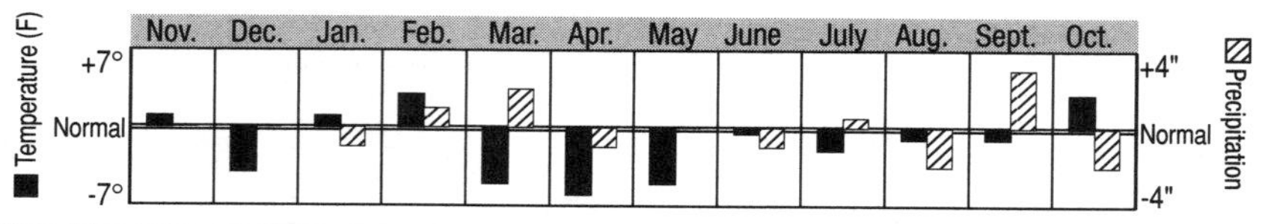

"My Prostate Problems Are Gone . . . Bless You"

By Jack Everett, Medical Journalist

BALTIMORE, MD — Just released: the all-new and revised edition of ***Miraculous Breakthroughs for Prostate and Impotency Problems***. This thorough healing guide for every man over 35 is now available to men who are concerned about their prostate — and to women who are concerned about their men.

Surgical procedures on the prostate are among the most commonly performed operations in America. With impotence and incontinence as common side effects, it's no wonder men fear the "cure" as much as the disease. This book defeats fear by telling all sides of the story, and gives every man reason for the hope of return to vigor and vitality.

It also tells you what doctors often don't — that for many men, nature offers far better alternatives than surgery.

For example: The patient decided to take the natural healer revealed in Chapter 3 as a general tonic, to build up his strength before scheduled prostate surgery. Very shortly after beginning the healing doses, the man noticed his prostate troubles were gone. His urologist canceled the surgery!

One prostate-related problem that bothers many men is frequent urination caused by a swollen or enlarged prostate, a condition doctors call BPH. One famous doctor routinely treats BPH with the natural remedy given on page 35.

He tells of a patient named Bill G., whose prostate was so swollen he visited the restroom every 20 minutes — yet in less than a month of this doctor's remedy, Bill's symptoms eased, and within two months he was sleeping through the night again.

Another patient, Larry R., 65, visited this doctor when his family physician told him his prostate should be surgically removed. The doctor prescribed two natural supplements revealed on page 36. Within 10 days, Larry noticed improvement. In a month, all signs of prostate problems had disappeared!

Even men with healthy prostates should follow this natural way of male health as a preventative measure. The table on page 38 tells exactly what to take.

Father Hohmann, a Catholic priest, was diagnosed with terminal prostate cancer. His doctor considered his case hopeless, and told the priest to make his peace and retire. But Father Hohmann wasn't ready to die. A local herbalist prescribed nature's remedy given on page 59.

According to the clergyman, his cure was "nothing less than a miracle."

Have your prostate battles left you feeling hopeless? See page 60 for the most potent natural remedy of all, with ability to help even cases declared hopeless.

This super-potent male remedy has been known to help bring relief to the toughest prostate complaints without doctors, drugs or surgery!

Not getting enough of the one essential mineral given on page 26 can lead to infertility and, in severe cases, impotency.

"An inexhaustible source of vigor offered by Mother Nature." What incredible male potency food is the famous European doctor talking about? The answer is on page 29.

Dr. Rudolf Sklenar, a German medical doctor, popularized the male potency elixir named on page 55 after he noticed the robust health of elderly Eastern European and Russian peasants. The men boasted of their lovemaking prowess well into their nineties.

Miraculous Breakthroughs is the owner's manual for the male body. Every man owes it to himself and his loved ones to review this book and the healing possibilities it offers.

Ringing endorsements and testimonies abound. "I'm not a health expert or any type of nutritional specialist, I am just an average guy — a guy who used to suffer from prostate disease. But thanks to William Fischer's latest book, I am no longer bothered by my prostate. I spent literally years searching for a doctor who could help me, but I found no relief. Finally, I gave up and resigned myself to living with the pain. My wife bought me a copy of ***Miraculous Breakthroughs***, but I was sure it would be of no use. Boy was I wrong!

"There was so much sound advice, I can't imagine any man not finding something that agrees with his body and his lifestyle. I was thrilled to discover that two products worked especially well for me. The answer to my problem was so simple." Mr. J.C.B., NY.

"Several years ago I developed some problems with my prostate gland. The troubles looked innocent enough at first, but they eventually grew and the situation got more serious. Someone loaned me a copy of the original edition.

"Well, before I knew it, my problem had eased up. My doctor surely was surprised (shocked would be a better word) and I made sure I always checked with him every so often. My prostate problems are gone. I'm happier than I've ever been and believe it or not, I feel I have the energy of someone half my age! Bless you." Mr. C.H., CA.

Right now you can receive a special press run of ***Miraculous Breakthroughs for Prostate and Impotency Problems*** directly from the publisher. Simply print your name, address and telephone number (in case they have any questions about your order) and the words "Prostate Book - Dept. PFA1" on a piece of paper and mail it along with a check or money order for only $19.95 plus $4.00 postage and handling **($23.95 total)** to: AGORA HEALTH BOOKS, Dept. PFA1, P.O. Box 977, Frederick, Maryland 21705-9838. (Make checks payable to Agora Health Books.) VISA/MasterCard/American Express send card number, signature, and expiration date.

For the fastest service call *toll-free* **1-888-821-3609** with your credit card handy and ask for Department **PFA1**.

You risk nothing by ordering now. That's because you're protected by the publisher's **365-Day Money-Back No-Risk Guarantee**. So you get a *full year* to read and use this life-enhancing book. If you're not *completely and utterly satisfied*, all you have to do is return it for a total refund of your purchase price. That's a great deal. But you must act now. Orders are filled on a first-come, first-served basis.

You and your loved ones will be glad you did.

REGION

7 GREATER OHIO VALLEY

FORECAST

SUMMARY: Overall, November through March will be typical, with temperatures near normal and precipitation and snowfall near or a bit below normal. The season will start cold and dry, with below-normal temperatures and precipitation the rule from November into early January. A reverse in the weather pattern will cause above-normal temperatures and precipitation from mid-January into early March. The remainder of March will be colder than normal. The coldest temperatures will occur in early and late December and early January.

April will be colder than normal, with below-normal rainfall in the west and above-normal rainfall in the east. May will be cooler and wetter than normal.

June will bring alternating warm and cool periods, with the first hot weather of the season in midmonth. July and August will be a bit cooler than normal, especially in the east. Rainfall will be near normal, with heavy rain in August bringing flooding to parts of the region. Hottest temperatures during the summer season will occur in mid-July and mid-August.

September will start warm, then turn cool. October, overall, will be much milder than normal, with many pleasant days. Rainfall in September and October will be well below normal.

NOV. 1998: Temp. 44.5° (0.5° below avg.); precip. 3" (0.5" below avg.). 1-7 Cool, periods of rain. 8-12 Sunny, cold. 13-16 Warmer, showers. 17-19 Mild, rainy. 20-24 Cold; rain, snow north. 25-27 Warm, then showers. 28-30 Cold, flurries.

DEC. 1998: Temp. 32° (3° below avg.); precip. 1" (2" below avg.). 1-5 Very cold, snow. 6-8 Rain, milder. 9-12 Cold, flurries. 13-20 Cold, occasional snow. 21-31 Very cold, then milder.

JAN. 1999: Temp. 31° (2° above avg.); precip. 1.5" (1" below avg.). 1-5 Cold, flurries. 6-10 Sunny, milder. 11-16 Periods of snow. 17-19 Milder. 20-25 Cold, snowy. 26-31 Sunny, cold.

FEB. 1999: Temp. 35° (3° above avg.); precip. 5" (2" above avg.). 1-6 Seasonable; rain, snow. 7-11 Chilly; rain, snow. 12-15 Mild, rain. 16-20 Raw, mild; snow north. 21-27 Turning colder, snow. 28 Warm.

MAR. 1999: Temp. 41° (2° below avg.); precip. 4" (1" above avg. northeast; 1" below southwest). 1-4 Rain, then cold. 5-9 Mild, few showers. 10-12 Rain, warm. 13-15 Cold, then mild. 16-22 Cold; rain, snow. 23-26 Sunny, chilly. 27-31 Rain, snow; then mild.

APR. 1999: Temp. 48° (5° below avg.); precip. 3" (1" below avg.; 1" above northeast). 1-3 Rain, warm. 4-10 Cold, then showers. 11-15 Cold, some sun. 16-19 Pleasant days, chilly nights. 20-22 Mild, then showers. 23-30 Cool, showers east.

MAY 1999: Temp. 61° (2° below avg.); precip. 6" (2" above avg.). 1-4 Rain, warm. 5-10 Seasonable; showers north. 11-13 Rain, cool. 14-19 Warm, thunderstorms. 20-25 Cool, few showers. 26-28 Warm, thunderstorms. 29-31 Sunny, cool.

JUNE 1999: Temp. 72° (2° above avg. northwest; 2° below southeast); precip. 2.5" (1" below avg.; 1" above central). 1-5 Showers, warm. 6-9 Chilly, rain. 10-15 Sunny, warmer. 16-19 Sunny, hot. 20-23 Thunderstorms, warm. 24-26 Cool, then warm. 27-30 Warm, thunderstorms.

JULY 1999: Temp. 74° (2° below avg.); precip. 4" (avg.; 1" above east). 1-4 Sunny, cool. 5-9 Warm, few thunderstorms. 10-14 Cool; then hot, thunderstorms. 15-19 Cool east; warm, showery west. 20-31 Seasonable, occasional thunderstorms.

AUG. 1999: Temp. 73.5° (1° above avg. west; 2° below east); precip. 3.5" (2" above avg. northwest; 2" below southeast). 1-4 Sunny, warm. 5-10 Thunderstorms, flooding. 11-19 Warm, thunderstorms. 20-22 Hot, humid. 23-31 Thunderstorms, cool.

SEPT. 1999: Temp. 67.5° (0.5° below avg.); precip. 2" (1" below avg.). 1-7 Hot, few thunderstorms. 8-13 Sunny, cool. 14-17 Showers; warm west, cool east. 18-22 Showers, seasonable. 23-26 Cool. 27-30 Cool, showers.

OCT. 1999: Temp. 60° (4° above avg.); precip. 0.5" (2" below avg.). 1-6 Sunny, pleasant. 7-12 Warm; showers east. 13-16 Sunny, cool. 17-23 Sunny, warm. 24-31 Mild, few showers.

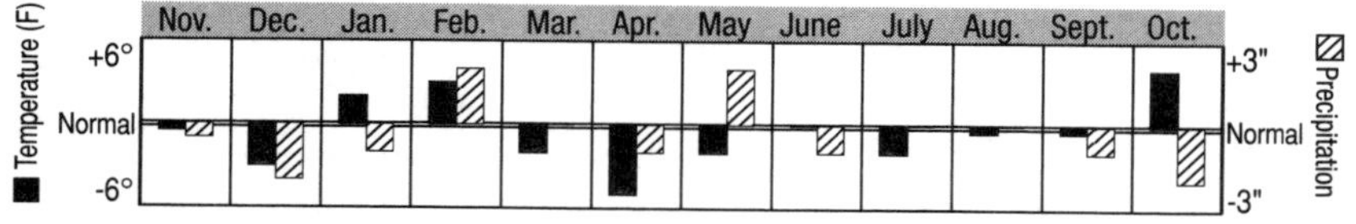

REGION

8 DEEP SOUTH

FORECAST

SUMMARY: November through March will bring near-normal temperatures overall, despite a cold start and end. A mild February will make up for colder weather in the other months. The coldest spells will be in early and mid-December and mid-January. Rainfall through January will be well below normal. February will be very wet; March will be near normal. Substantial snow and ice will occur in mid-December and mid- to late January.

Rainfall in April and May will be near or a bit below normal. April will be cool; May will be warm. The most widespread rain will occur in early to mid-April and early May.

Temperatures and rainfall from June through August will be slightly below normal. June will be cool and wet; July and August will get progressively hotter and drier. The hottest spells will be in early and mid-August. June will be the rainiest month of the season, with frequent heavy thunderstorms.

Below-normal rainfall will continue in September and October, with the best chances for rain in early and mid-September and late October. Temperatures will be a bit below normal in September and above normal in October.

NOV. 1998: Temp. 54° (avg.); precip. 3" (1" below avg.). 1-2 Showers, warm. 3-5 Cool, then warm. 6-9 Showers, cold. 10-14 Chilly, few showers. 15-20 Warmer, thunderstorms. 21-23 Rain, chilly. 24-30 Warm, then showers.

DEC. 1998: Temp. 43° (2° below avg.); precip. 2" (3" below avg.). 1-4 Sunny, cold. 5-9 Rain, mild. 10-15 Sunny, cold. 16-18 Milder. 19-25 Rapid changes. 26-31 Sunny, milder.

JAN. 1999: Temp. 38° (1° below avg.); precip. 2.5" (2" below avg.). 1-7 Mild, few showers. 8-16 Sunny, warm; then cold. 17-21 Sunny, chilly. 22-24 Rain; ice north. 25-31 Chilly, rain.

FEB. 1999: Temp. 48° (5° above avg.); precip. 8.5" (4" above avg.). 1-3 Warm, showers. 4-8 Heavy rain. 9-14 Rain, seasonable. 15-23 Warm, frequent showers. 24-28 Mild, then showers.

MAR. 1999: Temp. 51° (2° below avg.); precip. 5" (1" above avg.; 1" below north). 1-4 Sunny, warm. 5-7 Showers. 8-11 Warm, then showers. 12-14 Sunny, cool. 15-20 Chilly, heavy rain. 21-26 Cool, rain. 27-31 Sunny, warmer.

APR. 1999: Temp. 59° (4° below avg.); precip. 3.5" (1" below avg.). 1-4 Seasonable. 5-10 Rain. 11-14 Chilly, showers. 15-18 Sunny, seasonable. 19-25 Sunny, cool. 26-30 Showers, then seasonable.

MAY 1999: Temp. 73° (2° above avg.); precip. 4.5" (avg.). 1-7 Warm, then rainy; cool north. 8-12 Warm, few thunderstorms. 13-17 Sunny, warm. 18-24 Hot, few thunderstorms. 25-31 Warm, few thunderstorms.

JUNE 1999: Temp. 76° (2° below avg.); precip. 5.5" (2" above avg.). 1-8 Cool, showers. 9-13 Sunny, hot. 14-23 Humid, few thunderstorms. 24-30 Hot, humid; thunderstorms north.

JULY 1999: Temp. 80° (avg.); precip. 2.5" (1" below avg.). 1-8 Hazy, hot, humid. 9-15 Hot, few thunderstorms. 16-20 Sunny, hot. 21-31 Humid, few thunderstorms.

AUG. 1999: Temp. 81° (1° above avg.); precip. 0.5" (2.5" below avg.). 1-13 Heat wave, dry. 14-18 Hot, few thunderstorms. 19-23 Sunny, heat wave. 24-27 Thunderstorms, then cool. 28-31 Hot, thunderstorms.

SEPT. 1999: Temp. 73° (1° below avg.); precip. 2" (1.5" below avg.). 1-5 Warm, thunderstorms. 6-15 Sunny, warm. 16-22 Sunny, hot. 23-28 Thunderstorms, then cool. 29-30 Warm.

OCT. 1999: Temp. 67° (3° above avg.); precip. 2" (1" below avg.). 1-4 Hot days, comfortable nights. 5-8 Cool, showers. 9-23 Sunny, hot. 24-26 Showers, cool. 27-31 Rain, chilly.

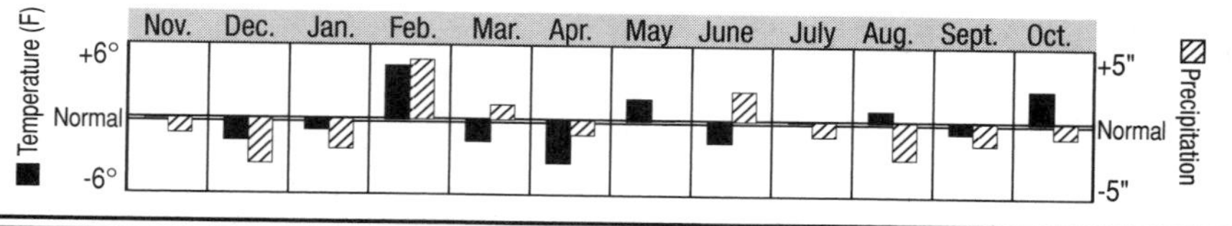

REGION

9 CHICAGO & SOUTHERN GREAT LAKES

FORECAST

SUMMARY: Temperatures from November through March will be near normal overall. November, December, and March will be colder than normal, while January and February will be milder than normal. Precipitation from November through March will be well below normal, with near- or below-normal snowfall. Widespread snowstorms will occur in mid- to late November and mid- to late February.

Temperatures in April and May will be 2 to 3 degrees below normal. Despite several rainy periods, April will be drier than normal overall. Heavy rain early in May and frequent thunderstorms later in the month will make May much wetter than normal.

The summer season will feature near-normal temperatures with below-normal rainfall. June will be relatively warm and dry. July will start and end hot, but cool periods will leave the month about 2 degrees below normal. July will also be on the dry side. Shower activity will pick up in August, which will have above-normal rainfall for the month and seasonably warm temperatures.

September and October will be much drier than normal, with drought a concern. Both months, but particularly October, will be warm.

NOV. 1998: Temp. 39° (1° below avg.); precip. 2" (0.5" below avg.). 1-7 Rainy, seasonable. 8-13 Some sun, colder. 14-19 Milder, occasional rain. 20-23 Cold, snow. 24-27 Mild, showers. 28-30 Sunny, seasonable.

DEC. 1998: Temp. 26° (2° below avg.); precip. 0.5" (2" below avg.). 1-6 Snow showers, cold. 7-10 Rain, then cold. 11-16 Cold, few flurries. 17-25 Very cold, snow showers. 26-31 Cloudy, milder.

JAN. 1999: Temp. 26° (4° above avg.); precip. 0.5" (1" below avg.). 1-6 Cold, then showers. 7-13 Sunny, mild. 14-18 Mild. 19-31 Cold, snow showers.

FEB. 1999: Temp. 27° (2° above avg.); precip. 2" (0.5" above avg.). 1-6 Cold, snow showers. 7-13 Mild, showers. 14-18 Mild, rainy episodes. 19-22 Snowstorm, colder. 23-26 Sunny, cold. 27-28 Rain, milder.

MAR. 1999: Temp. 35° (2° below avg.); precip. 1.5" (1" below avg.). 1-4 Chilly, flurries. 5-8 Sunny, milder. 9-13 Rain, then cold. 14-16 Mild. 17-23 Cold, showers, flurries. 24-31 Seasonable.

APR. 1999: Temp. 46° (3° below avg.); precip. 2" (1" below avg.). 1-5 Showers, then chilly. 6-9 Warm, rainy. 10-16 Showers, then cold. 17-19 Sunny, warm. 20-25 Showers, cool. 26-30 Warm; then cool, showers.

MAY 1999: Temp. 57° (2° below avg.); precip. 7.5" (4" above avg.). 1-4 Heavy rain. 5-10 Chilly, few showers. 11-15 Showers, warm. 16-18 Sunny, hot. 19-24 Cool, few showers. 25-27 Hot, then thunderstorms. 28-31 Cool; thunderstorms west.

JUNE 1999: Temp. 72° (2° above avg.); precip. 2" (2" below avg.). 1-4 Warm, showers. 5-13 Cool, then warm. 14-18 Sunny, hot. 19-30 Warm, humid, few thunderstorms.

JULY 1999: Temp. 72° (2° below avg.); precip. 3" (1" below avg.). 1-5 Sunny, hot. 6-11 Thunderstorms, cool. 12-21 Warm, few thunderstorms. 22-27 Cool, few thunderstorms. 28-31 Hot, humid.

AUG. 1999: Temp. 72° (avg.); precip. 4.5" (1" above avg.). 1-7 Showers, cool. 8-13 Sunny, hot. 14-22 Hot, humid, few thunderstorms. 23-27 Sunny, cool. 28-31 Seasonable, showers.

SEPT. 1999: Temp. 65° (1° above avg.); precip. 1.5" (2" below avg.). 1-5 Warm, thunderstorms. 6-9 Sunny, warm. 10-13 Showers, then cool. 14-20 Warm, few showers. 21-30 Sunny, warm.

OCT. 1999: Temp. 59° (7° above avg.); precip. 1" (2" below avg.). 1-5 Warm, few showers. 6-13 Sunny, warm. 14-22 Showers, warm. 23-31 Cool, mostly dry.

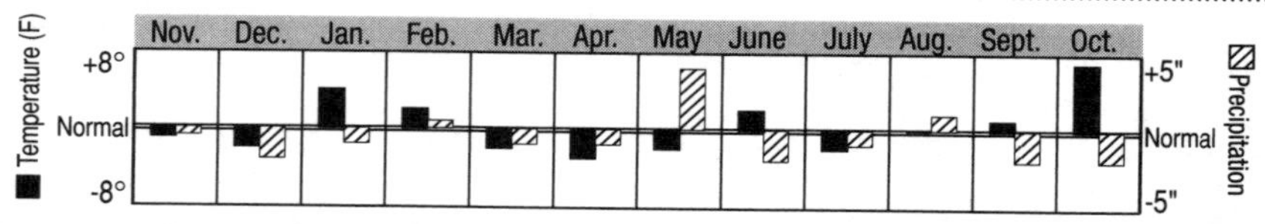

"SATURDAY AFTERNOON AT THE MOVIES"

$27.95 PER VIDEO TAPE

THE B-WESTERNS

2 TAPES FOR $50.00

4 ON A TAPE

VIGILANTES OF DODGE CITY - Bill Elliott, "Red Ryder"
RETURN OF THE LASH - Lash LaRue
SIX GUN LAW - Durango Kid
THE BOLD FRONTIERSMAN - Allan "Rocky" Lane

PONY POST - Johnny Mack Brown
FRONTIER LAW - Russell Hayden
SOUTH PACIFIC TRAIL - Rex Allen
BUCKAROO FROM POWDER RIVER - Durango Kid

LAW MEN - Johnny Mack Brown
WEST OF EL DORADO - Johnny Mack Brown
WILDFIRE - Bob Steele, Eddie Dean
SAGEBRUSH LAW - Tim Holt

RIDING THE CALIFORNIA TRAIL - G. Roland, The Cisco Kid
STAGECOACH EXPRESS - Don "Red" Barry
OUTLAWS OF STAMPEDE PASS - Johnny Mack Brown
DYNAMITE PASS - Tim Holt

LAND OF THE OUTLAWS - Johnny Mack Brown
OVERLAND MAIL ROBBERY - Bill Elliott
SILVER CITY KID - Allan "Rocky" Lane
LAW OF THE LASH - Lash LaRue

FLASHING GUNS - Johnny Mack Brown, Raymond Hatton
BORDER BADMEN - Buster Crabbe, Al "Fuzzy" St. John
SON OF BADMAN - Lash LaRue, Al "Fuzzy" St. John
CODE OF THE PRAIRIE - Sunset Carson

STAGECOACH TO DENVER - Allan Lane (Red Ryder)
BRANDED A COWARD - Johnny Mack Brown
THE SAN ANTONIO KID - Bill Elliott (Red Ryder)
CARSON CITY RAIDERS - Allan "Rocky" Lane

CALIFORNIA GOLD RUSH - Bill Elliott (Red Ryder)
MARSHALL OF RENO - Bill Elliott (Red Ryder)
SUN VALLEY CYCLONE - Bill Elliott (Red Ryder)
THE SHOWDOWN - Bill Elliott, Walter Brennan

THE 49ER'S - Bill Elliott
RUSTLERS OF DEVIL'S CANYON - "Rocky" Lane, Red Ryder
GREAT STAGECOACH ROBBERY - Bill Elliott, Red Ryder
CONQUEST OF CHEYENNE - Bill Elliott, Red Ryder

WILD HORSE RUSTLERS - Bob Livingston, Al "Fuzzy" St. John
0 **THE MYSTERY OF THE HOODED HORSEMAN** - Tex Ritter
GANGSTER OF THE FRONTIER - Tex Ritter
FLAMING BULLETS - Tex Ritter, Dave O'Brien, Texas Rangers

DAWN OF THE GREAT DIVIDE - Buck Jones, R. Hatton
1 **THE PIONEERS** - Tex Ritter
DOWN TEXAS WAY - Buck Jones, Tim McCoy, Raymond Hatton
BLAZING GUNS - Ken Maynard, Hoot Gibson

UTAH TRAIL - Tex Ritter, Charles King
2 **THE FEUD MAKER** - Bob Steele
ROGUE OF THE RANGE - Johnny Mack Brown
SONG OF THE GRINGO - Tex Ritter

ARIZONA WHIRLWIND - Ken Maynard, Hoot Gibson, Bob Steele
3 **THE GUNMAN FROM BODIE** - Buck Jones, Tim McCoy, R. Hatton
MARSHALL OF GUNSMOKE - Tex Ritter, Russell Hayden
ARIZONA BOUND - Buck Jones, Raymond Hatton, Tim McCoy

PALS OF THE SADDLE - Wayne, Corrigan, Terhune
4 **THE NIGHT RAIDERS** - Wayne, Corrigan, Terhune
THUNDERING TRAILS - Tyler, Steele, Davis
THE PHANTOM PLAINSMEN - Tyler, Steele, Davis

PRAIRIE GUNSMOKE - Bill Elliott, Tex Ritter
14A **BULLETS FOR BANDITS** - Bill Elliott, Tex Ritter
LONE STAR VIGILANTES - Bill Elliott, Tex Ritter
ROARING FRONTIERS - Bill Elliott, Tex Ritter

HIDDEN VALLEY OUTLAWS - Bill Elliott, "Gabby" Hayes
14B **TUCSON RAIDERS** - Bill Elliott, "Gabby" Hayes
BORDERTOWN GUNFIGHTERS - Bill Elliott, "Gabby" Hayes
WYOMING - Bill Elliott, "Gabby" Hayes

THE DENVER KID - Allan "Rocky" Lane
15 **THE MAN FROM RAINBOW VALLEY** - Monte Hale
ABILENE TRAIL - Whip Wilson
CHIP OF THE FLYING U - Johnny Mack Brown

THE LAST BANDIT - Bill Elliott
16 **CALLING WILD BILL ELLIOTT** - Bill Elliott, "Gabby" Hayes
LEADVILLE GUNSLINGER - Allan "Rocky" Lane
COVERED WAGON RAID - Allan "Rocky" Lane

TRAIL OF KIT CARSON - Allan "Rocky" Lane
17 **LAW OF THE GOLDEN WEST** - Monte Hale
PRIDE OF THE PLAINS - Bob Livingston
COWBOYS FROM TEXAS - Livingston, Hatton, Renaldo

DEATH RIDES THE RANGE - Ken Maynard
18 **BILLY THE KID'S FIGHTING PALS** - Bob Steele
PHANTOM RANCHER - Ken Maynard
SIX GUN MAN - Bob Steele

LAW OF THE VALLEY - Johnny Mack Brown
19 **THE THUNDERING TRAIL** - Lash LaRue
WACO - Bill Elliott
DESERT PASSAGE - Tim Holt

VIVA CISCO KID - Caesar Romaro
20 **MAN FROM MONTANA** - Johnny Mack Brown
FRONTIER INVESTIGATOR - Allan "Rocky" Lane
TRAIL TO LOREDO - Durango Kid

RIDE ON VAQUERO - Caesar Romaro as the "Cisco Kid"
21 **WHIRLWIND RAIDERS** - Durango Kid
CANYON RAIDERS - Whip Wilson
OUTLAW GOLD - Johnny Mack Brown

SOUTH OF MONTEREY - Gilbert Roland as the "Cisco Kid"
22 **LONE TEXAS RANGER** - Bill Elliott - Red Ryder
KING OF DODGE CITY - Bill Elliott, Tex Ritter
NORTH FROM LONE STAR - Bill Elliott, Tex Ritter

FRONTIER FEUD - Johnny Mack Brown
23 **RANGE LAW** - Johnny Mack Brown
CONQUEST OF CHEYENNE - Bill Elliott - Red Ryder
THE MISSOURIANS - Monte Hale

TO ORDER:
PHONE 724-349-4455 OR FAX 724-357-8406
OR SEND CHECK OR MONEY ORDER TO:
JIM SPOTTS, RARE SERIALS - FA
ROUTE 422 EAST, PENN RUN, PA 15765
Web: http://members.aol.com/rareserial/index.html
E-mail: rareserial@aol.com

Free Shipping - USA Only

REGION

NORTHERN GREAT PLAINS–GREAT LAKES

FORECAST

SUMMARY: Temperatures this winter will average 5 to 6 degrees colder than normal. An arctic blast in mid-November will inaugurate the season. Especially frigid temperatures will also occur in early and mid-December, the latter part of January, and early February. While precipitation will be a bit below normal from November through March, snowfall will be near or above normal. Watch for a blizzard in early December, with snowstorms in mid-February and mid-March.

Cold weather will continue in April and May, with temperatures about 5 degrees below normal. Precipitation will also be well below normal, despite some snow in early April.

Look for a dramatic warm-up in June, with heat waves in midmonth and at the end. Rainfall will continue below normal, with heavy local thunderstorms. July will start with record heat and end with another heat wave, but cool spells in between will bring monthly temperatures to a bit below normal. Rainfall for July will be a bit above normal. August will be much rainier than normal, with flooding possible. The last two weeks of August will be hot.

September and October will be warmer and drier than normal. October will begin with record heat.

NOV. 1998: Temp. 27° (5° below avg.); precip. 1.5" (avg.). 1-3 Mild, showers. 4-7 Cold, some sun. 8-15 Warm; then cold, flurries, showers. 16-22 Wintry blast, snow showers. 23-30 Mild, then showers.

DEC. 1998: Temp. 11° (8° below avg.); precip. 1.5" (0.5" above avg.). 1-4 Frigid. 5-8 Blizzard. 9-17 Cold, flurries. 18-25 Frigid, snow showers. 26-31 Milder.

JAN. 1999: Temp. 10.5° (4° below avg. west; 1° above east); precip. 1" (avg.). 1-18 Mild, mainly dry. 19-26 Frigid, flurries. 27-31 Cold, snowy intervals.

FEB. 1999: Temp. 10° (6° below avg.); precip. 0.5" (0.5" below avg.). 1-6 Bitter cold. 7-17 Sunny, relatively mild. 18-23 Cold, snowy. 24-28 Milder.

MAR. 1999: Temp. 21° (7° below avg.); precip. 1" (0.5" below avg.). 1-10 Cold, then milder. 11-15 Cold, then snowstorm. 16-19 Cold. 20-25 Milder, some sun. 26-31 Snow, rain; then mild.

APR. 1999: Temp. 37° (7° below avg.); precip. 1" (1" below avg.). 1-4 Rain to snow, cold. 5-11 Fast changes. 12-18 Sunny, warmer. 19-24 Sunny days, cold nights. 25-30 Few showers.

MAY 1999: Temp. 52° (4° below avg.); precip. 2" (1" below avg.). 1-3 Rain to snow. 4-10 Chilly, rainy periods. 11-14 Sunny. 15-20 Showers. 21-26 Sunny, warm. 27-31 Showers.

JUNE 1999: Temp. 70° (5° above avg.); precip. 3" (1" below avg.). 1-4 Showers, thunderstorms. 5-8 Sunny, warm. 9-11 Humid, thunderstorms. 12-18 Heat wave. 19-23 Humid, thunderstorms. 24-30 Hot; thunderstorms east.

JULY 1999: Temp. 71° (2° below avg.); precip. 4.5" (1" above avg.). 1-3 Scorching. 4-8 Thunderstorms, then cooler. 9-13 Thunderstorms. 14-18 Seasonable; thunderstorms east. 19-25 Hot; then showers, cool. 26-31 Sunny, hot.

AUG. 1999: Temp. 70° (1° below avg.); precip. 6.5" (3" above avg.). 1-3 Sunny. 4-7 Heavy rain, local flooding. 8-17 Warm, humid; thunderstorms. 18-22 Sunny, hot. 23-25 Thunderstorms, cool. 26-31 Sunny, hot.

SEPT. 1999: Temp. 59.5° (0.5° above avg.); precip. 2.5" (0.5" below avg.). 1-10 Warm; then showers, cool. 11-15 Sunny days, cool nights. 16-20 Rainy. 21-27 Sunny, pleasant. 28-30 Warm.

OCT. 1999: Temp. 52° (6° above avg.); precip. 1" (1" below avg.). 1-5 Hot, then cooler. 6-12 Sunny, warm. 13-18 Sunny, cool; then warm. 19-27 Pleasant days, cool nights. 28-31 Showers, mild.

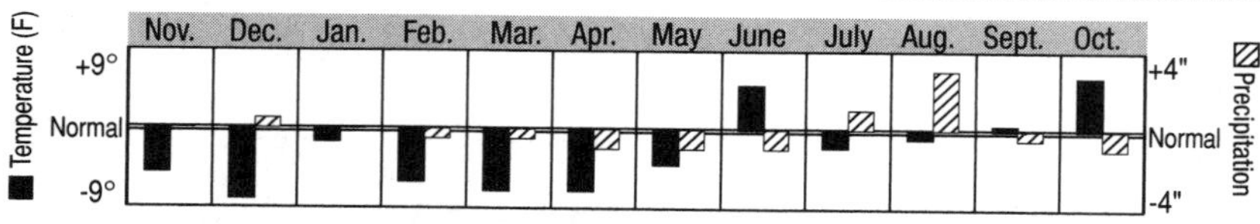

REGION

CENTRAL GREAT PLAINS

FORECAST

SUMMARY: Temperatures from November through March will be about 1 degree below normal on the average, with below-normal precipitation and snowfall. Colder-than-normal temperatures will be the rule early in the season, with November and December some 2 to 4 degrees below normal. Temperatures thereafter will be close to normal: a bit below in the west, a bit above in the east. The coldest periods will occur in mid-December and late January. The best chance for a big snowstorm is in early February, with other snowy periods in early December and late January.

April and May will be cool and dry, with April temperatures some 5 degrees below normal and May temperatures about 2 degrees below normal. April showers will occur early and late in the month.

June will be dramatically warmer, with hot weather from midmonth on. Rainfall will still be below normal, though frequent thunderstorms are likely. July and August will have typical hot, humid weather and scattered thunderstorms. The hottest weather will be in late July, when several new record highs may be set.

September and October will be warmer and drier than normal. Rainfall will be limited to early September and late October in many places.

NOV. 1998: Temp. 39° (2° below avg.); precip. 1.5" (1" below avg.). 1-5 Showers, cool. 6-17 Flurries, then mild. 18-22 Cold, few flurries. 23-25 Milder. 26-30 Showers, then cold.

DEC. 1998: Temp. 25° (4° below avg.); precip. 1" (1" below avg.). 1-5 Cold, snowy periods. 6-8 Mild east, snowstorm west. 9-23 Cold, few flurries. 24-31 Milder.

JAN. 1999: Temp. 26° (2° above avg.); precip. 0.5" (0.5" below avg.). 1-9 Sunny, chilly; then mild. 10-18 Sunny, seasonable. 19-31 Cold, occasional snow.

FEB. 1999: Temp. 27° (2° below avg.; 1° above east); precip. 1" (0.5" below avg.; 1" above east). 1-5 Snowstorm. 6-10 Sunny, cold. 11-15 Mild, rain; snow east. 16-22 Rain east, chilly west. 23-28 Flurries; showers east.

MAR. 1999: Temp. 39° (1° below avg.); precip. 0.5" (1.5" below avg.). 1-9 Mild, some sun. 10-15 Sunny, chilly. 16-24 Rain, snow. 25-31 Sunny, pleasant.

APR. 1999: Temp. 47° (5° below avg.); precip. 1" (2" below avg.). 1-5 Warmer. 6-13 Showers, then cool. 14-24 Seasonable. 25-30 Showers, cool.

MAY 1999: Temp. 60° (2° below avg.); precip. 2" (2" below avg.; avg. east). 1-9 Damp, chilly. 10-14 Warm. 15-20 Hot; then thunderstorms, cool. 21-25 Seasonable. 26-31 Showers, hot; then cool.

JUNE 1999: Temp. 76° (4° above avg.); precip. 3" (1" below avg.). 1-6 Thunderstorms. 7-10 Sunny east, thunderstorms west. 11-18 Sunny, hot. 19-30 Hot, humid, few thunderstorms.

JULY 1999: Temp. 76° (2° below avg.); precip. 3.5" (1" below avg. north; 1" above south). 1-9 Humid, thunderstorms. 10-14 Sunny, cool. 15-27 Seasonable, few thunderstorms. 28-31 Stifling heat.

AUG. 1999: Temp. 77° (2° above avg.); precip. 4.5" (1" above avg.). 1-13 Hot, humid, few thunderstorms. 14-20 Cool, then hot. 21-25 Frequent thunderstorms. 26-31 Hot, humid.

SEPT. 1999: Temp. 69° (3° above avg.); precip. 1" (2" below avg.). 1-8 Hot, few thunderstorms. 9-13 Cool. 14-18 Sunny, hot. 19-30 Warm, mainly dry.

OCT. 1999: Temp. 63° (8° above avg.); precip. 1.5" (1.5" below avg.). 1-9 Sunny, warm. 10-15 Sunny, cool. 16-23 Warm, showers. 24-31 Mild, few showers.

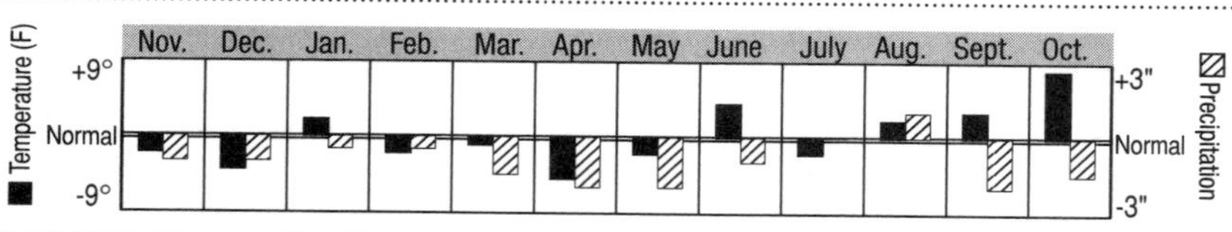

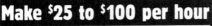

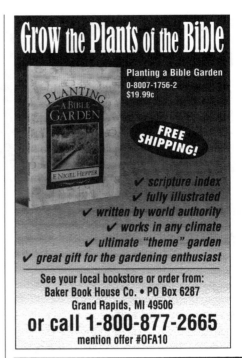

REGION

12 TEXAS–OKLAHOMA

F O R E C A S T

SUMMARY: Temperatures from November through March will be a bit colder than normal in the north and a degree or so warmer in the south, with below-normal precipitation. Cold air in early February will reach down to the Rio Grande Valley. The rainiest periods will be in early December and mid-February, with snow or ice across the north in early December, late January, and early February.

April will be relatively cool and wet, especially in the south. After a heavy rainstorm in early May, most of the rain activity will shift northward, with increasing heat and humidity the rule across most of the region.

Though June will start off wet, June through August will be drier than normal. The most widespread thunderstorms will be in mid-July and mid- to late August. Temperatures in the summer season will be about 2 degrees hotter than normal. The worst of the heat will occur in early and mid-August, when several record highs may be shattered.

September and October overall will be 4 to 5 degrees above average in temperature. Rainfall is expected to be well below normal.

NOV. 1998: Temp. 56° (avg.); precip. 0.5" (1.5" below avg.). 1-3 Warm; showers north. 4-9 Seasonable. 10-13 Cool; rain south. 14-19 Sunny, warm. 20-23 Cool, showers. 24-30 Sunny, seasonable.

DEC. 1998: Temp. 49° (2° below avg. north; 2° above south); precip. 0.5" (1" below avg.). 1-5 Cold; rain, ice north. 6-11 Sunny, mild. 12-15 Cold, sprinkles. 16-25 Clear, cool. 26-31 Sunny, warm.

JAN. 1999: Temp. 47° (2° above avg.); precip. 0.5" (1" below avg.). 1-9 Sunny, mild. 10-20 Sunny, cool. 21-31 Snow north, rain central, warm south.

FEB. 1999: Temp. 50° (2° below avg. north; 2° above south); precip. 1.5" (1" below avg. north; 1" above south). 1-4 Colder. 5-9 Snow, ice; drizzle south. 10-14 Rain, cool. 15-21 Clear, milder. 22-28 Sunny, warm north; rain south.

MAR. 1999: Temp. 56.5° (0.5° below avg.); precip. 0.5" (2" below avg.). 1-10 Clear, warm. 11-15 Cool. 16-20 Chilly, sprinkles. 21-25 Warm; then showers, cool. 26-31 Sunny, warm.

APR. 1999: Temp. 62° (4° below avg.); precip. 3" (2" below avg. north; 2" above south). 1-9 Clear, warm. 10-14 Cool, showers. 15-18 Warmer. 19-23 Thunderstorms, then cool. 24-30 Warm north, rainy south.

MAY 1999: Temp. 73° (1° above avg.); precip. 5.5" (1" above avg.; 2" below south). 1-7 Heavy rain, local flooding. 8-17 Sunny, warm. 18-20 Thunderstorms north. 21-25 Sunny, hot. 26-31 Periods of rain.

JUNE 1999: Temp. 82° (2° above avg.); precip. 2.5" (1" below avg.). 1-13 Seasonable, dry south; rainy elsewhere. 14-19 Sunny, warm. 20-30 Hot, humid, few thunderstorms.

JULY 1999: Temp. 85° (1° above avg.); precip. 1.5" (1" below avg.). 1-20 Hot, humid, few thunderstorms. 21-27 Frequent thunderstorms north. 28-31 Sunny, hot.

AUG. 1999: Temp. 87° (4° above avg.; 1° below south); precip. 1" (2" below avg.). 1-22 Heat wave, widely scattered thunderstorms. 23-26 Thunderstorms, then cooler. 27-31 Sunny, hot; cloudy south.

SEPT. 1999: Temp. 80° (4° above avg.); precip. 1" (3" below avg.). 1-8 Sunny, hot. 9-13 Thunderstorm, then cool. 14-20 Sunny, hot. 21-30 Warm, few thunderstorms.

OCT. 1999: Temp. 72° (5° above avg.); precip. 1" (2" below avg.). 1-7 Hot north, rain south. 8-13 Sunny, hot. 14-23 Cool, few thunderstorms. 24-31 Sunny, warm.

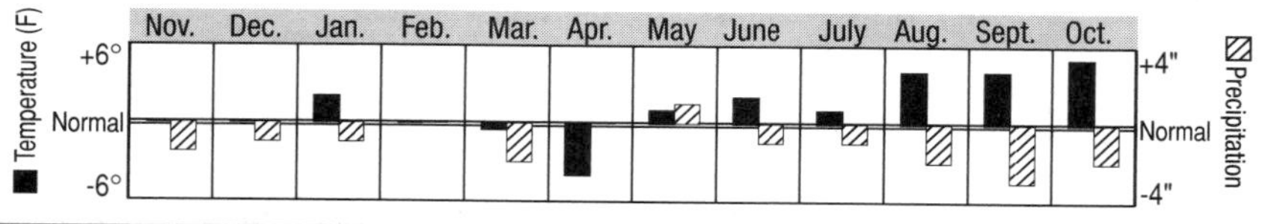

REGION 13

ROCKY MOUNTAINS

FORECAST

SUMMARY: November through March will be about 1 degree below normal, with above-normal precipitation and snowfall. Although the season as a whole will be close to normal, look for major swings from month to month. November will bring a cold start. December and January will have relatively mild temperatures but well-above-normal snowfall. February and early March will be exceptionally cold, possibly record-setting, but with little snow. The rest of March will be milder, with a snowstorm in midmonth.

April and early May will be snowier than usual, especially in the central mountains. Elsewhere, both months will have many sunny, mild days, with close-to-normal precipitation.

June through August will be 2 to 3 degrees cooler than normal, with below-normal rainfall. Hottest temperatures will be in mid- and late July and mid-August.

The first part of September will bring delightful weather, but the month will end with showers and cooler days. Warm periods in early and mid-October will give a last hint of summer, but colder weather at the end of the month will remind us that another winter is on the way.

NOV. 1998: Temp. 41° (1° below avg.; 5° below north); precip. 1" (avg.). 1-5 Rain north, warm south. 6-14 Seasonable. 15-21 Cold, heavy rain to snow. 22-30 Seasonable, flurries.

DEC. 1998: Temp. 33° (5° above avg.); precip. 2" (1" above avg.). 1-4 Mild; showers north. 5-9 Cold, rain to snow. 10-18 Sunny, milder. 19-25 Flurries north, mild south. 26-31 Cold, heavy rain and snow.

JAN. 1999: Temp. 31° (5° above avg.); precip. 3" (2" above avg.). 1-5 Cold, snow showers. 6-10 Sunny, milder. 11-16 Dry, seasonable. 17-24 Windy, periods of rain and snow. 25-31 Colder, snow showers.

FEB. 1999: Temp. 22° (10° below avg.); precip. 0.5" (0.5" below avg.). 1-7 Sunny, very cold. 8-15 Cold, few flurries. 16-22 Mild, then cooler. 23-28 Periods of rain and snow.

MAR. 1999: Temp. 37° (2° below avg.); precip. 1" (1" below avg.). 1-8 Sunny, cold; then milder. 9-16 Showers, colder. 17-23 Snow, then mild. 24-31 Mild; showers north.

APR. 1999: Temp. 48° (2° below avg. south; 2° above avg. north); precip. 1" (1" below avg.). 1-6 Showers; then flurries, cold. 7-14 Sunny, mild. 15-22 Periods of rain, mountain snows. 23-30 Mild days, chilly nights.

MAY 1999: Temp. 55° (2° below avg.); precip. 2.5" (0.5" above avg.). 1-4 Occasional rain. 5-7 Sunny, warm. 8-17 Showers. 18-23 Warming. 24-31 Showers, cool.

JUNE 1999: Temp. 63° (3° below avg.); precip. 1.5" (avg.). 1-7 Showers, then warm. 8-16 Showers, cool; then warm. 17-25 Thunderstorms, cool. 26-30 Sunny, warm.

JULY 1999: Temp. 72° (2° below avg.); precip. 0.5" (0.5" below avg.). 1-6 Sunny, warm. 7-10 Cool, few showers. 11-15 Sunny, hot. 16-20 Warm, showers. 21-31 Hot, few thunderstorms.

AUG. 1999: Temp. 69° (3° below avg.); precip. 0.5" (0.5" below avg.). 1-7 Warm; showers north. 8-14 Seasonable. 15-21 Sunny, hot; thunderstorm east. 22-27 Sunny, warm. 28-31 Thunderstorms, cool.

SEPT. 1999: Temp. 65° (2° above avg.); precip. 0.5" (0.5" below avg.). 1-10 Warm days, chilly nights. 11-16 Hot, showers. 17-22 Sunny, warm. 23-30 Showers, then cool.

OCT. 1999: Temp. 54° (1° above avg.); precip. 1" (avg.). 1-9 Warm. 10-17 Seasonable, showers. 18-25 Sunny, warm. 26-31 Showers, then cold.

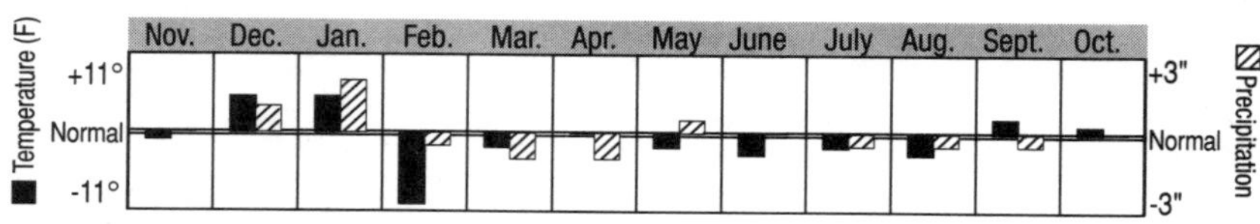

REGION

14 DESERT SOUTHWEST

FORECAST

SUMMARY: November through March will be a bit milder and drier than normal. November will feature warm, sunny days and chilly nights. December and January will be 3 to 5 degrees warmer than normal, with sunshine and some high clouds. Showers and thunderstorms will be infrequent. February will bring a noticeable change, with numerous showers and cool temperatures. Watch for snow in the eastern part of the region in early February. Clouds will give way to sunshine in March, with warm weather by month's end.

April showers will yield to sunshine, but temperatures will be cooler than normal. May will be sunny and warm.

Temperatures from June through August will average about 2 degrees below normal, but that's still hot. The hottest temperatures will occur in late June, the second week of July, and mid- and late August. The period will bring near-normal rainfall, with the most widespread thunderstorms in mid-July and early August.

September and October will be 3 to 4 degrees hotter than normal, with well-below-normal rainfall. The best chance for showers or thunderstorms is in mid-September and early and late October.

NOV. 1998: Temp. 58° (1° above avg.); precip. 0" (0.6" below avg.). 1-10 Sunny, pleasant. 11-17 Sunny days, chilly nights. 18-21 Scattered showers. 22-30 Sunny days, chilly nights.

DEC. 1998: Temp. 51° (3° above avg.); precip. 0.3" (0.7" below avg.). 1-8 Scattered showers, cool. 9-17 Sunny, seasonable. 18-31 Sunny, warm.

JAN. 1999: Temp. 52° (5° above avg.); precip. 0.3" (0.3" below avg.). 1-7 Sunny days, chilly nights. 8-19 Sunny, warm. 20-26 Cool, scattered thunderstorms. 27-31 High clouds, mild.

FEB. 1999: Temp. 47° (5° below avg.); precip. 1.1" (0.5" above avg.). 1-7 Chilly, showers; snow east. 8-13 Cool, showers. 14-19 Sunny, seasonable. 20-28 Clouds, sun, few showers.

MAR. 1999: Temp. 57° (1° below avg.); precip. 0" (0.6" below avg.). 1-6 Cool, some clouds. 7-10 Sunny, warm. 11-15 Chilly, then mild. 16-31 Sunny, cool; then warm.

APR. 1999: Temp. 63° (3° below avg.); precip. 0.1" (0.3" below avg.). 1-6 Warm; then cool, showers. 7-14 Sunny, warm. 15-25 Cool, widely scattered showers. 26-30 Sunny, warm.

MAY 1999: Temp. 74° (avg.); precip. 0" (0.3" below avg.). 1-4 Some clouds, cool. 5-8 Sunny, warm. 9-18 Sunny, pleasant. 19-24 Sunny, hot. 25-31 Clouds, sun, sparse showers.

JUNE 1999: Temp. 84° (avg.); precip. 0.3" (avg.). 1-7 Sunny, hot. 8-17 Hot; scattered thunderstorms east. 18-22 Sunny, seasonable. 23-30 Hot; scattered thunderstorms east.

JULY 1999: Temp. 85° (3° below avg.); precip. 1" (avg.). 1-7 Warm, humid, few thunderstorms. 8-13 Sunny, hot. 14-22 Warm, humid, heavy local thunderstorms. 23-31 Warm, scattered showers.

AUG. 1999: Temp. 84° (3° below avg.); precip. 1" (0.5" below avg.). 1-7 Cool, frequent thunderstorms. 8-15 Sunny, hot. 16-22 Clouds, thunderstorms. 23-31 Hot, few thunderstorms.

SEPT. 1999: Temp. 84° (3° above avg.); precip. 0.3" (0.7" below avg.). 1-9 Sunny, hot. 10-13 Cool, scattered thunderstorms. 14-24 Sunny, hot. 25-30 Sunny, cooler.

OCT. 1999: Temp. 75° (4° above avg.); precip. 0.1" (0.7" below avg.). 1-6 Hot, humid, few thunderstorms. 7-11 Sunny, hot. 12-24 Sunny, warm. 25-31 Showers, cold nights.

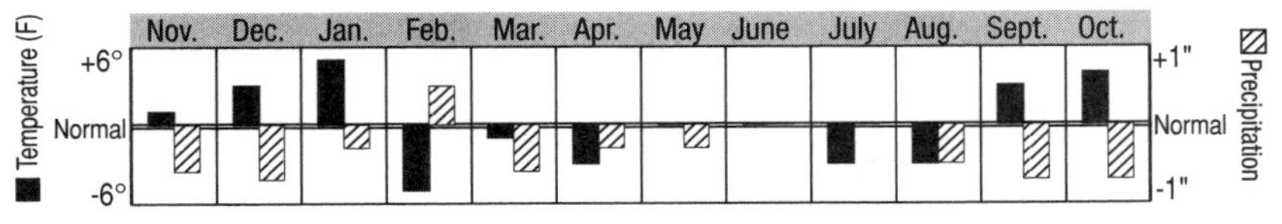

REGION

15 PACIFIC NORTHWEST

FORECAST

SUMMARY: November through March will be about 2 degrees milder and much wetter than normal. A number of storms will bring heavy rain from November through January. Rainfall in February and March will be closer to normal, with the heaviest in late February and early and late March. Cold air will bring snow all the way to the coast in late January and early and mid-February, and snowfall overall will be above normal.

April and May will turn warmer and drier. Rain in early April will be followed by sunshine and warm temperatures. Hot weather will occur in mid- to late May.

June through August will be cooler and rainier than normal, mainly because of a cool and damp June. July will be pleasant overall, with sunshine and comfortable temperatures. August will start and end on the cool side, with a hot spell in midmonth. Thunderstorms in the latter half of August will shepherd in cooler temperatures.

September will start with delightful weather, followed by rain around midmonth. October will be damp, with cooler temperatures by month's end.

NOV. 1998: Temp. 43° (3° below avg.); precip. 8" (2" above avg.). 1-5 Rainy, cool. 6-8 Warmer, heavy rain. 9-15 Mild, rainy periods. 16-19 Much colder, some sun. 20-24 Snow changing to heavy rain. 25-30 Cool, rain.

DEC. 1998: Temp. 44° (2° above avg.); precip. 10" (4" above avg.). 1-6 Seasonable, rain. 7-15 Cool, dry; then rainy, warmer. 16-23 Cold, rain, snow. 24-26 Stormy. 27-31 Rain, cool.

JAN. 1999: Temp. 44° (3° above avg.); precip. 11" (5" above avg.). 1-4 Some sun, chilly. 5-10 Stormy, flooding rains. 11-17 Occasional rain. 18-21 Heavy rain. 22-26 Mild, occasional rain. 27-31 Cold; rain, then snow.

FEB. 1999: Temp. 38° (6° below avg.); precip. 3.5" (1" below avg.). 1-7 Rain, snow; then clear, cold. 8-11 Showers, flurries inland. 12-18 Chilly, showers. 19-21 Cold, snow showers. 22-25 Chilly, rain. 26-28 Occasional rain.

MAR. 1999: Temp. 44° (3° below avg.); precip. 5.5" (2" above avg.). 1-5 Cool, occasional rain. 6-9 Stormy, heavy rain. 10-17 Chilly, rainy intervals. 18-22 Sunny, mild. 23-31 Cool with rain, some heavy.

APR. 1999: Temp. 52° (2° above avg.); precip. 1.5" (1" below avg.). 1-3 Periods of rain. 4-11 Occasional rain, cool. 12-17 Sunny, warmer. 18-20 Cool, sprinkles. 21-25 Sunny, warm. 26-30 Some sun, pleasant.

MAY 1999: Temp. 59° (3° above avg.); precip. 1" (1" below avg.). 1-3 Showers, then mild. 4-9 Sun, then showers. 10-16 Showers, warm; then cool. 17-22 Sunny, hot. 23-29 Sunny, warm. 30-31 Showers.

JUNE 1999: Temp. 61° (2° below avg.); precip. 2.5" (1" above avg.). 1-10 Hot; then showers, cool. 11-22 Seasonable, occasional rain. 23-30 Some sun, cool.

JULY 1999: Temp. 69° (1° above avg.); precip. 0.5" (0.5" below avg.). 1-7 Sunny, cool. 8-15 Warm, scattered showers. 16-24 Sunny, cool; then hot. 25-31 Sunny, pleasant.

AUG. 1999: Temp. 68° (1° below avg.); precip. 1" (avg.). 1-3 Sunny, cool. 4-8 Rain, chilly. 9-15 Sunny, pleasant. 16-20 Hot, thunderstorms; then cool. 21-26 Sunny, warm. 27-31 Thunderstorms, cool.

SEPT. 1999: Temp. 65° (1° above avg.); precip. 1.5" (0.5" below avg.). 1-12 Sunny, warm. 13-15 Rainy. 16-23 Seasonable. 24-30 Warm, few showers.

OCT. 1999: Temp. 57° (1° above avg.); precip. 4.5" (1" above avg.). 1-12 Rain, then pleasant. 13-17 Few showers. 18-31 Rainy, turning cool.

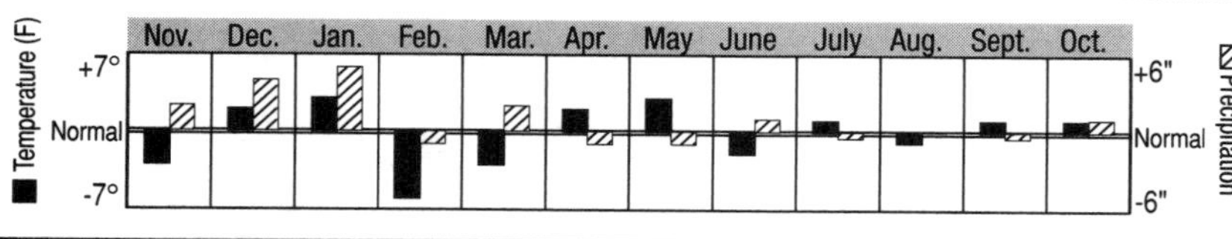

REGION 16

CALIFORNIA

FORECAST

SUMMARY: It will be another relatively stormy winter season, although the latter part will be more tranquil. December and January in particular will bring unsettled weather. Temperatures from November through January will average 2 to 3 degrees milder than normal. A major shift in the weather pattern will occur in late January, and February and March will feature below-normal rainfall and temperatures. Mountain snowfall will be above normal, with the heaviest snowfall from November through January and again in April.

April and May will be relatively cool and damp. Watch for heavy local rains and gusty winds in mid-April and early and mid-May. Hot temperatures will reach all the way to the coast in mid- to late May.

Temperatures from June through August will average near normal in the north and the interior and 1 to 2 degrees above normal from Los Angeles to San Diego. Hottest periods in the Valley will occur in early and late July and in early and mid-August. The hottest weather in coastal sections will wait until late August. Precipitation will be about average for the season.

September and October will be drier than normal, with near-normal temperatures in coastal sections and slightly cooler-than-normal weather in the Valley.

NOV. 1998: Temp. 57° (2° above avg.); precip. 2" (0.5" below avg.). 1-6 Sunny, warm; then cool. 7-16 Showers, then warm. 17-27 Cool, showers. 28-30 Sunny, cool.

San Francisco
Fresno
Los Angeles

DEC. 1998: Temp. 53° (3° above avg.); precip. 5" (5" above avg. north; avg. south). 1-3 Pleasant. 4-13 Stormy; heavy rains north. 14-18 Mild, some sun. 19-24 Rain north, dry south. 25-31 Stormy; thunderstorms north.

JAN. 1999: Temp. 51° (2° above avg.); precip. 7" (4" above avg.). 1-4 Showers. 5-15 Rainy north, pleasant south. 16-20 Heavy rain, especially north. 21-31 Seasonable, some rain.

FEB. 1999: Temp. 47° (5° below avg.); precip. 1" (2" below avg.). 1-9 Seasonable. 10-16 Sunny, pleasant. 17-20 Sunny, cool. 21-28 Heavy local showers.

MAR. 1999: Temp. 54° (1° below avg.); precip. 0.5" (2" below avg.). 1-10 Cool, few showers. 11-22 Sunny, warmer. 23-31 Sun, clouds, seasonable.

APR. 1999: Temp. 56° (2° below avg.); precip. 2.5" (1" above avg.). 1-6 Warm, then showers. 7-13 Sunny, pleasant. 14-18 Heavy rain, chilly. 19-26 Sun, clouds, warm. 27-30 Cool, few showers.

MAY 1999: Temp. 61° (2° below avg.); precip. 1.3" (1" above avg.). 1-2 Thunderstorms. 3-7 Sunny, seasonable. 8-15 Showers, some heavy. 16-22 Sunny, hot. 23-31 Clouds coast, sunny inland.

JUNE 1999: Temp. 66.5° (3° below avg. north; 2° above south); precip. 0.1" (avg.). 1-6 Clouds, cool. 7-15 Sunny, warm. 16-24 Scattered showers. 25-30 Sunny, seasonable.

JULY 1999: Temp. 70° (avg.); precip. 0" (avg.). 1-4 Sunny, hot. 5-13 Sunny, seasonable. 14-20 Sunny, pleasant. 21-31 Sunny, hot.

AUG. 1999: Temp. 67° (3° below avg.; 2° above southwest); precip. 0" (avg.). 1-4 Sunny, hot. 5-15 Sunny, warm; then hot. 16-23 Sunny, seasonable. 24-28 Clouds north, hot south. 29-31 Cool.

SEPT. 1999: Temp. 65° (2° below avg.); precip. 0.2" (0.1" below avg.). 1-12 Sunny, warm. 13-16 Cloudy north, hot south. 17-21 Sunny. 22-25 Showers. 26-30 Sunny, hot.

OCT. 1999: Temp. 62° (avg.); precip. 0.4" (0.4" below avg.). 1-6 Hot, then cool. 7-14 Seasonable, few showers. 15-21 Sunny, pleasant. 22-31 Cloudy, few showers.

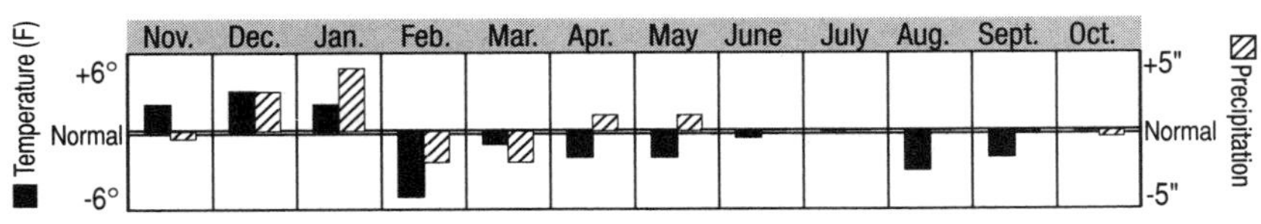

Plummeting temperatures in the Plains, snow in Tampa, fierce blizzards in the East — the worst that winter can bring — set weather records 100 years ago. Meteorologists are just beginning to understand the forces that led to . . .

– Corbis-Bettmann

The Great ARCTIC OUTBREAK *of* 1899

by Clifford Nielsen

– Washingtoniana Div., M. L. King Library, Washington, D.C.

Among what are known as "Arctic outbreaks" — unusual pushes of frigid northern air to relatively southern latitudes in North America, Europe, and Asia — the Great Arctic Outbreak of 1899, just 100 years ago, was the most widespread ever recorded in the United States.

The emerging pattern of unusually cold weather may have been evident in Wisconsin the year before. The greatest snowstorm ever recorded in the eastern part of that state deposited 30 inches of snow in Racine and created drifts of up to 15 feet in Milwaukee. As unexpected as that 1898 storm was, it did not begin to compare with the severity of the following winter.

The first indication of what was in store

The Arctic outbreak of 1899 triggered the Great Eastern Blizzard that buried the White House under more than 20 inches of new snow.

for 1899 was a temperature drop to -61° F in Montana on February 11. The cold air swiftly flowed south, causing the coldest morning temperatures ever recorded in the eastern Plains, Texas, and the Gulf Coast. As newspaper headlines began warning of the "Great Arctic Breakout of 1899," temperatures on February 12 plummeted to -22° F in Kansas City and -8° F in Fort Worth.

On the Gulf Coast, ice floes blocked the Mississippi River at New Orleans, the first such occurrence since 1784. On February 13, temperatures sank to 6.8° F in New Orleans, -1° F in Mobile, 7° F in Pensacola, and -2° F in Tallahassee, the lowest temperature ever recorded in Florida.

In the East, the outbreak not only caused low temperatures, including a chilly -15° F in Washington, D.C., but record snowfalls as well. The massive pool of Arctic air picked up moisture and became known as the Great Eastern Blizzard of '99. The storm dropped 20.5 inches of snow in Washington, D.C., on February 14, bringing the total snow cover there to 34 inches.

In the South, downtown Charleston, South Carolina, experienced its greatest modern snowfall — 3.5 inches. Incredibly, the same storm system brought enough snow to Tampa, Florida, to make snowballs, and snowflakes were seen in the air at Fort Myers, 120 miles to the south.

THE ARCTIC SEESAW:

Linking the Circumpolar Vortex, Solar Cycles, and the Quasi-Biennial Oscillation *(whew!)*

Unusual as the outbreak of 1899 was, it seemed to fit the pattern of a phenomenon that climatologists call the *seesaw effect*. Most of these, like the famous seesaw of pressure patterns in the tropical Pacific and Indian Oceans that leads to El Niño events, are still not fully understood by scientists.

The puzzle of the Arctic outbreak seesaw was first discovered in the late 1700s by the missionary Hans Saabi, who was proselytizing in Greenland. In a diary he kept from 1769 to 1778, Saabi wrote: "In Greenland, all winters are severe, yet they are not alike. The Danes have noticed that when the winter in Denmark was severe, as we perceive it, the winter in Greenland in its manner was mild, and conversely." Within a few years after Saabi's journal writings, a German named Granau created a table, based on weather records, of all the seesaws between 1700 and 1800. He may have missed some, but Granau noted 15 times when either unusual warmth or cold recorded in Germany was matched by the opposite condition in Greenland.

Little scientific progress was made in explaining the mysterious seesaw effect until the 1950s. Then, after the great advances in weather reporting during World War II, the explanation of Arctic warming (with simultaneous chilling farther south) could easily be seen on weather maps, which record both temperature and pressure gradients. The circumpolar vortex (a whirlpool of air at the poles), which is normally frigidly cold in winter, occasionally expands, causing northern temperatures within the vortex to become unusually warm, while colder temperatures move south. Expansions usually occur first in the stratosphere, above the troposphere (the atmospheric layer in which weather occurs).

But the pattern seemed chaotic. Expansions of the vortex were recorded in 1957 and 1958; then five years passed before another. During the next eight years, five more widespread expansions occurred. A complicating factor was that expansions in the stratospheric Arctic vortex did not always propagate down to the troposphere.

In the early 1980s, a pattern was discovered that may in time allow us to forecast the next Arctic intrusion that threatens to be as widespread and severe as that of 1899. Karin Labitzke, a researcher at the Free University of Berlin, noted that the Arctic vortex often expanded during periods of high solar activity, as in 1958, 1968 to 1970, and 1979 to 1981. But with equal frequency (1957, 1963, 1966, 1971, 1973, 1977, 1985, and 1987), the expansion was noted during periods of low solar activity. The connection seemed chaotic, and a comparison of graphs of solar cycles and vortex expansions resulted in a complete muddle (see figure 1).

The only other factor that seemed influential was the direction of the winds 20-plus miles above the equator, known as the quasi-biennial oscillation (QBO). The QBO is another puzzling seesaw that makes accurate weather forecasting a risky business. Given the spin of Earth, there seems to be no reason for these high winds to blow from any direction but east. Yet about every 30 months, they gradually start blowing from the west, propagating down through the stratosphere, only to reverse direction in another 30 months or so.

Working with Harry van Loon at the National Center for Atmospheric Research in Boulder, Colorado, Labitzke charted expansions of the vortex against solar cycles and the direction of the QBO. Finally, a strong and discrete pattern emerged (see figures 2a and 2b). When the QBO winds are from the west, the vortex expands during high solar activity and contracts during low solar activity. When the winds are easterly, the opposite effect happens: The vortex expands during low solar activity and contracts during high solar activity.

QBO winds from the west
+ high solar activity
= Arctic outbreaks

QBO winds from the east
+ low solar activity
= Arctic outbreaks

Analysis shows that the chance is less than 1 in 100 that either of these patterns could occur by accident. A journey back through the major national news stories about cold weather since the QBO measurements were first made in the early 1950s shows more than a few strong correlations. One example is the bitter winter of 1971 in Europe. It was colder in Milan than in Moscow. Temperatures fell to -29° F in France and -13° F in Venice, and thousands of cars that were headed for the Riviera were stranded by high snow drifts in France. Solar activity was low and the QBO wind was from the east. Other examples document widespread cold snaps while solar activity was quiet and the QBO wind was from the east. In 1973, recently elected West Virginia Governor Jay Rockefeller refused to move his inauguration indoors even though zero temperatures were forecast. Twenty-five people suffered from frostbite that day, prompting West Virginia wags to comment, "We always knew it would be a cold day in hell when a New Yorker got elected governor of West Virginia."

In January 1985, Hurd Willett, a pro-

UTBREAK ON THE CENTENNIAL OF THE 1899 EVENT.

fessor at MIT and an outspoken solar forecaster, made a forecast for the second Reagan inaugural. "Don't plan any outside ceremonies or activities," he advised. The 1985 inaugural, held during a period of low sunspot count and an easterly QBO, was the coldest on record.

Even as this article was being completed, an Arctic outbreak on March 9, 1998, plunged temperatures to well below normal from the Dakotas south. Although this outbreak did not result in the same heavy storminess as did the 1899 outbreak, temperatures reached near-record lows as far south as Florida, including a hard-freeze 23° F in Tallahassee, Florida, on March 12.

A quick check of the status of the solar cycle and the QBO shows that the sunspot count had accelerated rapidly during the last months of 1997. However, during this time, the QBO was blowing from the east and extremely cold air remained locked in the Arctic. By March, when the sunspot count had risen past 100, the QBO had turned and winds were blowing strongly from the west, opening the door to an Arctic outbreak.

Given the fact that sunspot count is expected to increase to as many as 130 or 140 by the winter of 1998-99, and that westerly QBO winds are expected to increase in velocity, the chances are good for another severe Arctic outbreak on the centennial of the 1899 event. □□

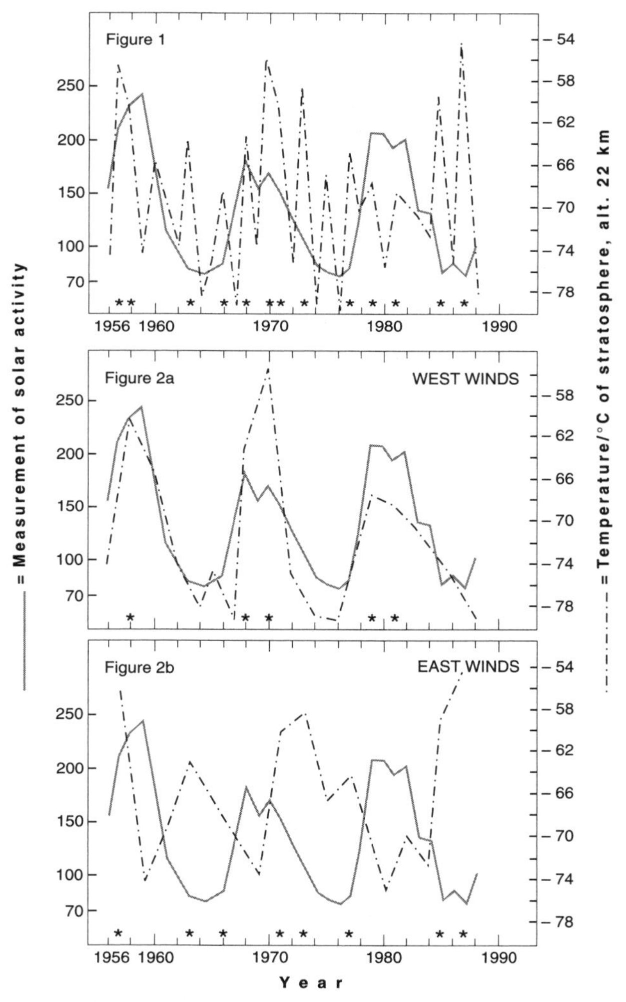

Figure 1 shows no correlation between solar cycles and Arctic outbreaks; figures 2a and 2b incorporate the QBO winds, and patterns clarify.

This article is excerpted from the author's book-length manuscript, *The Sun, Changing Climate, and the Coming Ice.*

A primer for gardeners who want to please their taste buds as well as their eyes.

Landscaping

So landscaping fever has grabbed you, and you are ready to head out to your favorite nursery or are thumbing through a catalog, checking out what's available in bushes. Decisions, decisions. Should your bushes offer tasty berries? Or should they offer good looks? Waver no more! There are plenty of ornamentals that bear edible berries as well.

THE BASICS

Berry bushes are easy to grow and are rarely threatened by pests, although birds may want to share the crop with you. A berry bush can be as trouble-free to grow as a forsythia or lilac, but as with any shrub, it will need some basic attention.

■ Check out site conditions for adequate soil drainage before you plant. If a bucketful of water stands in a foot-deep hole for more than 12 hours after you pour it in, the site is too boggy for most bushes. In that case, either plant your bush atop a wide mound of soil to get its roots up and out of the waterlogged zone, or choose a new, better site.

■ Make sure the site you choose has abundant sunlight. Most berry bushes require at least six hours per day. That sweetness in a blueberry fruit is the result of the conversion of the Sun's energy to sugar.

■ Prune regularly. Required of many berry bushes — as well as forsythias, lilacs, and other strictly ornamental bushes — pruning allows stems to bathe in light and air, which keeps a bush productive and limits disease problems.

Pruning is not really needed, however, until your

by Lee Reich

with Berries

plant's fourth winter. With your hand pruner or lopping shears (the latter if stems are thicker than about ½ inch), cut a few of the oldest, thickest stems back to ground level or to vigorous, low side shoots. The more new shoots that a bush makes each year, the more old ones you will have to prune away. The only other pruning needed is to clip back stems that look out of place. After all, you are growing these plants for beauty as well as for food.

SHRUBS
Offering Berries and Beauty

Blueberry is an attractive and tasty plant to begin with. For one thing, blueberries of some kind can be grown almost all over the country. In warmer regions, such as the Southeast, plant rabbiteye blueberries or southern highbush blueberries. In more northern areas, northern highbush blueberries and lowbush blueberries, adaptable well into most regions of Canada, are the ones to grow. Or try hybrids of the two, known as "half-highs."

Besides producing delectable fruits, blueberries are truly year-round ornamentals. Spring brings clusters of blossoms that dangle from stems like dainty white bells. Summer's soft green leaves, tinged slightly blue, turn to a fiery red in autumn, matching those of burning bush, an ornamental grown *just* for its fall color. In winter, the red of blueberry stems adds welcome color, especially against a snowy backdrop.

Attention to birds and to soil are two keys to success with blueberries. If birds try to monopolize all the berries, drape netting over the bushes while the fruits are ripening. Or take your chances and see how many berries the birds leave for you if you do nothing at all. (But remember, blueberries must hang on the bush for a few days after they first turn blue in order to achieve full ripeness by human standards.

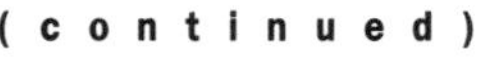

(continued)

– photos: Michael McConkey/Edible Landscaping

Nanking cherry in full bloom *(top)* and in fruit, ready for picking.

– photos: Michael McConkey/Edible Landscaping

Elderberries *(top)* are borne on handsome plants and make good jam and jelly. The highbush cranberry *(above)* bears glossy-red berries that birds love (they're good for sauce, too).

Birds may not wait.)

Blueberries require soil that is acidic and rich in humus. Provide these conditions by mixing a generous bucketful of peat moss into each planting hole. If your soil is quite alkaline, remove the soil from the planting hole and install the bushes in bottomless containers sunk into the ground and filled with a prepared mix of equal parts peat moss and sand.

Two blueberry relatives also ideal for "edible landscaping" are **salal** and **lingonberry.** The salal, native to the Pacific Northwest, bears sweet-tart fruits. The leaves are so decorative that florists use them as greens, under the name lemonleaf. The lingonberry is a low grower that is decked out in dark and lustrous green leaves all year. The tart red berries, tasty fresh-picked or made into sauce or jam, cling to the stems through winter. Both plants spread by underground runners to form colonies, and they enjoy the same soil conditions as their blueberry kin.

More cosmopolitan in its soil likes and dislikes, and also adapted throughout the country, is **juneberry.** Tree forms and bush forms of juneberries exist, and all sport cheery, white flowers in early spring, blazing orange and purple foliage in fall, and neat growth habits. The berries resemble blueberries but are, in fact, related to apples. They are sweet and juicy, with the richness of sweet cherries and a hint of almond.

Ironically, juneberries are more often planted for their ornamental qualities than for their fruits. You even find them planted around shopping malls, their fruits overlooked by passersby who do not know that the berries are edible. Now you know.

Nanking cherry is another bush more often planted as an ornamental than as a fruit-bearer. This bush has just one "season of interest" (to use the

conditions by mixing a bucketful of peat moss into each planting hole.

landscaping term), but what interest it has! In early spring, the whole bush bursts into a dense cloud of pinkish white blossoms.

Plant two Nanking cherries for cross-pollination, and just about all those flowers will go on to develop into fruits. The fruits are true cherries, small and varying from bush to bush in flavor from semisweet to semitart, and in color from almost white to deep red. Birds may eat some, but no matter. Production is so profuse that you will not notice the loss.

Viburnums are a familiar group of ornamental shrubs, and a few types also yield edible berries. Admittedly, none bear fruits that you would stuff right into your mouth,

SHRUBS FOR THE EDIBLE LANDSCAPE

Common Name	Botanical Name	Hardiness Zones	Height x Width (in feet)	Use: F=fresh, C=cooked (jam, jelly, pie), J=juice
Highbush blueberry, northern type	*Vaccinium corymbosum*	4-7	6-9 x 5	F, C
Highbush blueberry, southern type	*Vaccinium corymbosum*	6-10	6-9 x 5	F, C
Lowbush blueberry	*Vaccinium angustifolium*	3-7	1-2 x spreading ground cover	F, C
Rabbiteye blueberry	*Vaccinium ashei*	7-9	10-15 x 5-8	F, C
Salal	*Gaultheria shallon*	6-9	2-6 x 2-6	C
Lingonberry	*Vaccinium vitis-idaea*	2-6	0.5-2 x spreading ground cover	F, C
Juneberry	*Amelanchier spp.*	3-8	6-40 x 4-20	F, C
Nanking cherry	*Prunus tomentosum*	3-6	8-12 x 8-12	F, C, J
Nannyberry	*Viburnum lentago*	2-7	12-20 x 6-10	F
Highbush cranberry	*Viburnum trilobum*	2-7	8-12 x 8-12	C
Elderberry	*Sambucus nigra*	2-9	6-10 x 3-6	C
Red currant; white currant	*Ribes spp.*	3-5	5 x 5	F, C, J
Clove currant	*Ribes odoratum*	4-7	4 x 6	F, C

Currant is among the top performers for ornamental bushes. It is also

– photos: Michael McConkey/Edible Landscaping

The clove currant, *Ribes odoratum,* is known for its fragrant spring blooms *(top)* and tart, aromatic fruit *(above).*

but they are good for a nibble or to cook up into jam. **Nannyberry** is a viburnum that offers the nibble, with black fruits that are sweet even if they are more seed than flesh, and that change from green to yellow to pink to blue-black during ripening. **Highbush cranberry** is another edible viburnum, one that yields, as the name implies, berries that are glossy red and tart, perfect for sauce. This is not the Thanksgiving cranberry, but it can be used in the same way. Both nannyberry and highbush cranberry bushes are smothered with clusters of small, creamy-white flowers in spring, and any highbush cranberry fruits that you or the birds leave will festoon the shrub well into winter.

Elderberry is related to the viburnums and, like the two mentioned above, is native through much of the country. You may have admired the wide, flat-topped bunches of flowers staring out at you from along roadsides, so welcome after early spring's flurry of flowering shrubs has passed. The small, dark-blue berries are not too tasty right off the bush, but they cook up into a fine pie or jam.

Currant is among the top performers for ornamental bushes bearing edible berries. It is also among the few berry bushes that bear well in par-

among the few berry bushes that bear well in partial shade.

SOURCES FOR PLANTS

■ Edible Landscaping Nursery, Rte. 2 Box 77, Afton, VA 22920; 800-524-4156; www.eat-it.com.

■ Raintree Nursery, 391 Butts Rd., Morton, WA 98356; 360-496-6400; fax 888-770-8358; www.raintreenursery.com.

■ St. Lawrence Nurseries, 325 State Hwy. 345, Potsdam, NY 13676; 315-265-6739; www.sln.potsdam.ny.us.

■ Tripple Brook Farm, 37 Middle Rd., Southampton, MA 01073; 413-527-4626; fax 413-527-9853.

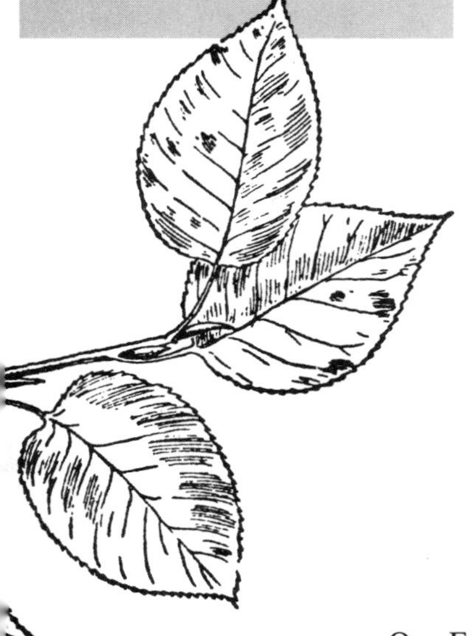

tial shade. Red and white currants are cool-weather plants, thriving best in the northern half of the country. Toward the southern end of their range, they actually prefer shade to full sun.

Red currants are the most common of the currants, but do not overlook equally beautiful white currants, essentially the same fruit except for the color. For these two plants, the fruits provide much of the show, as they dangle from the branches like ropes of rubies or pearls. The delicate spheres, when backlit by sunlight, are so translucent that you can see the seeds floating within.

Perhaps the star performer among bushes for edible landscaping is a relatively unknown currant called the clove currant. The shrub was a common dooryard plant around the turn of the century. The name hints at why it was planted near the house: In spring, the flowers pour out a spicy, clove-like fragrance. And if fragrance and fruit are not enough, the abundant flowers put on quite a show. Each is a long, yellow trumpet with a spot of red in its center. And if fragrance, fruit, and sunny blossoms are still not enough, this plant — a native of the upper Midwest — is also tough, able to withstand drought, heat, and cold, as well as insects, diseases, and even deer. The tart fruit is aromatic and is good fresh or in jam.

The above bushes are merely a sampler. Other "edible ornamentals" are adapted to certain regions only. For example, if you live in a warm winter area, where currants would languish, you might choose from among subtropicals such as strawberry guava, feijoa, and cherry-of-the-Rio-Grande.

Note that the definition of *berry* — a small fruit borne on a bush — has been hazy. After all, botanically speaking, an orange is a berry and a juneberry is not. We've also excluded some true berries, such as mulberries, because they grow on trees. And the mulberry is not the only ornamental tree that bears edible fruits. There is also . . . but that's another story. □□

Lee Reich is the author of *Uncommon Fruits Worthy of Attention* (Addison-Wesley Publishing Co., Inc., 1991; out of print).

Outdoor Planting Table

1 9 9 9

The best time to plant flowers and vegetables that bear crops above ground is during the *light* of the Moon; that is, from the day the Moon is new to the day it is full. Flowering bulbs and vegetables that bear crops below ground should be planted during the *dark* of the Moon; that is, from the day after it is full to the day before it is new again. The Moon Favorable columns at right give these Moon days, which are based on the Moon's phases for 1999 and the safe periods for planting in areas that receive frost. Consult page 162 for dates of frosts and lengths of growing seasons. See calendar pages 60-86 for the exact days of the new and full Moons.

Aboveground Crops Marked (*)

☞ E means Early **☞ L means Late**

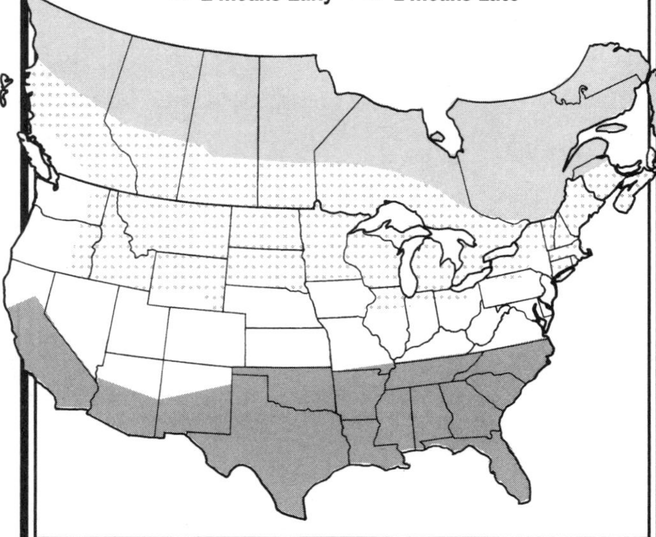

*	Barley	
*	Beans	(E)
		(L)
	Beets	(E)
		(L)
*	Broccoli Plants	(E)
		(L)
*	Brussels Sprouts	
*	Cabbage Plants	
	Carrots	(E)
		(L)
*	Cauliflower Plants	(E)
		(L)
*	Celery Plants	(E)
		(L)
*	Collards	(E)
		(L)
*	Corn, Sweet	(E)
		(L)
*	Cucumber	
*	Eggplant Plants	
*	Endive	(E)
		(L)
*	Flowers	(All)
*	Kale	(E)
		(L)
	Leek Plants	
*	Lettuce	
*	Muskmelon	
	Onion Sets	
*	Parsley	
	Parsnips	
*	Peas	(E)
		(L)
*	Pepper Plants	
	Potato	
*	Pumpkin	
	Radish	(E)
		(L)
*	Spinach	(E)
		(L)
*	Squash	
	Sweet Potatoes	
*	Swiss Chard	
*	Tomato Plants	
	Turnips	(E)
		(L)
*	Watermelon	
*	Wheat, Spring	
*	Wheat, Winter	

Planting Dates	Moon Favorable	Planting Dates	Moon Favorable	Planting Dates	Moon Favorable	Planting Dates	Moon Favorable
6/1-30	6/13-28	5/15-6/21	5/15-30, 6/13-21	3/15-4/7	3/17-31	2/15-3/7	2/16-3/2
5/30-6/15	5/30, 6/13-15	5/7-6/21	5/15-30, 6/13-21	4/15-30	4/16-30	3/15-4/7	3/17-31
—	—	6/15-7/15	6/15-28, 7/12-15	7/1-21	7/12-21	8/7-31	8/11-26
5/25-6/10	5/31-6/10	5/1-15	5/1-14	3/15-4/3	3/15-16, 4/1-3	2/7-28	2/7-15
6/15-7/8	6/29-7/8	7/15-8/15	7/29-8/10	8/15-31	8/27-31	9/1-30	9/1-8, 9/26-30
6/1-25	6/13-25	5/15-31	5/15-30	3/7-31	3/17-31	2/15-3/15	2/16-3/2
—	—	6/15-7/7	6/15-28	8/1-20	8/11-20	9/7-30	9/9-25
6/1-25	6/13-25	5/15-31	5/15-30	3/7-4/15	3/17-31	2/11-3/20	2/16-3/2, 3/17-20
6/1-25	6/13-25	5/15-31	5/15-30	3/7-4/15	3/17-31	2/11-3/20	2/16-3/2, 3/17-20
5/25-6/10	5/31-6/10	5/15-31	5/31	3/7-31	3/7-16	2/15-3/7	2/15, 3/3-7
6/15-7/8	6/29-7/8	6/15-7/21	6/29-7/11	7/7-31	7/7-11, 7/29-31	8/1-9/7	8/1-10, 8/27-9/7
6/1-25	6/13-25	5/15-31	5/15-30	3/15-4/7	3/17-31	2/15-3/7	2/16-3/2
—	—	6/15-7/21	6/15-28, 7/12-21	7/1-8/7	7/12-28	8/7-31	8/11-26
6/1-30	6/13-28	5/15-6/30	5/15-30, 6/13-28	3/7-31	3/17-31	2/15-28	2/16-28
—	—	7/15-8/15	7/15-28, 8/11-15	8/15-9/7	8/15-26	9/15-30	9/15-25
6/1-25	6/13-25	5/15-31	5/15-30	3/7-4/7	3/17-31	2/11-3/20	2/16-3/2, 3/17-20
—	—	7/1-8/7	7/12-28	8/15-31	8/15-26	9/7-30	9/9-25
5/30-6/20	5/30, 6/13-20	5/10-6/15	5/15-30, 6/13-15	4/1-17	4/16-17	3/15-31	3/17-31
—	—	6/15-30	6/15-28	7/7-21	7/12-21	8/7-31	8/11-26
5/30-6/15	5/30, 6/13-15	5/7-6/20	5/15-30, 6/13-20	4/7-5/15	4/16-30, 5/15	3/7-4/15	3/17-31
6/15-30	6/15-28	6/1-30	6/13-28	4/7-5/15	4/16-30, 5/15	3/7-4/15	3/17-31
6/1-25	6/13-25	5/15-31	5/15-30	4/7-5/15	4/16-30, 5/15	2/15-3/20	2/16-3/2, 3/17-20
—	—	6/7-30	6/13-28	7/15-8/15	7/15-28, 8/11-15	8/15-9/7	8/15-26
6/1-30	6/13-28	5/7-6/21	5/15-30, 6/13-21	4/15-30	4/16-30	3/15-4/7	3/17-31
6/1-15	6/13-15	5/15-31	5/15-30	3/7-4/7	3/17-31	2/11-3/20	2/16-3/2, 3/17-20
6/25-7/15	6/25-28, 7/12-15	7/1-8/7	7/12-28	8/15-31	8/15-26	9/7-30	9/9-25
6/1-15	6/1-12	5/15-31	5/31	3/7-4/7	3/7-16, 4/1-7	2/15-4/15	2/15, 3/3-16, 4/1-15
6/1-30	6/13-28	5/15-6/30	5/15-30, 6/13-28	3/1-31	3/1-2, 3/17-31	2/15-3/7	2/16-3/2
6/1-30	6/13-28	5/15-6/30	5/15-30, 6/13-28	4/15-5/7	4/16-30	3/15-4/7	3/17-31
6/1-25	6/1-12	5/15-6/7	5/31-6/7	3/1-31	3/3-16	2/1-28	2/1-15
6/1-15	6/13-15	5/15-31	5/15-30	3/1-31	3/17-31	2/20-3/15	2/20-3/2
5/10-31	5/10-14, 5/31	4/1-30	4/1-15	3/7-31	3/7-16	1/15-2/4	1/15-16, 2/1-4
5/20-31	5/20-30	4/15-5/7	4/16-30	3/7-31	3/17-31	1/15-2/7	1/17-31
7/10-25	7/12-25	7/15-31	7/15-28	8/7-31	8/11-26	9/15-30	9/15-25
6/1-30	6/13-28	5/15-6/30	5/15-30, 6/13-28	4/1-30	4/16-30	3/1-20	3/1-2, 3/17-20
6/1-25	6/1-12	5/1-31	5/1-14, 5/31	4/1-30	4/1-15	2/10-28	2/10-15
6/1-30	6/13-28	5/15-31	5/15-30	4/23-5/15	4/23-30, 5/15	3/7-20	3/17-20
5/15-6/5	5/31-6/5	4/15-30	4/15	3/7-31	3/7-16	1/21-3/1	2/1-15
7/10-31	7/10-11, 7/29-31	8/15-31	8/27-31	9/7-30	9/7-8, 9/26-30	10/1-21	10/1-8
6/1-25	6/13-25	5/15-31	5/15-30	3/15-4/20	3/17-31, 4/16-20	2/7-3/15	2/16-3/2
7/20-8/5	7/20-28	7/15-9/7	7/15-28, 8/11-26	8/1-9/15	8/11-26, 9/9-15	10/1-21	10/9-21
6/1-30	6/13-28	5/15-6/15	5/15-30, 6/13-15	4/15-30	4/16-30	3/15-4/15	3/17-31
6/1-30	6/1-12, 6/29-30	5/15-6/15	5/31-6/12	4/21-5/2	5/1-2	3/23-4/6	4/1-6
5/15-31	5/15-30	5/1-31	5/15-30	3/15-4/15	3/17-31	2/7-3/15	2/16-3/2
6/1-15	6/13-15	5/15-31	5/15-30	4/7-30	4/16-30	3/7-20	3/17-20
5/10-31	5/10-14, 5/31	4/7-30	4/7-15	3/15-31	3/15-16	1/20-2/15	2/1-15
—	—	7/1-8/15	7/1-11, 7/29-8/10	8/1-20	8/1-10	9/1-10/15	9/1-8, 9/26-10/8
6/1-30	6/13-28	5/15-6/30	5/15-30, 6/13-28	4/15-5/7	4/16-30	3/15-4/7	3/17-31
5/15-6/10	5/15-30	4/7-30	4/16-30	3/1-20	3/1-2, 3/17-20	2/15-28	2/16-28
8/5-30	8/11-26	8/11-9/15	8/11-26, 9/9-15	9/15-10/20	9/15-25, 10/9-20	10/15-12/7	10/15-24, 11/7-23, 12/7

Frosts and Growing Seasons

Courtesy of National Climatic Center

Dates given are normal averages for a light freeze (32° F); local weather and topography may cause considerable variations. The possibility of frost occurring after the spring dates and before the fall dates is 50 percent. The classification of freeze temperatures is usually based on their effect on plants, with the following commonly accepted categories: **Light freeze:** 29° to 32° F — tender plants killed; little destructive effect on other vegetation. **Moderate freeze:** 25° to 28° F — widely destructive effect on most vegetation; heavy damage to fruit blossoms and tender and semihardy plants. **Severe freeze:** 24° F and colder — heavy damage to most plants.

CITY	Growing Season (days)	Last Frost Spring	First Frost Fall
Mobile, AL	272	Feb. 27	Nov. 26
Juneau, AK	133	May 16	Sept. 26
Phoenix, AZ	308	Feb. 5	Dec. 15
Tucson, AZ	273	Feb. 28	Nov. 29
Pine Bluff, AR	234	Mar. 19	Nov. 8
Eureka, CA	324	Jan. 30	Dec. 15
Sacramento, CA	289	Feb. 14	Dec. 1
San Francisco, CA	*	*	*
Denver, CO	157	May 3	Oct. 8
Hartford, CT	167	Apr. 25	Oct. 10
Wilmington, DE	198	Apr. 13	Oct. 29
Miami, FL	*	*	*
Tampa, FL	338	Jan. 28	Jan. 3
Athens, GA	224	Mar. 28	Nov. 8
Savannah, GA	250	Mar. 10	Nov. 15
Boise, ID	153	May 8	Oct. 9
Chicago, IL	187	Apr. 22	Oct. 26
Springfield, IL	185	Apr. 17	Oct. 19
Indianapolis, IN	180	Apr. 22	Oct. 20
South Bend, IN	169	May 1	Oct. 18
Atlantic, IA	141	May 9	Sept. 28
Cedar Rapids, IA	161	Apr. 29	Oct. 7
Topeka, KS	175	Apr. 21	Oct. 14
Lexington, KY	190	Apr. 17	Oct. 25
Monroe, LA	242	Mar. 9	Nov. 7
New Orleans, LA	288	Feb. 20	Dec. 5
Portland, ME	143	May 10	Sept. 30
Baltimore, MD	231	Mar. 26	Nov. 13
Worcester, MA	172	Apr. 27	Oct. 17
Lansing, MI	140	May 13	Sept. 30
Marquette, MI	159	May 12	Oct. 19
Duluth, MN	122	May 21	Sept. 21
Willmar, MN	152	May 4	Oct. 4
Columbus, MS	215	Mar. 27	Oct. 29
Vicksburg, MS	250	Mar. 13	Nov. 18
Jefferson City, MO	173	Apr. 26	Oct. 16
Fort Peck, MT	146	May 5	Sept. 28
Helena, MT	122	May 18	Sept. 18
Blair, NE	165	Apr. 27	Oct. 10
North Platte, NE	136	May 11	Sept. 24
Las Vegas, NV	259	Mar. 7	Nov. 21
Concord, NH	121	May 23	Sept. 22
Newark, NJ	219	Apr. 4	Nov. 10
Carlsbad, NM	223	Mar. 29	Nov. 7
Los Alamos, NM	157	May 8	Oct. 13
Albany, NY	144	May 7	Sept. 29
Syracuse, NY	170	Apr. 28	Oct. 16
Fayetteville, NC	212	Apr. 2	Oct. 31
Bismarck, ND	129	May 14	Sept. 20
Akron, OH	168	May 3	Oct. 18
Cincinnati, OH	195	Apr. 14	Oct. 27
Lawton, OK	217	Apr. 1	Nov. 5
Tulsa, OK	218	Mar. 30	Nov. 4
Pendleton, OR	188	Apr. 15	Oct. 21
Portland, OR	217	Apr. 3	Nov. 7
Carlisle, PA	182	Apr. 20	Oct. 20
Williamsport, PA	168	Apr. 29	Oct. 15
Kingston, RI	144	May 8	Sept. 30
Charleston, SC	253	Mar. 11	Nov. 20
Columbia, SC	211	Apr. 4	Nov. 2
Rapid City, SD	145	May 7	Sept. 29
Memphis, TN	228	Mar. 23	Nov. 7
Nashville, TN	207	Apr. 5	Oct. 29
Amarillo, TX	197	Apr. 14	Oct. 29
Denton, TX	231	Mar. 25	Nov. 12
San Antonio, TX	265	Mar. 3	Nov. 24
Cedar City, UT	134	May 20	Oct. 2
Spanish Fork, UT	156	May 8	Oct. 12
Burlington, VT	142	May 11	Oct. 1
Norfolk, VA	239	Mar. 23	Nov. 17
Richmond, VA	198	Apr. 10	Oct. 26
Seattle, WA	232	Mar. 24	Nov. 11
Spokane, WA	153	May 4	Oct. 5
Parkersburg, WV	175	Apr. 25	Oct. 18
Green Bay, WI	143	May 12	Oct. 2
Janesville, WI	164	Apr. 28	Oct. 10
Casper, WY	123	May 22	Sept. 22

***Frosts do not occur every year.**

A Month-by-Month Astrological Timetable for 1999

The following yearlong chart is based on the Moon signs and shows the *most favorable* times each month for certain activities. BY CELESTE LONGACRE

	JAN.	FEB.	MAR.	APR.	MAY	JUNE	JULY	AUG.	SEPT.	OCT.	NOV.	DEC.
Give up smoking	3, 18, 22	4, 14, 27	4, 18, 26	10, 14, 27	7, 12, 20	4, 8, 16, 21	1, 5, 14, 28	10, 15, 24	2, 11, 21	8, 18, 23	4, 14, 19	2, 12, 17, 29
Begin diet to lose weight	3, 8	4, 14	4, 14	10, 14	7, 12	4, 8	1, 6	2, 4	7, 26	4, 8	4, 27	2, 25, 29
Begin diet to gain weight	18, 22, 31	19, 27	18, 26	23, 27	20, 25	16, 21	14, 18	15, 24	11, 21	18, 23	14, 19	12, 17
Cut hair to encourage growth	24, 25	21, 22	20, 21, 31	27, 28, 29	25, 26	21, 22	18, 19	15, 16	11, 12	21, 22	21, 22	19, 20
Cut hair to discourage growth	8, 9	4, 5, 6	4, 5	12, 13	10, 11, 14	10, 11	8, 9	1, 27, 28	1, 27, 28	8, 26	4, 5, 6	2, 3, 29, 30
Have dental care	6, 7	2, 3	1, 2, 3, 29	25, 26	22, 23	19, 20	16, 17	12, 13	9, 10	6, 7	2, 3, 29, 30	1, 27, 28
End old projects	15, 16	14, 15	15, 16	14, 15	13, 14	11, 12	11, 12	9, 10	7, 8	7, 8	6, 7	5, 6
Start a new project	18, 19	17, 18	18, 19	17, 18	16, 17	14, 15	14, 15	12, 13	10, 11	10, 11	9, 10	8, 9
Entertain	3, 4, 31	1, 27, 28	26, 27	23, 24	20, 21	16, 17	14, 15	10, 11	6, 7	4, 5, 31	1, 27, 28	25, 26
Go fishing	13, 14	9, 10, 11	9, 10	5, 6	2, 3, 30, 31	26, 27	23, 24	20, 21	16, 17	13, 14	10, 11	7, 8
Plant above-ground crops	20, 21, 29	17, 25, 26	24, 25	20, 21	18, 19, 27, 28	14, 15, 23, 24	21, 22	17, 18	13, 14, 23, 24	11, 12, 21, 22	17, 18	14, 15
Plant below-ground crops	1, 2, 11, 12	7, 8	6, 7, 16	3, 4, 12, 13	1, 10, 11	6, 7	3, 4, 12, 31	1, 8, 9, 27, 28	4, 5	2, 3, 29, 30	7, 26, 27	4, 5, 23, 24
Destroy pests and weeds	22, 23	19, 20	18, 19	14, 15	12, 13	8, 9	5, 6	2, 3, 29, 30	25, 26	23, 24	19, 20	16, 17, 18
Graft or pollinate	1, 2, 20, 21	16, 17, 25, 26	16, 17, 24, 25	12, 13, 20, 21	10, 11, 18, 19	6, 7, 14, 15	3, 4, 12, 13, 31	1, 8, 9, 27, 28	4, 5, 23, 24	2, 3, 21, 22, 30	17, 18, 25, 26	14, 15, 23, 24
Prune to encourage growth	22, 23	19, 20	18, 19	23, 24	20, 21	26, 27	23, 24	19, 20	16, 17	13, 14	9, 10	8, 17, 18
Prune to discourage growth	13, 14	9, 10	9, 10	14, 15	12, 13	8, 9	5, 6	2, 3, 29	7, 26	4, 5	27, 28	25, 26
Harvest above-ground crops	24, 25	21, 22	20, 21	25, 26	22, 23	19, 20	16, 17	12, 13	18, 19	16, 17	21, 22	9, 10
Harvest below-ground crops	6, 7	2, 3	1, 2	8, 9	5, 6	10, 11	8, 9	4, 5	1, 27, 28	6, 7, 26	2, 3, 30	1, 27, 28
Cut hay	22, 23	19, 20	18, 19	14, 15	12, 13	8, 9	6, 7	2, 3, 29, 30	25, 26	23, 24	19, 20	17, 18
Begin logging	16, 17	12, 13	11, 12	8, 9	5, 6	1, 2, 28, 29	26, 27	22, 23	18, 19	16, 17	12, 13	9, 10
Set posts or pour concrete	16, 17	12, 13	11, 12	8, 9	5, 6	1, 2, 28, 29	26, 27	22, 23	18, 19	16, 17	12, 13	9, 10
Breed	11, 12	7, 8	6, 7, 8	3, 4, 30	1, 27, 28	23, 24	21, 22	17, 18	13, 14	11, 12	7, 8	4, 5, 31
Wean	3, 8	4, 14	4, 14	10, 14	7, 12	4, 8	1, 6	2, 4	7, 26	4, 8	4, 27	2, 25, 29
Castrate animals	18, 19	14, 15	14, 15	10, 11	7, 8	4, 5	1, 2, 28, 29	24, 25	21, 22	18, 19	14, 15	12, 13
Slaughter	11, 12	7, 8	6, 7, 8	3, 4, 30	1, 27, 28	23, 24	21, 22	17, 18	13, 14	11, 12	7, 8	4, 5, 31

GARDENING BY THE MOON'S SIGN

It is important to note that *the placement of the planets through the signs of the zodiac is not the same in astronomy and astrology.* The *astrological* placement of the Moon, by sign, is given in the chart below. (The *astronomical,* or actual, placement is given in the Left-Hand Calendar Pages 60-86.)

For planting, the most fertile signs are the three water signs: Cancer, Scorpio, and Pisces. Taurus, Virgo, and Capricorn are good second choices for sowing.

Weeding and plowing are best done when the Moon occupies the sign of Aries, Gemini, Leo, Sagittarius, or Aquarius. Insect pests can also be handled at these times. Transplanting and grafting are best done under a Cancer, Scorpio, or Pisces Moon. Pruning is best done under an Aries, Leo, or Sagittarius Moon, with growth encouraged during the waxing stage (between new and full Moon) and discouraged during waning (the day after full to the day before new Moon). (The dates of the Moon's phases can be found on pages 60-86.) Clean out the garden shed when the Moon occupies Virgo so that the work will flow smoothly. Fences or permanent beds can be built or mended when Capricorn predominates. Avoid indecision when under the Libra Moon.

Moon's Place in the Astrological Zodiac

	NOV. 98	DEC. 98	JAN. 99	FEB. 99	MAR. 99	APR. 99	MAY 99	JUNE 99	JULY 99	AUG. 99	SEPT. 99	OCT. 99	NOV. 99	DEC. 99
1	ARI	TAU	CAN	LEO	VIR	LIB	SCO	CAP	AQU	PSC	TAU	CAN	LEO	VIR
2	ARI	TAU	CAN	VIR	VIR	SCO	SAG	CAP	AQU	ARI	GEM	CAN	VIR	LIB
3	TAU	GEM	LEO	VIR	VIR	SCO	SAG	AQU	PSC	ARI	GEM	CAN	VIR	LIB
4	TAU	GEM	LEO	LIB	LIB	SCO	SAG	AQU	PSC	TAU	CAN	LEO	LIB	SCO
5	GEM	CAN	LEO	LIB	LIB	SAG	CAP	AQU	ARI	TAU	CAN	LEO	LIB	SCO
6	GEM	CAN	VIR	LIB	SCO	SAG	CAP	PSC	ARI	GEM	LEO	VIR	LIB	SAG
7	CAN	LEO	VIR	SCO	SCO	CAP	AQU	PSC	TAU	GEM	LEO	VIR	SCO	SAG
8	CAN	LEO	LIB	SCO	SCO	CAP	AQU	ARI	TAU	CAN	LEO	LIB	SCO	SAG
9	LEO	VIR	LIB	SAG	SAG	CAP	PSC	ARI	TAU	CAN	VIR	LIB	SAG	CAP
10	LEO	VIR	SCO	SAG	SAG	AQU	PSC	TAU	GEM	LEO	VIR	SCO	SAG	CAP
11	LEO	VIR	SCO	SAG	CAP	AQU	PSC	TAU	GEM	LEO	LIB	SCO	SAG	CAP
12	VIR	LIB	SCO	CAP	CAP	PSC	ARI	GEM	CAN	VIR	LIB	SCO	CAP	AQU
13	VIR	LIB	SAG	CAP	CAP	PSC	ARI	GEM	CAN	VIR	SCO	SAG	CAP	AQU
14	LIB	SCO	SAG	AQU	AQU	ARI	TAU	CAN	LEO	LIB	SCO	SAG	AQU	PSC
15	LIB	SCO	CAP	AQU	AQU	ARI	TAU	CAN	LEO	LIB	SCO	CAP	AQU	PSC
16	LIB	SCO	CAP	PSC	PSC	TAU	GEM	LEO	VIR	LIB	SAG	CAP	AQU	ARI
17	SCO	SAG	CAP	PSC	PSC	TAU	GEM	LEO	VIR	SCO	SAG	CAP	PSC	ARI
18	SCO	SAG	AQU	PSC	ARI	GEM	CAN	VIR	LIB	SCO	CAP	AQU	PSC	ARI
19	SAG	CAP	AQU	ARI	ARI	GEM	CAN	VIR	LIB	SAG	CAP	AQU	ARI	TAU
20	SAG	CAP	PSC	ARI	TAU	CAN	LEO	VIR	SCO	SAG	CAP	PSC	ARI	TAU
21	SAG	AQU	PSC	TAU	TAU	CAN	LEO	LIB	SCO	SAG	AQU	PSC	TAU	GEM
22	CAP	AQU	ARI	TAU	GEM	LEO	VIR	LIB	SCO	CAP	AQU	PSC	TAU	GEM
23	CAP	AQU	ARI	GEM	GEM	LEO	VIR	SCO	SAG	CAP	PSC	ARI	GEM	CAN
24	AQU	PSC	TAU	GEM	CAN	LEO	LIB	SCO	SAG	AQU	PSC	ARI	GEM	CAN
25	AQU	PSC	TAU	CAN	CAN	VIR	LIB	SCO	CAP	AQU	ARI	TAU	CAN	LEO
26	AQU	ARI	GEM	CAN	LEO	VIR	LIB	SAG	CAP	AQU	ARI	TAU	CAN	LEO
27	PSC	ARI	GEM	LEO	LEO	LIB	SCO	SAG	CAP	PSC	TAU	GEM	LEO	VIR
28	PSC	TAU	GEM	LEO	LEO	LIB	SCO	CAP	AQU	PSC	TAU	GEM	LEO	VIR
29	ARI	TAU	CAN	—	VIR	LIB	SAG	CAP	AQU	ARI	GEM	CAN	VIR	LIB
30	ARI	TAU	CAN	—	VIR	SCO	SAG	CAP	PSC	ARI	GEM	CAN	VIR	LIB
31	—	GEM	LEO	—	LIB	—	SAG	—	PSC	TAU	—	LEO	—	SCO

Secrets of the Zodiac

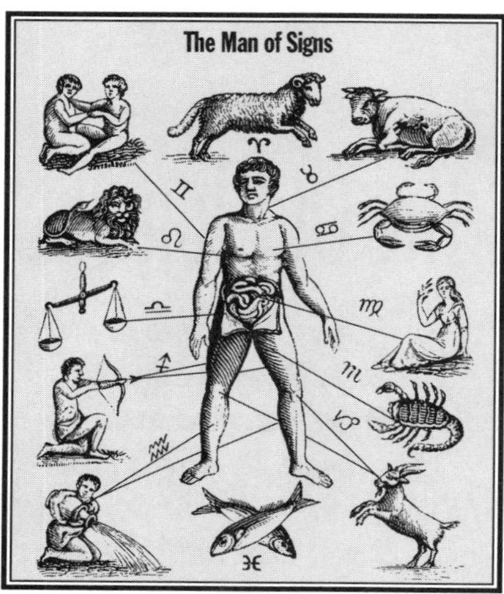

Ancient astrologers associated each of the signs with a part of the body over which they felt the sign held some influence. The first sign of the zodiac — Aries — was attributed to the head, with the rest of the signs moving down the body, ending with Pisces at the feet.

♈	**Aries, head. ARI Mar. 21-Apr. 20**
♉	**Taurus, neck. TAU Apr. 21-May 20**
♊	**Gemini, arms. GEM May 21-June 20**
♋	**Cancer, breast. CAN June 21-July 22**
♌	**Leo, heart. LEO July 23-Aug. 22**
♍	**Virgo, belly. VIR Aug. 23-Sept. 22**
♎	**Libra, reins. LIB Sept. 23-Oct. 22**
♏	**Scorpio, secrets. SCO Oct. 23-Nov. 22**
♐	**Sagittarius, thighs. SAG Nov. 23-Dec. 21**
♑	**Capricorn, knees. CAP Dec. 22-Jan. 19**
♒	**Aquarius, legs. AQU Jan. 20-Feb. 19**
♓	**Pisces, feet. PSC Feb. 20-Mar. 20**

Astrology and Astronomy

Astrology is a tool we use to time events according to the *astrological* placement of the two luminaries (the Sun and the Moon) and eight planets in the 12 signs of the zodiac. Astronomy, on the other hand, is the charting of the *actual* placement of the known planets and constellations, taking into account precession of the equinoxes. As a result, *the placement of the planets in the signs of the zodiac are not the same astrologically and astronomically.* (The Moon's *astronomical* place is given in the Left-Hand Calendar Pages [60-86] and its *astrological* place is given in Gardening by the Moon's Sign, page 166.)

Modern astrology is a study of synchronicities. The planetary movements do not *cause* events. Rather, they *explain* the "flow," or trajectory, that events tend to follow. Because of free will, you can choose to plan a schedule in harmony with the flow, or you can choose to swim against the current.

The dates given in A Month-by-Month Astrological Timetable (page 164) have been chosen with particular care to the astrological passage of the Moon. However, since other planets also influence us, it's best to take a look at *all* indicators before seeking advice on major life decisions. A qualified astrologer can study the current relationship of the planets and your own personal birth chart to assist you in the best possible timing for carrying out your plans.

Planet Mercury Does What?

Sometimes when we look out from our perspective here on Earth, the other planets appear to be traveling backward through the zodiac. (They're not actually moving backward; it just looks that way to us.) We call this *retrograde*.

Mercury's retrograde periods, which occur three or four times a year, can cause travel delays and misconstrued communications. Plans have a way of unraveling, too. However, this is an excellent time to be researching or looking into the past. Intuition is high during these periods, and coincidences can be extraordinary.

When Mercury is retrograde, astrologers advise us to keep plans flexible, allow extra time for travel, and avoid signing contracts. It's OK and even useful to look over projects and plans, because we may see them with different eyes at these times. However, our normal system of checks and balances might not be active, so it's best to wait until Mercury is direct again to make any final decisions. In 1999, Mercury will be retrograde from March 10 to April 2, July 12 to August 6, and November 5 to November 25. *– Celeste Longacre*

PASS the MUSTARD!

by Victoria Doudera

Take a long look at that common condiment sitting so calmly in your fridge. Mustard is actually a mysterious mixture, with as many identities as a secret agent. Is it yellow, or is it brown? A tiny seed or a pungent salad green? An exotic spice or an all-too-familiar flavoring? Mustard can be fruity, mild, or fiery — as ubiquitous as the spread at a picnic or as worldly as the sauce in an upscale restaurant.

Mustard is a plant of the genus *Brassica* and a member of the Cruciferae family, which includes broccoli, Brussels sprouts, cabbage, collards, kale, kohlrabi, and turnips. The dark-green leaves are harvested when they are young and tender. Peppery mustard leaves, or "greens," have always been a popular ingredient in southern soul food, and like their dark leafy cousins, they are an excellent source of vitamins A and C.

The mustard plant bears yellow flowers and slender pods containing tiny seeds. In Biblical times, the mustard seed, which was the smallest seed then known, symbolized the potential of a new religion and the power of faith: "The kingdom of heaven is like to a grain of mustard seed . . . which indeed is the least of all seeds: but when it is grown, it is the greatest among herbs. . . . If ye have faith as a grain of mustard seed, . . . nothing shall be impossible unto you." (Matthew 13:31-32 and 17:20.)

There are three types of mustard seeds — *B. alba,* white; *B. juncea,* brown or Asian; and *B. nigra,* black (rarely grown or used today). White mustard seeds are the largest, but curiously, also the mildest. They are the main ingredient in our yellow, or "ballpark," mustards. (The yellow color comes from turmeric.) Brown seeds, more pungent, are blended with white seeds to make proper English mustards and are often used alone in pickling, as a seasoning, and in the preparation of spicy Oriental mustards. Genuine Dijon mustard, the *moutarde de choix* in France, legally must contain either brown or black seeds (French mustard producers nowadays mainly use brown mustard seeds).

Powdered mustard, the kind sitting in your kitchen cabinet, is simply finely ground seeds from which the oil has been removed. It is unique among spices: Unlike other, more aromatic seasonings, powdered mustard in its dry form is no more powerful than cornstarch. Mustard's pungency is created only by the action of an enzyme (myrosin, for you chemistry buffs) released when mustard mixes with water. This chemical reaction is at its most flavorful after 10 or 15 minutes. After that, exposure to air causes the zest to dissipate.

Mustard is an ancient spice, originating in Asia and known since prehistoric times. The Chinese have mixed their sharp mustards for thousands of years, and today we continue to dip our egg rolls into the same simple paste made from ground brown mustard seeds and cold water. Two thousand years ago, the Romans planted *sinapis* — mustard — everywhere they conquered, including Merrie Olde England. By the 13th century, the French had established the city of Dijon as the mecca of mustards. Mustard grinders, used like pepper mills, were a fixture on medieval tables. The court of King Philip VI of France was said to have consumed 100 gallons of mustard while entertaining the Duke of Burgundy and his entourage.

In 18th-century France, mustard mixing became an esteemed culinary art. Like gourmet purveyors of mustard today, there were some exotic concoctions: caper, rose-water, anchovy, truffle, and even vanilla mustards. The gender-conscious French served both a fiery "gentlemen's mustard" (see recipe on page 174) and a more demure version, the "ladies' mustard."

Why was all this mustard being spread? Was it because the condiment could mask a malodorous mutton, or boost a blah boar? Or was it just because people liked it? "The myth that food in medieval times didn't taste good, or that meat was 'tainted,' has pretty much been debunked," says food historian Kathleen Curtin. "Mustard was used because it was available and affordable, while other flavorings, like ginger, sugar, and dried fruits, were very expensive."

To this side of the Atlantic, the Pilgrims "most certainly brought mustard on the *Mayflower,*" believes Curtin, who studies the history of food at Plimoth Plantation in Plymouth, Massachusetts. Captain John Smith, the Pilgrims' military leader, listed mustard as a necessary provision for sailors, for taste as well as medicinal value. John Gerard described the many curative attributes of mustard in *The Herbal,* written in 1633: "The seed of Mustard pound with vineger, is an excellent sauce, good to be eaten with any grosse meates either fish or flesh, because it doth helpe digestion, warmeth the stomacke, and provoketh appetite." And mustard's healing powers weren't only internal: Even today, a mustard plaster can be used as a poultice.

According to mustard authority John Hemingway, seeds as well as processed mustard products began to be imported into North America in the 1700s. In

A tale without love is like beef without mustard: insipid.

– Anatole France

Must-Sees for Mustard Lovers

The annual Napa Valley (California) Mustard Festival, held when the wild mustard blooms (February and March), features mustard tasting, mustard competitions, mustard art, a mustard photography contest (with monetary awards), and the "Mustard Street Mystery." Call 707-259-9020 for more information.

The Mount Horeb Mustard Museum, in Mount Horeb, Wisconsin, boasts the world's largest collection of mustards (more than 2,800 at last count). You can taste hundreds of exotic concoctions, watch "MustardPiece Theatre," see antique mustard pots, and purchase delicious mustards from the retail shop and slather it on some fine Wisconsin sausage. Call 800-438-6878 for more information, or look up the museum's Web site at www.mustardweb.com.

– Bob Kreisel/courtesy Summers-McCann

Wild mustard in the Napa Valley.

northern California, beginning in 1768, a Catholic priest named Father Serra spread mustard seeds with the Gospel along the Mission trail. In 1790, Thomas Jefferson decided to try his hand with mustard production at Monticello, planting seeds purchased from a grocer in Paris.

The Reverend Sylvester Graham (of graham cracker fame), founder of the Society for the Suppression of Feasting, was a mustard malcontent. Graham and his followers believed that excessive consumption of lively spices would ruin the nation's morals. Mustard and other degenerate foods would "result in the hormonal boisterousness that leads men to take advantage of pliant women," wrote Graham, whose crusade against condiments in the late 1800s quickly ran out of steam.

Soon a new use for mustard arose: tangy sauce for tiny sardines. Raye's Mustard Mill, founded by J. W. Raye in Eastport, Maine, in 1899, was one of the early suppliers of mustard for the sardine canneries along the East Coast. When Nancy Raye, granddaughter of the mill's founder, took over in 1991, the sardine industry had long since waned, and Raye's Mustard Mill was dying. Under her direction, the mill began grinding out a variety of gourmet, or "specialty," mustards, using brown and white seeds and mixing them with well water or distilled vinegar. Raye's is the only place in the United States still producing mustard the old-fashioned way. Other companies use powdered mustard; Raye's grinds whole seeds with four enormous one-ton stones, a process that yields a clean, sharp flavor.

At last count, there were 2,052 specialty mustards on the American market. The average American now consumes about a half-pound of mustard per year, compared with the two tablespoons each per year that our grandparents enjoyed. (That's still way below the French, who consume two pounds each per year.) Most of the world's condiment mustard seed is grown in the Canadian prairies, plus a bit in Montana and North Dakota.

As in the 1700s, inventive mustard mixers have come up with some amazing concoctions: black olive, pineapple habanero, and raspberry mustards, to name a few. Try your hand at mixing your own. You'll be part of a proud and ancient tradition of folks around the world who passed the mustard.

(continued on page 174)

French Gentlemen's Mustard

1 tablespoon powdered mustard
1 tablespoon cold water
1/8 teaspoon salt

Blend all the ingredients into a smooth paste and set aside for 10 minutes for flavor to develop. Spread on pâté, or maybe on *le hot dog*.

Whole-Grain Apricot Mustard

(From Chef Andrew Sutton of Auberge du Soleil)

2 tablespoons whole mustard seeds
1/2 cup whole-fruit apricot jam
1/2 cup water

In a small saucepan, combine all ingredients. Simmer gently for 15 minutes. Set aside to cool, then refrigerate overnight.

Mustard Gingerbread

Here's an old recipe found in a handwritten cookbook from Mystic, Connecticut, and printed in The Spice Cookbook, *by Avanelle Day and Lillie Stuckey.*

2-1/4 cups flour
1-1/2 teaspoons baking powder
1/2 teaspoon salt
1/2 teaspoon baking soda
1/2 teaspoon ground cloves
1 teaspoon powdered mustard
1 teaspoon ground cinnamon
1 teaspoon ground ginger
1/2 cup shortening
1/2 cup sugar
1 cup molasses
1 large egg
1 cup hot water

Sift together flour, baking powder, and salt and set aside. Add baking soda and spices, including mustard, to shortening and mix well. Gradually blend in sugar and molasses. Beat in egg. Add flour mixture alternately with hot water. Beat for ½ minute. Turn batter into a well-greased, lightly floured 9x9-inch pan.

Bake at 350° F for 45 minutes, or until a toothpick inserted into center comes out clean. Cool in pan 10 minutes, then turn out onto wire rack. Serve warm with whipped cream.

Whole-Grain Mustard Risotto

(From Chef S. Patrick Finney of the Napa Valley Wine Train)

8 cups chicken stock or bouillon
2 tablespoons olive oil
1 yellow onion, finely chopped
3 cups Arborio rice
3 tablespoons whole-grain deli mustard
1/2 cup grated Parmesan cheese, plus additional for garnish

In a saucepan, bring stock to a low simmer. In a heavy sauté pan over low heat, add olive oil and sauté onion until transparent, then add rice and stir thoroughly. Add a ladleful of stock so that the rice is just covered with liquid. Stir. As the stock is absorbed, add a little more, stirring after each addition. Don't let the rice become dry.

Once all the liquid has been absorbed, remove the rice from the heat. Fold in the mustard and ½ cup of the cheese. Cover and let set for 10 minutes. Garnish with additional cheese, to taste.

Mustard Greens Pesto

(From Chef Peter McCaffrey of Wine Valley Catering)

2 bunches mustard greens
4 cloves garlic
1 tablespoon pine nuts
1 cup olive oil
salt and pepper
Parmesan cheese (optional)

Puree all ingredients except cheese in blender until smooth. Adjust seasonings and serve over fettucine, with Parmesan cheese, if desired. □□

The *Best Apple Pie* in the WHOLE WIDE WORLD

(or mighty close to it)

■ Amy Fuqua, of Boulder, Colorado, won first prize with this double-crust apple pie at the National Pie Championship two years ago. The pie is a classic, from the lard- and butter-shortened crust to the blend of spices in the filling. But there's one twist: The apples are baked twice. Amy said it took a lot of experimenting to find the apple with the strength of texture and taste to hold up to the double baking. She tried 'Jonathan', 'Granny Smith', and 'Golden Delicious' apples before settling on 'Winesap', her favorite for pies. She actually modified the spices found in standard recipes to let the apple taste predominate.

Autumn is the best time of the year for making apple pies because the apples are so fresh and crisp, says Amy. If 'Winesap' apples are not available, try 'Cortland'. 'McIntosh' is good early in the harvest; 'Northern Spy', later in the season. In any case, the key to a good pie is to use the most freshly picked apples, because storage tends to make apples mushy and bland.

Although Amy and her family are vegetarians, they make an exception for something as important as piecrust. The lard/butter blend is easy to handle and distinctive in taste and flakiness.

AMY'S APPLE PIE

FLAKY PIECRUST:

2 cups flour
1/2 teaspoon salt
3/4 cup lard, chilled
1/4 cup butter, chilled
1/3 cup ice water

Mix flour and salt. Cut lard and butter into the flour with a wire pastry blender until it is the texture of cornmeal. Mix in water, tossing with a fork, and using only enough to allow dry ingredients to be formed into a ball. Divide dough in half, and roll out each half into a pie-size circle. Chill crusts on cookie sheets, well wrapped in plastic wrap, for a few hours or overnight.

PIE FILLING:

12 'Winesap' apples
1/3 cup granulated sugar
1/2 teaspoon cinnamon
1/8 teaspoon nutmeg
1/8 teaspoon ground cloves
1 tablespoon fresh lemon juice
6 tablespoons melted butter
1/3 cup brown sugar
1 large tablespoon cornstarch
juice from baked apples

Preheat oven to 375° F. Peel, core, and dice apples. Mix with sugar, spices, lemon juice, and butter. Bake in a covered dish for 40 minutes. Remove from oven and set aside.

In a small saucepan, mix the brown sugar and cornstarch, and carefully pour in the juices from the baked apples. Stir over high heat until bubbly and thick. Pour this sauce over the baked apples and stir.

Line a 9-inch pie plate with one crust. Fill with apple mixture. Cover with top crust and crimp. Prick the top crust to make steam vents.

Bake at 450° F for 15 minutes, then lower heat to 350° F and bake for 35 minutes. Remove from oven when golden brown and bubbly. Cool and serve. ***Makes 6 to 8 servings.***

□□

This recipe and many others can be found in *Best Home Baking — Irresistible Recipes from America's Blue Ribbon Bakers,* by Polly Bannister and the editors of *The Old Farmer's Almanac* (Time-Life Books, 1998), part of *The Old Farmer's Almanac* Home Library Series. To order, call 800-277-8844.

WINNING RECIPES

in the 1998 RECIPE CONTEST

CHICKEN

First Prize

Mediterranean Chicken

6 boneless chicken breast halves, skin removed
1/4 cup ranch dressing
1 package (8 ounces) cream cheese, softened
1 package (3 ounces) sun-dried tomatoes, chopped, softened in boiling water, and drained
1/3 cup grated fresh Parmesan cheese
1/4 cup sliced, ripe pitted olives
1 clove garlic, minced
6 fresh basil leaves
1 cup ground pistachio nuts
1/2 cup Italian-style bread crumbs
lemon slices and additional fresh basil leaves, for garnish

Place chicken between two sheets of waxed paper and flatten to ¼-inch thickness with a meat mallet. Place chicken in a shallow dish and pour the ranch dressing over the pieces, turning to coat. Marinate for 1 hour.

Meanwhile, place cream cheese, tomatoes, Parmesan, olives, garlic, and basil in a food processor, and process until smooth. Chill for ½ hour. Remove chicken breasts from the marinade. Place 1½ tablespoons of cream-cheese filling in the center of each breast. Roll up and secure with toothpicks.

In a shallow bowl, mix the pistachio nuts and bread crumbs. Coat each stuffed breast with nut mixture. Place chicken, seam side down, in an ungreased 13x9-inch baking dish. Bake at 375° F for 45 minutes. **Makes 6 servings.**

Liz Barclay,
Annapolis, Maryland

Second Prize

Star-Spangled Chicken with Fireworks Salsa

SALSA:

1 each red, yellow, and green bell pepper
1 can (20 ounces) pineapple tidbits, well drained
1-1/2 teaspoon Chipotle chili puree or powder, to taste
1/2 small red onion, diced
1 tablespoon fresh lime juice
1 tablespoon melted jalapeño jelly, or to taste
1 to 2 teaspoons finely minced fresh cilantro leaves

Halve peppers, removing stems, seeds, and large ribs. Set aside half of each color. Dice remaining pepper halves and place in a nonreactive bowl with the remaining salsa ingredients. Stir well. Allow salsa to meld at room temperature for at least 1 hour before serving. Taste and adjust seasonings as desired.

Cut remaining pepper halves into strips and small star shapes for garnish; dice trimmings and add to salsa.

CHICKEN:

6 boneless chicken breast halves (6 to 8 ounces each), skin removed
2 tablespoons apricot jam
2 tablespoons mango chutney
1 cup mayonnaise
2 teaspoons Worcestershire sauce
1 tablespoon grainy mustard
2 tablespoons fresh lime or lemon juice

Place chicken breasts in a big resealable plastic bag. Whisk remaining ingredients together to make a marinade and pour over chicken. Seal bag and place in refrigerator for several hours or overnight, turning occasionally.

Heat barbecue cooker to glowing. Remove chicken from marinade; pour marinade into a small bowl. Spray grill with nonstick vegetable spray and place 4 to 6 inches from medium-hot coals. Put chicken on grill and cook, basting with marinade and turning occasionally, until chicken is cooked through. Allow about 6 to 8 minutes per side, until juices are no longer pink.

Place dollops of salsa on each serving plate and put a chicken breast half in the center. Garnish with the pepper stars. **Makes 6 servings.**

Diane Halferty,
Tucson, Arizona

Third Prize

Moroccan-Style Chicken Breasts with Spiced Couscous

CHICKEN:

2 cans (16 ounces each) Italian-style stewed tomatoes with juice
1 cup chopped onion
2 tablespoons chopped garlic
1-1/2 cups chopped, unpeeled, seeded zucchini
1/2 teaspoon salt
1/2 teaspoon coarsely cracked black pepper
1 tablespoon ground cinnamon
1 teaspoon ground ginger
1/4 cup honey
6 boneless chicken breast halves, skin removed

In a large, heavy casserole, mix all ingredients except the chicken breasts; stir to blend, then add the chicken breasts. Turn to coat. Cover and cook over medium-low heat until chicken is tender, about 45 minutes.

COUSCOUS:

2-1/4 cups chicken broth
1 teaspoon ground turmeric
1/2 cup chopped roasted red pepper (from a jar)
1 package (10 ounces) couscous
toasted sesame seeds, for garnish

About 15 minutes before serving, place broth, turmeric, and red pepper in a medium saucepan. Cover and bring to a boil. Remove from heat, stir in couscous, and let stand for 5 minutes.

To serve, spoon couscous onto a serving platter, arrange the chicken on top, and pour the sauce over the chicken. Sprinkle with sesame seeds to garnish, if desired.

Makes 6 servings.

Marilou Robinson,
Portland, Oregon

Special thanks to Sylvia Wright and Rich Roth for recipe judging and testing. – *Ed.*

Honorable Mention

Swiss-Crusted Molasses Mustard Chicken

1 tablespoon fresh lime juice
1 tablespoon mayonnaise
1 tablespoon Dijon mustard
1 tablespoon dark molasses
1/2 cup bread crumbs, seasoned
1/4 cup yellow cornmeal
1 teaspoon Old Bay seasoning
1/8 teaspoon ground white pepper
6 skinless chicken thighs
1 tablespoon canola oil
1/3 cup white wine
1/2 cup chunky salsa
6 slices Swiss cheese
lime slices, for garnish

In a bowl, combine lime juice, mayonnaise, mustard, and molasses. In another bowl, combine bread crumbs, cornmeal, chicken seasoning, and pepper. Dip chicken pieces in molasses mixture to coat both sides, then into crumb mixture. In a large skillet, heat the oil. Brown the chicken thighs evenly on both sides over medium heat, about 5 minutes per side.

Place thighs in a 10-inch casserole dish. Add the wine. Cover and bake at 350° F for 35 to 40 minutes, until tender. Top each piece with a tablespoon of salsa and a slice of cheese. Return to oven just long enough to melt the cheese. Serve immediately, spooning any sauce over the chicken. Garnish with lime slices. **Makes 6 servings.**

Karen Martis,
Merrillville, Indiana

ANNOUNCING *The* 1999 RECIPE CONTEST

Fruit Desserts

For 1999, cash prizes (first prize, $100; second prize, $75; third prize, $50) will be awarded for the best original recipes for fruit desserts (made from scratch). All entries become the property of Yankee Publishing Incorporated, which reserves all rights to the materials submitted. Winners will be announced in the 2000 edition of *The Old Farmer's Almanac.* Deadline is February 1, 1999. Please type all recipes. Address: Recipe Contest, *The Old Farmer's Almanac,* P.O. Box 520, Dublin, NH 03444; or send E-mail (subject: Fruit Desserts Contest) to almanac@yankeepub.com.

Winning Essays

in the 1998 ESSAY CONTEST

THE MOST USEFUL INVENTION OF THE 20TH CENTURY

Dear Readers: We received such a variety of responses to this contest that the judges, usually a decisive group, were overwhelmed, dazzled, and then ultimately stumped at the prospect of choosing only three winners. Instead, we are sending a small cash prize to each of the entrants listed below, all of whom had great ideas about the most useful invention of the 20th century.

– THE EDITORS

■ The **five-gallon plastic bucket** may well be the most useful thing you have. Put your cow's grain in it, sit on another one while she eats, and milk her into a third one.

– Ronald Curell, Mayville, Michigan

■ From lock picking to ejecting a stubborn computer disk, the **paper clip** has got to be the most useful invention. I have abused and misused them, making zipper pulls, button extenders, and hooks for reaching in nooks and crannies; cleaning fuzz from a keyboard; resetting my watch; and releasing air from an overinflated tire. I have even clipped papers together!

– Bonnie Meador, Scottsville, Kentucky

■ **Scotch tape.** My father always taped a dime to his bicycle frame so that if he ever got lost or had a flat tire on a bike ride, he could call us. I do the same today, except that I have to use a dime and a quarter.

– John Whittemore, Morganton, North Carolina

■ A notable percentage of today's scientists and astronauts were inspired by Gene Roddenberry's invention of **Star Trek.**

– Bill Niesslein, New Cumberland, West Virginia

■ **Teflon.** Its electrical and low-friction properties are outstanding. It can withstand temperatures exceeding 500° F (260° C). Teflon's nonstick reputation has not gone unnoticed by our nation's top political leaders. Truly bipartisan in nature, Teflon works equally well on both Democrats and Republicans.

– Andrew Burnett, Smithville, New Jersey

■ I can't say enough about **automatic transmissions.** But the thing I like the most is the **intermittent windshield wiper** when it's sprinklin' or spittin' rain.

– Jerry Fry, Freeman, Missouri

■ **Mr. Coffee.** This is one guy any woman would like to have lying around the house all day. He never complains or gets underfoot.

– Ruthanne Buchanan, Defuniak Springs, Florida

■ One small button overshadows all the others: the **mute button on the TV remote.** This small, insignificant button has saved marriages and opened communication between parents and children.

– Leroy Terry, Shreveport, Louisiana

■ **Ziploc bags.** They are not just for food. I use them for my sewing projects, coupons, small toys, photos, garden seeds, travel. I can (and do) live without a computer, but don't take away my Ziploc baggies.

– Kelly Jo Bickett, Malden, Illinois

■ **Television** put vaudeville, motion pictures, newsreels, musical comedy, and sports events into the nation's living rooms. In 1969, television showed us Neil Armstrong walking on the Moon.

– Barbara L. Sherman, Marion, Ohio

■ I don't like to admit it, but **plastic** is the most useful invention of the century. I am a Peace Corps volunteer living in Africa. In a place where function must always take precedence over form, a plastic tub for carrying water is preferable to a heavy steel or earthenware container.

– Michael Sterner, Dakar, Senegal

■ **Velcro.** No more buttons, pins, zippers, shoestrings. No more notebooks coming apart. Velcro holds the world together.

– Zella Wilson, Graceville, Florida

■ As a 75-year-old grandmother with seven children and 14 grandchildren, I feel the best things ever produced are **disposable diapers** and **sanitary napkins.** Having washed my share of both, I can tell you they freed up the women of this country from two miserable tasks.

– Honor Twomey, Hampden, Massachusetts

■ The handheld **potato peeler.** It can peel, slice, shave, and de-eye. In a lifetime of use, my only real concern is remembering not to throw out the peeler with the peelings.

– Martha Herp, Louisville, Kentucky

■ Hands down, the most useful invention of the 20th century is none other than the P-38 handy-dandy **portable can opener.** It's small enough to fit on a key chain or rides well in any pocket. One was enclosed with every C ration, for your dining pleasure.

– Chrystle White, Orlando, Florida

■ **Rock 'n' roll music** stands as the greatest discovery of this century. Elvis Presley, the king of rock 'n' roll, was to popular music what Babe Ruth was to baseball and Henry Ford to the automobile.

– Robert Ruane Jr., Binghamton, New York

■ All I have to do is mention **duct tape** and most of you will be nodding your head in agreement. At one time or another, many of the other "most useful inventions of the 20th century" have been repaired with duct tape. I bet there's even a roll or two lying around the offices of *The Old Farmer's Almanac.*

– Martin Zybura, Monroe, New York

[The duct tape's right here, along with a can of WD-40. – *Ed.*]

■ The **blow-dryer.** My husband uses mine for drying his deodorant, defrosting the freezer, thawing pipes, sealing contact paper to a surface, and curing a headache with a shot of warm air to the forehead. Pretty good for motorized air, huh?

– Barbara Poole, Lincoln, Nebraska

■ Freedom from girdles came in a package labeled **panty hose.** Figures softened and so did the dispositions of half the adult population. What could be more useful than that?

– Marilyn Fontana, Pittsfield, Massachusetts

■ The **Post-it note.** What makes this removable adhesive most valuable is its ability to remind me that things change. Even the things we hold most dear are only temporary, it tells me; cleave tight, but know when to let go.

– Karen Shaffer, State College, Pennsylvania

■ Maybe the most useful thing of all is the **OFF switch** on all the other inventions.

– Karl Beauregard, Warren, Rhode Island

ANNOUNCING
The 1999 ESSAY CONTEST

My Favorite 20th-Century Memory

Are you a survivor of the Hurricane of '38? Did you see Babe Ruth hit a home run, or did you watch Lindbergh's ticker-tape parade after he crossed the Atlantic? Was Dr. Benjamin Spock your pediatrician? If you were present at a great event or crossed paths with a notable personality, we'd like to hear about it. Send us a brief, personal recollection of your unique and memorable encounter with a great event or character of the last 100 years. Cash prizes (first prize, $100; second prize, $75; third prize, $50) will be awarded for the best original 200-word essay on this subject. All entries become the property of Yankee Publishing Incorporated, which reserves all rights to the materials submitted. Winners will be announced in the 2000 edition of *The Old Farmer's Almanac* and posted on our Web site at www.almanac.com. Deadline is February 1, 1999. Please type all essays. Address: Essay Contest, *The Old Farmer's Almanac*, P.O. Box 520, Dublin, NH 03444; or send E-mail (subject: Essay Contest) to almanac@yankeepub.com.

ANSWERS TO MR. SMITH'S MADDENING Mind-Manglers

from page 112.

1. 6 rugs with 6 tables each = 36 tables
36 tables with 6 creatures each = 216 creatures
36 tables + 216 creatures = 252 objects
252 objects with 6 legs each = 1,512 legs in the room

2. Mr. Willoughby sells the land for 90% of $8,000 = $7,200
Mrs. Hansen sells the land for 110% of $7,200 = $7,920
Result: Mr. Willoughby has lost $720 ($7,920 – $7,200)

3. 1 knife = 2 spoons
3 spoons = 1 knife and 1 fork
1 plate = 1 knife and 1 spoon
1 fork = 4 ounces
3 spoons = 1 knife and 1 fork
3 spoons = 2 spoons and 1 fork
1 fork = 1 spoon

Therefore:
Spoon = 4 ounces
Knife = 8 ounces
Plate = 12 ounces

4. If Waldo averaged 48 miles per hour, then 72 miles took him 1.5 hours (72 ÷ 48 = 1.5). To be on time for a 12:30 P.M. appointment, Waldo would have had to leave at 11:00 A.M. Because he was 10 minutes late, he must have left at 11:10 A.M.

5. Emily started with $17. You can solve this two ways:

a) Work backward:
$60 + $12 = $72
$72 ÷ 3 = $24
$24 + $10 = $34
$34 ÷ 2 = $17

b) Write an equation:
$3(2n - 10) - 12 = 60$
$6n - 30 - 12 = 60$
$6n - 42 = 60$
$6n = 102$
$n = 17$

6. . . . 6, 3, 2, 0
The digits are listed in alphabetical order.

7. Only the middle statement is true: ⅓ exceeds ¼ by 1/12; ⅓ of ¼ is 1/12.

8. 90 days!
January has 31 days that are multiples of 1.
February has 14 days that are multiples of 2.
March has 10 days that are multiples of 3.
April has 7 days that are multiples of 4.
May has 6 days that are multiples of 5.
June has 5 days that are multiples of 6.
July has 4 days that are multiples of 7.
August has 3 days that are multiples of 8.
September has 3 days that are multiples of 9.
October has 3 days that are multiples of 10.

November has 2 days that are multiples of 11.
December has 2 days that are multiples of 12.

9. Paul = 1 minute
John = 2 minutes
George = 5 minutes
Ringo = 10 minutes

Method:

Paul and John cross	=	2 minutes
Paul goes back	=	1 minute
George and Ringo cross	=	10 minutes
John goes back	=	2 minutes
Paul and John cross again	=	2 minutes
Total	=	17 minutes

10. Use a field of 100 acres.

First swipe:
60% of 100 acres = 60 acres
There are now 40 acres left.

Second swipe:
60% of 40 acres = 24 acres
There are now 16 acres left.

Third swipe:
60% of 16 acres = 9.6 acres
A total of 93.6 acres (60 + 24 + 9.6) of the original 100 will be harvested; therefore, 93.6% of the entire crop will be harvested by MASH after the third swipe!

Answers to "A Special Millennium Countdown Activity,"

from the 1998 Almanac, page 209.

Charades:
1. Quicksand
2. Almanac

Conundrums:
1. Because her son never sets.
2. Jonah, because the whale could not keep him down.
3. Johnny, 7 cents. Tommy, 5 cents.

Puzzles:
1. XL
2.

3	8	7
10	6	2
5	4	9

Anagrams:
1. Astronomers
2. Catalogues
3. Lawyers

Easter Sunday (1999-2003)

Christian churches that follow the Gregorian calendar (Eastern Orthodox churches follow the Julian calendar) celebrate Easter on the first Sunday after the full Moon that occurs on or just after the vernal equinox.

In	Easter will fall on
1999	April 4
2000	April 23
2001	April 15
2002	March 31
2003	April 20

Triskaidekaphobia

Here are a few conclusions on Friday the 13th:

Of the 14 possible configurations for the annual calendar (see any perpetual calendar), the occurrence of Friday the 13th is this:

- **6 of 14 years have one Friday the 13th.
6 of 14 years have two Fridays the 13th.
2 of 14 years have three Fridays the 13th.
There is no year without one Friday the 13th, and no year with more than three.**
- **There is only one Friday the 13th in 1999. The next year to have three Fridays the 13th is 2009.**
- **The reason we say "Fridays the 13th" is that no one can pronounce "Friday the 13ths."**

Table of Measures

Apothecaries'

1 scruple = 20 grains
1 dram = 3 scruples
1 ounce = 8 drams
1 pound = 12 ounces

Avoirdupois

1 ounce = 16 drams
1 pound = 16 ounces
1 hundredweight = 100 pounds
1 ton = 2,000 pounds
1 long ton = 2,240 pounds

Cubic Measure

1 cubic foot = 1,728 cubic inches
1 cubic yard = 27 cubic feet
1 cord = 128 cubic feet
1 U.S. liquid gallon = 4 quarts = 231 cubic inches
1 Imperial gallon = 1.20 U.S. gallons = 0.16 cubic feet
1 board foot = 144 cubic inches

Dry Measure

2 pints = 1 quart
4 quarts = 1 gallon
2 gallons = 1 peck
4 pecks = 1 bushel

Liquid Measure

4 gills = 1 pint
2 pints = 1 quart
4 quarts = 1 gallon
63 gallons = 1 hogshead
2 hogsheads = 1 pipe or butt
2 pipes = 1 tun

Linear Measure

1 foot = 12 inches
1 yard = 3 feet
1 rod = 5½ yards
1 mile = 320 rods = 1,760 yards = 5,280 feet
1 Int. nautical mile = 6,076.1155 feet
1 knot = 1 nautical mile per hour
1 furlong = ⅛ mile = 660 feet = 220 yards
1 league = 3 miles = 24 furlongs
1 fathom = 2 yards = 6 feet
1 chain = 100 links = 22 yards
1 link = 7.92 inches
1 hand = 4 inches
1 span = 9 inches

Square Measure

1 square foot = 144 square inches
1 square yard = 9 square feet
1 square rod = 30¼ square yards = 272¼ square feet
1 acre = 160 square rods = 43,560 square feet
1 square mile = 640 acres = 102,400 square rods
1 square rod = 625 square links
1 square chain = 16 square rods
1 acre = 10 square chains

Household Measures

120 drops of water = 1 teaspoon
60 drops thick fluid = 1 teaspoon
2 teaspoons = 1 dessertspoon
3 teaspoons = 1 tablespoon
16 tablespoons = 1 cup
2 cups = 1 pint
2 pints = 1 quart
4 quarts = 1 gallon
3 tablespoons flour = 1 ounce
2 tablespoons butter = 1 ounce
2 cups granulated sugar = 1 pound
3¾ cups confectioners' sugar = 1 pound
3½ cups wheat flour = 1 pound
5⅓ cups dry coffee = 1 pound
6½ cups dry tea = 1 pound
2 cups shortening = 1 pound
1 stick butter = ½ cup
2 cups cornmeal = 1 pound
2¾ cups brown sugar = 1 pound
2⅜ cups raisins = 1 pound
9 eggs = 1 pound
1 ounce yeast = 1 scant tablespoon

Metric

1 inch = 2.54 centimeters
1 centimeter = 0.39 inch
1 meter = 39.37 inches
1 yard = 0.914 meters
1 mile = 1,609.344 meters = 1.61 kilometers
1 kilometer = .62 mile
1 square inch = 6.45 square centimeters
1 square yard = 0.84 square meter
1 square mile = 2.59 square kilometers
1 square kilometer = 0.386 square mile
1 acre = 0.40 hectare
1 hectare = 2.47 acres
1 cubic yard = 0.76 cubic meter
1 cubic meter = 1.31 cubic yards
1 liter = 1.057 U.S. liquid quarts
1 U.S. liquid quart = 0.946 liter
1 U.S. liquid gallon = 3.78 liters
1 gram = 0.035 ounce
1 ounce = 28.349 grams
1 kilogram = 2.2 pounds
1 pound avoirdupois = 0.45 kilogram

Get Rid Of Canada Geese

GOOSE BE GONE™

Repel Geese And Ducks From Grass And Turf.

How Does It Work? Goose Be Gone™ is a completely save EPA approved taste aversion agent. The active ingredient is an incredibly bitter part of the concord grape. (methyl anthranilate) Geese and ducks have a strong aversion to this particular taste. When sprayed on grass, turf or plants the resulting taste is disgusting to geese and ducks but harmless to the vegetation. Birds give up and leave because their food source is now inedible.

How Is Goose Be Gone™ Applied? Spray on grass after diluting 1 gallon of concentrate with water. This will treat 1 acre of 2" tall grass. The height of the grass determines how much GBG you need. The taller the grass the more GBG you will need to treat an acre.

1/2 Gallon $50.00 plus $5.00 shipping.

1 Gallon $80.00 • 3 or more Gallons 70.00 each.
12 or more gallons $66.00 each. ©1998

Is It Safe? Yes.

Goose Be Gone™ is a food grade, biodegradable repellent regulated by EPA. It will not harm children or pets or the grasses and plants to which it is applied.

Is It Legal? Yes.

The use of this product complies with all government rules and regulations. It is legal to use against protected birds such as the Canada Goose.

Mail coupon with check, money order or credit card information to:

Shipping Charge UPS delivery: **Phone: (816) 221-3581**
Each 2 gallons add $12.00 One gallon add $8.00
For example 5 gallons 12+12+8=$32.00 total shipping

Rosedale Chemical
Department, GG8
PO Box 3042
Rosedale KS 66103

Steam Tractors Real Live Steam

©1998

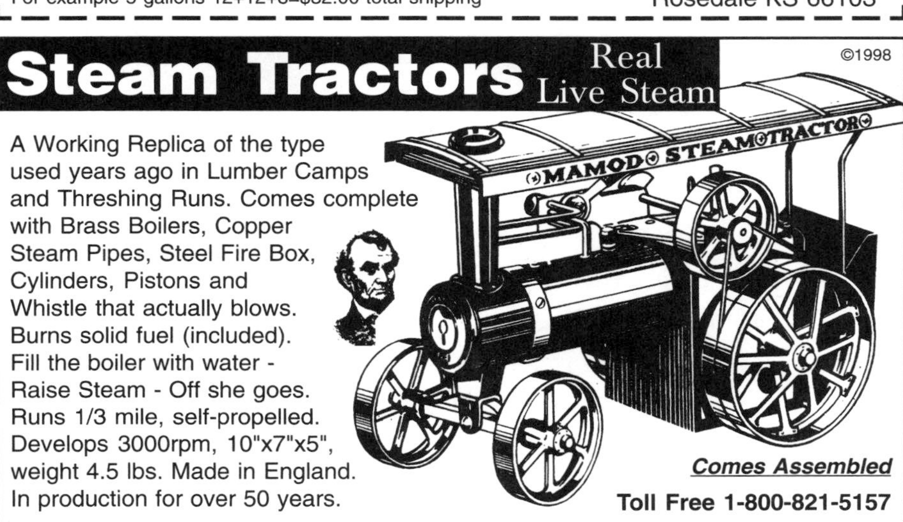

A Working Replica of the type used years ago in Lumber Camps and Threshing Runs. Comes complete with Brass Boilers, Copper Steam Pipes, Steel Fire Box, Cylinders, Pistons and Whistle that actually blows. Burns solid fuel (included). Fill the boiler with water - Raise Steam - Off she goes. Runs 1/3 mile, self-propelled. Develops 3000rpm, 10"x7"x5", weight 4.5 lbs. Made in England. In production for over 50 years.

Comes Assembled

Toll Free 1-800-821-5157

To order by mail: Send check/money order or credit card # and expiration date to:

Order Working Steam Tractor $140.00
Extra Solid Fuel $8.00 Per Box Of 20 Tabs.
Please add $5.00 shipping per order.

Satisfaction Guaranteed

DutchGuard, Dept. OFT
PO Box 411687
Kansas City MO 64141

Why Elvis Presley Carried His

and Nine Other Little-Known Items About "The King"

by Christine Schultz

Forty-five years ago, on the last day of July 1954, a young man named Elvis Presley stuttered and shook nervously as he prepared to go onstage for his first outdoor performance at Overton Park in Memphis, Tennessee. Just that month, he had cut a recording of "That's All Right, Mama" with Sun Records, and it had become his first hit. When he stepped out onstage and started to sing, the crowd went wild. He couldn't understand why and leaned over to ask his manager what was happening. "I'm not really sure," the manager told Elvis, "but every time you wiggle your left leg, they start to scream. Whatever it is, just don't stop." For the next 23 years, he didn't.

– UPI/Corbis-Bettmann

Elvis had launched a new kind of music, combining country, rock, and gospel. His name gained international recognition, but despite his popularity, there are still some amazing facts about Elvis that most people don't know.

(continued on page 188)

Own Utensils

Elvis in 1956, at age 21, the year he starred on The Ed Sullivan Show *and zoomed to national fame. His famous "gyrations"* (left) *often wore out the toes of his loafers.*

– UPI/Corbis-Bettmann

– UPI/Corbis-Bettmann

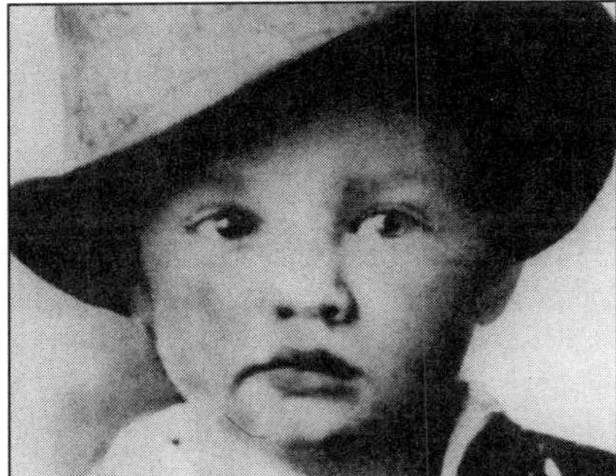

Elvis at age three.

1

Elvis was said to be lonely for the identical twin he lost at birth. The boy was stillborn a half hour before Elvis came into the world at 4:35 A.M. on January 8, 1935, at his parents' home in Tupelo, Mississippi. Mother Gladys rhymed the name of the twin with Elvis Aaron, calling him Jesse Garon, for their paternal grandfather.

2

Elvis never learned to read music, never composed any tunes, and never wrote any lyrics of his own. "He and Jerry Lee Lewis are the only important performers in rock and roll history who wrote none of their own material," says biographer Dave Marsh. Elvis learned everything by ear. His memory was photographic and encyclopedic. He impressed musicians at the Grand Ole Opry with his knowledge of trivia and memorized his lines in Hollywood movies without effort.

As a child, Elvis picked up a few pointers from the music director at his Pentecostal church, a man named Aaron Kennedy (Elvis's middle namesake), but that was the only boost he got. "When I was four or five," Elvis once said, "all I looked forward to were Sundays, when we all could go to church. That was the only singing training I ever had."

3

His first guitar was a cigar box with a hole cut in it and a string pulled across the hole. In elementary school, he bought a guitar for $5. When he turned ten, his mother took him to the store to buy him a better guitar for his birthday. But at that point, what Elvis wanted more than anything else was a gun or a bicycle. He threw a temper tantrum in front of the music store owner.

4

Like his father, Vernon Presley, Elvis was a natural blond. However, Elvis preferred the darker color of his mother's hair, so as a teenager he decided to darken his hair. He did it gradually over a three-year period. Once a month, Elvis used a hair-dye kit to touch up his hair, his eyebrows, and his famous sideburns. In fact, Elvis was so conscious about his looks that he had a minor adjustment to the bridge of his nose.

5

Elvis was a black belt in two styles of karate: Tae Kwon Do and Kang Rhee. He read an article about karate while he was in the army, stationed in Germany, and found an instructor nearby. He later went all the way to Paris to track down a respected Korean karate teacher. Back home in Memphis, he continued his training and eventually worked martial arts moves and clothing into his acting scenes. He preferred to be called by his karate name, The Tiger, but was more often referred to by the nickname actor Danny Thomas had given him: Dollface.

6

Elvis's pink Cadillac was originally blue. He bought the 1955 Cadillac

with white interior after receiving his first big earnings as an entertainer. He had it painted pink because pink had been one of his favorite colors since boyhood.

7

Elvis spawned a lipstick craze. Since Elvis admirers often wrote marriage proposals and messages of love on his Cadillac and on the buildings where he performed, Elvis came out with autographed lipstick shades of "hound-dog orange," "cruel red," "tender pink," and "tutti-frutti red." His ads said, "Always keep me on your lips," and the girls apparently did, because sales were estimated at more than $20 million a year.

8

Elvis had a food obsession that some called an eating "hobby." A typical sitting was said to have included eight cheeseburgers; two bacon, lettuce, and tomato sandwiches; and three milk shakes. At Graceland, his cooks were on call 24 hours a day. One of his favorite snacks was a grilled peanut-butter-and-banana sandwich.

According to his cousin, when Elvis went to a restaurant, he brought his own spoon, knife, and fork, a habit he had developed as a child even when he ate at relatives' homes. He was also compulsive about brushing his teeth after every meal.

9

Elvis was a sleepwalker and insomniac. When he was young, his mother took the inside knob off his bedroom door at night so that he wouldn't wander off and hurt himself.

10

Elvis dabbled in numerology and was also somewhat superstitious. If a black cat crossed the road ahead of his car, he would search for another route, even if it took him miles out of the way. He was careful always to dress in the same order: first the right sleeve, then the right pant leg, right sock, and right shoe, before dressing his left side. His cousin once said, "Elvis was superstitious to the point of being suspicious of anyone who wasn't superstitious." □□

Elvis loved his 1955 Cadillac (now on display across from Graceland, in Memphis).

– Michael Ochs Archives/Venice, CA

What was it really like to be sent to "the Rock," the harshest and most escapeproof prison in the country? Isolation, silence, boredom — and the torture of hearing a woman's laughter drifting across San Francisco Bay.

It's not as dim as you'd think inside. Daylight comes in from high windows. The floor of the main drag they call "Broadway" gleams so you can almost see your reflection. The cell bars shine — 336 cells, not counting the 42 solitary confinement and isolation cells in D-block. At the end of each cell block is a place for guards, one for every three prisoners. Electronic gates guard the cell blocks; barbed-wire fences ring the whole place; beyond are rocks, a lot of cold water called San Francisco Bay, and a mile and a half away, the hills of San Francisco. From the exercise yard, you get a glimpse of clouds floating by or the Golden Gate Bridge.

Your five-by-nine cell has a narrow bed, a toilet, a sink, a table, and a single bare bulb that seems to highlight every pimple in the ugly green walls. All the cell doors slam shut for the night at 5:30 P.M. Lights-out isn't until 9:30 P.M. You might read a letter — censored, of course, of anything remotely criminal, violent, sexual, or even newsworthy. You probably think about ways to escape and what you'd do first if you got out. Or you just sit and wait.

Once the lights are out, it's quiet, but you can hear bodies turning in their beds. Someone lights a cigarette. From far away, a woman's laughter — a punishment, that sound — drifts on a summer breeze from the St. Francis Yacht Club across the Bay.

You could be anybody. You could be Robert Stroud (a.k.a. "the Birdman"), who murdered a man; or Alvin "Creepy" Karpis,

"Alcatraz Was Never

by Jamie Kageleiry

who kidnapped someone and killed a cop; or Floyd Hamilton, Bonnie and Clyde's driver; or a "fish" — that's a new guy. What you did to deserve this was probably something big. You were a "public enemy," a famous criminal

Alcatraz opened as a federal prison in 1933. Among the public enemies sent here was Al Capone, who arrived by tugboat *(above)* in August of 1934.

like Al Capone or the likable George "Machine Gun" Kelly, and J. Edgar Hoover was looking to make an example of you. Maybe you did rob a bank or kill a man, but you ended up on Alcatraz for only one reason, the same as everybody else: You didn't follow the rules at another federal pen.

But it doesn't matter who you are, because the biggest thing identifying you is this: You're inside Alcatraz, the harshest and most escapeproof prison in the history of the United States penal system. *(continued)*

Who Was the Birdman of Alcatraz?

The Birdman, title character in Alcatraz's most famous film, was a Hollywood fabrication on several accounts. For one, convict Robert Stroud was nothing like the gentle Burt Lancaster but rather a loose cannon, a certifiable psychotic known for his meanness. It angered the guards to see him portrayed as he was in the film. But the biggest thing was that Stroud never kept birds at Alcatraz — he wasn't allowed to. Stroud kept his birds at Leavenworth — the prison he occupied before being sent on to Alcatraz. But "Birdman of Leavenworth" just doesn't sound the same, does it?

Robert Stroud, "the Birdman" of Alcatraz.

No Good for Nobody"

– Alcatraz photos in this article: Golden Gate National Recreation Area, Don Denevi Collection

Above: James A. Johnston *(left)*, Alcatraz's tough first warden; and Frank Heaney *(right)*, the prison's youngest guard, in 1946. Heaney still visits "the Rock" as guest author at the island's bookstore.

Top row: "Machine Gun" Kelly *(left)* and Alvin "Creepy" Karpis were among the gangsters at Alcatraz. Middle row: Brothers Clarence *(left)* and John Anglin, ringleaders with Frank Morris *(at right)* of the 1962 escape attempt.

At 6:30 the next morning, you hear a loud clang and you're up. You have 20 minutes to brush your teeth, make your bed, get dressed, and march single file down Broadway to the dining hall, where, after the shriek of a whistle and a body count, you all sit down at once. You have 20 minutes to eat your breakfast, and you'd better eat all of it or you're sent to the "hole" — that's solitary. Then another whistle blows, and you all stand up in the same instant and file out — to work, if you're lucky, or back to your cell.

It's another day at Alcatraz. You will have many more to come. Because you ain't leaving here, they like to say, unless you're dead. And even corpses leave in handcuffs and shackles.

Alcatraz sits on a 22-acre island (called "la Isla de los Alcatraces," or Isle of the Pelicans) in the middle of San Francisco Bay. The island is rocky and has no fresh water. The structure that became Alcatraz Federal Prison was completed 87 years ago in 1912. Before that, during the Gold Rush, the island was a fortress guarding ships in San Francisco Bay. During the Civil War and after, it was a makeshift military prison.

By 1933 the military didn't need Alcatraz anymore, but FBI Director Hoover did. For 29 years, until the last prisoner, #1576, filed out in 1963, Alcatraz's 336 cells were filled with America's most incorrigible convicts.

Life here was tough. There was no TV, no radio, no newspapers, few magazines, no place to buy cigarettes or candy. Until the early forties, there was a "no talk" rule among prisoners. Showers were allowed twice a week, and shaving was mandatory. Even if you were a model prisoner, visitors were rarely allowed, and monitored conversations (in English only) were held through glass. Once Al Capone's mother came to visit him but kept setting off the alarms in the metal detector. An officer's wife took her to a dressing room to search her and discovered that Mrs. Capone's corset was full of metal hooks. Mortified, she exploded in a volley of Italian when she reached the visiting area, which was against the rules. The whole visit was such a disaster that she never came back to see her son.

The library was stocked with 15,000 books, which prisoners could request from a catalog in their cells; Zane Grey and Jack London were popular, as was Culbertson's *Beginner's Book of Bridge*.

An unarmed guard patrols "Broadway," the nickname prisoners gave the busiest hallway in the cell house.

Prisoners considered work a privilege. You could sweep the cell house; "yardbirds" cleaned up the exercise yard. You'd wait for an opening in the "industries" — the prison enterprises that produced uniforms or made brushes. The best job, library orderly, went to the long-term inmates. Ultimately, work

Voices of Alcatraz

"I never saw a naked man yet who could maintain any sort of dignity."

– James Johnston, Alcatraz's first warden, on the requisite strip search of new prisoners

"As far as I could tell, he [Machine Gun Kelly] was one of the most stable prisoners on the island. He wasn't like a lot of them who always blamed someone else. He wasn't bitter about things and recognized it was his own fault that he was on Alcatraz."

– Frank Heaney, Alcatraz's youngest guard

"The 'no talk' rule is the hardest thing in Alcatraz life. It's the toughest pen I've ever seen. The hopelessness of it gets to you."

– parolee William Ambrose, to the San Francisco Chronicle

"Why lock your doors on Alcatraz?"

– Jolene Babyak, daughter of an associate warden. In her book Eyewitness on Alcatraz, *she described her island childhood as "delightful"*

"Well, at first the old foghorns would drive you crazy. But you got used to 'em. There was a lot to despise about the place. But I really hated those damn birds."

– former convict Nathan Glenn Williams

or no work, it was all degrees of boredom.

D-block held isolation cells (which had bars like conventional cells, but except for a ten-minute shower once a week, the prisoners weren't allowed to leave them) as well as six cells for solitary confinement. Solitary was dark and silent — the doors were solid steel. The maximum stay in a cell like this was supposed to be 19 days, but there are stories about men who served years here and lost their minds. Some were here for refusing to finish their meals, or for hitting a guard, or for speaking to each other before the "no talk" rule was rescinded.

Jim Quillen served time in the "Hole" for an attempted escape. "There was nothing in the cell except a cold metal bed frame, a toilet, a sink, and you," he said years later. "There was total silence because of the soundproof door. If not for the interruption of meals, it would be easy to confuse night and day. . . . It was cold, because of the limited clothing you were allowed. Worse than being cold, though, was the feeling of isolation from the world. Being unable to see or hear is a very awesome experience. I invented a game simply to retain my sanity. I would tear a button from my coveralls, then fling it into the air, turn around in circles several times, and with my eyes closed get on the floor on my hands and knees and search for the button. I would repeat the entire routine over and over until I was exhausted or my knees were so sore, I could not continue."

Inmates in the recreation yard playing cards. The only "card" game allowed was bridge, using dominoes rather than cards. Cards would wear out too fast or blow away, and the cellulose coating could be scraped off to make an explosive.

Quillen, Alcatraz's youngest prisoner, served his 19 days and went back to the main prison. Working in the kitchen one day in the early 1950s, he got to talking to the youngest guard at the prison, Frank Heaney. It turned out that Quillen and Heaney had grown up a block apart in Berkeley, but after that, their paths in life had diverged. Though it took Jim Quillen a few decades longer, he *did* turn his life around. Today he and Heaney occasionally visit as guest authors at Alcatraz.

As a guard, Heaney lived in bachelor quarters in a converted military chapel. He paid $10 a month for his room, which included getting his laundry done. Guards could play billiards, bowl, dance, or play cards. They could go into San Francisco on the boat *The Warden Johnston*. The wardens' and guards' families lived in little houses on the island. There was a playground, places for fishing and crabbing, and flowers in abundance. The kids commuted to school in San Francisco. Women and children could not have contact with prisoners. Many spoke about how safe they felt: Criminals from the mainland weren't about to try burglarizing anyone on Alcatraz, and the prison itself was famously "escapeproof."

But was it? There's no proof that anyone ever made it to freedom, but a few came close. Alcatraz's most fabled escape attempt was in June of 1962. After months of preparation, three inmates — Frank Lee Morris and brothers John and Clarence Anglin — placed dummy heads in their beds, sawed through vents with stolen tools, and escaped into the utility shaft. From there they went to the roof, cutting more bars in a vent there. They climbed down a drainpipe and made it to the water, where they made a raft from stolen raincoats. Personal items were later found floating in the water, but no bodies ever surfaced. It's part of Alcatraz legend that Morris and the Anglins may still be out there somewhere. *(continued on page 198)*

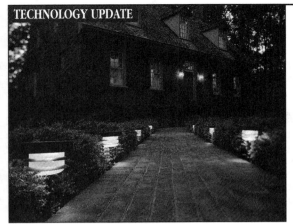

By 1962 it had become clear that America's super prison was more expensive than any other federal prison, and it was in need of massive repairs. Attorney General Robert Kennedy ordered it closed.

On March 21, 1963, Alcatraz's cell doors — the ones that had made Americans feel safer in their beds at night for 29 years — slammed shut for the last time. This time, though, they slammed behind the convicts. The last 27 prisoners marched single file down Broadway in shackles and leg irons on their way to other prisons. Frank Weatherman, prisoner #1576, was the last to get on the boat to San Francisco. Heading down the gangplank, he turned to the guys from the newspapers and said, "All of us are glad to get off. Alcatraz was never no good for nobody."

The last prisoners filed out of Alcatraz as it closed in 1963.

Alcatraz in the Movies

As soon as it opened, Alcatraz became the subject of intrigue and speculation, perhaps because it was always shut up tight against the media. Close to a dozen movies have been based on "the Rock," including:

- ***Alcatraz Island*, 1937**
- ***King of Alcatraz*, 1938**
- ***Seven Miles from Alcatraz*, 1942**
- ***Birdman of Alcatraz*, 1962**
- ***The Enforcer*, 1974**
- ***Escape from Alcatraz*, 1979**
- ***Murder in the First*, 1994**
- ***The Rock*, 1996**

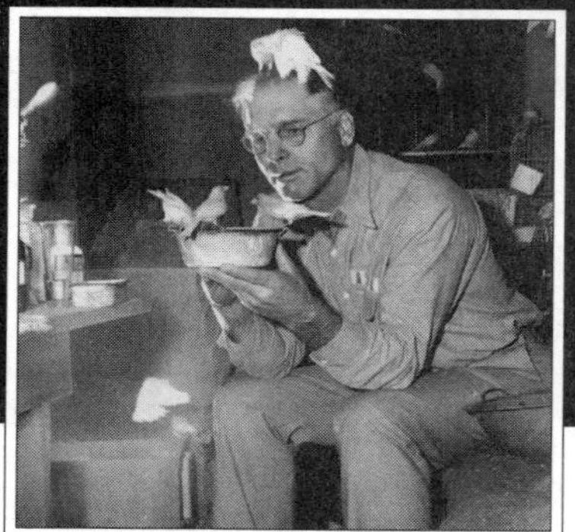

– Photofest

Burt Lancaster as prisoner Stroud in *Birdman of Alcatraz*.

Now part of the Golden Gate National Recreation Area, Alcatraz Island is managed by the National Park Service. For visitor information, contact Golden Gate National Recreation Area, Fort Mason, Building 201, San Francisco, CA 94123; 415-556-0560. Alcatraz is also accessible via the World Wide Web at www.nps.gov/alcatraz. For ferry reservations, call the Blue and Gold Line, 415-705-5555. □□

UNEXPECTED USES FOR HOUSEHOLD ITEMS

SALT

■ **Rub salt on fruit stains while still wet, then put item in the wash.**

■ For mildew spots, rub in some buttermilk and salt, and let item dry in the sun.

■ **If you spill wine or fruit juice on your tablecloth, pour salt on the spot at once to absorb the stain.**

■ Apply a paste of salt and olive oil to ugly heat rings on your table. Let sit for about an hour, and then wipe off with a soft cloth.

■ **To catch a wild bird easily, first sprinkle some salt on its tail.**

■ Sprinkle salt on a piece of paper and run your sticky iron over it a few times while the iron is hot. You should notice a big improvement next time you use the iron.

■ **To restore some of the color to faded fabric, soak it in a strong solution of salt and water.**

■ You can get rid of an evil spell by throwing a pinch of salt over your left shoulder.

■ **Mix a tablespoon of salt into the water of a vase of cut flowers to keep them fresh longer.**

VINEGAR

■ Bring a solution of 1 cup vinegar and 4 tablespoons baking soda to a boil in teapots and coffeepots to rid them of mineral deposits.

■ **A solution of vinegar and baking soda will easily remove cooking oil from your stovetop.**

■ Clean the filter on your humidifier by removing it and soaking it in a pan of white vinegar until all the sediment is off.

■ **Vinegar naturally breaks down uric acid and soapy residue, leaving baby clothes and diapers soft and fresh. Add a cup of vinegar to each load during the rinse cycle.**

■ Saturate a cloth with vinegar and sprinkle with baking soda, then use it to clean fiberglass tubs and showers. Rinse well and rub dry for a spotless shine.

■ **To remove chewing gum, rub it with full-strength vinegar.**

■ For a clean oven, combine vinegar and baking soda, then scrub.

■ **Soak paint stains in hot vinegar to remove them.**

BAKING SODA

■ Add baking soda to your bath water to relieve sunburned or itchy skin.

■ **Make a paste of baking soda and water, and apply to a burn or an insect bite for relief.**

■ Clean your refrigerator with a solution of 1 teaspoon baking soda to 1 quart of warm water.

■ **Pour a cup of baking soda into the opening of your clogged drain and then add a cup of hot vinegar. After a few minutes, flush the drain with a quart of boiling water.**

■ To remove perspiration stains, make a thick paste of baking soda and water. Rub paste into the stain, let sit for an hour, and launder as usual.

■ **If you crave sweets, rinse your mouth with 1 teaspoon baking soda dissolved in a glass of warm water. Don't swallow the mixture; spit it out. Your craving should disappear at once.**

■ Tough meat can be tenderized by rubbing it with baking soda. Let stand for several hours before rinsing and cooking. □ □

Animal Terminology

Animal	Male	Female	Young
Ant	Male-ant (reproductive)	Queen (reproductive), worker (nonreproductive)	Antling
Antelope	Ram	Ewe	Calf, fawn, kid, yearling
Ass	Jack, jackass	Jenny	Foal
Bear	Boar, he-bear	Sow, she-bear	Cub
Beaver	Boar	Sow	Kit, kitten
Bee	Drone	Queen or queen bee, worker (nonreproductive)	Larva
Buffalo	Bull	Cow	Calf, yearling, spike-bull
Camel	Bull	Cow	Calf, colt
Caribou	Bull, stag, hart	Cow, doe	Calf, fawn
Cat	Tom, tomcat, gib, gibcat, boarcat, ramcat	Tabby, grimalkin, malkin, pussy, queen	Kitten, kit, kitling, kitty, pussy
Cattle	Bull	Cow	Calf, stot, yearling, bullcalf heifer
Chicken	Rooster, cock, stag, chanticleer	Hen, partlet, biddy	Chick, chicken, poult, cockerel, pullet
Deer	Buck, stag	Doe	Fawn
Dog	Dog	Bitch	Whelp
Duck	Drake, stag	Duck	Duckling, flapper
Elephant	Bull	Cow	Calf
Fox	Dog	Vixen	Kit, pup, cub
Giraffe	Bull	Cow	Calf
Goat	Buck, billy, billie, billie-goat, he-goat	She-goat, nanny, nannie, nannie-goat	Kid
Goose	Gander, stag	Goose, dame	Gosling
Horse	Stallion, stag, horse, stud	Mare, dam	Colt, foal, stot, stag, filly, hog-colt, hogget
Kangaroo	Buck	Doe	Joey
Leopard	Leopard	Leopardess	Cub
Lion	Lion, tom	Lioness, she-lion	Shelp, cub, lionet
Moose	Bull	Cow	Calf
Partridge	Cock	Hen	Cheeper
Quail	Cock	Hen	Cheeper, chick, squealer
Reindeer	Buck	Doe	Fawn
Seal	Bull	Cow	Whelp, pup, cub, bachelor
Sheep	Buck, ram, male-sheep, mutton	Ewe, dam	Lamb, lambkin, shearling, yearling, cosset, hog
Swan	Cob	Pen	Cygnet
Swine	Boar	Sow	Shoat, trotter, pig, piglet, farrow, suckling
Termite	King	Queen	Nymph
Walrus	Bull	Cow	Cub
Whale	Bull	Cow	Calf
Zebra	Stallion	Mare	Colt, foal

Collective
Colony, nest, army, state, swarm
Herd
Pace, drove, herd
Sleuth, sloth
Family, colony
Swarm, grist, cluster, nest, hive, erst
Troop, herd, gang
Flock, train, caravan
Herd
Clowder, clutter (kindle or kendle of kittens)
Drove, herd
Flock, run, brood, clutch, peep
Herd, leash
Pack (cry or mute of hounds, leash of greyhounds)
Brace, team, paddling, raft, bed, flock, flight
Herd
Leash, skulk, cloud, troop
Herd, corps, troop
Tribe, trip, flock, herd
Flock (on land), gaggle, skein (in flight), gaggle or plump (on water)
Haras, stable, remuda, herd, string, field, set, pair, team
Mob, troop, herd
Leap
Pride, troop, flock, sawt, souse
Herd
Covey
Bevy, covey
Herd
Pod, herd, trip, rookery, harem
Flock, drove, hirsel, trip, pack
Herd, team, bank, wege, bevy
Drift, sounder, herd, trip (litter of pigs)
Colony, nest, swarm, brood
Pod, herd
Gam, pod, school, herd
Herd

More Animal Collectives

army of caterpillars, frogs
bale of turtles
band of gorillas
bed of clams, oysters
brood of jellyfish
business of flies
cartload of monkeys
cast of hawks
cete of badgers
charm of goldfinches
chatter of budgerigars
cloud of gnats, flies, grasshoppers, locusts
colony of penguins
congregation of plovers
convocation of eagles
crash of rhinoceri
descent of woodpeckers
dole of turtles
down of hares
dray of squirrels
dule of turtle doves
exaltation of larks
family of sardines
flight of birds
flock of lice
gang of elks
hatch of flies
horde of gnats
host of sparrows
hover of trout
husk of hares
knab of toads
knot of toads, snakes
murder of crows
murmuration of starlings
mustering of storks
nest of vipers
nest or nide of pheasants
pack of weasels
pladge of wasps
plague of locusts
scattering of herons
sedge or siege of cranes
smuck of jellyfish
span of mules
spring of teals
steam of minnows
tittering of magpies
troop of monkeys
troubling of goldfish
volery of birds
watch of nightingales
wing of plovers
yoke of oxen

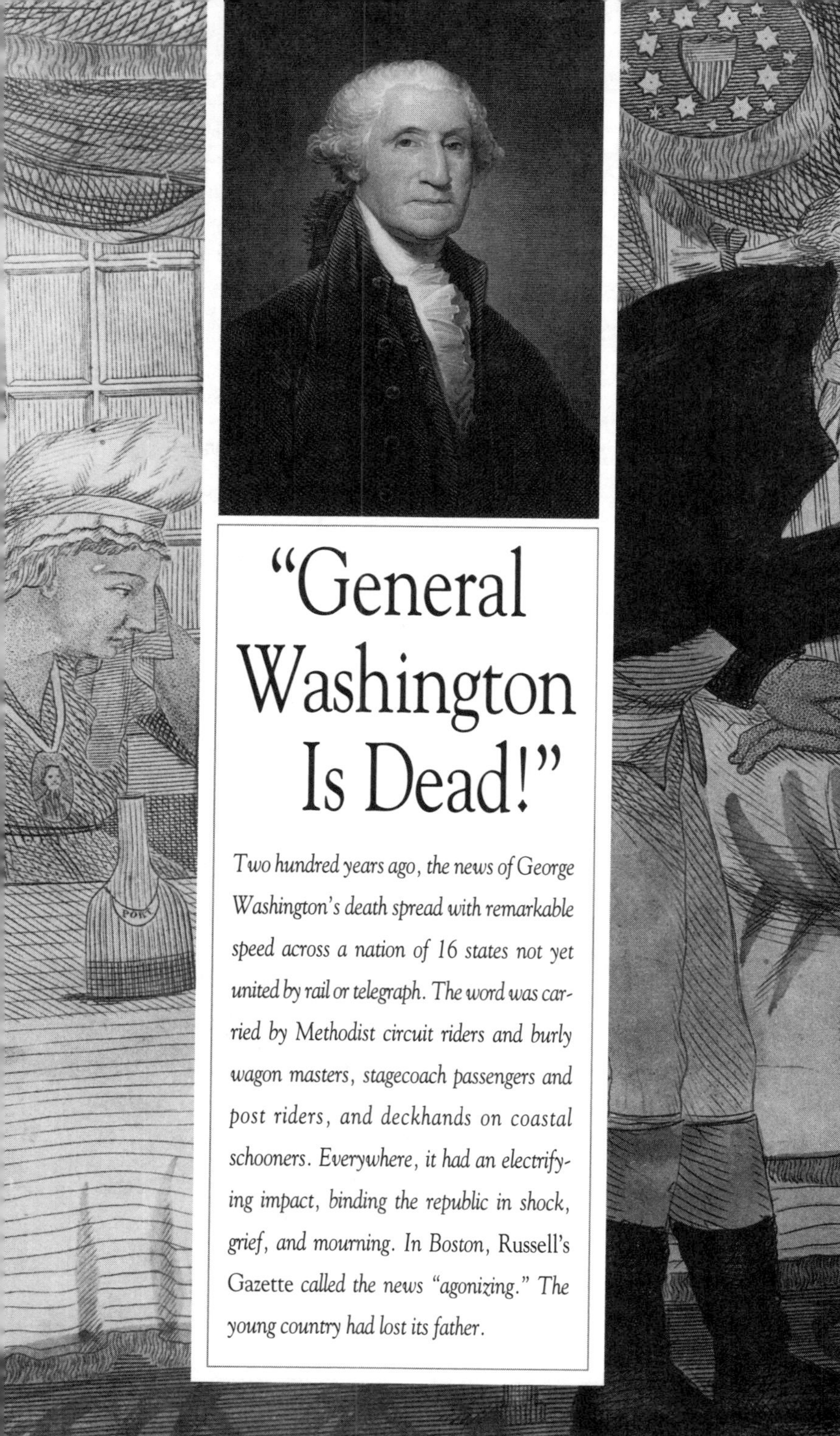

"General Washington Is Dead!"

Two hundred years ago, the news of George Washington's death spread with remarkable speed across a nation of 16 states not yet united by rail or telegraph. The word was carried by Methodist circuit riders and burly wagon masters, stagecoach passengers and post riders, and deckhands on coastal schooners. Everywhere, it had an electrifying impact, binding the republic in shock, grief, and mourning. In Boston, Russell's Gazette *called the news "agonizing." The young country had lost its father.*

– The Mount Vernon Ladies' Association

George Washington died at Mount Vernon, at the age of 67, on Saturday, December 14, 1799, at 10:20 in the evening. According to his secretary's letter to Congress, written the following day, the former president's illness was short, and the cause of his death was "an inflammatory sore throat, which proceeded from a cold of which he made but little complaint Friday." Historians now believe that it was either a raging pneumonia or a strep infection.

The general's illness was so brief that the news of his passing reached Congress, which was meeting in Philadelphia, before the legislators even learned that the former president had been sick. On December 18, a passenger jumped from a stagecoach and relayed the news to Congressman John Marshall. Visibly moved, Marshall reported to his colleagues that this "distressing intelligence is not certain." Official word arrived the next day. "Our Washington," as Marshall called him, was gone. By then, the general was already entombed.

Washington had been placed in a vault at Mount Vernon in the mid-afternoon of December 17. The ceremony became the template for memorial services that absorbed the nation over the next two months. Alexandria, Virginia's, military establishment provided the honor guard of horse and foot, arms reversed. A small band, with drums muffled, played the dirge. The general's riderless horse was armed with saddle holsters and pistols; his coffin was borne by young officers from the Virginia militia.

Washington's tomb at Mount Vernon, where he was buried three days after his death.

As the brief Anglican and Masonic burial services were conducted at the tomb and a short eulogy was delivered by Washington's pastor, the booming salute of 11 artillery

by Taylor Sanders

pieces on shore answered the sharp crack of minute guns firing from a rocking schooner out on the gray Potomac River. With each salvo, a Masonic banner fluttered in the breeze: "Washington in glory; America in tears."

On January 6, President John Adams issued an official proclamation urging Americans to gather on Washington's birthday, February 22, "publickly to testify their grief" with "suitable Eulogies, Orations, and Discourses, or by Public Prayers." During the six-week mourning period, well over 300 eulogies were delivered in nearly 200 hamlets, towns, and cities — Federalist Massachusetts alone held more than 100 memorial services in some 60 places. Speakers from Natchez to New Haven declared Washington "the American Moses" and held his example up proudly against such lesser men as Cromwell, Napoleon, Caesar, and Alexander the Great.

Lexington, Kentucky

It usually took from three to four weeks for travelers to cover the 650 miles from Philadelphia to Kentucky. Perhaps the news of Washington's death finally arrived in Lexington the third week in January with the "handsome assortment," as reported in the local *Gazette*, of trade goods, including velvet, coarse muslin, books, Bibles, screws, saws, Cuban sugar, and rifles. On January 21, the *Gazette* also reported that the town trustees had voted to "join the procession on Saturday next from respect of the Revolutionary hero, George Washington, Commander-in-Chief of the Revolutionary Army of the United States, who led his country to Independence and then resumed his station as a private citizen in 1783."

Washington was revered for his wartime leadership. Here, Cornwallis surrenders at Yorktown, 1781.

The theme of Washington, the American Cincinnatus, who had returned to the plow after saving the republic, was an important one throughout the mourning period, and the Society of the Cincinnati, an organization of Washington's fellow Continental officers, organized numerous memorial services.

By March 6, the local paper published Washington's last testament. In October, shops were selling copies of his will printed on white silk, alongside Dr. Gann's Anti-Bilious Pills and Hamilton's Grand Restorative for Dissipated Pleasures and Immoderate Use of Tea.

Lexington, Virginia

Back across the Appalachians in Lexington, Virginia, local people felt an unusual connection with Washington. A few years prior to his death, Washington endowed the struggling local college with the equivalent of $50,000 of canal stock, among the largest bequests to any college in the early republic. The school, Liberty Hall, was renamed Washington Academy in his honor. Captain William Lyle, veteran of the decisive battle of Guilford Courthouse in North Carolina, called together the local trustees of the college and began planning a memorial service to take place on Washington's birthday, February 22, 1800, already a holiday at the school.

On February 22, a procession of stu-

A view of Washington Academy, a school endowed by the general with a gift of $50,000 in canal stock.

dents, faculty, trustees, veterans, and "a respectable number of citizens" slowly moved from the campus to the courthouse, where the college's rector delivered a fitting eulogy. The pragmatic Scotch-Irish trustees, who viewed Washington's death as the "most distressing circumstance that ever befel the U. States" and who deeply felt the "loss of our common parent," met afterward and voted to use their anticipated benefaction, recently recorded in Washington's will, to make repairs at the college, to buy new library books, and to pay off its £500 debt.

Philadelphians marched on High Street to mourn Washington, December 26, 1799.

Philadelphia

Philadelphians, who were enjoying their final months as citizens of the nation's capital, would not be denied a state funeral — even if they had no corpse. They settled for a spectacular mock funeral service, held the day after Christmas. It was a magnified replica of the simpler Mount Vernon service, remembered especially for Congressman Henry "Light Horse Harry" Lee's famous "First in war, first in peace, and first in the hearts of his countrymen . . ." speech that included the oft-repeated theme that the "purity" of Washington's "private character gave effulgence to his public virtues."

For the next two months, as the nation mourned, posted sentries in Philadelphia guarded an empty bier. On January 8, 1800, a writer in the Pennsylvania *Gazette* summed up a loss he shared with his fellow citizens: "When Washington lived we had one common mind — one common head — one common heart — we were united — we were safe."

New York City

New Yorkers read of Washington's death in city newspapers on December 21. Black-bordered headlines announced "Columbia Mourns," and grim skulls and crossbones bracketed the text. Washington, one news sheet noted, had been the "perfect model of all that is *virtuous, noble, great, and dignified* in man." New York selected the last day of the year for its solemnities and tapped Gouverneur Morris as the principle eulogist. His theme was Washington's wisdom and his "judgement" that "was always clear because his mind was pure." A huge crowd listened in "extacy" and burst into applause at its end.

Earlier that same week, the managers of the city's Park Theater organized a striking

New York City (shown early 1800s) offered eulogies and tableaux to lament the loss.

tableau based on a popular illustration, "An America Lamenting Her Loss." As the curtain rose, an overflow audience (including women "covered with badges of mourning") discovered a Greek tomb, a portrait of the general, and a hero's crown of oak above a sword, shield, helmet, and national flag. An American eagle wept streams of blood and hoisted in its beak a scroll announcing "A Nation's Tears."

Boston

Word of Washington's death began to spread in Federalist Boston on Christmas Eve, three days after the news hit New York City. Because of their political leanings, Revolutionary heritage, and Washington's role in driving the British out of the city in 1776, Bostonians felt a special bond with the dead Virginian. Their celebration, perhaps more so than any other, revealed the general's power — in death as in life — to unify and inspire the public.

On January 9, businesses closed throughout the city, ships in the harbor flew flags at half-staff, guns barked, and bells tolled to honor the "memory of the great, the good, and beloved Washington." The crowd — 6,000 men, women, and children wearing mourning ribbons and bands — gathered at the new State House. Precisely at noon, they became a common unit, marching six abreast. The procession began with schoolboys and their teachers, followed by a multitude of local bodies that ranged from militia companies and Masons to physicians, lawyers, clergy, and mechanics, with "not enumerated" citizens bringing up the rear.

With silent dignity, the mourners began to walk through the narrow brick streets, ending at the Old South Meeting House, where all the various elements took designated places and listened to George Richards Minot's eulogy. A local paper noted, "The assemblage of all ranks in society, from venerable age to lisping infancy, to pay tribute to the virtues and services of Washington, was inexpressibly interesting."

Some speakers could not let pass unnoticed that the news of the national savior's death had arrived during the Christmas season. By the second week of February, with the tide of hero worship rising all about them, some New Englanders had second thoughts about an unrepublican lurch toward untempered pride and sanctification. Congregationalists from Connecticut to Rhode Island cautioned against transforming even so virtuous a man into a saint!

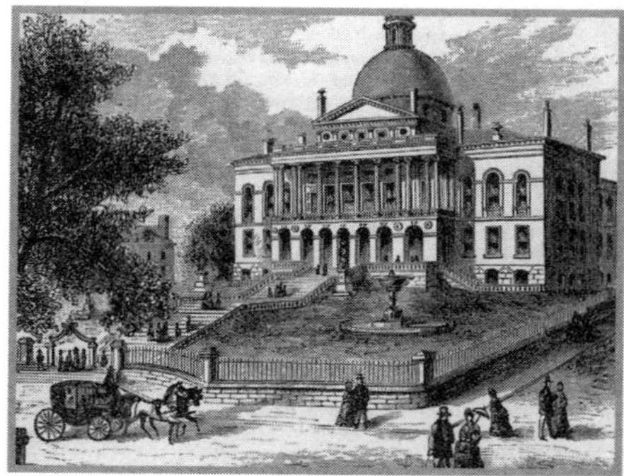

Thousands of Boston mourners gathered at the State House to march in honor of their lost hero.

Abigail Adams, with her usual eloquent common sense, brought the whole matter firmly back to earth: "Simple truth is his best, his greatest eulogy. She alone can render his fame immortal."

Europe

Praise did not stop at the nation's shores. Within two weeks of the great Boston event and at about the same time it reached Lexington, Kentucky, the news spread to England on ships like the *Active*, home at last from Virginia "in a very leaky state" after a stormy passage.

On January 25, the phlegmatic London *Times* briefly reported Washington's death, including the "remarkable circumstance, which redounds to his eternal honour, that while President . . . he never appointed one of his own relations to any office of trust or emolument."

By February 4, 1800, American diplomat John Quincy Adams, posted to the continent, had just heard the sad news "by way of England."

A month later, Adams wrote the American Secretary of State describing the honors that Napoleon had paid to Washington: French battle standards had been draped in black; Washington's bust was to be placed in the Tuileries, beside other modern and ancient heroes; eulogies were delivered in Paris (despite a simmering, unofficial naval war between France and the United States).

At about the same time that Adams heard of Washington's death, a Dartmouth College student wrote to a friend. Young Daniel Webster's letter of February 5 was filled with foreboding, as chilling as a New Hampshire winter. The recent news of Washington's death started Webster reflecting on current politics, racked by tumult, diplomatic intrigue, partisan strife, scandals, and a scurrilous press. As the country began the savage presidential campaign of 1800, one that teemed with epithets like *Tory, atheist, bigot, poltroon,* and *traitor,* the young Federalist feared calamity and civil war.

During the early weeks of 1800, ancient rites of mourning and remembrance had calmed conflict and briefly united a nervous republic. Webster, already wise beyond his years, summed up the major thrust of that remarkable and unprecedented wintry season of national grief. Webster's hope, indeed the prayer of the entire country, was that the spirit of the dead Virginian might still endure to "guard the liberties of his country" and "direct the sword of freedom . . ." But what lay ahead, he pondered, now that General Washington, "the great political cement," is dead? □□

Daniel Webster, ca. 1804. After Washington's death, the 18-year-old student wrote of his fears of civil war.

– Dartmouth College Library

Taylor Sanders is a professor of history at Washington and Lee University (formerly Washington Academy) in Lexington, Virginia, a school endowed by George Washington. Washington and Lee celebrates its 250th anniversary in 1999. Sanders is a member of the Society of the Cincinnati in the State of Maryland.

Editor's Note: If you'd like to see some of George Washington's original hand-written letters as well as his hand-written family tree, the stem of an Indian peace pipe he once smoked, hair from his head (reddish in his youth, gray in his senior years), and literally hundreds of other Washington items, drop by the Huntington Library in San Marino, California, between October 6, 1998, and May 30, 1999. During the last three months of the exhibit, even Washington's famous dentures will be on display. For more information, call the Huntington Library at 626-405-2141.

In Search of New Year's Eve, A.D. 999

What really happened 1,000 years ago in Europe at the end of the first millennium A.D.? Was it an apocalyptic frenzy of fear and panic, as some historians have asserted, or was it a transition little noted and even less documented? Here's one writer's look at the evidence (what there is of it).

by Andrew Rothovius

As we approach the end of the second millennium of our Western time reckoning, we often hear references to the panic and fear that gripped Christendom throughout western Europe as the midnight hour neared on December 31, 999. Vast crowds, it is asserted, kneeled in the streets and public squares, bewailing their sins in momentary expectation of the fiery end of the world and the Last Judgment. For months, all ordinary pursuits of life had come to a standstill. People had given away their property in their rush to prepare for Doomsday.

It is a dramatic and awful scenario. And it is almost certainly fictional. French historian Henri Foçillon, who died in 1944, was the first researcher whose findings started to dispel the notion that had become prevalent among historians in the 19th century — that of panic-stricken throngs cowering in abject dread as the last hours of 999 slipped away. Foçillon's documentation has been supported by other prominent European scholars, yet it has been mostly ignored by writers, who find the alleged panic to be a more exciting story.

Admittedly, there is a kernel of truth in the panic legend. About three or four decades before the climactic year 1000, fearful anticipation of a possible apocalypse in that year began to stir locally in France and central Europe. The church sought to counteract this anxiety by declaring that so long as the Holy Roman Empire lasted in any of its forms — whether in the French monarchy founded by Charlemagne, or in the Holy Roman Empire of the German Kaisers — the world would not come to an end, for its ultimate salvation was still being worked out. Moreover, it was heresy for man to think he could know the unknowable — the moment of the Last Judgment — which resided only in the mind of God.

The message proved effective. Events that might have been seen as portents of doom — several poor harvests and resulting famines in the closing years of the 10th century, eruptions of Vesuvius in 988, 991, and 999, and a brilliant comet in 989

— were not generally interpreted as omens of calamity. In fact, to many chroniclers of the age, the worst of all the horrendous hardships since the fall of Rome centuries earlier seemed to be behind them.

This optimism was inspired by the remarkable pope, Sylvester II, who presided over Western Christendom at the end of its first millennium. Born Gerbert of Aurillac, in southern France, the pope possessed a wide-ranging curiosity and capability in many fields, including navigation, mathematics, and musical notation. There is no record that he had to calm a frightened crowd at the Vatican on the last night of 999. In fact, there appear to be no documented accounts at all of a remarkable New Year's Eve of 999, whether joyous or fearful. (Historical records, particularly those documenting the lives of ordinary people at that time, are scarce.)

We *do* know that western Europe was on the verge of a great cultural awakening. Pope Sylvester encouraged a revival of church-building, most often employing gleaming white limestone in the emerging Romanesque style. Stonework had become a lost art during the post-Roman centuries and had to be learned all over again.

With the reintroduction of stone construction, new languages — French and its close kin Provençal, Spanish, and Italian — were emerging in Europe out of the Latin that had been the universal tongue of the Roman Empire. To the north and east, the Teutonic languages of the tribes that had toppled Rome were evolving into English, Dutch, German, and Norse.

Looking around him at these signs of the fresh dawning of a continental civilization, the German chronicler Dietmar of Merseburg hailed "the radiant dawn [that] rose over the world . . . when the thousandth year since the saving birth had come." It is hard to discern in his words any reflection of panic and fear at the end of the first millennium. The people may not have had fireworks and champagne on that New Year's Eve 1000 years ago, but the evidence shows a society looking forward to the next millennium. □□

Tide Corrections

Many factors affect the times and heights of the tides: the coastal configuration, the time of the Moon's southing (crossing the meridian) at a location, and the phase of the Moon. This table of tidal corrections can be used to calculate the *approximate* times and heights of the high water at the places shown. The figures for Full Sea on the Left-Hand Calendar Pages 60-86 are the times of high tide at Commonwealth Pier in Boston Harbor. The heights of some of these tides, reckoned from Mean Lower Low Water, are given on the Right-Hand Calendar Pages 61-87. To obtain the times and heights of high water at any of the following places, apply the time difference to the daily times of high water at Boston (pages 60-86) and the height difference to the heights at Boston (pages 61-87).

Estimations derived from this table are not meant to be used for navigation. *The Old Farmer's Almanac* accepts no responsibility for errors or any consequences ensuing from the use of this table.

National Ocean Service (NOS) tide tables for the East Coast, West Coast, and Caribbean regions are available from Reed's Nautical Almanacs, Thomas Reed Publications, Inc., 13A Lewis St., Boston, MA 02113; 800-995-4995. Tide predictions for many other reference stations around the country are also listed at NOS's Web site, www.opsd.nos.noaa.gov/tp4days.html.

	Time Difference: Hr. Min.	Height Feet
MAINE		
Bar Harbor	–0 34	+0.9
Belfast	–0 20	+0.4
Boothbay Harbor	–0 18	–0.8
Chebeague Island	–0 16	–0.6
Eastport	–0 28	+8.4
Kennebunkport	+0 04	–1.0
Machias	–0 28	+2.8
Monhegan Island	–0 25	–0.8
Old Orchard	0 00	–0.8
Portland	–0 12	–0.6
Rockland	–0 28	+0.1
Stonington	–0 30	+0.1
York	–0 09	–1.0
NEW HAMPSHIRE		
Hampton	+0 02	–1.3
Portsmouth	+0 11	–1.5
Rye Beach	–0 09	–0.9

	Time Difference: Hr. Min.	Height Feet
MASSACHUSETTS		
Annisquam	–0 02	–1.1
Beverly Farms	0 00	–0.5
Boston	0 00	0.0
Cape Cod Canal		
East Entrance	–0 01	–0.8
West Entrance	–2 16	–5.9
Chatham Outer Coast	+0 30	–2.8
Inside	+1 54	*0.4
Cohasset	+0 02	–0.07
Cotuit Highlands	+1 15	*0.3
Dennis Port	+1 01	*0.4
Duxbury–Gurnet Pt.	+0 02	–0.3
Fall River	–3 03	–5.0
Gloucester	–0 03	–0.8
Hingham	+0 07	0.0
Hull	+0 03	–0.2
Hyannis Port	+1 01	*0.3
Magnolia–Manchester	–0 02	–0.7
Marblehead	–0 02	–0.4
Marion	–3 22	–5.4
Monument Beach	–3 08	–5.4
Nahant	–0 01	–0.5
Nantasket	+0 04	–0.1
Nantucket	+0 56	*0.3
Nauset Beach	+0 30	*0.6
New Bedford	–3 24	–5.7
Newburyport	+0 19	–1.8
Oak Bluffs	+0 30	*0.2
Onset–R.R. Bridge	–2 16	–5.9
Plymouth	+0 05	0.0
Provincetown	+0 14	–0.4
Revere Beach	–0 01	–0.3
Rockport	–0 08	–1.0
Salem	0 00	–0.5
Scituate	–0 05	–0.7
Wareham	–3 09	–5.3
Wellfleet	+0 12	+0.5
West Falmouth	–3 10	–5.4
Westport Harbor	–3 22	–6.4
Woods Hole		
Little Harbor	–2 50	*0.2
Oceanographic Inst.	–3 07	*0.2
RHODE ISLAND		
Bristol	–3 24	–5.3
Narragansett Pier	–3 42	–6.2
Newport	–3 34	–5.9
Pt. Judith	–3 41	–6.3
Providence	–3 20	–4.8
Sakonnet	–3 44	–5.6
Watch Hill	–2 50	–6.8
CONNECTICUT		
Bridgeport	+0 01	–2.6

	Time Difference: Hr. Min.	Height Feet
Madison	–0 22	–2.3
New Haven	–0 11	–3.2
New London	–1 54	–6.7
Norwalk	+0 01	–2.2
Old Lyme		
Highway Bridge	–0 30	–6.2
Stamford	+0 01	–2.2
Stonington	–2 27	–6.6
NEW YORK		
Coney Island	–3 33	–4.9
Fire Island Light	–2 43	*0.1
Long Beach	–3 11	–5.7
Montauk Harbor	–2 19	–7.4
New York City–Battery	–2 43	–5.0
Oyster Bay	+0 04	–1.8
Port Chester	–0 09	–2.2
Port Washington	–0 01	–2.1
Sag Harbor	–0 55	–6.8
Southampton		
Shinnecock Inlet	–4 20	*0.2
Willets Point	0 00	–2.3
NEW JERSEY		
Asbury Park	–4 04	–5.3
Atlantic City	–3 56	–5.5
Bay Head–Sea Girt	–4 04	–5.3
Beach Haven	–1 43	*0.24
Cape May	–3 28	–5.3
Ocean City	–3 06	–5.9
Sandy Hook	–3 30	–5.0
Seaside Park	–4 03	–5.4
PENNSYLVANIA		
Philadelphia	+2 40	–3.5
DELAWARE		
Cape Henlopen	–2 48	–5.3
Rehoboth Beach	–3 37	–5.7
Wilmington	+1 56	–3.8
MARYLAND		
Annapolis	+6 23	–8.5
Baltimore	+7 59	–8.3
Cambridge	+5 05	–7.8
Havre de Grace	+11 21	–7.7
Point No Point	+2 28	–8.1
Prince Frederick		
Plum Point	+4 25	–8.5
VIRGINIA		
Cape Charles	–2 20	–7.0
Hampton Roads	–2 02	–6.9
Norfolk	–2 06	–6.6
Virginia Beach	–4 00	–6.0
Yorktown	–2 13	–7.0
NORTH CAROLINA		
Cape Fear	–3 55	–5.0
Cape Lookout	–4 28	–5.7
Currituck	–4 10	–5.8

	Time Difference: Hr. Min.	Height Feet
Hatteras		
Inlet	–4 03	–7.4
Kitty Hawk	–4 14	–6.2
Ocean	–4 26	–6.0
SOUTH CAROLINA		
Charleston	–3 22	–4.3
Georgetown	–1 48	*0.36
Hilton Head	–3 22	–2.9
Myrtle Beach	–3 49	–4.4
St. Helena		
Harbor Entrance	–3 15	–3.4
GEORGIA		
Jekyll Island	–3 46	–2.9
St. Simon's Island	–2 50	–2.9
Savannah Beach		
River Entrance	–3 14	–5.5
Tybee Light	–3 22	–2.7
FLORIDA		
Cape Canaveral	–3 59	–6.0
Daytona Beach	–3 28	–5.3
Fort Lauderdale	–2 50	–7.2
Fort Pierce Inlet	–3 32	–6.9
Jacksonville		
Railroad Bridge	–6 55	*0.1
Miami Harbor Entrance	–3 18	–7.0
St. Augustine	–2 55	–4.9
CANADA		
Alberton, PE	–5 45**	–7.5
Charlottetown, PE	–0 45**	–3.5
Halifax, NS	–3 23	–4.5
North Sydney, NS	–3 15	–6.5
Saint John, NB	+0 30	+15.0
St. John's, NF	–4 00	–6.5
Yarmouth, NS	–0 40	+3.0

* Where the difference in the "Height/Feet" column is so marked, height at Boston should be multiplied by this ratio.

** Varies widely; accurate only within 1½ hours. Consult local tide tables for precise times and heights.

Example: The conversion of the times and heights of the tides at Boston to those of Rye Beach, New Hampshire, is given below:

Sample tide calculation July 1, 1999:

High tide Boston (p. 76)	1:30 A.M., EDT
Correction for Rye Beach	–0:09 hrs.
High tide Rye Beach	1:21 A.M., EDT
Tide height Boston (p. 77)	10.3 ft.
Correction for Rye Beach	–0.9 ft.
Tide height Rye Beach	9.4 ft.

The Twilight Zone

How to Determine the Length of Twilight and the Times of Dawn and Dark

Astronomical twilight is the period of time between dawn (when the Sun is 18 degrees below the horizon) and sunrise, and again between sunset and dark (when the Sun is 18 degrees below the horizon). The latitude of a place and the time of year determine the length of twilight. To find the latitude of your city or the city nearest you, consult the **Time Correction Tables,** page 214. Check that figure against the chart at the right for the appropriate date, and you will have the length of twilight in your area.

To determine when dawn will break and when dark will descend, apply the length of twilight to the times of sunrise and sunset at any specific place. (Follow the instructions given in "How to Use This Almanac," page 34, to determine sunrise/sunset times for a given locality.) **Subtract** the length of twilight from the time of sunrise for dawn. **Add** the length of twilight to the time of sunset for dark.

Latitude	25° N to 30° N	31° N to 36° N	37° N to 42° N	43° N to 47° N	48° N to 49° N
	H M	H M	H M	H M	H M
Jan. 1 to Apr. 10	1 20	1 26	1 33	1 42	1 50
Apr. 11 to May 2	1 23	1 28	1 39	1 51	2 04
May 3 to May 14	1 26	1 34	1 47	2 02	2 22
May 15 to May 25	1 29	1 38	1 52	2 13	2 42
May 26 to July 22	1 32	1 43	1 59	2 27	—
July 23 to Aug. 3	1 29	1 38	1 52	2 13	2 42
Aug. 4 to Aug. 14	1 26	1 34	1 47	2 02	2 22
Aug. 15 to Sept. 5	1 23	1 28	1 39	1 51	2 04
Sept. 6 to Dec. 31	1 20	1 26	1 33	1 42	1 50

	Boston, Mass. (latitude 42° 22')	Phoenix, Ariz. (latitude 33° 27')
Sunrise, August 1	5:36 A.M.	6:47 A.M.
Length of twilight	–1:52	–1:38
Dawn breaks	3:44 A.M., EDT	5:09 A.M., MDT
Sunset, August 1	8:04 P.M.	8:34 P.M.
Length of twilight	+1:52	+1:38
Dark descends	9:56 P.M., EDT	10:12 P.M., MDT

Tidal Glossary

Apogean Tide: A monthly tide of decreased range that occurs when the Moon is farthest from Earth (at apogee).

Diurnal: Experiencing one high water and one low water during a tidal day of approximately 24 hours.

Mean Lower Low Water: The arithmetic mean of the lesser of a daily pair of low waters, observed over a specific 19-year cycle called the National Tidal Datum Epoch.

Neap Tide: A tide of decreased range that occurs twice a month, when the Moon is in quadrature (during the first and last quarter Moons, when the Sun and the Moon are at right angles to each other relative to Earth).

Perigean Tide: A monthly tide of increased range that occurs when the Moon is closest to Earth (at perigee).

Semidiurnal: Having a period of half a tidal day. East Coast tides, for example, are semidiurnal, with two highs and two lows during a tidal day of approximately 24 hours.

Spring Tide: A tide of increased range that occurs at times of syzygy each month. Named not for the season of spring, but from the German *springen* ("to leap up"), a spring tide also brings a lower low water.

Syzygy: The nearly straight-line configuration that occurs twice a month, when the Sun and the Moon are in conjunction (on the same side of Earth at the new Moon) and when they are in opposition (on opposite sides of Earth at the full Moon). In both cases, the gravitational effects of the Sun and the Moon reinforce each other, and tidal range is increased.

Vanishing Tide: A mixed tide of considerable inequality in the two highs or two lows, so that the "high low" may become indistinguishable from the "low high." The result is a vanishing tide, where no significant difference is apparent.

Gestation and Mating Table

	Proper age for first mating	Period of fertility, in years	No. of females for one male	Period of gestation in days Range	Average
Ewe	90 lb. or 1 yr.	6		142-154	147 / 151[8]
Ram	12-14 mo., Well matured	7	50-75[2] / 35-40[3]		
Mare	3 yr.	10-12		310-370	336
Stallion	3 yr.	12-15	40-45[4] / Record 252[5]		
Cow	15-18 mo.[1]	10-14		279-290[6] 262-300[7]	283
Bull	1 yr., well matured	10-12	50[4] / Thousands[5]		
Sow	5-6 mo. or 250 lb.	6		110-120	115
Boar	250-300 lb.	6	50[2] / 35-40[3]		
Doe goat	10 mo. or 85-90 lb.	6		145-155	150
Buck goat	Well matured	5	30		
Bitch	16-18 mo.	8		58-67	63
Male dog	12-16 mo.	8			
She cat	12 mo.	6		60-68	63
Doe rabbit	6 mo.	5-6		30-32	31
Buck rabbit	6 mo.	5-6	30		

[1]Holstein & beef: 750 lb.; Jersey: 500 lb. [2]Handmated. [3]Pasture. [4]Natural. [5]Artificial. [6]Beef; 8-10 days shorter for Angus. [7]Dairy. [8]For fine wool breeds.

Bird and Poultry Incubation Periods, in Days

Chicken......21	Goose 30-34	Guinea........26-28
Turkey........28	Swan 42	Canary........14-15
Duck 26-32	Pheasant ..22-24	Parakeet......18-20

Gestation Periods, Wild Animals, in Days

Black bear 210	Seal 330
Hippo...................225-250	Squirrel, gray 44
Moose..................240-250	Whale, sperm..........480
Otter.....................270-300	Wolf.....................60-63
Reindeer 210-240	

Maximum Life Spans of Animals in Capitivity, in Years

Ant (queen) ...... 18+	Eagle 55	Mouse (house) 6
Badger 26	Elephant 75	Mussel (freshwater) ... 70-80
Beaver .... 15+	Giraffe 36	Octopus 2-3
Box turtle (Eastern) 138	Goat (domestic) 20	Quahog 150
Camel .... 35+	Goldfish 41	Rabbit .... 18+
Cat (domestic) 34	Goose (domestic) .. 20	Squirrel, gray 23
Chicken (domestic) 25	Gorilla .... 50+	Tiger 26
Chimpanzee 51	Horse 62	Toad 40
Coyote .... 21+	Housefly .... .04 (17 days)	Tortoise (Marion's) .... 152+
Dog (domestic) 29	Kangaroo 30	Turkey (domestic) .. 16
Dolphin 25	Lion 29	
Duck (domestic) ... 23	Monarch butterfly .. 1+	

	Recurs if not bred	Estrual cycle incl. heat period (days)		In heat for		Usual time of ovulation
	Days	Avg.	Range	Avg.	Range	
Mare	21	21	10-37	5-6 days	2-11 days	24-48 hours before end of estrus
Sow	21	21	18-24	2-3 days	1-5 days	30-36 hours after start of estrus
Ewe	16½	16½	14-19	30 hours	24-32 hours	12-24 hours before end of estrus
Goat	21	21	18-24	2-3 days	1-4 days	Near end of estrus
Cow	21	21	18-24	18 hours	10-24 hours	10-12 hours after end of estrus
Bitch	pseudo-pregnancy	24		7 days	5-9 days	1-3 days after first acceptance
Cat	pseudo-pregnancy		15-21	3-4 if mated	9-10 days in absence of male	24-56 hours after coitus

Time Correction Tables

The times of sunrise/sunset and moonrise/moonset, selected times for observing the visible planets, and the transit times of the bright stars are given for **Boston only** on pages 60-86, 46-47, and 50. Use the **Key Letter** shown to the right of each time on those pages with these tables to find the number of minutes that should be added to or subtracted from Boston time to give the correct time for your city. (Because of the complexities of calculation for different locations, times may not be precise to the minute.) If your city is not listed, find the city closest to you in latitude and longitude and use those figures. **Boston's latitude is 42° 22' and its longitude is 71° 03'.** Canadian cities appear at the end of the list. For a more complete explanation of the use of Key Letters and these tables, see "How to Use This Almanac," page 34.

Time Zone Code: Codes represent *standard time.* Atlantic is -1, Eastern is 0, Central is 1, Mountain is 2, Pacific is 3, Alaska is 4, and Hawaii–Aleutian is 5.

City	North Latitude °	'	West Longitude °	'	Time Zone Code	Key Letters A min.	B min.	C min.	D min.	E min.
Aberdeen, SD	45	28	98	29	1	+37	+44	+49	+54	+59
Akron, OH	41	5	81	31	0	+46	+43	+41	+39	+37
Albany, NY	42	39	73	45	0	+ 9	+10	+10	+11	+11
Albert Lea, MN	43	39	93	22	1	+24	+26	+28	+31	+33
Albuquerque, NM	35	5	106	39	2	+45	+32	+22	+11	+ 2
Alexandria, LA	31	18	92	27	1	+58	+40	+26	+ 9	– 3
Allentown–Bethlehem, PA	40	36	75	28	0	+23	+20	+17	+14	+12
Amarillo, TX	35	12	101	50	1	+85	+73	+63	+52	+43
Anchorage, AK	61	10	149	59	4	–46	+27	+71	+122	+171
Asheville, NC	35	36	82	33	0	+67	+55	+46	+35	+27
Atlanta, GA	33	45	84	24	0	+79	+65	+53	+40	+30
Atlantic City, NJ	39	22	74	26	0	+23	+17	+13	+ 8	+ 4
Augusta, GA	33	28	81	58	0	+70	+55	+44	+30	+19
Augusta, ME	44	19	69	46	0	–12	– 8	– 5	– 1	0
Austin, TX	30	16	97	45	1	+82	+62	+47	+29	+15
Bakersfield, CA	35	23	119	1	3	+33	+21	+12	+ 1	– 7
Baltimore, MD	39	17	76	37	0	+32	+26	+22	+17	+13
Bangor, ME	44	48	68	46	0	–18	–13	– 9	– 5	– 1
Barstow, CA	34	54	117	1	3	+27	+14	+ 4	– 7	–16
Baton Rouge, LA	30	27	91	11	1	+55	+36	+21	+ 3	–10
Beaumont, TX	30	5	94	6	1	+67	+48	+32	+14	0
Bellingham, WA	48	45	122	29	3	0	+13	+24	+37	+47
Bemidji, MN	47	28	94	53	1	+14	+26	+34	+44	+52
Berlin, NH	44	28	71	11	0	– 7	– 3	0	+ 3	+ 7
Billings, MT	45	47	108	30	2	+16	+23	+29	+35	+40
Biloxi, MS	30	24	88	53	1	+46	+27	+11	– 5	–19
Binghamton, NY	42	6	75	55	0	+20	+19	+19	+18	+18
Birmingham, AL	33	31	86	49	1	+30	+15	+ 3	–10	–20
Bismarck, ND	46	48	100	47	1	+41	+50	+58	+66	+73
Boise, ID	43	37	116	12	2	+55	+58	+60	+62	+64
Brattleboro, VT	42	51	72	34	0	+ 4	+ 5	+ 5	+ 6	+ 7
Bridgeport, CT	41	11	73	11	0	+12	+10	+ 8	+ 6	+ 4
Brockton, MA	42	5	71	1	0	0	0	0	0	– 1
Brownsville, TX	25	54	97	30	1	+91	+66	+46	+23	+ 5
Buffalo, NY	42	53	78	52	0	+29	+30	+30	+31	+32
Burlington, VT	44	29	73	13	0	0	+ 4	+ 8	+12	+15
Butte, MT	46	1	112	32	2	+31	+39	+45	+52	+57
Cairo, IL	37	0	89	11	1	+29	+20	+12	+ 4	– 2
Camden, NJ	39	57	75	7	0	+24	+19	+16	+12	+ 9
Canton, OH	40	48	81	23	0	+46	+43	+41	+38	+36
Cape May, NJ	38	56	74	56	0	+26	+20	+15	+ 9	+ 5
Carson City–Reno, NV	39	10	119	46	3	+25	+19	+14	+ 9	+ 5

City	North Latitude °	'	West Longitude °	'	Time Zone Code	Key Letters A min.	B min.	C min.	D min.	E min.
Casper, WY	42	51	106	19	2	+19	+19	+20	+21	+22
Charleston, SC	32	47	79	56	0	+64	+48	+36	+21	+10
Charleston, WV	38	21	81	38	0	+55	+48	+42	+35	+30
Charlotte, NC	35	14	80	51	0	+61	+49	+39	+28	+19
Charlottesville, VA	38	2	78	30	0	+43	+35	+29	+22	+17
Chattanooga, TN	35	3	85	19	0	+79	+67	+57	+45	+36
Cheboygan, MI	45	39	84	29	0	+40	+47	+53	+59	+64
Cheyenne, WY	41	8	104	49	2	+19	+16	+14	+12	+11
Chicago–Oak Park, IL	41	52	87	38	1	+ 7	+ 6	+ 6	+ 5	+ 4
Cincinnati–Hamilton, OH	39	6	84	31	0	+64	+58	+53	+48	+44
Cleveland–Lakewood, OH	41	30	81	42	0	+45	+43	+42	+40	+39
Columbia, SC	34	0	81	2	0	+65	+51	+40	+27	+17
Columbus, OH	39	57	83	1	0	+55	+51	+47	+43	+40
Cordova, AK	60	33	145	45	4	–55	+13	+55	+103	+149
Corpus Christi, TX	27	48	97	24	1	+86	+64	+46	+25	+ 9
Craig, CO	40	31	107	33	2	+32	+28	+25	+22	+20
Dallas–Fort Worth, TX	32	47	96	48	1	+71	+55	+43	+28	+17
Danville, IL	40	8	87	37	1	+13	+ 9	+ 6	+ 2	0
Danville, VA	36	36	79	23	0	+51	+41	+33	+24	+17
Davenport, IA	41	32	90	35	1	+20	+19	+17	+16	+15
Dayton, OH	39	45	84	10	0	+61	+56	+52	+48	+44
Decatur, AL	34	36	86	59	1	+27	+14	+ 4	– 7	–17
Decatur, IL	39	51	88	57	1	+19	+15	+11	+ 7	+ 4
Denver–Boulder, CO	39	44	104	59	2	+24	+19	+15	+11	+ 7
Des Moines, IA	41	35	93	37	1	+32	+31	+30	+28	+27
Detroit–Dearborn, MI	42	20	83	3	0	+47	+47	+47	+47	+47
Dubuque, IA	42	30	90	41	1	+17	+18	+18	+18	+18
Duluth, MN	46	47	92	6	1	+ 6	+16	+23	+31	+38
Durham, NC	36	0	78	55	0	+51	+40	+31	+21	+13
Eastport, ME	44	54	67	0	0	–26	–20	–16	–11	– 8
Eau Claire, WI	44	49	91	30	1	+12	+17	+21	+25	+29
Elko, NV	40	50	115	46	3	+ 3	0	– 1	– 3	– 5
Ellsworth, ME	44	33	68	25	0	–18	–14	–10	– 6	– 3
El Paso, TX	31	45	106	29	2	+53	+35	+22	+ 6	– 6
Erie, PA	42	7	80	5	0	+36	+36	+35	+35	+35
Eugene, OR	44	3	123	6	3	+21	+24	+27	+30	+33
Fairbanks, AK	64	48	147	51	4	–127	+ 2	+61	+131	+205
Fall River–New Bedford, MA	41	42	71	9	0	+ 2	+ 1	0	0	– 1
Fargo, ND	46	53	96	47	1	+24	+34	+42	+50	+57
Flagstaff, AZ	35	12	111	39	2	+64	+52	+42	+31	+22
Flint, MI	43	1	83	41	0	+47	+49	+50	+51	+52
Fort Myers, FL	26	38	81	52	0	+87	+63	+44	+21	+ 4
Fort Scott, KS	37	50	94	42	1	+49	+41	+34	+27	+21
Fort Smith, AR	35	23	94	25	1	+55	+43	+33	+22	+14
Fort Wayne, IN	41	4	85	9	0	+60	+58	+56	+54	+52
Fresno, CA	36	44	119	47	3	+32	+22	+15	+ 6	0
Gallup, NM	35	32	108	45	2	+52	+40	+31	+20	+11
Galveston, TX	29	18	94	48	1	+72	+52	+35	+16	+ 1
Gary, IN	41	36	87	20	1	+ 7	+ 6	+ 4	+ 3	+ 2
Glasgow, MT	48	12	106	38	2	– 1	+11	+21	+32	+42
Grand Forks, ND	47	55	97	3	1	+21	+33	+43	+53	+62
Grand Island, NE	40	55	98	21	1	+53	+51	+49	+46	+44
Grand Junction, CO	39	4	108	33	2	+40	+34	+29	+24	+20
Great Falls, MT	47	30	111	17	2	+20	+31	+39	+49	+58
Green Bay, WI	44	31	88	0	1	0	+ 3	+ 7	+11	+14
Greensboro, NC	36	4	79	47	0	+54	+43	+35	+25	+17

City	North Latitude °	'	West Longitude °	'	Time Zone Code	Key Letters A min.	B min.	C min.	D min.	E min.
Hagerstown, MD	39	39	77	43	0	+35	+30	+26	+22	+18
Harrisburg, PA	40	16	76	53	0	+30	+26	+23	+19	+16
Hartford–New Britain, CT	41	46	72	41	0	+ 8	+ 7	+ 6	+ 5	+ 4
Helena, MT	46	36	112	2	2	+27	+36	+43	+51	+57
Hilo, HI	19	44	155	5	5	+94	+62	+37	+ 7	–15
Honolulu, HI	21	18	157	52	5	+102	+72	+48	+19	– 1
Houston, TX	29	45	95	22	1	+73	+53	+37	+19	+ 5
Indianapolis, IN	39	46	86	10	0	+69	+64	+60	+56	+52
Ironwood, MI	46	27	90	9	1	0	+ 9	+15	+23	+29
Jackson, MI	42	15	84	24	0	+53	+53	+53	+52	+52
Jackson, MS	32	18	90	11	1	+46	+30	+17	+ 1	–10
Jacksonville, FL	30	20	81	40	0	+77	+58	+43	+25	+11
Jefferson City, MO	38	34	92	10	1	+36	+29	+24	+18	+13
Joplin, MO	37	6	94	30	1	+50	+41	+33	+25	+18
Juneau, AK	58	18	134	25	4	–76	–23	+10	+49	+86
Kalamazoo, MI	42	17	85	35	0	+58	+57	+57	+57	+57
Kanab, UT	37	3	112	32	2	+62	+53	+46	+37	+30
Kansas City, MO	39	1	94	20	1	+44	+37	+33	+27	+23
Keene, NH	42	56	72	17	0	+ 2	+ 3	+ 4	+ 5	+ 6
Ketchikan, AK	55	21	131	39	4	–62	–25	0	+29	+56
Knoxville, TN	35	58	83	55	0	+71	+60	+51	+41	+33
Kodiak, AK	57	47	152	24	4	0	+49	+82	+120	+154
LaCrosse, WI	43	48	91	15	1	+15	+18	+20	+22	+25
Lake Charles, LA	30	14	93	13	1	+64	+44	+29	+11	– 2
Lanai City, HI	20	50	156	55	5	+99	+69	+44	+15	– 6
Lancaster, PA	40	2	76	18	0	+28	+24	+20	+17	+13
Lansing, MI	42	44	84	33	0	+52	+53	+53	+54	+54
Las Cruces, NM	32	19	106	47	2	+53	+36	+23	+ 8	– 3
Las Vegas, NV	36	10	115	9	3	+16	+ 4	– 3	–13	–20
Lawrence–Lowell, MA	42	42	71	10	0	0	0	0	0	+ 1
Lewiston, ID	46	25	117	1	3	–12	– 3	+ 2	+10	+17
Lexington–Frankfort, KY	38	3	84	30	0	+67	+59	+53	+46	+41
Liberal, KS	37	3	100	55	1	+76	+66	+59	+51	+44
Lihue, HI	21	59	159	23	5	+107	+77	+54	+26	+ 5
Lincoln, NE	40	49	96	41	1	+47	+44	+42	+39	+37
Little Rock, AR	34	45	92	17	1	+48	+35	+25	+13	+ 4
Los Angeles–Pasadena–Santa Monica, CA	34	3	118	14	3	+34	+20	+ 9	– 3	–13
Louisville, KY	38	15	85	46	0	+72	+64	+58	+52	+46
Macon, GA	32	50	83	38	0	+79	+63	+50	+36	+24
Madison, WI	43	4	89	23	1	+10	+11	+12	+14	+15
Manchester–Concord, NH	42	59	71	28	0	0	0	+ 1	+ 2	+ 3
McAllen, TX	26	12	98	14	1	+93	+69	+49	+26	+9
Memphis, TN	35	9	90	3	1	+38	+26	+16	+ 5	– 3
Meridian, MS	32	22	88	42	1	+40	+24	+11	– 4	–15
Miami, FL	25	47	80	12	0	+88	+57	+37	+14	– 3
Miles City, MT	46	25	105	51	2	+ 3	+11	+18	+26	+32
Milwaukee, WI	43	2	87	54	1	+ 4	+ 6	+ 7	+ 8	+ 9
Minneapolis–St. Paul, MN	44	59	93	16	1	+18	+24	+28	+33	+37
Minot, ND	48	14	101	18	1	+36	+50	+59	+71	+81
Moab, UT	38	35	109	33	2	+46	+39	+33	+27	+22
Mobile, AL	30	42	88	3	1	+42	+23	+ 8	– 8	–22
Monroe, LA	32	30	92	7	1	+53	+37	+24	+ 9	– 1
Montgomery, AL	32	23	86	19	1	+31	+14	+ 1	–13	–25
Muncie, IN	40	12	85	23	0	+64	+60	+57	+53	+50
Nashville, TN	36	10	86	47	1	+22	+11	+ 3	– 6	–14
Newark–East Orange, NJ	40	44	74	10	0	+17	+14	+12	+ 9	+ 7

City	North Latitude °	'	West Longitude °	'	Time Zone Code	Key Letters A min.	B min.	C min.	D min.	E min.
New Haven, CT	41	18	72	56	0	+11	+ 8	+ 7	+ 5	+ 4
New London, CT	41	22	72	6	0	+ 7	+ 5	+ 4	+ 2	+ 1
New Orleans, LA	29	57	90	4	1	+52	+32	+16	– 1	–15
New York, NY	40	45	74	0	0	+17	+14	+11	+ 9	+ 6
Norfolk, VA	36	51	76	17	0	+38	+28	+21	+12	+ 5
North Platte, NE	41	8	100	46	1	+62	+60	+58	+56	+54
Norwalk–Stamford, CT	41	7	73	22	0	+13	+10	+ 9	+ 7	+ 5
Oakley, KS	39	8	100	51	1	+69	+63	+59	+53	+49
Ogden, UT	41	13	111	58	2	+47	+45	+43	+41	+40
Ogdensburg, NY	44	42	75	30	0	+ 8	+13	+17	+21	+25
Oklahoma City, OK	35	28	97	31	1	+67	+55	+46	+35	+26
Omaha, NE	41	16	95	56	1	+43	+40	+39	+37	+36
Orlando, FL	28	32	81	22	0	+80	+59	+42	+22	+ 6
Ortonville, MN	45	19	96	27	1	+30	+36	+40	+46	+51
Oshkosh, WI	44	1	88	33	1	+ 3	+ 6	+ 9	+12	+15
Palm Springs, CA	33	49	116	32	3	+28	+13	+ 1	–12	–22
Parkersburg, WV	39	16	81	34	0	+52	+46	+42	+36	+32
Paterson, NJ	40	55	74	10	0	+17	+14	+12	+ 9	+ 7
Pendleton, OR	45	40	118	47	3	– 1	+ 4	+10	+16	+21
Pensacola, FL	30	25	87	13	1	+39	+20	+ 5	–12	–26
Peoria, IL	40	42	89	36	1	+19	+16	+14	+11	+ 9
Philadelphia–Chester, PA	39	57	75	9	0	+24	+19	+16	+12	+ 9
Phoenix, AZ	33	27	112	4	2	+71	+56	+44	+30	+20
Pierre, SD	44	22	100	21	1	+49	+53	+56	+60	+63
Pittsburgh–McKeesport, PA	40	26	80	0	0	+42	+38	+35	+32	+29
Pittsfield, MA	42	27	73	15	0	+ 8	+ 8	+ 8	+ 8	+ 8
Pocatello, ID	42	52	112	27	2	+43	+44	+45	+46	+46
Poplar Bluff, MO	36	46	90	24	1	+35	+25	+17	+ 8	+ 1
Portland, ME	43	40	70	15	0	– 8	– 5	– 3	– 1	0
Portland, OR	45	31	122	41	3	+14	+20	+25	+31	+36
Portsmouth, NH	43	5	70	45	0	– 4	– 2	– 1	0	0
Presque Isle, ME	46	41	68	1	0	–29	–19	–12	– 4	+ 2
Providence, RI	41	50	71	25	0	+ 3	+ 2	+ 1	0	0
Pueblo, CO	38	16	104	37	2	+27	+20	+14	+ 7	+ 2
Raleigh, NC	35	47	78	38	0	+51	+39	+30	+20	+12
Rapid City, SD	44	5	103	14	2	+ 2	+ 5	+ 8	+11	+13
Reading, PA	40	20	75	56	0	+26	+22	+19	+16	+13
Redding, CA	40	35	122	24	3	+31	+27	+25	+22	+19
Richmond, VA	37	32	77	26	0	+41	+32	+25	+17	+11
Roanoke, VA	37	16	79	57	0	+51	+42	+35	+27	+21
Roswell, NM	33	24	104	32	2	+41	+26	+14	0	–10
Rutland, VT	43	37	72	58	0	+ 2	+ 5	+ 7	+ 9	+11
Sacramento, CA	38	35	121	30	3	+34	+27	+21	+15	+10
St. Johnsbury, VT	44	25	72	1	0	– 4	0	+ 3	+ 7	+10
St. Joseph, MI	42	5	86	26	0	+61	+61	+60	+60	+59
St. Joseph, MO	39	46	94	50	1	+43	+38	+35	+30	+27
St. Louis, MO	38	37	90	12	1	+28	+21	+16	+10	+ 5
St. Petersburg, FL	27	46	82	39	0	+87	+65	+47	+26	+10
Salem, OR	44	57	123	1	3	+17	+23	+27	+31	+35
Salina, KS	38	50	97	37	1	+57	+51	+46	+40	+35
Salisbury, MD	38	22	75	36	0	+31	+23	+18	+11	+ 6
Salt Lake City, UT	40	45	111	53	2	+48	+45	+43	+40	+38
San Antonio, TX	29	25	98	30	1	+87	+66	+50	+31	+16
San Diego, CA	32	43	117	9	3	+33	+17	+ 4	– 9	–21
San Francisco–Oakland–San Jose, CA	37	47	122	25	3	+40	+31	+25	+18	+12
Santa Fe, NM	35	41	105	56	2	+40	+28	+19	+ 9	0

City	North Latitude °	'	West Longitude °	'	Time Zone Code	Key Letters A min.	B min.	C min.	D min.	E min.
Savannah, GA	32	5	81	6	0	+70	+54	+40	+25	+13
Scranton–Wilkes-Barre, PA	41	25	75	40	0	+21	+19	+18	+16	+15
Seattle–Tacoma–Olympia, WA	47	37	122	20	3	+ 3	+15	+24	+34	+42
Sheridan, WY	44	48	106	58	2	+14	+19	+23	+27	+31
Shreveport, LA	32	31	93	45	1	+60	+44	+31	+16	+ 4
Sioux Falls, SD	43	33	96	44	1	+38	+40	+42	+44	+46
South Bend, IN	41	41	86	15	0	+62	+61	+60	+59	+58
Spartanburg, SC	34	56	81	57	0	+66	+53	+43	+32	+23
Spokane, WA	47	40	117	24	3	–16	– 4	+ 4	+14	+23
Springfield, IL	39	48	89	39	1	+22	+18	+14	+10	+ 6
Springfield–Holyoke, MA	42	6	72	36	0	+ 6	+ 6	+ 6	+ 5	+ 5
Springfield, MO	37	13	93	18	1	+45	+36	+29	+20	+14
Syracuse, NY	43	3	76	9	0	+17	+19	+20	+21	+22
Tallahassee, FL	30	27	84	17	0	+87	+68	+53	+35	+22
Tampa, FL	27	57	82	27	0	+86	+64	+46	+25	+ 9
Terre Haute, IN	39	28	87	24	0	+74	+69	+65	+60	+56
Texarkana, AR	33	26	94	3	1	+59	+44	+32	+18	+ 8
Toledo, OH	41	39	83	33	0	+52	+50	+49	+48	+47
Topeka, KS	39	3	95	40	1	+49	+43	+38	+32	+28
Traverse City, MI	44	46	85	38	0	+49	+54	+57	+62	+65
Trenton, NJ	40	13	74	46	0	+21	+17	+14	+11	+ 8
Trinidad, CO	37	10	104	31	2	+30	+21	+13	+ 5	0
Tucson, AZ	32	13	110	58	2	+70	+53	+40	+24	+12
Tulsa, OK	36	9	95	60	1	+59	+48	+40	+30	+22
Tupelo, MS	34	16	88	34	1	+35	+21	+10	– 2	–11
Vernal, UT	40	27	109	32	2	+40	+36	+33	+30	+28
Walla Walla, WA	46	4	118	20	3	– 5	+ 2	+ 8	+15	+21
Washington, DC	38	54	77	1	0	+35	+28	+23	+18	+13
Waterbury–Meriden, CT	41	33	73	3	0	+10	+ 9	+ 7	+ 6	+ 5
Waterloo, IA	42	30	92	20	1	+24	+24	+24	+25	+25
Wausau, WI	44	58	89	38	1	+ 4	+ 9	+13	+18	+22
West Palm Beach, FL	26	43	80	3	0	+79	+55	+36	+14	– 2
Wichita, KS	37	42	97	20	1	+60	+51	+45	+37	+31
Williston, ND	48	9	103	37	1	+46	+59	+69	+80	+90
Wilmington, DE	39	45	75	33	0	+26	+21	+18	+13	+10
Wilmington, NC	34	14	77	55	0	+52	+38	+27	+15	+ 5
Winchester, VA	39	11	78	10	0	+38	+33	+28	+23	+19
Worcester, MA	42	16	71	48	0	+ 3	+ 2	+ 2	+ 2	+ 2
York, PA	39	58	76	43	0	+30	+26	+22	+18	+15
Youngstown, OH	41	6	80	39	0	+42	40	+38	+36	+34
Yuma, AZ	32	43	114	37	2	+83	+67	+54	+40	+28
CANADA										
Calgary, AB	51	5	114	5	2	+13	+35	+50	+68	+84
Edmonton, AB	53	34	113	25	2	– 3	+26	+47	+72	+93
Halifax, NS	44	38	63	35	– 1	+21	+26	+29	+33	+37
Montreal, QC	45	28	73	39	0	– 1	+ 4	+ 9	+15	+20
Ottawa, ON	45	25	75	43	0	+ 6	+13	+18	+23	+28
Peterborough, ON	44	18	78	19	0	+21	+25	+28	+32	+35
Saint John, NB	45	16	66	3	– 1	+28	+34	+39	+44	+49
Saskatoon, SK	52	10	106	40	1	+37	+63	+80	+101	+119
Sydney, NS	46	10	60	10	– 1	+ 1	+ 9	+15	+23	+28
Thunder Bay, ON	48	27	89	12	0	+47	+61	+71	+83	+93
Toronto, ON	43	39	79	23	0	+28	+30	+32	+35	+37
Vancouver, BC	49	13	123	6	3	0	+15	+26	+40	+52
Winnipeg, MB	49	53	97	10	1	+12	+30	+43	+58	+71

The OLD FARMER'S GENERAL STORE

A special section featuring unique mail-order products for all our readers who shop by mail.

WEATHER STATIONS

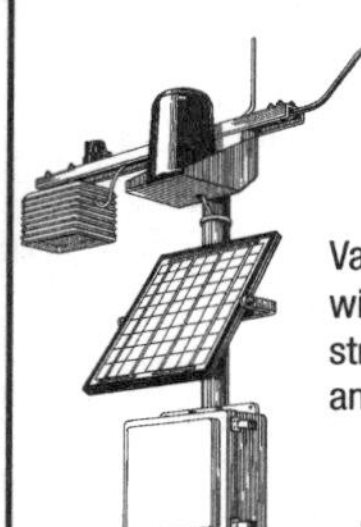

Professional-quality weather stations for home or industry.

Various models track temperature, wind, rain, evapotranspiration, heat-stress index, UV index, degree-days, and more. Priced from 150^{00}.

For a free catalog of all our stations and accessories, call

1-800-678-3669

OLD0199

Davis Instruments

3465 Diablo Avenue, Hayward, CA 94545-2778 • www.davisnet.com

LULU BELLE & SCOTTY

send $1 for your Catalog.

bringing you 100's of unforgettable recordings from the good old days.

The Music Barn

PO Box 1164 Lewiston NY 14092

www.themusicbarn.com

AMERICA'S OLDEST & LARGEST RARE BREED HATCHERY

FREE COLOR CATALOG

Over 140 varieties Baby Chicks, Bantams, Turkeys, Game Birds, Peacocks, Waterfowl, Guineas, plus Books, Equipment, Eggs, Incubators, & Medicine.

1-800-456-3280

(24 hours a day)

MURRAY MC MURRAY HATCHERY

C100, WEBSTER CITY, IOWA 50595-0458

VISIT OUR WEBSITE

http://www.mcmurrayhatchery.com

SAWMILL $3795.

FREE INFORMATION

Norwood Sawmills

90 Curtwright Dr., Unit 3

Amherst, N.Y. 14221

1-800-661-7746

Bargain Books

America's biggest selection. **Save up to 80%** on recent publishers' overstocks. **Save 30% or more** on current books and best sellers! Gardening, Nature, Biography, History—over 60 subject areas. **FREE CATALOG.**

Hamilton 5696 Oak, Falls Village, CT 06031-5005

60% MORE JUICE FROM YOUR APPLES!

Complete home cider press and fruit grinder, 3 models to choose from, completely assembled or in kit form. The secret is the cast iron "APPLE EATER" grinder which reduces the fruit to a fine pulp and will grind a bushel of whole apples in 5 minutes. Tub holds full bushel of pulped fruit. Heavy 1½" acme screw and cast iron crossbeam. Hardwood construction. Call or send $1.00 for catalog.

HAPPY VALLEY RANCH (913) 849-3103

16577 W. 327 DEPT 17 • PAOLA, KS 66071

www.happyvalleyranch.com

SLEEP WARM & RELAXED

Automatic Bed Warming Pad makes electric blankets obsolete, all sizes, plus dual controls, 12V/115V for RV's. Also foot, back,&pet warmers. Free booklet explains advantages & savings. **Special Low Prices** direct from factory. Patented Products Inc. Box A/F99 Danville, OH 43014 800-990-4622

KITES

FREE COLOR CATALOG

Choose from over 200 exciting kites.

• Many unusual & innovative designs.

Call or write for your catalog today!

Into The Wind • **(800) 541-0314**

1408-FA Pearl St., Boulder, CO 80302

Save Money—

saw your own lumber

With a Wood-Mizer!

LT15 Personal Sawmill

- Cut logs up to 28" D. x 9' L.
- Extra bed sections permit longer lengths.
- Easily transportable.

(Shown with optional loading ramps.)

▶ Free $2 Catalog* *With purchase of All Products Video @ $10.

Wood-Mizer®

8180 West 10th Street Dept BH13

Indianapolis, IN 46214-2400

www.woodmizer.com

1-800-553-0219

RONNIGER'S SEED & POTATO CO.

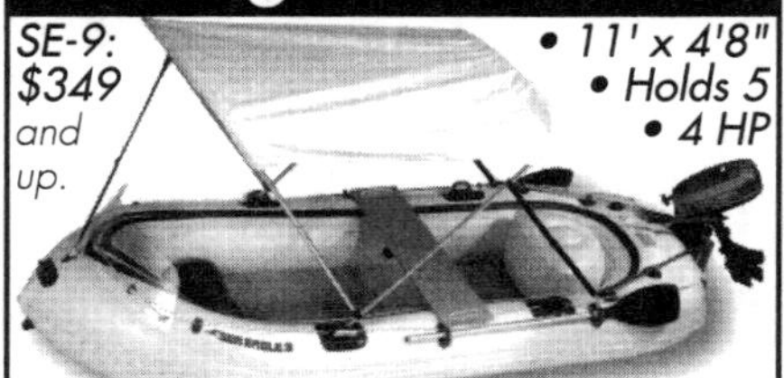

FREE! FREE!

Nationally Famous JENASOL "Miracle Bullets" Multi Vitamin Formula includes ROYAL JELLY, GINSENG and YOHIMBE BARK. Send for 1 month supply FREE or visit us at:

WWW.JENASOLVITAMINS.COM

Please enclose $1.00 to cover cost of post. & hdlg.: JENASOL, INC., Dept. B-11-A, Hallandale, FL 33009

Vanilla

Since 1888 we've been making pure vanilla extract using only the world's best, most flavorful and most expensive Madagascar Bourbon Vanilla bean.

CHARLES H. BALDWIN & SONS
1 Center Street, Dept. A
West Stockbridge, MA 01266

Quart $27.50 Pint $16.50 8 Oz. $9.50

MasterCard and Visa call 413-232-7785

(plus $5.00 shipping - orders over $50.00 add 10%)

Work at Home

Earn up to $40,000 a year in medical billing and claims!

Now get free facts on how you can train at home for America's fastest-growing, money-making at-home career. Plenty of high-pay office jobs, too! Call Toll-Free **1-800-388-8765, Dept. GXI98,** or write School of Medical Claims Processing, **Dept. GXI98,** At-Home Professions, 2001 Lowe St., Fort Collins, CO 80525. 1047

---

2 SEAT BIKE

Drives Like a Car!
Easy to Pedal
Multi-Speed
Street Legal
1, 2 & 4 Seater
Free Literature
RHOADES CAR
1-615-822-2737 Ext. 2686
www.4wc.com/?2686

FREE

Catalogs

Get your Spring catalog first, Fall edition in season from...

Vigor, hardiness, unequalled selections including varieties not available anywhere else. 64 pages of delightful reading. Send for your catalogs today.

J.E. Miller Nurseries, Dept. 400
5060 W. Lake Road, Candalgua NY 14424

COTTAGE TOILETS

SUN-MAR

COMPOSTING TOILETS

*Many models including **non-electric**.*

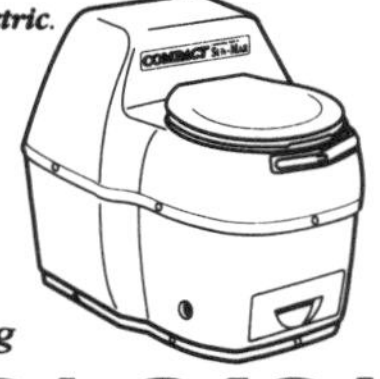

- **NO Septic**
- **NO Odor**

FREE:
24 Page Color Catalog

1-800-461-2461

600 Main Street, Tonawanda, New York 14150

Scooters, scooter lifts, Ramps, GEL batteries, & lift chairs available. *Delivery included. Save hundreds of $$.*

Free Catalog

Quality & Savings You Deserve!

1-800-229-1317 CALL TODAY

Scooter Discounters

PUBLISH YOUR BOOK!

Our FREE step-by-step Self Publishing Guide gives you all features and prices up-front. You're ensured quality with in-house printing and bindery services. We offer low minimum quantities – only 200 books! Call or write for our FREE guide.

MORRIS
PUBLISHING
3212 E. Hwy 30
Kearney, NE 68847

***800-650-7888**, ext. OFA9*

http://morrispublishing.com

CLASSIFIED ADVERTISING

For information, contact Donna Stone, 800-729-9265, ext. 214.

ALTERNATIVE ENERGY

BUILD WATER-, WIND-, AND SOLAR-powered appliances. Thirty plants. Details $3. MCOD, 3203 Bordero, Thousand Oaks CA 91362.

HYDROELECTRIC SYSTEMS since 1973. Free brochure, guide, U.S. $15. WPM, Box 9723, Midland TX 79708. E-mail wpm@tech-center.com.

ASTROLOGY/OCCULT

BIORHYTHMS. Your physical, emotional, intellectual cycles charted in color. Interpretation guide. Six months ($14). Twelve months ($20). Send name, birth date. CYCLES, Dept. FAB, 2251 Berkely Ave., Schenectady NY 12309.

PSYCHIC SAMPLES. Unlimited calling. 800-647-7813. Adults over 18 only.

FREE METAPHYSICAL CATALOG. Feng shui, incense, oils, and brews. Moonrise Magic, 505-332-2665; www.moonrisebooks.com.

LOOKING FOR LOVE, HAPPINESS, SUCCESS? Live psychic readings 800-581-6699 and 900-263-5744. Dial direct 268-404-5549 and 011-592-1787. 18+. International rates.

FREE OCCULT CATALOG! Over 5,000 books, jewelry, ritual items, incense, music, etc. AzureGreen, PO Box 48-OFA, Middlefield MA 01243. 413-623-2155.

ASTROLOGY. Personalized, comprehensive natal chart ($14). Progressed chart for current year ($14). Both ($20). Send name, birth date, birth time, birthplace. CYCLES, Dept. FAA, 2251 Berkely Ave., Schenectady NY 12309.

TAKE CONTROL OF YOUR FUTURE. Contact your personal psychic 800-941-8355. No credit card, no problem 900-993-5688 and 268-404-4529, tarot 011-592-246-680. 18+. International rates.

ANNABELL GOD-GIFTED POWERFUL PSYCHIC, 36 years experience. Specializing in reuniting loved ones, health, happiness, and money. Guarantee immediate results. Call anytime 817-608-0424.

MISS LISA, astrology reader, extraordinary powers; call for help for love or money. 3810 Memorial Dr., Waycross GA 31501. 912-283-3206.

FREE: ONE BLACK OR WHITE MAGIC SPELL! Tell me what you need! EKSES, PO Box 9315(B), San Bernardino CA 92427-9315.

LIVE PROFESSIONAL PSYCHICS. Expert advice on where to meet your soul mate. Call 900-226-9800 ext. 8168. $3.99/min. 18+. Serve-U 619-645-8434.

LUCK, LOVE, AND MONEY can be yours. Over 5,000 spiritual items. $1 for catalog. Church Goods, Dept. F, 801 W. Jackson, Chicago IL 60607.

WICCACRAFT, learn the power, live the magic. Learn at home. Free information, PO Box 1366, Nashua NH 03061. 603-880-7237.

LET EARTH'S RELIGION EMPOWER YOU! The school of Wicca, PO Box 297OP, Hinton WV 25951-0297.

FREE SAMPLES! Best live psychics! 18+ from 69¢/min. 800-207-6338 and 900-745-0118. Live tarot: 268-404-4959 and 011-592-580-330.

FREE LUCKY NUMBERS. Send birth date and self-addressed envelope. Mystic, Box 2009-R, Jamestown NC 27282.

AMAZING OCCULT DISCOVERIES develop supernatural powers safely, easily! Free experiments. Williamsburg, Box 3483-RL, New York NY 10008.

CATALOG. Complete spiritual, occult needs. Oils, incense, herbs, books, etc. $3. Power Products, Box 442F, Mars Hill NC 28754.

LIVE PSYCHICS. 1-on-1. 900-407-7784 ext. 9217. $3.99 per min. Must be 18 years. Serv-U 619-645-8434.

THE MOST COMPLETE metaphysical, magical, psychic-power correspondence course ever. Become a recognized professional. Earn unlimited income with our university doctoral-degree program. Reasonable rates. Priesthood, 2401 Artesia Blvd., 12-188FA, Redondo Beach CA 90278.

ACCURATE, INSIGHTFUL TELEPHONE READINGS with radio/television psychics, authors, teachers Stephen & Tasha Halpert. Over 20 years experience. Visa/MC 508-839-0111.

PSYCHIC SPIRITUAL ADVISOR helps restore broken love, health, happiness. Telephone readings help even miles away. Remarkable results. Visa/MC 707-579-5123.

SISTER ODESSA, spiritual healer and advisor. Are you unhappy, suffering from pain? I guarantee results. 912-273-4059.

SISTER ROGERS, psychic reader and advisor. Can help you with problems, love, business, marriage, and health. 903-454-4406.

BROTHER DANIEL, Louisiana bayou spiritualist. Stop searching, end confusion. Remove pain, sorrow, and all your problems. 561-460-9993.

ASTROLOGICAL CHARTS, interpreted reports, 25+ pages. Natal, current year progressed, $15. Both $25. Send birth date, birthplace, time. Yvette Duval, Box 562524, Miami FL 33256.

APPAREL

FREE CATALOG! Great Martini gear, golf hats, T-shirts, piques, towels, and more! Martini Lovers Unite! 888-827-3447. www.martiniman.com.

AUTOMOTIVE

AUTOMOBILE/TRUCK/MOTORCYCLE literature wanted: 1900-1975. I buy sales brochures, manuals, toys, racing memorabilia, etc. Walter Miller, 6710 Brooklawn, Syracuse NY 13211. 315-432-8282. Fax 315-432-8256.

WINTON AUTOMOBILE, BICYCLE, AND DIESEL LITERATURE, postcards, letters, factory magazines. *The Auto ERA,* ephemera, photos, miscellaneous memorabilia. Anything Winton. Bernie Golias, PO Box 392, Twinsburg OH 44087. Phone 330-425-4744 or fax 330-425-4840.

GOVERNMENT-SEIZED vehicles from $100. Fords, Mercedes, Chevys, Corvettes, surplus. Buyers guide. 800-513-4343 ext. S-2838.

BEER & WINE MAKING

WINEMAKERS-BEERMAKERS. Free illustrated catalog. Fast service. Since 1967. Kraus, Box 7850-YB, Independence MO 64054. 800-841-7404.

BOAT KIT & PLANS

BOAT KITS, PLANS & SUPPLIES. Huge catalog $5. CLARKCRAFT, 16-29 Aqualane, Tonawanda NY 14150. 716-873-2640. www.clarkcraft.com.

BOOKS/MAGAZINES/CATALOGS

HAWAIIAN LUAU of taste treats. Original Macadima Nut Korn Krunch, 100% Kona coffee and new 100% Hawaiian coffee, Poi Ilio coffee, scrumptious gourmet chocolates, Hawaiian macadamia nuts, factory-direct prices. Free catalog. Kona Confections, PO Box 2579, Kailua-Kona, HI 96745. 800-437-7477. Check out our Web site www.konaconfections.com.

FREE BOOKLETS: Life, death, soul, resurrection, pollution crisis, hell, Judgment Day, restitution. Bible Standard(OF), PO Box 67, Chester Springs PA 19425-0067.

MAP COLLECTOR'S KIT. For the beginning map collector. Great introduction gift. Bowditch & Crandall, Inc., 781-721-7666. www.bowcran.com. E-mail jackm7453@msn.com.

SEND mailing addresses of your favorite country gift shops or $2 to: Famous Catalog, 654 W. Morrison St., Frankfort IN 46041. www.mathewswire.com. E-mail mwire@iquest.net.

MANUSCRIPTS WANTED, ALL TYPES. Publisher with 75-year tradition. *Author's Guide to Subsidy Publishing.* 800-695-9599.

LOSE WEIGHT, improve your health, and increase your potential! Life-altering book shows how. Money-back guarantee. Send $12.95 to High Living, Fitness Book, PO Box 719, Lahaska PA 18931.

FREE ISSUE! Gardening, livestock, alternative energy, making a living. Great magazine! 1/2 year for $9.95 with a free extra issue. 800-835-2418. www.backwoodshome.com.

MAKE $$$ ON GARAGE SALES. Send $8.95 for book plus $2 s/h. Sanchez, 4140 Oceanside Blvd. #159-357, Oceanside CA 92056.

FREE BOOK LIST! Astrology, metaphysics, motivation, inspiration, religion. Box 5588(OFA), Santa Fe NM 87502-5588. www.sunbooks.com.

GRACE LIVINGSTON HILL BOOK COLLECTORS! We stock them all! Phone 800-854-8571 for free lists.

BUSINESS OPPORTUNITIES

NATIONAL DIRECTORY: Home workers wanted by over 100 companies. Good pay. Free newsletter. Gulf Books, Box 263484, Tampa FL 33685-3484.

$400 WEEKLY ASSEMBLING PRODUCTS from home. For free information, send SASE to Home Assembly-FA, PO Box 216, New Britain CT 06050-0216.

1,500 ITEMS BELOW WHOLESALE. A real business opportunity. PO Box 4821, Warrington FL 32507.

LET THE GOVERNMENT FINANCE your small business. Grants/loans to $800,000. Free recorded message. 707-448-0270. (KE1).

EARN THOUSANDS STUFFING ENVELOPES. Money never stops. Send SASE to Lightning Quick Mail Distributors, PO Box 18027, Philadelphia PA 19147.

$1,000 WEEKLY processing envelopes! $1 each! Weekly pay! Send stamped envelope: PrimeSource, Box 700-FA, Worth IL 60482.

GET PAID $268.20/roll taking easy snapshots at home! Film supplied. Phototek, Box 3706-FO, Idyllwild CA 92549. 909-659-9757 ext. 207. www.phototek.net.

RECORD VIDEOTAPES AT HOME! Easy $1,800 weekly income! Free start-up information kit! CMS VIDEO, Dept. 174, 210 Lorna Square, Birmingham AL 35216-5439.

PIANO TUNING PAYS: Learn with home correspondence course. American Tuning School, 17070 Telfer, Dept. FA, Morgan Hill CA 95037. 800-497-9793.

$3,500 or more weekly! Little or no investment. LSASE. $1. Richardson's, Box 307-F9, Rittman OH 44270-1378.

$29,000 IN BACKYARD, growing profitable plants with hydroponics. Start with $80. Free booklet. Growers, Box 2010-FA, Pt. Townsend WA 98368.

EARN $80-$300 DAILY! Easy home mail-order system. Free report. LaPacifica, Box 80717FA99, Bakersfield CA 93380-0717.

CASINO MANIA! Win consistently. Slot machines, blackjack, craps, roulette, and bingo. Free info packet. Write JSA, Box 7038, North Arlington NJ 07031.

AMAZING SECRET. Make money at home the old-fashioned way. Free information. Toll-free 888-693-5703.

LEARN SMALL-BUSINESS MANAGEMENT at home. Free information. Call 800-326-9221, or write Lifetime Career Schools, Dept. OBO919, 101 Harrison St., Archbald PA 18403.

NO EXPERIENCE NECESSARY! $400 to $900 weekly potential. Own hours. For information, write to V.P. Enterprise, PO Box 1196, Hightstown NJ 08520.

$80,000 FROM ONE ACRE! Grow ginseng, golden seal. Information, long SASE. Lee's, Box 68276-FA9, New Augusta IN 46268.

LET THE GOVERNMENT start your business. Free business incorporation. 202-298-0526. www.capitalpublications.com.

BUY IT WHOLESALE

FREE BULK-CANDY CATALOG! Old-fashioned specialty candies — home, work, travel, resale. Peters Candies, Inc., 138-F2 West Court St., Cincinnati OH 45202.

49,457 PRODUCTS, FACTORY DIRECT. Taiwan, Hong Kong, Mexico! Save 500%-900%. Echomark, Box 739-FA9, Shalimar FL 32579-0739.

CATTLE

DISCOVER DEXTER CATTLE: Small, dual-purpose, intelligent, hardy, unique. Contact Rosemary Fleharty, The American Dexter Cattle Association, Route 1 Box 378, Concordia MO 64020. Telephone: 660-463-7704;www.members.aol.com/dexteramer.

CARNIVOROUS PLANTS

CARNIVOROUS (insect-eating) plants, seeds, supplies, and books. Peter Paul's Nurseries, Canandaigua NY 14424-8713. www.peterpauls.com.

COLLECTIBLES/NOSTALGIA

BUYING PRE-1975 COMIC BOOKS! Top prices paid. Free catalog of comics for sale. Nostalgia Zone, 3149-1/2 Hennepin Ave. S., Minneapolis MN 55406. 612-822-2806.

ALADDIN LAMPS and parts. Kerosene lamps, repair service, beautiful, collectible. Catalog $1. MGS Co., Box 11-FA, Mitcheville TN 37119.

CIVIL WAR and other firearms, swords, uniforms, flags, buckles, letters, colts, Winchesters. Singles or collections, Jerry 800-686-0222.

COMPOSTING TOILETS

PHOENIX COMPOSTING TOILETS. Odorless, waterless, low maintenance. Cabin, home, or public facility. Graywater Systems. 888-862-3854.

CRAFTS

INDIAN CRAFTS. Free brochure showing materials used. Recommended to Indian Guides, Scout troops, etc. Cleveland Leather, 2629 Lorain Ave., Cleveland OH 44113.

DEER CONTROL

DEER PROBLEMS? We can help! Free catalog. Call Deerbusters, 800-248-DEER (3337). www.deerbusters.com.

GARDEN CATALOGS

FREE GARDENING CATALOG. Seeds: vegetable, herb, oriental. Trees, shrubs, supplies, greenhouses, beneficial insects. Mellingers, Dept. 720N Range Rd., North Lima OH 44452-9731.

EXPLORE THE MIRACLE OF BEEKEEPING. A successful garden needs honeybees. To get started, call 800-233-7929 for free 78-page catalog.

EDUCATION/INSTRUCTION

BECOME A PRIVATE INVESTIGATOR. Approved home study. Free literature. P.C.D.I., Atlanta, Georgia. 800-362-7070 Dept. JRK554.

LEARN TO LEGALLY ELIMINATE SOCIAL SECURITY and income taxes. SASE. Preferred $ervices, 203 Argonne B209, Long Beach CA 90803.

BECOME A MEDICAL BILLING/CLAIMS SPECIALIST. Home study. P.C.D.I., Atlanta, Georgia. 800-362-7070 Dept. MCK554.

LEARN FLOWER ARRANGING! Start business or hobby. Free brochure on home study program. Call 800-326-9221, or write Lifetime Career Schools, Dept. OBO219, 101 Harrison St., Archbald PA 18403.

COMPLETE HIGH SCHOOL AT HOME. Diploma awarded. Low tuition. Est. 1897 — Accredited. Telephone 800-531-9268 for free information, or write to AMERICAN SCHOOL, Dept. #348, 220 E. 170th St., Lansing IL 60438.

BECOME A VETERINARY ASSISTANT/animal care specialist. Home study. Exciting careers for animal lovers. Free literature package. 800-362-7070 Dept. CCK554.

LEARN LANDSCAPING at home. Free brochure. Call 800-326-9221, or write Lifetime Career Schools, Dept. OBO119, 101 Harrison St., Archbald PA 18403.

BECOME A HOME INSPECTOR. Approved home study. Free literature. P.C.D.I., Atlanta, Georgia. 800-362-7070 Dept. PPK554.

BECOME A MEDICAL TRANSCRIPTIONIST. Home study. Free career literature. P.C.D.I., Atlanta, Georgia. 800-362-7070 Dept. YYK554.

WILDERNESS WAY primitive skills, tracking, nature-awareness school. Complimentary catalog. 774 Glenmary Dr., Owego NY 13827. 607-687-9186.

LEARN TAX PREPARATION. Approved home study. Free career literature. P.C.D.I., Atlanta, Georgia. 800-362-7070 Dept. TPK 554.

FARM & GARDEN

DISCOVER NEWEST PLANTS FOR YOUR GARDEN in *New Varieties to Know and Grow,* 1999 edition. Photograph-intensive book complete with detailed cultural requirements and advice from experts. Oakleaf Publications, PO Box 58649, Cincinnati OH 45258. 888-256-OAKLEAF (9285).

TROY-BILT® OWNERS. Discount parts catalog, send stamp. Replacement tines $64. Kelley's, Manilla IN 46150. 317-398-9042. www.svs.net/kelley/index.htm.

NEPTUNE'S HARVEST ORGANIC fish fertilizers. Pleasant smelling. Commercially proven. Outperforms chemicals. Wholesale/Retail/Catalog. 800-259-GROW (4769).

FINANCIAL/LOANS BY MAIL

NEED MONEY? Credit challenges? Business opportunity based on operating lines of credit. Extremely high approval rates. Very attractive interest rates. Call toll-free for application. 800-828-7475.

FLAGS

FLAGS! American, state, NASCAR, MIA/POW, Confederate, historical. Color catalog send $2. Flags & Things, PO Box 356, Dillsburg PA 17019.

FOR THE HOME

DRINKING WATER PROBLEMS? Large or small, we solve them with a Pure Water distillation system. Dealer inquiries are also welcome. Call us at 800-875-5915.

DIGITAL RAIN GAUGES. Measure rainfall without stepping outdoors. Wireless, self-emptying, accurate. $99.95 and $149.95, plus s&h. MC/Visa. Free information. MAMINO DIST-F998, PO Box 113, Belleville IL 62222.

FUND-RAISING

MAKE GOOD MONEY for your school, group, or organization selling *The Old Farmer's Almanac* publications and calendars to friends and neighbors. Great products sell themselves! Great prices! Great opportunity! Call today 800-424-6906. *The Old Farmer's Almanac* Fund-raising, 220 South St., Bernardston MA 01337. www.gbimkt.com.

GENEALOGY

HAROLD PUTNAM'S. *The Putnams of Salem Village*. Hardcover $20. The Putnam's, PO Box 3821, Vero Beach FL 32964.

GIFTS

FREE GIFT OF YOUR CHOICE! With order of personalized children's storybook. Call for full-color brochures. 888-869-7116.

AMAZING GIFTS FOR EVERYONE. NFL/MLB collectible clocks. Save big! Order free catalog now! Send $3 s/h to Armu, 8322-K Dalesford, Baltimore MD 21234-5010. Web site: www.armuproducts.com.

NEVER GIVE THE WRONG GIFT AGAIN! Unique gift idea allows recipients to pick their own gift. Call 888-869-7116 for catalog.

GINSENG

GINSENG SEED $12/oz., roots $20/100; goldenseal roots $25/100. Information $1. Ginseng-OFA, Flag-pond TN 37657

HEALTH CARE

FREE CATALOG! Edgar Cayce natural remedies, dental products, homeopathy, oils, shampoos, vitamins, herbs, etc. The Heritage Store, PO Box 444-FA, Virginia Beach VA 23458. 800-862-2923.

FREE CATALOG! National-brand vitamins up to 60% off! Kal, Schiff, Twinlab, and more! 800-858-2143.

FREE MAGNETIC CATALOG and information report. Distributors wanted. American Health Service. 800-635-7070.

LOSE WEIGHT NOW! No drugs, no stimulants, no diets! Research-based and proven that it works. Call free 888-900-9881.

NEARSIGHTEDNESS CURE! Radical new breakthrough. Easy, self-method. Free brochure: World Innovations, RR #2-F, Sexsmith, AB T0H 3C0 Canada. 403-568-2137.

WHAT YOU DON'T KNOW is killing you! Mineral content of North American soils at all-time low. You are at risk! Learn how to easily protect your health. Call 403-225-2051.

DR. BROSS CAN HELP IMPOTENCY and enlarge size and firmness. 15 million satisfied customers. Cat. #89FA Pump, instructional video, magazine, shipping. $29.95. METCO, Dept. 89FA, Box 7020, Tarzana CA 91357. Visa/MC/AMEX. 800-378-4689. Fax 818-345-4643.

HEARING-AID BATTERIES AND ACCESSORIES. Lowest prices, Rayovac Zinc Air, no shipping charges. 336-774-0103. www.powerpalace.com.

JOINT PAIN? Thousands have found relief from arthritis without drugs or stimulants. You can learn simple solution. Call free 888-751-2323.

DEATH BEGINS IN THE COLON. Headaches, indigestion, constipation, diarrhea, heartburn, fatigue, irritable bowel, gas, and big stomach all have been directly attributed to a toxic colon. Raw dietary fiber and enzymes are the answer. Call 800-610-1958 to reclaim your health.

HEARING AIDS. Quality hearing instruments and accessories, repairs, affordable prices, reliable service. Better Hearing Aids and Supplies, PO Box 6015, Wilmette IL 60091. Fax 773-465-5576.

HELP WANTED

GREAT EXTRA-INCOME IDEA! Assemble craft products at home! Guaranteed! Call now! 800-377-6000 ext. 8440.

$1,093/WEEK! WORK AT HOME. Get paid watching TV, listening to music, and reading! Learn how. Send $1 s/h to JobsAmerica, 611 Pennsylvania S.E. 8676F9, Washington DC 20003-4303.

$400 WEEKLY ASSEMBLING PRODUCTS from home. For free information, send SASE to Home Assembly-A, PO Box 216, New Britain CT 06050-0216.

HOME TYPISTS, PC users needed. $45,000 income potential. Call 800-513-4343 ext. B-2838.

EASY WORK! EXCELLENT PAY! Assemble products at home. Call toll-free 800-467-5566 ext. 12627.

HERBS

FREE GRANDMA'S HOME-REMEDIES BOOKLET. Collection of recipes, herbs, and folklore. Send long stamped envelope. Champion's RX-Herb Store, 2369 Elvis Presley, Memphis TN 38106.

HERB LABELS and engraved garden markers featuring botanical name: any herb or variety; request free brochure. Write to The Still-Roome, 1214 W. Boston Post Rd. #A244, Mamaroneck NY 10543-3327. E-mail herbs@westnet.com.

INVENTIONS/PATENTS

INVENTIONS, IDEAS, NEW PRODUCTS! Presentation to industry/exhibition at national innovation exposition. Patent services. 800-288-IDEA(4332).

PATENT IT ECONOMICALLY! Free details. Licensed since 1958. Near Washington, DC; Ph.D. Associates, 800-546-2649.

LIVE BAIT

WORM CASTINGS AND COMPOSTING. Redworms breeders 1,000 $18. Bedruns 2,000 $19. Postpaid instructions. Smith's Worms Co., Boston GA 31626.Visa/MC 912-498-1605.

MUSIC/RECORDS/TAPES

CASH FOR OLD RECORDS! Illustrated 72-page catalog, including thousands of specific prices we pay for 78s on common labels (Columbia, Decca, Victor, etc.), information about scarce labels, shipping instruction, etc. Send $2 (refundable). Discollector, Box 691035(FA), San Antonio TX 78269.

ACCORDIONS, CONCERTINAS, button boxes. New, used, buy, sell, trade, repair. Hohners, Martin guitars. Catalog $5. Castiglione, Box 40-A, Warren MI 48090. 810-755-6050.

NURSERY STOCK

TREE SEEDLINGS, Christmas trees, windbreaks, reforestation, wildlife habitat. Wholesale prices. Free catalog. FLICKINGERS' NURSERY, Box 245A, Sagamore PA 16250. 800-368-7381.

EVERGREEN TREE SEEDLINGS direct from grower. Free catalog. Carino Nurseries, Box 538, Dept. AL, Indiana PA 15701. www.carinonurseries.com.

OF INTEREST TO ALL

FOUNDATION GRANTS for individuals, to $180,000 for widely varied uses. Free recorded message: 707-448-2668. (2KE1).

NATIONAL MENTAL-HEALTH MAINTENANCE. "Treating your chronic anxiety" written program contains breakthrough information and individualized therapies. Don't forget students! Send $14.95 (NY residents add sales tax). NMHM, PO Box 38013, Albany NY 12203-8013.

TWELVE-MONTH BIORHYTHM CHARTS. $7. Send birth date and year. John Morgan, 1208 Harris, Bartlesville OK 74006.

BELLS IN YOUR EARS? Amazing natural remedy. 100 capsules $13.95, $3.50 s/h. International Concepts, 60 Martin Creek Ct., Stockbridge GA 30281.

ANGRY? Turn anger's energy into powers for happiness, success, security. Order today. Powerful booklet by Vernon Howard. *Conquer Harmful Anger 100 Ways.* $2. NewLife, PO Box 2230-CS, Pine AZ 85544. www.anewlife.org.

OUTDOOR SPORTS/ACTIVITIES

BAIT SECRETS for freshwater and saltwater fishing detailed in six packet booklets. Gulf Books, Box 263484, Tampa FL 33685-3484. www.gulfbooks.com.

PERENNIALS

SELECT NORTHERN PERFORMANCE DAYLILIES. More bloom. Catalog. Scrub Oak Farm, PO Box 817, West Tisbury MA 02575-0817.

PERSONALS

MEET LATIN LADIES! Mexico, South America. Magazines, videos, tours. Free brochures! TLC, Box 924994-AL, Houston TX 77292-4994. 713-896-9224. www.tlcworldwide.com.

RUSSIAN LADIES, truly beautiful, educated, seek relationship. 3,000 selected from 80,000+ ladies. Exciting tours, videos. Free color catalog — 500 photos! Euro182, PO Box 888851, Atlanta GA 30356. 770-458-0909. www.euroladies.com.

BEAUTIFUL ASIAN LADIES overseas seek love, marriage. Lowest rates! Free brochure: PR, Box 1245FA, Benicia CA 94510. 707-747-6906.

ATTENTION: SISTER LIGHT, Spartanburg, South Carolina. One free reading when you call. I will help in all problems. 864-576-9397 or 864-978-6767.

BEAUTIFUL LADIES desire life mates! Exciting Thailand tours! Free pen-pal catalog! TAWL, Box 937(FT), Kailua-Kona HI 96745-0937. 808-329-5559. www.tawl.com.

LATIN, ORIENTAL LADIES seek friendship, marriage. Free photo-brochure. LATINS, Box 1716-OF, Chula Vista CA 91912.

MOTHER DOROTHY, reader and adviser. Advice on all problems — love, marriage, health, business, and nature. Gifted healer, she will remove your sickness, sorrow, pain, bad luck. ESP. Results in three days. Write or call about your problems. 1214 Gordon St., Atlanta GA 30310. 404-755-1301.

ASIAN BEAUTIES! Worldwide! Pen pals, marriage! Color brochure $2. P.I.C., Box 461873-FA, Los Angeles CA 90046. www.pacisl.com.

NICE SINGLES, Christian values. Amazing results. Free magazine. Singles, PO Box 310-OFA, Allardt TN 38504.

LONELY? UNLUCKY? UNHAPPY? Lost nature? Lost love? Linda solves all problems quickly. Free readings. 912-995-3611.

MOTHER DORA can influence others. Bring luck. Help with all problems. Correct wrongs. Results! 912-888-5999.

SISTER RUBY helps in all problems. One free reading by phone. Removes bad luck. 912-776-3069.

ASIAN WOMEN desire marriage! Overseas. $2 for details, photos! Sunshine International, Box 5500-YH, Kailua-Kona HI 96745-5500. Web site www.sunshine-girls.com.

REV. FIXXER. Emergencies, fast, lottery, luck, courts, love, addictions, health. Fix/unfix. MOJOS — anything. 616-778-3009.

ELIZABETH POWERS, truly gifted healer. Do you feel there is evil influence following you? Everything you do in life not going your way? Are you tired of searching for answers? Do you want peace of mind in love, business, family, friends, health, etc.? I can help overcome your enemies and guide you through life's toughest problems. "Don't give up." The answer is only a phone call away; all readings private and confidential. 2062 Thomasville Rd., Tallahasse FL 32312. 850-297-1808.

FREE INFORMATION FOR UNMARRIED Catholics. Large membership. Unlimited choice. Established 1980. Sparks, Box 872-F9, Troy NY 12181.

ASIAN DREAM GIRLS abroad desire love, marriage. Lowest price! Tours! Free brochure. ADG, Box 4821FA, Sanford FL 32772. 407-321-8558.

DOMINIQUE REVEALS FUTURE, love, finance; helps all problems. Reunites lovers immediately. One free reading. 423-472-3035.

MEET WOMEN WORLDWIDE FOR LOVE AND MARRIAGE! World's #1 correspondence service since 1974. Complimentary 32-page photo-magazine. Cherry Blossoms, PO Box 190-FA, Kapaau HI 96755. 800-322-3267 ext. 71. Web site: www.blossom.com/ad71.html. E-mail cherry@blossoms.com.

LOUISIANA SPIRITUALIST. 39 years experience removing bad luck. Unhappy in love, fast help with all problems. Sister Mary 561-466-0589.

DO YOU NEED HELP in love, sickness, work? I can help; call now for one free reading. Ms. Gina 860-456-9429.

SISTER JOSIE can solve all problems in life such as love, business, health, marriage, financial. 706-353-9259.

POULTRY

GOSLINGS, DUCKLINGS, CHICKS, turkeys, guineas, books. Picture catalog $1. Pilgrim Goose Hatchery, OF-99, Williamsfield OH 44093.

FREE CATALOG. Baby chicks, ducks, geese, turkeys, game birds, Canadian honkers, wood ducks. Eggs to incubators. Books and supplies. Call 800-720-1134. Stromberg's, Pine River 45 MN 56474-0400.

GOSLINGS, DUCKLINGS, CHICKS, guineas, turkeys, bantams, pheasants, quail, swans. Books, medications. Hoffman Hatchery, Gratz PA 17030.

REAL ESTATE

OZARK MOUNTAIN OR LAKE ACREAGES. From $50/month, nothing down, environmental protection codes, huge selection. Free catalog. WOODS & WATERS, Box 1-FA, Willow Springs MO 65793. 888-634-6222. www.ozarkland.com.

THE BEST REALTORS in central Massachusetts. Call Louise Erskine Real Estate 508-752-0466.

GOVERNMENT LAND now available for claim. Up to 160 acres/person. Free recorded message. 707-448-1887. (4KE1).

ESCAPE TO THE HILLS OF SOUTH-CENTRAL KENTUCKY. Secluded country properties. Inexpensive homes. Call Century 21, Vibbert Realty, 800-267-2600 for free brochure.

ARKANSAS LAND. Free lists! Recreational, investment, retirement homes, acreages. Gatlin Farm Agency, Box 790, Waldron AR 72958. Toll-free 800-562-9078 ext. OFA.

LET THE GOVERNMENT PAY for your new or existing home. Over 100 different programs available. Free recorded message: 707-448-3210. (8KE1)

RECIPES

DELICIOUS RUSSIAN RECIPES. Appetizers to amazing deserts. Send $5 to M. Rath, 2046 N. Cambridge Ave., Milwaukee WI 53202.

ONE-SKILLET WONDERS — 8 quick, delicious, nutritious meals prepared in a single skillet. $1 plus SASE to JOBE, 1165 Ferguson Rd., Gloster LA 71030.

FUDGE! ALMOST BETTER THAN "SEX." $3 + SASE. Workshop (Fudge-A), 417 Busse, Marengo IL 60152.

HOMEMADE CREOLE CREAMY PRALINES recipe with secrets. $3. SASE. Lyn, 1057 Vieux Chene Dr., Broussard LA 70518.

HAGGIS & MORE! *Guide to Traditional Scottish Fare.* $5 and SASE. Workshop (Haggis-A), 417 Busse, Marengo IL 60152.

BERKSHIRE BERRIES®. Home of original garlic-raspberry jelly; offer flavors of New England made by The Berry People™. Jams, jellies, maple syrup, honey, switchel, and more. 800-5-BERRY'S (23-7797). Web site: www.berkshireberries.com

SOUPS, SOUPS & MORE SOUPS! 100+ sensational recipes. $10. Workshop (Soup-A), 417 Busse, Marengo IL 60152.

LOW-FAT HOMESTYLE COOKBOOK. "Over 100 delicious familiar homestyle recipes (with fat reduced) . . . that keep the great taste your family loves." *Women's Circle*/Feb. 1996. Also included in *Best of the Best from Colorado Cookbooks.* $10 (s/h included). Brook Forest Publishing, PO Box 1224, Conifer CO 80433.

CANNERS! Best lids and prices. Regular (#70) 60 dozen @ $49.50 case. Widemouthed (#86) 36 dozen same price. Check/money order to Gardener's Kitchen, PO Box 322, Monument Beach MA 02553.

BARBECUE SAUCE, recipes from Arkansas. Send $3 to WPF, PO Box 503, Clarksville AR 72830.

FOOLPROOF CHICKEN SOUP, incredible! Send $2 plus SASE to Mugs' Kitchen, PO Box 6264, Ashland VA 23005.

CABBAGE SOUP DIET, healthy, natural, superb, weight-loss recipe, $5. Box 562524, Miami FL 33256.

RELIGION

GOD GAVE ME VISION, February 98. Must tell all people; send $5 plus SASE to Voice in the Wind, 230 46th St. N., St. Petersburg FL 33713.

FREE ADULT OR CHILD Bible study courses. Project Philip, Box 35-A, Muskegon MI 49443.

BIBLICAL ANSWERS to questions pastors hate. SASE. Ja-dam, PO Box 259, Avenel NJ 07001-0259.

AND GOD CRIED. . . . Unique perspective. If God shares our suffering, why does he permit the evil that causes suffering? Booklet $1. Clearwater Bible Students, PO Box 8216, Clearwater FL 33758.

CHRISTIAN PROGRAM debt freedom — monthly gifts. Free information. LSASE. 25 Pleasant St. (1005), Lynn MA 01902-4429.

SEEDS

ENDANGERED/HEIRLOOM vegetable, herb, flower seeds. Catalogs $1. Greenseeds-FA, 4N381 Maple Ave., Bensenville IL 60106. Web site: www.grandmasgarden.com.

EXOTIC HOUSEPLANTS. Flowering tropicals, medicinal herbs. Rare container plants, seeds, and supplies. Free catalog 800-793-8186. E-mail plantplace@aol.com.

RARE HILARIOUS peter, female, and squash pepper seeds. $3 per pkg. 2 for $5. All three $7.50 and over 100 more rare peppers. SEEDS, 2119 Hauss Nursery Rd., Atmore AL 36502.

FRAGRANCE. Seeds for fragrant, rare, and old-fashioned plants. Catalog $1. THE FRAGRANT PATH, PO Box 328F, Ft. Calhoun NE 68023.

GOURDS. More than 15 different shapes and sizes! The Gourd Garden and Curiosity Shop, 4808 E. C-30A, Santa Rosa Beach FL 32459. 850-231-2007.

TOBACCO KIT. Everything to grow tobacco for cigarettes, cigars, chew. Even Far North! Free catalog. 800-793-8186.

OPIUM POPPY SEEDS guaranteed fertile. 10,000 seeds for $10. Not intended for illegal use. Jones Seed Company, PO Box 2002, Douglas GA 31534.

FREE CATALOG. Finest-quality vegetable, flower & herb seeds obtainable. Burrell, Box 150-FA, Rocky Ford CO 81067.

GROW YOUR OWN pesticide-free tobacco and healing plants. Also seeds for hot peppers, houseplants, vines, specialty vegetables. Free catalog. EONS/FA, PO Box 4604, Hallandale FL 33008. 954-455-0229.

WANTED

CASH IMMEDIATELY FOR dental gold, old jewelry, coins. Free recycling kit. 800-947-1718 or Laidnear, 2213 Paradise Rd., Las Vegas NV 89104.

MAGIC STUFF. Houdini items, vintage magic posters, Mysto sets. Trombly, 7112 Loch Lomond Dr., Bethesda MD 20817. 800-673-8158.

WANTED: AUTOGRAPHS, signed photos, letters, documents of famous people. Gray, 300 Boylston St. #510, Boston MA 02116. 617-426-4912.

WE BUY ROYALTIES and minerals in producing oil and gas wells. Please write Marienfeld Royalty Corp., PO Box 25914, Houston TX 77265, or call 800-647-2580, or visit www.marienfeld.com.

WEATHER VANES

WEATHER VANES AND CUPOLAS — 50% off sale! America's largest selection. Immediate delivery. Free catalog 800-724-2548.

WILDFLOWERS

WILDFLOWERS, nursery-propagated woodland and prairie native plants for sun, shade, and wetlands. Catalog $1. Contact Cattail Meadows, Ltd., PO Box 39391, Dept. GC, Solon OH 44139.

MISCELLANEOUS

BURIED TREASURE, water, mineral deposits. Sensitive equipment allows locating from a distance. Brochure free. Simmons Scientific, Box 10057PA, Wilmington NC 28405.

JEHOVAH'S WITNESSES, friends, family, find out facts the society doesn't want you to know. Free and confidential. JW FACTS, Box 454, Metaline Falls WA 99153. Web site: www.macgregorministries.org.

STAINLESS STEEL high-pressure steam cleaners, to 4,000 PSI, 210° F, factory-direct cost. Financing. 800-324-2822.

FREE DEGREES! Counseling, metaphysics, hypnotherapy, parapsychology! Ministerial license! P.U.L.C., Box 276265-FR, Sacramento CA 95827.

THE ROSICRUCIANS offer a positive home-study system for the spiritually minded. For the authentic, traditional Rosicrucian teachings: ARC, PO Box 4764, Dallas TX 75208. www.arcgl.org.

The Old Farmer's Almanac accepts classified ads for products and services we feel will be of interest to our readers. However, we cannot verify the quality or reliability of the products or services offered.

ATTENTION CLASSIFIED ADVERTISERS!

Here's a great opportunity from the publishers of *The Old Farmer's Almanac*! Put our popular and powerful family of publications right to work for your business. For special group rates, Web classifieds, or more information, contact Donna Stone: 800-729-9265, ext. 214; fax 603-563-8252; E-mail donnas@yankeepub.com. Or write to *The Old Farmer's Almanac,* Attn: Donna Stone, P.O. Box 520, Dublin, NH 03444.

CLOSING DATES:

The Good Cook's Companion Traditional Holiday Recipes
Circulation 400,000. $6 per word........August 21, 1998

The Gardener's Companion
Circulation 400,000. $6 per word........November 2, 1998

The HomeOwner's Companion
Circulation 400,000. $6 per word........January 2, 1999

☞ Put The Old Farmer's Almanac Family of Products to Work for Your Business

The Old Farmer's Almanac products are available with your company's custom imprint at some very special pricing. Now your business can share in the marketing impact we can provide from over 200 years of experience and customer commitment. The key promotional-products distributors listed below can custom-design a single promotion or a special 12-month campaign for your business.

The Old Farmer's Almanac Family of Products

Ask Your Promotional-Products Distributor to Custom-Tailor a Successful Program for Your Company.

Just call *The Old Farmer's Almanac* Special Markets experts today at 800-729-9265, ext. 220, and we will fill you in on all the details. Web site: www.almanac.com/specialprod.html

BANKERS ADVERTISING COMPANY, Iowa City IA ● BILL LARSEN & ASSOCIATES, Tacoma WA ● CYRK, INC., Gloucester MA ● FORBES MARKETING, Exeter NH ● GOLDMAN ASSOCIATES, St. Louis MO ● HA-LO PROMOTIONAL PRODUCTS, Niles IL ● IDEA MAN, Los Angeles CA ● JII/SALES PROMOTIONS ASSOCIATES, INC., Red Oak IA ● KAESER & BLAIR, INC., Batavia OH ● LEE WAYNE, Sterling IL ● NEWTON MFG., Newton IA ● SPARTAN PROMOTIONAL GROUP, Oakdale MN ● TASCO INDUSTRIES, Dallas TX ● THE VERNON CO., Newton IA

Knowledge of germ theory is the mighty lever tha

We're not talking theology or

reincarnation. You may be alive

today simply because your great-

grandmother remembered to

wash her hands after leaving a

sickroom. by John Fleischman

Ladies and gentlemen, let us propose a toast to the greatest invention of the 20th century — the American mortality rate. You have a better chance of living longer today than ever before in human history. It's a fact of modern life that we all take for granted. But have you ever considered your chances of never having been born? What if Mom had died of typhoid as a baby? What if Dad had never been born because *his* father had died young?

Your chances of being here at all were about 50-50. If death rates at the beginning of the century had not changed and all other factors had remained the same, we would be a nation of 139 million people instead of 270 million, say Kevin M. White and Samuel H. Preston, demographers at the University of Pennsylvania.

"Half of the population owes its existence to twentieth-century mortality improvements," White and Preston wrote in the September 1996 issue of *Population and Development Review*. The demographers reached this conclusion by using "counterfactual projections." That is, they set up a what-if experiment. Think of it as a demographic history of the United States that never happened. What if no significant progress had been made in American public health and medicine after 1900? White and Preston calculated that fully half the people now alive either would have died young or would be absent because one of their parents would not have survived to reproductive age.

Mortality is a concept that warms the hearts of insurance underwriters, theologians, and demographers. The rest of us take it more personally, thinking of it in terms of our own "life expectancy." The increase in American life expectancy in this century has been amazing. Life expectancy at birth in 1900 was 47.3 years; in 1994, it was 75.7 years. In 1900, fewer than 60 percent of women could expect to reach the age of 50. In 1992, it was calculated that 95 percent of women would reach age 50. The baby boomers may now be in the throes of 50-something angst, but they should consider the alternative to suffering through an "over the hill" party.

opened a new philosophy of life for most of us.

In their counterfactual history of the United States, White and Preston recalculated population growth across the century in five-year increments, using the real improvements in life span that occurred. The big impacts came early in the century, and the younger age-groups experienced the greatest benefits. Since 1950, improvements in survival rates have been slower and have had the greatest impact on the elderly. If the U.S. mortality rate had remained stuck at the 1950 level, the U.S. population would nevertheless be 94 percent of its size today.

Researchers have made great advances in medicine over the past 100 years, but at least half of us owe our very lives to one big breakthrough: Preston credits the acceptance of the germ theory of disease and the changes it brought to the practice of medicine, the handling of food, and the treatment of water. Simple sanitation was the innovation with the greatest impact on human life in the past century, indeed the past 1,000 years. Knowledge of germ theory is the mighty lever that opened a new philosophy of life for most of us. We can expect to live. We can expect our children to live.

The instruments of that optimism are all around us. We expect reasonably safe drinking water, organized waste disposal, and nosy inspectors in restaurants and food plants. We think doctors should wash their hands and don gloves between operations. We isolate or treat carriers of contagious diseases. We float in a sea of antiseptics, antibiotics, and preservatives. We freeze, sterilize, refrigerate, irradiate, and seal all that can spoil. We flush, dump, burn, treat, recycle, and isolate all that can carry pathogens. We test the workplace for dangers. We keep tabs on the toxic.

If we can stay clean and out of the way of runaway trucks or runaway cancer cells, the U.S. Census Bureau is expecting 274,634,000 of us to be on hand for the Fourth of July, 2000. On our nation's birthday, surely it would be fitting to celebrate that which has made America so great and so populous. My fellow Americans, let us all hail hot and cold running water — and soap. Three cheers for the pursuit of life, liberty, and cleanliness!

ONE DIFFERENCE BETWEEN MEN AND WOMEN

Everyone knows that women live longer than men and that there are more old women than old men. The current ratio of men to women in the 85-plus age-group is 0.38 (i.e., 2/5 of a man for every woman), compared with a more equal 0.79 (or 4/5) in 1900. Why is that? Women in this century have benefited more than men from declines in mortality after the first years of life. Seven out of eight women over age 84 would not be alive today if 1900 mortality rates had continued, say White and Preston.

But men have benefited the most from decreases in infant and childhood mortality. In 1900, 15 percent of males died in the critical first year of life, while only 12 percent of females died. In the first decade of the century, there was a tremendous decline in infant mortality. Today the mortality rate for babies of both sexes is under 1 percent. The ratio of old men to old women in 2000 will be unbalanced but closer, because more baby boys were surviving by 1915.

WHERE TO WATCH THE POPCLOCK

The U.S. Census Bureau's Web site (www.census.gov) is a candy jar for those who can't resist the lure of numbers. For the exact population figures of the United States or the world, calculated to the second, go to www.census.gov/main/www/popclock.html.

Anecdotes and PLEASANTRIES

A motley collection of useful (and useless) facts, stories, advice, and observations compiled mostly from reader correspondence received over the past 12 months.

A Valiant Attempt to Prove the Ol' "Balancing Egg" Theory

As we all know (and can agree on), the equinoxes come at those two times of the year that the Sun crosses the celestial equator and the length of day is approximately the same as the length of night all over the world. In 1999, the vernal (spring) equinox is on March 20 at 8:46 P.M., EST; the autumnal (fall) equinox is on September 23 at 7:31 A.M., EDT.

What we all *don't* agree on is whether or not it's possible to stand a raw egg on its end during the five minutes before and the five minutes after the exact moment of an equinox. Folklore says you can do it, but only at those times.

THE ARGUMENT FOR:

"I can make raw eggs stand on their fat ends only at the times of the fall or spring equinoxes. I know people think it's hogwash, but I don't care. It works."

– L. S., Hammonton, New Jersey

"It has something to do with the balance of night and day when everything is in harmony."

– R. T., Green Bay, Wisconsin

"It works because gravity is balanced when the Sun is over Earth's equator."

– B.R.D., Nashville, Tennessee

"The Sun exerts a greater gravitational attraction at that time so the eggs are sort of pulled upright for a few minutes."

– C.D.B., Jacksonville, Florida

(Editor's Note: The statements of these four Almanac readers are typical of the vast majority of mail we receive each fall and spring on this subject.)

THE ARGUMENT AGAINST:

"There is no astronomical reason that a raw egg can be balanced at the times of the equinoxes — any more than at any other time. As to the gravity argument, Earth's pull on the egg is nearly 300,000 times greater than that of the Moon and more than 1,600 times greater than that of the Sun, so the minor variations in the gravitational pull of the Sun or the Moon would not affect one's ability to balance an egg on its end. That depends on the egg. Some balance; some don't. Anytime."

– Dr. George Greenstein, astronomer for The Old Farmer's Almanac

THE TEST:

Last spring, a few minutes before 2:55 P.M., EST, on March 20 (the precise moment of the 1998 vernal equinox), several editors of this Almanac attempted to balance 24 raw eggs — some white, some brown, slightly cool from refrigeration — on their fat ends. We were successful with 19. Two slumped over within a half hour;

– Brian Jenkins

17 remained standing until the end of the work day, at which point we put them back into their egg cartons.

Three days later we tried again, with the same eggs, same room, and same editors — and again were able to stand 19 on end. Some people present said that three days was still too close to the spring equinox and that we'd never be able to do it, say, a month later. Some blamed El Niño.

We intend to try again this December — at the winter solstice, exactly the halfway point between the equinoxes. Meanwhile, looks as if you might be right, George.

Almanac editors successfully stood eggs upright on the vernal equinox — and again three days later.

The Best "If Only" of the Decade

■ I remember reading recently in Smiley Ander's *Advocate* column that a few years ago, two U.S. senators, William B. Sprong and Hiram Fong, sponsored a bill in Congress recommending the ringing of church bells all over the country to hail the arrival in Hong Kong of the United States table-tennis team after its successful tour of China.

Unfortunately, their bill was defeated, thus depriving Congress of the opportunity to pass the Sprong-Fong Hong Kong Ping-Pong Ding-Dong Bill.

– courtesy of E. R., Seattle, Washington

Letter from a Schoolteacher

Dear Folks at the Almanac,

I am a kindergarten teacher here in Massachusetts. Since lots of my students are children of friends in my neighborhood, they know me by my first name. But in order to teach respect for elders and so forth, I like being called by my last name when I'm in school.

So at the beginning of last year, I said, as usual, to my class of mostly five-year-olds, "Outside you know me as 'Midge,' but here in school, I want you to call me 'Mrs. Landry.' OK?" Everyone nodded in agreement.

One little boy, Timmy Booth, immediately turned to his neighbor, and in the same serious tone of voice I had used, said, "Joshua, outside you know me as 'Timmy,' but here in school, I want you to call me . . ." He paused for a second, then said, ". . . Bat Man!"

I collapsed in laughter. Thought you might find a place for this true story in your '99 edition.

Yours truly,
Mrs. Midge Landry
Lowell, Massachusetts

(continued)

How to Easily Estimate Distances

(A Bona Fide "Rule of Thumb")

Your arm is about ten times longer than the distance between your eyes. That fact, together with a bit of applied trigonometry, can be used to estimate the distance between you and any object of approximately known size.

Imagine, for example, that you're standing on the side of a hill, trying to decide how far it is to the top of a low hill on the other side of the valley. Just below the hilltop is a barn, which you feel reasonably sure is about 100 feet wide on the side facing you.

Hold one arm straight out in front of you, elbow straight, thumb pointing up. Close one eye, and align one edge of your thumb with one edge of the barn. Without moving your head or arm, switch eyes, now sighting with the eye that was closed and closing the other. Your thumb will appear to jump sideways as a result of the change in perspective.

How far did it move? (Be sure to sight the same edge of your thumb when you switch eyes.) Let's say it jumped about five times the width of the barn, or about 500 feet. Now multiply that figure by the handy constant 10 (the ratio of the length of your arm to the distance between your eyes), and you get the distance between you and the barn — 5,000 feet, or about one mile. The accompanying diagram should make the whole process clear.

With a little practice, you'll find that you can perform a quick thumb-jump estimate in just a few seconds, and the result will usually be more accurate than an out-and-out guess. At a minimum, it will provide some assurance that the figure is in the ballpark — which, in many cases, is as close as you need to get.

– courtesy of Jon Vara, Marshfield, Vermont

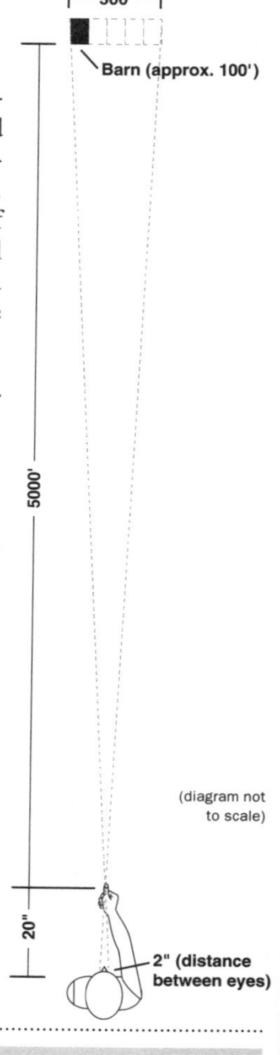

Proof That Canadian Women Are the Most Amorous

(Well, except for Turkish women)

■ Last winter, Harlequin, the world's leading publisher of romance fiction, released its annual Romance Report — and many people were surprised at some of the findings.

For instance, conventional wisdom may hold that women in the 1990s are suffering from a serious shortage of time — especially for love. But Harlequin, which is based in Toronto, surveyed 6,200 women in 21 countries and found that 56 percent say they have ample time for making love. In Canada, however, 74 percent of the women surveyed reported having enough time, eclipsed only by Turkish women at 78 percent.

Said Harlequin vice president Katherine Orr, "Finally, we Canadians are getting the recognition we deserve."

– courtesy of P.F.R., Toronto, Ontario

A Horrifying Mouse Fact

■ A female mouse gives birth to six young ones just three weeks after mating. Then she's ready to mate again in two days. She can produce between six and ten litters a year. The offspring are ready to mate in only two months. So a single female's children, grandchildren, great-grandchildren, and great-great grandchildren are capable of producing offspring during the same year — which, conceivably, could be as many as 30,000 new mice!

– courtesy of What's Buggin' You? Michael Bohdan's Guide to Home Pest Control, *Santa Monica Press, 1998 (call 800-784-9553 to order)*

And... a Simple Way to Build Your Own Mousetrap

■ Take a beer or soda can and punch a small hole in the center of both ends. Cut a piece of wire two feet long and thread it through the can. Suspend the can over a five-gallon pail by attaching the ends of the wire to the same places the handle is attached to the pail. Next, coat the can with peanut butter. Pour a few inches of water into the pail and, finally, place a little ramp from the floor or ground to the lip of the pail. The mouse will smell the peanut butter, walk up the ramp, and jump on the can, which will roll the mouse into the water. Voilà! One less mouse for your cat to worry about.

– from Weekly Market Bulletin, *New Hampshire Department of Agriculture, courtesy of R.D.H., Manchester, New Hampshire*

Only 100 Years Since...

THE FIRST SPEEDING TICKET

On May 20, 1899, a New York City bicycle policeman arrested 26-year-old Jacob German for speeding — the first police action of its kind. The spatially gifted policeman determined that German was driving his electric taxicab at 12 miles per hour along Lexington Avenue and, pursuing the speedster, saw him round the corner of 23rd Street (always a crowded place) at the same speed. The city's speed limit for motor vehicles was 8 miles per hour between streets and 4 miles per hour around corners. The cab driver was locked up.

THE FIRST TRAFFIC FATALITY

The first fatality caused by an automobile in the United States occurred in New York City on September 13, 1899. According to Peter Salwen, author of *Upper West Side Story: A History and Guide* (Abbeville Press, 1989), Henry H. Bliss, a 68-year-old realtor, alighted from a trolley on West 72nd Street in front of the Dakota Apartments, turned to help the lady behind him, and was knocked down and run over by an electric cab. Bliss was taken to Roosevelt Hospital, where he died from his injuries; cab driver Arthur Smith was arrested and held on $1,000 bail. In the 100 years since that fatal evening, some 3,000,000 people have died in traffic accidents.

A U.S. PRESIDENT FIRST RODE IN A CAR

At the age of 56, President William McKinley (born in Niles, Ohio) rode in a Stanley Steamer. The date was October 14, 1899.

– courtesy of Randy Miller, East Alstead, New Hampshire

Why Is One Side of the "V" of Flying Geese Longer than the Other?

or

A Very Shaggy Goose Story

■ Those in the know tell us that wild geese always fly in a "V" so that the leader cuts into the wind and thus creates currents that make it somewhat easier for those behind him to fly. However, no one has come up with the answer to why one side of the "V" is always longer than the other — that is, until now.

It seems that Richard Hargroder, a veterinarian in Opelousas, Louisiana, has been pondering the question for years. While watching the geese formations over the Mississippi Flyway each fall, he noticed that the lead goose in a "V" would occasionally drop back and another would fly forward to assume the lead position. But no matter how many times this leadership change took place, one side of the "V" remained longer. He consulted books, naturalists, and several of his colleagues, but no one knew why this was always so.

Then, last fall, the answer finally dawned on him. The mystery of a lifetime was finally solved. It was such a simple thing that he was annoyed with himself for not having discovered it years before. The reason one side of the "V" of flying geese is always longer than the other, he realized, is that the longer side contains more geese.

– adapted from a radio broadcast on KSLO-AM and KOGM-FM and courtesy of Wandell Allegood, Opelousas, Louisiana

Some Good and Bad News About Cows

GOOD: Cows enjoy being together. Scientists (who call this "social facilitation") now say that cows eat more in groups than when fed separately. Also, when hanging out in close proximity to each other, they're more content and less fearful.

BAD: A Maryland study indicated that, in fending off stable flies, cows make as many as 14,400 defensive shake-off movements in a 12-hour period. Also, they can "donate" as much as two pints of blood per day to the flies they cannot shake off.

GOOD: Thanks to the work of Dutch scientists, cows can now milk themselves — with the help of a computer. Wearing a computer chip in their collars, the high-tech cows approach the robotic milking machine whenever they feel the urge to be milked. The farmer, perhaps sleeping in that morning, is alerted by beeper if anything goes wrong.

BAD: This new self-milking machine is very expensive — about $250,000 — and it still has some glitches to be worked out. (For instance, the machine's robots have trouble milking cows with very big or low-hanging udders.)

– courtesy of C.R.G., Des Moines, Iowa

(continued)

For Those Who Would Like to Know Who Discovered How to Make a Turkey REALLY Tender

■ In 1746, Benjamin Franklin — yes, our own Benjamin Franklin of Revolutionary War fame — was all but laughed out of England's Royal Society for suggesting, as he put it, "the sameness of lightning with electricity." But Ben let his detractors have their fun, and he continued to experiment with electricity, using whatever was at hand: glass tubes, salt cellars, thimbles, vinegar, cruets, cakes of wax, pump handles, and even gold leaf filched from the binding of a book. His purpose was to find a practical use for this mysterious and powerful "juice" he'd discovered.

One day he found exactly that. Before beheading a turkey in preparation for dinner, he happened, either by design or error — we're not sure which — to electrocute the bird. The resulting turkey meat was found to be uncommonly tender — best he'd ever eaten.

Today, it's common practice to run electricity through a carcass immediately after slaughter to achieve the same result. So nobody's laughing now. Thanks, Ben.

– courtesy of Clare Innes, Harrisville, New Hampshire

It's Not Always Easy for an FBI Man to Order Pizza

(Here's proof)

The following is quoted from remarks made during a conference on global organized crime, sponsored by the Center for Strategic and International Studies:

It seems that FBI agents conducted a raid on a psychiatric hospital near San Diego that was under investigation for some sort of medical fraud. After hours of reviewing thousands of medical records, the dozens of agents involved had worked up quite an appetite. So the agent in charge of the investigation called a nearby pizza parlor to deliver a quick dinner for his colleagues. Because they were taping all conversations at the hospital at the time, the following conversation was recorded:

Agent: Hello. I would like to order 19 large pizzas and 67 cans of soda.

Pizza Man: And where would you like them delivered?

Agent: We're over at the psychiatric hospital.

Pizza Man: The psychiatric hospital?

Agent: That's right. I'm an FBI agent.

Pizza Man: You're an FBI agent?

Agent: That's correct. Just about everybody here is.

Pizza Man: And you're at the psychiatric hospital?

Agent: That's correct. And make sure you don't go through the front doors. We have them locked. You will have to go around to the back to the service entrance to deliver the pizzas.

Pizza Man: And you say you're all FBI agents?

Agent: That's right. We've been here all day and we're starving.

Pizza Man: How are you going to pay for all of this?

Agent: I have my checkbook right here.

Pizza Man: And you're all FBI agents?

Agent: That's right. Everyone here is an FBI agent. Can you remember to bring the pizzas and sodas to the service entrance in the rear? We have the front doors locked.

Pizza Man: I don't think so.

– courtesy of M.R.B., Houston, Texas

1998

JANUARY

S	M	T	W	T	F	S
—	—	—	—	1	2	3
4	5	6	7	8	9	10
11	12	13	14	15	16	17
18	19	20	21	22	23	24
25	26	27	28	29	30	31

FEBRUARY

S	M	T	W	T	F	S
1	2	3	4	5	6	7
8	9	10	11	12	13	14
15	16	17	18	19	20	21
22	23	24	25	26	27	28
—	—	—	—	—	—	—

MARCH

S	M	T	W	T	F	S
1	2	3	4	5	6	7
8	9	10	11	12	13	14
15	16	17	18	19	20	21
22	23	24	25	26	27	28
29	30	31	—	—	—	—

APRIL

S	M	T	W	T	F	S
—	—	—	1	2	3	4
5	6	7	8	9	10	11
12	13	14	15	16	17	18
19	20	21	22	23	24	25
26	27	28	29	30	—	—

MAY

S	M	T	W	T	F	S
—	—	—	—	—	1	2
3	4	5	6	7	8	9
10	11	12	13	14	15	16
17	18	19	20	21	22	23
24	25	26	27	28	29	30
31	—	—	—	—	—	—

JUNE

S	M	T	W	T	F	S
—	1	2	3	4	5	6
7	8	9	10	11	12	13
14	15	16	17	18	19	20
21	22	23	24	25	26	27
28	29	30	—	—	—	—
—	—	—	—	—	—	—

JULY

S	M	T	W	T	F	S
—	—	—	1	2	3	4
5	6	7	8	9	10	11
12	13	14	15	16	17	18
19	20	21	22	23	24	25
26	27	28	29	30	31	—
—	—	—	—	—	—	—

AUGUST

S	M	T	W	T	F	S
—	—	—	—	—	—	1
2	3	4	5	6	7	8
9	10	11	12	13	14	15
16	17	18	19	20	21	22
23	24	25	26	27	28	29
30	31	—	—	—	—	—

SEPTEMBER

S	M	T	W	T	F	S
—	—	1	2	3	4	5
6	7	8	9	10	11	12
13	14	15	16	17	18	19
20	21	22	23	24	25	26
27	28	29	30	—	—	—

OCTOBER

S	M	T	W	T	F	S
—	—	—	—	1	2	3
4	5	6	7	8	9	10
11	12	13	14	15	16	17
18	19	20	21	22	23	24
25	26	27	28	29	30	31

NOVEMBER

S	M	T	W	T	F	S
1	2	3	4	5	6	7
8	9	10	11	12	13	14
15	16	17	18	19	20	21
22	23	24	25	26	27	28
29	30	—	—	—	—	—

DECEMBER

S	M	T	W	T	F	S
—	—	1	2	3	4	5
6	7	8	9	10	11	12
13	14	15	16	17	18	19
20	21	22	23	24	25	26
27	28	29	30	31	—	—

1999

JANUARY

S	M	T	W	T	F	S
—	—	—	—	—	1	2
3	4	5	6	7	8	9
10	11	12	13	14	15	16
17	18	19	20	21	22	23
24	25	26	27	28	29	30
31	—	—	—	—	—	—

FEBRUARY

S	M	T	W	T	F	S
—	1	2	3	4	5	6
7	8	9	10	11	12	13
14	15	16	17	18	19	20
21	22	23	24	25	26	27
28	—	—	—	—	—	—
—	—	—	—	—	—	—

MARCH

S	M	T	W	T	F	S
—	1	2	3	4	5	6
7	8	9	10	11	12	13
14	15	16	17	18	19	20
21	22	23	24	25	26	27
28	29	30	31	—	—	—
—	—	—	—	—	—	—

APRIL

S	M	T	W	T	F	S
—	—	—	—	1	2	3
4	5	6	7	8	9	10
11	12	13	14	15	16	17
18	19	20	21	22	23	24
25	26	27	28	29	30	—
—	—	—	—	—	—	—

MAY

S	M	T	W	T	F	S
—	—	—	—	—	—	1
2	3	4	5	6	7	8
9	10	11	12	13	14	15
16	17	18	19	20	21	22
23	24	25	26	27	28	29
30	31	—	—	—	—	—

JUNE

S	M	T	W	T	F	S
—	—	1	2	3	4	5
6	7	8	9	10	11	12
13	14	15	16	17	18	19
20	21	22	23	24	25	26
27	28	29	30	—	—	—
—	—	—	—	—	—	—

JULY

S	M	T	W	T	F	S
—	—	—	—	1	2	3
4	5	6	7	8	9	10
11	12	13	14	15	16	17
18	19	20	21	22	23	24
25	26	27	28	29	30	31
—	—	—	—	—	—	—

AUGUST

S	M	T	W	T	F	S
1	2	3	4	5	6	7
8	9	10	11	12	13	14
15	16	17	18	19	20	21
22	23	24	25	26	27	28
29	30	31	—	—	—	—
—	—	—	—	—	—	—

SEPTEMBER

S	M	T	W	T	F	S
—	—	—	1	2	3	4
5	6	7	8	9	10	11
12	13	14	15	16	17	18
19	20	21	22	23	24	25
26	27	28	29	30	—	—
—	—	—	—	—	—	—

OCTOBER

S	M	T	W	T	F	S
—	—	—	—	—	1	2
3	4	5	6	7	8	9
10	11	12	13	14	15	16
17	18	19	20	21	22	23
24	25	26	27	28	29	30
31	—	—	—	—	—	—

NOVEMBER

S	M	T	W	T	F	S
—	1	2	3	4	5	6
7	8	9	10	11	12	13
14	15	16	17	18	19	20
21	22	23	24	25	26	27
28	29	30	—	—	—	—
—	—	—	—	—	—	—

DECEMBER

S	M	T	W	T	F	S
—	—	—	1	2	3	4
5	6	7	8	9	10	11
12	13	14	15	16	17	18
19	20	21	22	23	24	25
26	27	28	29	30	31	—
—	—	—	—	—	—	—

2000

JANUARY

S	M	T	W	T	F	S
—	—	—	—	—	—	1
2	3	4	5	6	7	8
9	10	11	12	13	14	15
16	17	18	19	20	21	22
23	24	25	26	27	28	29
30	31	—	—	—	—	—

FEBRUARY

S	M	T	W	T	F	S
—	—	1	2	3	4	5
6	7	8	9	10	11	12
13	14	15	16	17	18	19
20	21	22	23	24	25	26
27	28	29	—	—	—	—
—	—	—	—	—	—	—

MARCH

S	M	T	W	T	F	S
—	—	—	1	2	3	4
5	6	7	8	9	10	11
12	13	14	15	16	17	18
19	20	21	22	23	24	25
26	27	28	29	30	31	—
—	—	—	—	—	—	—

APRIL

S	M	T	W	T	F	S
—	—	—	—	—	—	1
2	3	4	5	6	7	8
9	10	11	12	13	14	15
16	17	18	19	20	21	22
23	24	25	26	27	28	29
30	—	—	—	—	—	—

MAY

S	M	T	W	T	F	S
—	1	2	3	4	5	6
7	8	9	10	11	12	13
14	15	16	17	18	19	20
21	22	23	24	25	26	27
28	29	30	31	—	—	—
—	—	—	—	—	—	—

JUNE

S	M	T	W	T	F	S
—	—	—	—	1	2	3
4	5	6	7	8	9	10
11	12	13	14	15	16	17
18	19	20	21	22	23	24
25	26	27	28	29	30	—
—	—	—	—	—	—	—

JULY

S	M	T	W	T	F	S
—	—	—	—	—	—	1
2	3	4	5	6	7	8
9	10	11	12	13	14	15
16	17	18	19	20	21	22
23	24	25	26	27	28	29
30	31	—	—	—	—	—

AUGUST

S	M	T	W	T	F	S
—	—	1	2	3	4	5
6	7	8	9	10	11	12
13	14	15	16	17	18	19
20	21	22	23	24	25	26
27	28	29	30	31	—	—
—	—	—	—	—	—	—

SEPTEMBER

S	M	T	W	T	F	S
—	—	—	—	—	1	2
3	4	5	6	7	8	9
10	11	12	13	14	15	16
17	18	19	20	21	22	23
24	25	26	27	28	29	30
—	—	—	—	—	—	—

OCTOBER

S	M	T	W	T	F	S
1	2	3	4	5	6	7
8	9	10	11	12	13	14
15	16	17	18	19	20	21
22	23	24	25	26	27	28
29	30	31	—	—	—	—
—	—	—	—	—	—	—

NOVEMBER

S	M	T	W	T	F	S
—	—	—	1	2	3	4
5	6	7	8	9	10	11
12	13	14	15	16	17	18
19	20	21	22	23	24	25
26	27	28	29	30	—	—
—	—	—	—	—	—	—

DECEMBER

S	M	T	W	T	F	S
—	—	—	—	—	1	2
3	4	5	6	7	8	9
10	11	12	13	14	15	16
17	18	19	20	21	22	23
24	25	26	27	28	29	30
31	—	—	—	—	—	—

A Reference Compendium

compiled by Mare-Anne Jarvela

Calendar

Weather

The Garden

Household

Leap Years

The actual length of a year (the rotation of Earth around the Sun) is 365.2422 days. If we didn't have leap years, the seasons would shift about a quarter of a day every year, and after 100 years the seasons would be off by 25 days. The extra leap day adjusts this drift.

A year is a leap year if it is divisible by 4, but century years are not leap years unless they are divisible by 400. So, the years 1700, 1800, and 1900 were not leap years, but the year 2000 will be one, the first century leap year since 1600.

Glossary of Time

Atomic Time (TA) Scale: A time scale based on atomic or molecular resonance phenomena. Elapsed time is measured by counting cycles of a frequency locked to an atomic or molecular transition.

Date: A unique instant defined in a specified time scale. NOTE: The date can be conventionally expressed in years, months, days, hours, minutes, seconds, and fractions.

Greenwich Mean Time (GMT): A 24-hour system based on mean solar time plus 12 hours at Greenwich, England. Greenwich Mean Time can be considered approximately equivalent to **Coordinated Universal Time (UTC),** which is broadcast from all standard time and frequency radio stations. However, GMT is now obsolete and has been replaced by UTC.

International Atomic Time: An atomic time scale based on data from a worldwide set of atomic clocks. It is the internationally agreed-upon time reference conforming to the definition of the second, the fundamental unit of atomic time in the International System of Units (SI).

Leap Second: An intentional time step of one second used to adjust UTC. An inserted second is called a positive leap second, and an omitted second is called a negative leap second. A positive leap second is presently needed about once per year.

Mean Solar Time: Apparent solar time corrected for the effects of orbital eccentricity and the tilt of Earth's axis relative to the ecliptic plane; that is, corrected by the equation of time, which is defined as the hour angle of the true Sun minus the hour angle of the mean Sun.

Second: The basic unit of time or time interval in the International System of Units (SI), which is equal to 9 192 631 770 periods of radiation corresponding to the transition between the two hyperfine levels of the ground state of cesium-133 as defined at the 1967 Conference Generale des Poids et Mesures.

Sidereal Time: The measure of time defined by the apparent diurnal motion of the vernal equinox; hence, a measure of the rotation of Earth with respect to the reference frame that is related to the stars rather than the Sun. One sidereal day is equal to about 23 hours, 56 minutes, and 4.090 seconds of mean solar time.

– National Institute of Standards and Technology (NIST)

Glossary of Almanac Oddities

Many readers have expressed puzzlement over the rather obscure notations that appear on our Right-Hand Calendar Pages (pages 61-87). These "oddities" have long been fixtures in the Almanac, and we are pleased to provide some definitions. (Once explained, it may seem that they are not so odd after all!)

■ Ember Days (Movable)

The *Almanac* traditionally marks the four periods formerly observed by the Roman Catholic and Anglican churches for prayer, fasting, and the ordination of clergy. These Ember Days are the Wednesdays, Fridays, and Saturdays that follow in succession after 1) the First Sunday in Lent; 2) Pentecost (Whitsunday); 3) the Feast of the Holy Cross (September 14); and 4) the Feast of St. Lucy (December 13). (The word *ember* is perhaps a corruption of the Latin *quatuor tempora,* "four times.")

Folklore has it that the weather on each of the three days foretells weather for three successive months — that is, in September Ember Days, Wednesday forecasts weather for October, Friday for November, and Saturday for December.

■ Plough Monday (January)

The first Monday after the Epiphany; so called because it was the end of the Christmas holidays, when men returned to their plough — or daily work. It was customary for farm laborers to draw a plough through the village, soliciting money for a "plough-light," which was kept burning in the parish church all year. In some areas, the custom of blessing the plough is maintained.

■ Three Chilly Saints (May)

Mammertius, Pancratius, and Gervatius, three early Christian saints, whose feast days occur on May 11, 12, and 13, respectively. Because these days are traditionally cold (an old French saying goes: "St. Mammertius, St. Pancras, and St. Gervais do not pass without a frost"), they have come to be known as the Three Chilly Saints.

■ Midsummer Day (June 24)

Although it occurs near the summer solstice, to the farmer it is the midpoint of the growing season, halfway between planting and harvest and an occasion for festivity. The English church considered it a "Quarter Day," one of the four major divisions of the liturgical year. It also marks the feast day of St. John the Baptist.

■ Cornscateous Air (July)

A term first used by the old almanac makers to signify warm, damp air. While it signals ideal climatic conditions for growing corn, it also poses a danger to those affected by asthma, pneumonia, and other respiratory problems.

■ Dog Days (July-August)

The hottest and most unhealthy days of the year. Also known as "Canicular Days," the name derives from the Dog Star, Sirius. The Almanac lists the traditional timing of Dog Days: The 40 days beginning July 3 and ending August 11, coinciding with the heliacal (at sunrise) rising of Sirius.

■ Cat Nights Begin (August)

The term harks back to the days when people believed in witches. An old Irish legend has it that a witch could turn herself into a cat eight times and then regain herself, but on the ninth time — August 17 — she couldn't change back. Hence the saying, "A cat has nine lives." Since August is a "yowly" time for cats, this may have prompted the speculation about witches on the prowl in the first place.

(continued on next page)

■ Harvest Home (September)

In both Europe and Britain, the conclusion of the harvest each autumn was once marked by great festivals of fun, feasting, and thanksgiving known as "Harvest Home." It was also a time to hold elections, pay workers, and collect rents. These festivals usually took place around the time of the autumnal equinox. Certain ethnic groups in this country, particularly the Pennsylvania Dutch, have kept the tradition alive.

■ St. Luke's Little Summer (October)

A spell of warm weather occurring about the time of the saint's feast day, October 18. This period is sometimes referred to as "Indian Summer."

■ Indian Summer (November)

A period of warm weather following a cold spell or a hard frost. While there are differing dates for the time of occurrence, for 206 years the Almanac has adhered to the saying, "If All Saints brings out winter, St. Martin's brings out Indian Summer." Accordingly, Indian Summer can occur between St. Martin's Day (November 11) and November 20. As for the origin of the term, some say it comes from the early Indians, who believed the condition was caused by a warm wind sent from the court of their southwestern God, Cautantowwit.

■ Halcyon Days (December)

A period (about 14 days) of calm weather, following the blustery winds of autumn's end. The ancient Greeks and Romans believed them to occur around the time of the winter solstice when the halcyon, or kingfisher, was brooding. In a nest floating on the sea, the bird was said to have charmed the wind and waves so the waters were especially calm during this period.

■ Beware the Pogonip (December)

The word *pogonip* is a meteorological term used to describe an uncommon occurrence — frozen fog. The word was coined by American Indians to describe the frozen fogs of fine ice needles that occur in the mountain valleys of the western United States. According to Indian tradition, breathing the fog is injurious to the lungs.

When Will the Moon Rise Today?

A lunar puzzle involves the timing of moonrise. Folks who enjoy the out-of-doors and the wonders of nature may wish to commit to memory the following gem:

The new Moon always rises at sunrise
And the first quarter at noon.
The full Moon always rises at sunset
And the last quarter at midnight.

Moonrise occurs about 50 minutes later each day than the day before. The new Moon is invisible because the Sun blots it out. One or two days after the date of the new Moon, you can see it in the western sky as a thin crescent setting just after sunset. (See pages 60-86 for exact moonrise times.)

Phases of the Moon

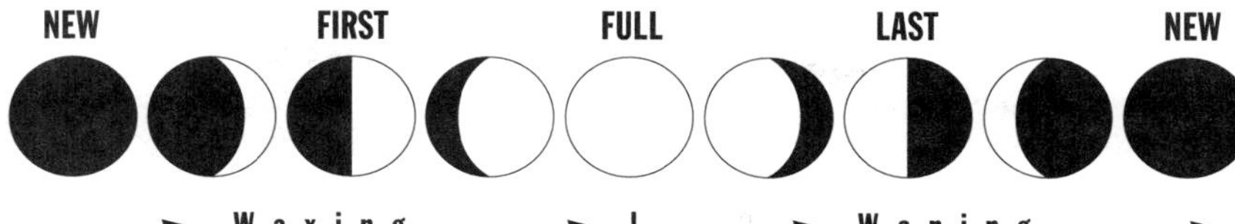

Month Names

JANUARY Named for the Roman god Janus, protector of gates and doorways. Janus is depicted with two faces, one looking into the past, the other into the future.

FEBRUARY From the Latin word *februa,* "to cleanse." The Roman Februalia was a month of purification and atonement.

MARCH Named for the Roman god of war, Mars. This was the time of year to resume military campaigns that had been interrupted by winter.

APRIL From the Latin word *aperio,* "to open (bud)," because plants begin to grow in this month.

MAY Named for the Roman goddess Maia, who oversaw the growth of plants. Also from the Latin word *maiores,* meaning "elders," who were celebrated during this month.

JUNE Named for the Roman goddess Juno, patroness of marriage and the well-being of women. Also from the Latin word *juvenis,* "young people."

JULY Named to honor Roman dictator Julius Caesar (100 B.C.- 44 B.C.). In 46 B.C., Julius Caesar made one of his greatest contributions to history: With the help of Sosigenes, he developed the Julian calendar, the precursor to the Gregorian calendar we use today.

AUGUST Named to honor the first Roman emperor (and grandnephew of Julius Caesar), Augustus Caesar (63 B.C.-A.D. 14)

SEPTEMBER From the Latin word *septem,* "seven," because this had been the seventh month of the early Roman calendar.

OCTOBER From the Latin word *octo,* "eight," because this had been the eighth month of the early Roman calendar.

NOVEMBER From the Latin word *novem,* "nine," because this had been the ninth month of the early Roman calendar.

DECEMBER From the Latin word *decem,* "ten," because this had been the tenth month of the early Roman calendar.

Full-Moon Names

Historically, the Indians of what are now the northern and eastern United States kept track of the seasons by giving a distinctive name to each recurring full Moon, this name being applied to the entire month in which it occurred. With some variations, the same Moon names were used throughout the Algonquin tribes from New England to Lake Superior.

NAME	MONTH	OTHER NAMES USED
Full Wolf Moon	January	Full Old Moon
Full Snow Moon	February	Full Hunger Moon
Full Worm Moon	March	Full Crow Moon, Full Crust Moon, Full Sugar Moon, Full Sap Moon
Full Pink Moon	April	Full Sprouting Grass Moon, Full Egg Moon, Full Fish Moon
Full Flower Moon	May	Full Corn Planting Moon, Full Milk Moon
Full Strawberry Moon	June	Full Rose Moon, Full Hot Moon
Full Buck Moon	July	Full Thunder Moon, Full Hay Moon
Full Sturgeon Moon	August	Full Red Moon, Full Green Corn Moon
Full Harvest Moon*	September	Full Corn Moon, Full Barley Moon
Full Hunter's Moon	October	Full Travel Moon, Full Dying Grass Moon
Full Beaver Moon	November	Full Frost Moon
Full Cold Moon	December	Full Long Nights Moon

*** The Harvest Moon is always the full Moon closest to the autumnal equinox. If the Harvest Moon occurs in October, the September full Moon is usually called the Corn Moon.**

Day Names

The Romans named the days of the week after the Sun, the Moon, and the five known planets. These names have survived in European languages, but English names also reflect an Anglo-Saxon influence.

LATIN	FRENCH	ITALIAN	SPANISH	SAXON	ENGLISH
Solis (Sun)	dimanche	domenica	domingo	Sun	Sunday
Lunae (Moon)	lundi	lunedì	lunes	Moon	Monday
Martis (Mars)	mardi	martedì	martes	Tiw (the Anglo-Saxon god of war, the equivalent of the Norse Tyr or the Roman Mars)	Tuesday
Mercurii (Mercury)	mercredi	mercoledì	miércoles	Woden (the Anglo-Saxon equivalent of the Norse Odin or the Roman Mercury)	Wednesday
Jovis (Jupiter)	jeudi	giovedì	jueves	Thor (the Norse god of thunder, the equivalent of the Roman Jupiter)	Thursday
Veneris (Venus)	vendredi	venerdì	viernes	Frigg (the Norse god of love and fertility, the equivalent of the Roman Venus)	Friday
Saturni (Saturn)	samedi	sabato	sábado	Saterne (Saturn, the Roman god of agriculture)	Saturday

Dining by the Calendar: Traditional Foods for Feasts and Fasts

JANUARY

Feast of the Circumcision: Black-eyed peas and pork (United States); oat-husk gruel or oatmeal porridge (Scotland).

Epiphany: Cake with a lucky bean baked in it; the one who finds the bean is the king or queen of the feast, in memory of the three wise men (France).

Robert Burns Day: Haggis — sheep's stomach stuffed with suet, chopped organ meat (heart, lungs, liver), onions, oatmeal, and seasonings (Scotland). Haggis is a traditional Scottish delicacy served on all holidays of national importance.

FEBRUARY

Candlemas Day: Pancakes eaten today will prevent hemorrhoids for a full year (French American).

St. Agatha: Round loaves of bread blessed by a priest (southern Europe).

Shrove Tuesday: Pancakes (England); oatcakes (Scotland); rabbit (Ireland). Rich foods are eaten to usher in the Lenten fast; pancakes use up the last of the eggs and butter.

Lent: Simnel, a large fruitcake baked so hard it has sometimes been mistaken by recipients for a hassock or footstool (Great Britain).

MARCH

St. David: Leeks, to be worn (Wales) or eaten raw (England). Recalls a Welsh victory over the Saxons in A.D. 640; the Welsh wore leeks in their hats to distinguish them from the enemy.

St. Benedict: Nettle soup (ancient monastic practice). Picking nettles, which irritate the skin, was a penance in keeping with the spirit of the monastic rule of St. Benedict.

Purim: Strong drink and three-cornered cookies flavored with poppy seed (Jewish). These cookies, called hamantaschen, are said to represent the three-cornered hat of Haman, the enemy of the Jewish people, whose downfall is celebrated on this holiday.

Maundy Thursday: Green foods or foods colored green (southern Europe). The medieval liturgical observance called for green vestments; in some parts of Europe, it is still called Green Thursday.

Good Friday: Hot cross buns. If made properly on this day, they will never get moldy (England).

APRIL

Easter: Lamb as symbol of sacrifice; ham.

Beltane, May Day Eve: Strong ale (England); oatcakes with nine knobs to be broken off one by one and offered to each of nine supernatural protectors of domestic animals (Scotland).

MAY

Ascension Day: Fowl, or pastries molded in the shape of birds, to commemorate the taking of Jesus into the skies (medieval Europe).

Whitsunday (Pentecost): Dove or pigeon in honor of the Holy Spirit (southern Europe); strong ale (England).

St. Dunstan: Beer. Cider pressed today will go bad (England).

Corpus Christi: Orange peel dipped in chocolate, chicken stuffed with sauerkraut (Basque Provinces).

JUNE

St. Anthony of Padua: Liver, possibly based on the pre-Christian custom of eating liver on the summer solstice.

Feast of St. John the Baptist: First fruits of spring harvest eaten.

JULY

St. Swithin: Eggs, because the saint miraculously restored intact a basket of eggs that had been broken by a poor woman taking them to market; he also looks after apples (medieval England).

(continued on next page)

St. James: Oysters, because James was a fisherman (England).

AUGUST

Lammas Day: Oatcakes (Scotland); loaves made from new grain of the season (England); toffee; seaweed pudding. Blueberries in baskets as an offering to a sweetheart are the last vestige of this holiday as a pagan fertility festival (Ireland).

St. Lawrence of Rome: Because the saint was roasted to death on a gridiron, it is courteous to serve only cold meat today (southern Europe).

Feast of the Assumption: Onions, possibly because they have always been considered wholesome and potent against evil (Polish American).

SEPTEMBER

St. Giles: Tea loaf with raisins (Scotland).

Nativity of Mary: Blackberries, possibly because the color is reminiscent of the depiction of the Virgin's blue cloak (Brittany).

Michaelmas Day: New wine (Europe); goose, originally a sacrifice to the saint (Great Britain); cake of oats, barley, and rye (Scotland); carrots (Ireland).

OCTOBER

Rosh Hashanah: Sweet foods; honey; foods colored orange or yellow to represent a bright, joyous, and sweet new year (Jewish).

Yom Kippur: Fast day; the day before, eat kreplach (filled noodles), considered by generations of mothers to be good and filling (Jewish).

St. Luke: Oatcakes flavored with anise and cinnamon (Scotland).

Sts. Simon and Jude: Dirge cakes, simple fried buns made for distribution to the poor. Also apples or potatoes, for divination (Scotland and England). Divination with apples is accomplished by peeling the fruit in one long strip and tossing the peel over one's shoulder. The letter formed by the peel is then interpreted.

All Hallows Eve: Apples and nuts for divination (England); buttered oat-husk gruel (Scotland); bosty, a mixture of potatoes, cabbage, and onions (Ireland).

NOVEMBER

All Saints Day: Chestnuts (Italy); gingerbread and oatcakes (Scotland); milk (central Europe); doughnuts, whose round shape indicates eternity (Tyrol).

All Souls Day: Skull-shaped candy (Mexico); beans, peas, and lentils, considered food of the poor, as penance for souls in purgatory (southern Europe).

St. Martin: Last religious feast day before the beginning of the Advent fast. Goose, last of fresh-killed meat before winter; blood pudding (Great Britain).

St. Andrew: Haggis — stuffed sheep's stomach (Scotland).

DECEMBER

St. Nicholas: Fruit, nuts, candy for children (Germany). Commemorates, in part, the miracle by which the saint restored to life three young boys who had been murdered by a greedy innkeeper.

St. Lucy: Headcheese; cakes flavored with saffron or cardamom, raisins, and almonds (Sweden). The saffron imparts a yellow color to the cakes, representing sunlight, whose return is celebrated at the solstice.

Christmas: Boar's head or goose, plum pudding, nuts, oranges (England); turkey (United States); spiced beef (Ireland).

St. John the Evangelist: Small loaves of bread made with blessed wine (medieval Europe). This is a feast on which wine is ritually blessed in memory of the saint, who drank poisoned wine and miraculously survived.

Chanukah: Latkes — potato pancakes (Jewish).

Holy Innocents Day: Baby food, pablum, Cream of Wheat, in honor of the children killed by King Herod of Judea (monastic observance).

St. Sylvester: Strong drink (United States); haggis, oatcakes and cheese, oat-husk gruel or porridge (Scotland). *– E. Brady*

Chinese Zodiac

The animal designations of the Chinese zodiac follow a 12-year cycle and are always used in the same sequence. The Chinese year of 354 days begins three to seven weeks into the western 365-day year, so the animal designation changes at that time, rather than on January 1.

RAT

Ambitious and sincere, you can be generous with your financial resources. Compatible with the dragon and the monkey. Your opposite is the horse.

1900	1960
1912	1972
1924	1984
1936	1996
1948	2008

RABBIT (HARE)

Talented and affectionate, you are a seeker of tranquility. Compatible with the sheep and the pig. Your opposite is the rooster.

1903	1963
1915	1975
1927	1987
1939	1999
1951	2011

HORSE

Physically attractive and popular, you like the company of others. Compatible with the tiger and the dog. Your opposite is the rat.

1906	1966
1918	1978
1930	1990
1942	2002
1954	2014

ROOSTER (COCK)

Seeking wisdom and truth, you have a pioneering spirit. Compatible with the snake and the ox. Your opposite is the rabbit.

1909	1969
1921	1981
1933	1993
1945	2005
1957	2017

OX (BUFFALO)

A leader, you are bright and cheerful. Compatible with the snake and the rooster. Your opposite is the sheep.

1901	1961
1913	1973
1925	1985
1937	1997
1949	2009

DRAGON

Robust and passionate, your life is filled with complexity. Compatible with the monkey and the rat. Your opposite is the dog.

1904	1964
1916	1976
1928	1988
1940	2000
1952	2012

SHEEP (GOAT)

Aesthetic and stylish, you enjoy being a private person. Compatible with the pig and the rabbit. Your opposite is the ox.

1907	1967
1919	1979
1931	1991
1943	2003
1955	2015

DOG

Generous and loyal, you have the ability to work well with others. Compatible with the horse and the tiger. Your opposite is the dragon.

1910	1970
1922	1982
1934	1994
1946	2006
1958	2018

TIGER

Forthright and sensitive, you possess great courage. Compatible with the horse and the dog. Your opposite is the monkey.

1902	1962
1914	1974
1926	1986
1938	1998
1950	2010

SNAKE

Strong-willed and intense, you display great wisdom. Compatible with the rooster and the ox. Your opposite is the pig.

1905	1965
1917	1977
1929	1989
1941	2001
1953	2013

MONKEY

Persuasive and intelligent, you strive to excel. Compatible with the dragon and the rat. Your opposite is the tiger.

1908	1968
1920	1980
1932	1992
1944	2004
1956	2016

PIG (BOAR)

Gallant and noble, your friends will remain at your side. Compatible with the rabbit and the sheep. Your opposite is the snake.

1911	1971
1923	1983
1935	1995
1947	2007
1959	2019

Clouds

1. High clouds (bases starting at an average of 20,000 feet)

Cirrus: thin feather-like crystal clouds.

Cirrostratus: thin white clouds that resemble veils.

Cirrocumulus: thin clouds that appear as small "cotton patches."

2. Middle clouds (bases starting at about 10,000 feet)

Altostratus: grayish or bluish layer of clouds that can obscure the Sun.

Altocumulus: gray or white layer or patches of solid clouds with rounded shapes.

3. Low clouds (bases starting near Earth's surface to 6,500 feet)

Stratus: thin, gray sheet-like clouds with low base; may bring drizzle and snow.

Stratocumulus: rounded cloud masses that form on top of a layer.

Nimbostratus: dark, gray shapeless cloud layers containing rain, snow, and ice pellets.

4. Clouds with vertical development (high clouds that form at almost any altitude and that reach up to 14,000 feet)

Cumulus: fair-weather clouds with flat bases and domeshaped tops.

Cumulonimbus: large, dark vertical clouds with bulging tops that bring showers, thunder, and lightning.

Snowflakes

Snowflakes are made up of six-sided crystals. If you look carefully at the snowflakes during the next snowstorm, you might be able to find some of the crystal types below. The temperature at which a crystal forms mainly determines the basic shape. Sometimes a snowflake is a combination of more than one type of crystal.

Capped columns (also called tsuzumi crystals) occur when colder than 12° F.

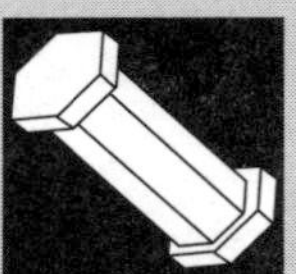

Columns (dense crystals, act like prisms) occur when colder than 12° F.

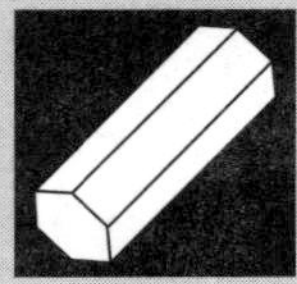

Needles (long and thin but still six-sided) occur at warmer temperatures, 21° to 25° F.

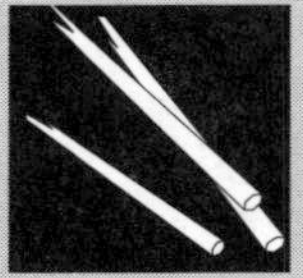

Plates (mirror-like crystals) occur under special weather conditions.

Spatial dendrites (irregular and feathery) occur in high-moisture clouds, 3° to 10° F.

Stellar crystals (beautiful, delicate crystals) occur under special weather conditions.

Windchill Table

As wind speed increases, the air temperature against your body falls. The combination of cold temperature and high wind creates a cooling effect so severe that exposed flesh can freeze. (Inanimate objects, such as cars, do not experience windchill.)

To gauge wind speed: At 10 miles per hour, you can feel wind on your face; at 20, small branches move and dust or snow is raised; at 30, large branches move and wires whistle; at 40, whole trees bend.

– courtesy Mount Washington Observatory

Wind Velocity (mph)	Temperature (° F)												
	50	41	32	23	14	5	–4	–13	–22	–31	–40	–49	–58
	Equivalent Temperature (° F) (Equivalent in cooling power on exposed flesh under calm conditions)												
5	48	39	28	19	10	1	–9	–18	–27	–36	–51	–56	–65
10	41	30	18	7	–4	–15	–26	–36	–49	–60	–71	–81	–92
20	32	19	7	–6	–18	–31	–44	–58	–71	–83	–96	–108	–121
30	28	14	1	–13	–27	–40	–54	–69	–81	–96	–108	–123	–137
40	27	12	–2	–17	–31	–45	–60	–74	–89	–103	–116	–130	–144
50	25	10	–4	–18	–33	–47	–62	–76	–90	–105	–119	–134	–148
	Little Danger				Increasing Danger				Great Danger				
	Danger from freezing of exposed flesh (for properly clothed person)												

Heat Index

As humidity increases, the air temperature feels hotter to your skin. The combination of hot temperature and high humidity reduces your body's ability to cool itself. For example, the heat you feel when the actual temperature is 90 degrees Fahrenheit with a relative humidity of 70 percent is 106 degrees.

	Temperature (° F)										
	70	75	80	85	90	95	100	105	110	115	120
Humidity (%)	Equivalent Temperature (° F)										
0	64	69	73	78	83	87	91	95	99	103	107
10	65	70	75	80	85	90	95	100	105	111	116
20	66	72	77	82	87	93	99	105	112	120	130
30	67	73	78	84	90	96	104	113	123	120	148
40	68	74	79	86	93	101	110	123	137	135	
50	69	75	81	88	96	107	120	135	150		
60	70	76	82	90	100	114	132	149			
70	70	77	85	93	106	124	144				
80	71	78	86	97	113	136					
90	71	79	88	102	122						
100	72	80	91	108							

Is It Raining, Drizzling, or Misting?

	Drops (per sq. ft. per sec.)	Diameter of Drops (mm)	Intensity (in. per hr.)
Cloudburst	113	2.85	4.00
Excessive rain	76	2.40	1.60
Heavy rain	46	2.05	.60
Moderate rain	46	1.60	.15
Light rain	26	1.24	.04
Drizzle	14	.96	.01
Mist	2,510	.10	.002
Fog	6,264,000	.01	.005

A Table Foretelling the Weather Through All the Lunations of Each Year (Forever)

This table is the result of many years of actual observation and shows what sort of weather will probably follow the Moon's entrance into any of its quarters. For example, the table shows that the week following January 17, 1999, will be cold with high winds because the Moon becomes new that day at 10:46 A.M., EST. (See Left-Hand Calendar Pages 60-86 for 1999 Moon phases.)

Editor's note: While the data in this table is taken into consideration in the yearlong process of compiling the annual long-range weather forecasts for *The Old Farmer's Almanac*, we rely far more on our projections of solar activity.

Time of Change	Summer	Winter
Midnight to 2 A.M.	Fair	Hard frost, unless wind is south or west
2 A.M. to 4 A.M.	Cold, with frequent showers	Snow and stormy
4 A.M. to 6 A.M.	Rain	Rain
6 A.M. to 8 A.M.	Wind and rain	Stormy
8 A.M. to 10 A.M.	Changeable	Cold rain if wind is west; snow if east
10 A.M. to noon	Frequent showers	Cold with high winds
Noon to 2 P.M.	Very rainy	Snow or rain
2 P.M. to 4 P.M.	Changeable	Fair and mild
4 P.M. to 6 P.M.	Fair	Fair
6 P.M. to 10 P.M.	Fair if wind is northwest; rain if wind is south or southwest	Fair and frosty if wind is north or northeast; rain or snow if wind is south or southwest
10 P.M. to midnight	Fair	Fair and frosty

This table was created more than 160 years ago by Dr. Herschell for the Boston Courier; *it first appeared in* The Old Farmer's Almanac *in 1834.*

Beaufort's Scale of Wind Speeds

"Used Mostly at Sea but of Help to All Who Are Interested in the Weather"

A scale of wind velocity was devised by Admiral Sir Francis Beaufort of the British Navy in 1806. The numbers 0 to 12 were arranged by Beaufort to indicate the strength of the wind from a calm, force 0, to a hurricane, force 12. Here's a scale adapted to land.

Beaufort Force	Description	When You See This	mph	km/h
0	Calm	Smoke goes straight up. No wind.	less than 1	0-1.6
1	Light air	Direction of wind is shown by smoke drift but not by wind vane.	1-3	1.7-5
2	Light breeze	Wind felt on face. Leaves rustle. Wind vane moves.	4-7	6-11
3	Gentle breeze	Leaves and small twigs move steadily. Wind extends small flag straight out.	8-12	12-19
4	Moderate breeze	Wind raises dust and loose paper. Small branches move.	13-18	20-29
5	Fresh breeze	Small trees sway. Waves form on lakes.	19-24	30-39
6	Strong breeze	Large branches move. Wires whistle. Umbrellas are hard to use.	25-31	40-50
7	Moderate gale	Whole trees are in motion. Hard to walk against the wind.	32-38	51-61
8	Fresh gale	Twigs break from trees. Very hard to walk against wind.	39-46	62-74
9	Strong gale	Small damage to buildings. Roof shingles are removed.	47-54	75-87
10	Whole gale	Trees are uprooted.	55-63	88-101
11	Violent storm	Widespread damage from wind.	64-72	102-116
12	Hurricane	Widespread destruction from wind.	73+	117+

Atlantic Hurricane Names for 1999

Arlene
Bret
Cindy
Dennis

Emily
Floyd
Gert
Harvey
Irene

Jose
Katrina
Lenny
Maria

Nate
Ophelia
Philippe
Rita
Stan

Tammy
Vince
Wilma

East-Pacific Hurricane Names for 1999

Adrian	Fernanda	Kenneth	Pilar	Wiley
Beatriz	Greg	Lidia	Ramon	Xina
Calvin	Hilary	Max	Selma	York
Dora	Irwin	Norma	Todd	Zelda
Eugene	Jova	Otis	Veronica	

Retired Atlantic Hurricane Names

These are some of the most destructive and costly storms whose names have been retired from the six-year rotating hurricane list.

Year Retired	Name	Year Retired	Name	Year Retired	Name	Year Retired	Name
1970	Celia	1979	David	1985	Gloria	1990	Klaus
1972	Agnes	1979	Frederic	1988	Gilbert	1991	Bob
1974	Carmen	1980	Allen	1988	Joan	1992	Andrew
1975	Eloise	1983	Alicia	1989	Hugo	1995	Opal
1977	Anita	1985	Elena	1990	Diana	1995	Roxanne

Fujita Scale (or F Scale) for Tornadoes

This is a system developed by Dr. Theodore Fujita to classify tornadoes based on wind damage. All tornadoes, and most other severe local windstorms, are assigned a single number from this scale according to the most intense damage caused by the storm.

F0 (weak) .... 40- 72 mph, light damage

F1 (weak) ...... 73-112 mph, moderate damage

F2 (strong). . 113-157 mph, considerable damage

F3 (strong)...... 158-206 mph, severe damage

F4 (violent). . 207-260 mph, devastating damage

F5 (violent) .... 261-318 mph, (rare) incredible damage

Richter Scale for Measuring Earthquakes

MAGNITUDE	POSSIBLE EFFECTS
1	Detectable only by instruments
2	Barely detectable, even near the epicenter
3	Felt indoors
4	Felt by most people; slight damage
5	Felt by all; damage minor to moderate
6	Moderately destructive
7	Major damage
8	Total and major damage

Devised by American geologist Charles W. Richter in 1935 to measure the magnitude of an earthquake.

Winter Weather Terms

Winter Storm Watch

■ Possibility of a winter storm. Be alert to changing weather conditions. Avoid unnecessary travel.

Winter Storm Warning

■ A severe winter storm has started or is about to begin in the forecast area. You should stay indoors during the storm. If you must go outdoors, wear several layers of lightweight clothing, which will keep you warmer than a single heavy coat. In addition, wear gloves or mittens and a hat to prevent loss of body heat. Cover your mouth to protect your lungs.

Heavy Snow Warning

■ Snow accumulations are expected to approach or exceed six inches in 12 hours but will not be accompanied by significant wind. This warning could also be issued if eight inches or more of snow accumulation is expected in a 24-hour period. During a heavy snow warning, freezing rain and sleet are not expected.

Blizzard Warning

■ Sustained winds or frequent gusts of 35 miles per hour or greater will occur in combination with considerable falling and/or blowing snow for a period of at least three hours. Visibility will often be reduced to less than ¼ mile in a blizzard.

Ice Storm Warning

■ A significant coating of ice, ½ inch thick or more, is expected.

Windchill Warning

■ Windchills reach life-threatening levels of minus 50 degrees Fahrenheit or lower.

Windchill Advisory

■ Windchill factors fall between minus 35 and minus 50 degrees Fahrenheit.

Sleet

■ Frozen or partially frozen rain in the form of ice pellets hit the ground so fast they bounce off with a sharp click.

Freezing Rain

■ Rain falls as a liquid but turns to ice on contact with a frozen surface to form a smooth ice coating called glaze.

Safe Ice Thickness *

Ice Thickness	Permissible Load
2 inches	One person on foot
3 inches	Group in single file
7½ inches	Passenger car (2-ton gross)
8 inches	Light truck (2½-ton gross)
10 inches	Medium truck (3½-ton gross)
12 inches	Heavy truck (8-ton gross)
15 inches	10 tons
20 inches	25 tons
30 inches	70 tons
36 inches	110 tons

*** Solid clear blue/black pond and lake ice**

☞ Slush ice has only half the strength of blue ice.

☞ Strength value of river ice is 15 percent less.

Source: American Pulpwood Association

A Beginner Garden

A good size for a beginner vegetable garden is 10x16 feet and features crops that are easy to grow. A plot this size, planted as suggested below, can feed a family of four for one summer, with a little extra for canning and freezing (or giving away).

Make your garden 11 rows of ten feet each of the following:

ROW	
1	Tomatoes (5 plants, staked)
2	Zucchini (4 plants)
3	Peppers (6 plants)
4	Cabbage
5	Bush beans
6	Lettuce
7	Beets
8	Carrots
9	Chard
10	Radish
11	Marigolds (to discourage rabbits!)

Ideally the rows should run north and south to take full advantage of the Sun.

Plants with Interesting Foliage

Airy/Fine Foliage
- Barrenwort, *Epimedium* spp.
- Maidenhair fern, *Adiantum pedatum*
- Meadow rue, *Thalictrum* spp.
- Silver mound, *Artemisia schmidtiana*

Linear Foliage
- Blazing star, *Liatris* spp.
- Daylily, *Hemerocallis* spp.
- Iris, *Iris* spp.
- Yucca, *Yucca* spp.

Textured Foliage
- Lamb's-ear, *Stachys byzantina*
- Sea holly, *Eryngium* spp.
- Silver sage, *Salvia argentea*
- Woolly thyme, *Thymus pseudolanuginosus*

Foliage with Attractive Shapes
- Cranesbill, *Geranium* spp.
- Foamflower, *Tiarella cordifolia*
- Hybrid lupine, *Lupinus* x *rus selianus*
- Lady's-mantle, *Alchemilla vulgaris*

Perennials for Cutting Gardens

Aster (*Aster*)
Baby's-breath (*Gypsophila*)
Bellflower (*Campanula*)
Black-eyed Susan (*Rudbeckia*)
Blanket flower (*Gaillardia*)
Chrysanthemum (*Chrysanthemum*)
Delphinium (*Delphinium*)
False sunflower (*Heliopsis*)
Flowering onion (*Allium*)
Foxglove (*Digitalis*)
Gay-feather (*Liatris*)
Globe thistle (*Echinops*)
Goldenrod (*Solidago*)
Iris (*Iris*)
Lavender (*Lavandula*)
Meadow rue (*Thalictrum*)
Peony (*Paeonia*)
Phlox (*Phlox*)
Purple coneflower (*Echinacea*)
Sea holly (*Eryngium*)
Speedwell (*Veronica*)
Tickseed (*Coreopsis*)
Yarrow (*Achillea*)

Herb Gardening

Name	Height (in inches)	Part Used
Anise	18	Seeds
Basil	20	Leaves
Borage	18	Leaves, flowers
Caraway	18	Seeds
Catnip	24	Leaves
Chamomile	10	Flowers
Chevril	15	Leaves
Chive	12	Leaves
Coriander	20	Leaves, seeds
Dill	36	Leaves, seeds
Hyssop	14	Leaves
Lemonbalm	20	Leaves
Marjoram	18	Leaves
Mint	24	Leaves
Rosemary	18	Leaves
Sage	16	Leaves
Savory	16	Leaves
Tarragon	20	Leaves
Thyme	7	Leaves

Herbs to Plant in Lawns

Choose plants that suit your soil and your climate. All these can withstand mowing and considerable foot traffic.

- Ajuga or bugleweed *(Ajuga reptans)*
- Corsican mint *(Mentha requienii)*
- Dwarf cinquefoil *(Potentilla tabernaemontani)*
- English pennyroyal *(Mentha pulegium)*
- Green Irish moss *(Sagiona subulata)*
- Pearly everlasting *(Anaphalis margaritacea)*
- Roman chamomile *(Chamaemelum nobile)*
- Rupturewort *(Herniaria glabra)*
- Speedwell *(Veronica officinalis)*
- Stonecrop *(Sedum ternatum)*
- Sweet violets *(Viola odorata* or *tricolor)*
- Thyme *(Thymus serpyllum)*
- White clover *(Trifolium repens)*
- Wild strawberries *(Fragaria virginiana)*
- Wintergreen or partridgeberry *(Mitchella repens)*

Herbs That Attract Butterflies

Catmint	*Nepeta*
Creeping thyme	*Thymus serpyllum*
Dill	*Anethum graveolens*
Mealy-cup sage	*Salvia farinacea*
Mint	*Mentha*
Oregano	*Origanum vulgare*
Parsley	*Petroselinum crispum*
Sweet marjoram	*Origanum majorana*

Heat-Loving Wildflowers

Asclepias tuberosa (butterfly weed)
Baptisia (wild indigo)
Echinacea purpurea (purple coneflower)
Liatris (blazing star)
Mirabilis (four-o'clock)
Monarda (bee balm)
Ratibida pinnata (prairie coneflower)
Rudbeckia (black-eyed Susan)

Flowers That Attract Butterflies

Allium	*Allium*
Aster	*Aster*
Bee balm	*Monarda*
Butterfly bush	*Buddleia*
Clove pink	*Dianthus*
Cornflower	*Centaurea*
Daylily	*Hemerocallis*
False indigo	*Baptisia*
Fleabane	*Erigeron*
Floss flower	*Ageratum*
Globe thistle	*Echinops*
Goldenrod	*Solidago*
Helen's flower	*Helenium*
Hollyhock	*Alcea*
Honeysuckle	*Lonicera*
Lavender	*Lavendula*
Lilac	*Syringa*
Lupine	*Lupinus*
Lychnis	*Lychnis*
Mallow	*Malva*
Milkweed	*Asclepias*
Pansy	*Viola*
Phlox	*Phlox*
Privet	*Ligustrum*
Purple coneflower	*Echinacea purpurea*
Purple loosestrife	*Lythrum*
Rock cress	*Arabis*
Sea holly	*Eryngium*
Shasta daisy	*Chrysanthemum*
Snapdragon	*Antirrhinum*
Stonecrop	*Sedum*
Sweet alyssum	*Lobularia*
Sweet rocket	*Hesperis*
Tickseed	*Coreopsis*
Zinnia	*Zinnia*

Flowers That Attract Hummingbirds

Beard tongue	*Penstemon*
Bee balm	*Monarda*
Butterfly bush	*Buddleia*
Catmint	*Nepeta*
Clove pink	*Dianthus*
Columbine	*Aquilegia*
Coral bells	*Heuchera*
Daylily	*Hemerocallis*
Desert candle	*Yucca*
Flag	*Iris*
Flowering tobacco	*Nicotiana alata*
Foxglove	*Digitalis*
Larkspur	*Delphinium*
Lily	*Lilium*
Lupine	*Lupinus*
Petunia	*Petunia*
Pincushion flower	*Scabiosa*
Red-hot poker	*Kniphofia*
Scarlet sage	*Salvia splendens*
Scarlet trumpet honeysuckle	*Lonicera sempervirens*
Soapwort	*Saponaria*
Summer phlox	*Phlox paniculata*
Verbena	*Verbena*
Weigela	*Weigela*

Note: Choose varieties in red and orange shades.

Forcing Blooms Indoors

Here is a list of some shrubs and trees that can be forced to flower indoors. (The trees tend to be stubborn and their blossoms may not be as rewarding as those of the shrubs.) The numbers indicate the approximate number of weeks they will take to flower.

Buckeye	5
Cherry	4
Cornelian dogwood	2
Crab apple	4
Deutzia	3
Flowering almond	3
Flowering dogwood	5
Flowering quince	4
Forsythia	1
Honeysuckle	3
Horse chestnut	5
Lilac	4
Magnolia	3
Pussy willow	2
Red maple	2
Redbud	2
Red-twig dogwood	5
Spicebush	2
Spirea	4
Wisteria	3

Source: Purdue University Cooperative Extension Service

Houseplant Harmonies

Experiments conducted in a controlled environment during the 1960s and 1970s suggest that you may want to consider the health and well-being of your houseplants when making musical selections.

Type of Music	Effect on Plant Growth
Classical	Lush and abundant growth; good root development
Indian Devotional	Lush and abundant growth; good root development
Country	No abnormal growth reaction
Silence	No abnormal growth reaction
Jazz	Abundant growth
Rock 'n' Roll	Poor growth; roots scrawny and sparse
White Noise	Plants died quickly

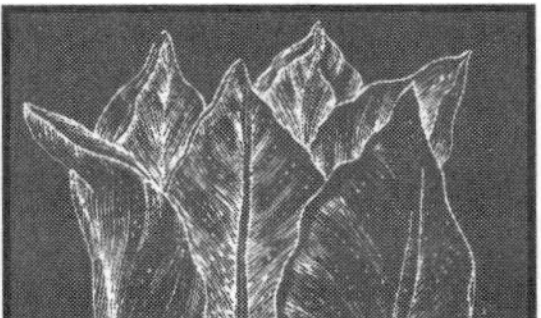

Forcing Bulbs Indoors

The technique is simple. Plant bulbs in pots of rich soil so tips are just even with pot rims. Store in a cold frame, cellar, or refrigerator at a cold temperature for two to several months. Water bulbs just enough to keep them from drying out. When roots can be seen poking out through bottoms of pots, bring them into a lighted room to flower.

The table below shows estimated times for rooting and ideal temperatures for flowering for some of the most common spring bulbs.

Name of Bulb	Time for Rooting	Temperature for Flowering
Chionodoxa (glory-of-the-snow)	10-14 weeks	55-60° F
Convallaria (lily-of-the-valley)	10-12 weeks	60-65° F
Crocus (crocus)	8-12 weeks	55-60° F
Freesia (freesia)	8-12 weeks	50-55° F
Galanthus (snowdrop)	9-12 weeks	55-60° F
Hyacinthus (hyacinth)	8-10 weeks	55-60° F
Iris reticulata (netted iris)	10-14 weeks	55-60° F
Muscari (grape hyacinth)	10-12 weeks	55-60° F
Narcissus (daffodil)	10-12 weeks	50-60° F
Puschkinia (striped squill)	8-12 weeks	50-55° F
Scilla (squill)	12-16 weeks	55-60° F
Tulipa (tulip)	12-16 weeks	55-60° F

Spring-Flowering Bulbs

These bulbs, planted in the fall, will be welcome heralds of spring.

	Planting Depth (inches)	Flower Height (inches)
Early-Spring Blooms		
Galanthus (snowdrop)	5	6
Crocus	5	6
Anemone blanda (Grecian windflower)	5	6
Muscari (grape hyacinth)	5	10
Greigii tulip	8	14
Hyacinth	8	14
Mid-Spring Blooms		
Daffodil	8	20
Darwin hybrid tulip	8	28
Fritillaria imperialis (crown imperial)	8	40
Late-Spring Blooms		
Spanish bluebell	5	10
Dutch iris	8	24
Late tulip	8	32
Allium giganteum (ornamental onion)	8	50

Planning Your Garden

Sow or plant in cool weather	Beets/chard, broccoli, brussels sprouts, cabbage, lettuce, onions, parsley, peas, radishes, spinach, turnips
Sow or plant in warm weather	Beans, carrots, corn, cucumbers, eggplant, melons, okra, peppers, squash tomatoes
One crop per season	Corn, eggplant, leeks, melons, peppers, potatoes, spinach (New Zealand), squash, tomatoes
Resow for additional crops	Beans, beets, cabbage family, carrots, kohlrabi, lettuce, radishes, rutabagas, spinach, turnips

Vegetable Seeds Best Sown in the Ground

Beans, bush and pole
Beets
Carrots
Collards
Corn
Cucumbers
Endive
Kale
Kohlrabi
Mustard greens
Parsnips
Peas
Potatoes
Radishes
Spinach
Squash, summer and winter
Swiss chard
Turnips

Vegetables and Herbs Best Started Indoors

Seeds	Weeks before last frost in spring
Basil	6
Broccoli	6-8
Brussels sprouts	4-8
Cabbage	6-8
Cauliflower	6-8
Celeriac	6-8
Celery	6-8
Chives	8-12
Eggplant	8-10
Leeks	8-12
Lettuce	4-6
Onions	10-12
Parsley	8
Peppers	8-10
Sweet marjoram	8
Tomatoes	6-8

Minimum Soil Temperature for Seeds to Germinate

Vegetable	Minimum Soil Temperature (°F)
Beans	48-50
Beets	39-41
Cabbage	38-40
Carrots	39-41
Corn	46-50
Melons	55-60
Onions	34-36
Peas	34-36
Radishes	39-41
Squash	55-60
Tomatoes	50-55

Critical Low Temperatures for Frost Damage to Vegetables

Vegetable	Temperature (°F)
Artichoke	31-32
Asparagus	30-31
Beans	31-32
Beets (roots)	29-30
Beets (tops)	31-32
Broccoli	29-30
Cabbage	26-28
Carrots	28-30
Cauliflower	27-29
Celery	31-32
Cucumbers	30-32
Kale	27-29
Muskmelon	33-34
Okra	29-30
Peas	28-30
Potato tubers	28-30
Pumpkins	31-32
Radishes	30-32
Spinach	30-32
Squash (summer)	31-33
Squash (winter)	30-32
Sweet corn	32-33
Sweet potatoes	32-33
Tomatoes	32-34
Watermelon	32-33

How Much Water Is Enough?

When confronted with a dry garden and the end of a hose, many gardeners admit to a certain insecurity about just how much water those plants really need. Here's a guide to help you estimate when and how much to water, assuming rich, well-balanced soil. Increase frequency during hot, very dry periods.

Vegetable	Critical time(s) to water
● Beans	When flowers form and during pod-formi and picking.
■ Beets	Before soil gets bone-dry.
■ Broccoli	Don't let soil dry out for 4 weeks after transplanting.
■ Brussels sprouts	Don't let soil dry out for 4 weeks after transplanting.
▲ Cabbage	Water frequently in dry weather for best crop.
■ Carrots	Before soil gets bone-dry.
▲ Cauliflower	Water frequently for best crop.
▲ Celery	Water frequently for best crop.
● Corn	When tassels form and when cobs swell.
▲ Cucumbers	Water frequently for best crop.
▲ Lettuce/Spinach	Water frequently for best crop.
■ Onions	In dry weather water in early stage to get plants going.
■ Parsnips	Before soil gets bone-dry.
● Peas	When flowers form and during pod-forming and picking.
● Potatoes	When the size of marbles.
▲ Squash (all types)	Water frequently for best crop.
● Tomatoes	For 3 to 4 weeks after transplanting and when flowers and fruit form.

▲ Needs a lot of water during dry spells. ● Needs water at critical

Number of gallons of water needed for a 5-foot row	Comments
2 per week depending on rainfall	Dry soil when pods are forming will adversely affect quantity and quality.
1 at early stage; 2 every 2 weeks	Water sparingly during early stages to prevent foliage from becoming too lush at the expense of the roots; increase water when round roots form.
1 to 1-1/2 per week	Best crop will result with no water shortage.
1 to 1-1/2 per week	Plants can endure dry conditions once they are established. Give 2 gallons the last 2 weeks before harvest for most succulent crop.
2 per week	If crop suffers some dry weather, focus efforts on providing 2 gallons 2 weeks before harvest. (Too much water will cause heads to crack.)
1 at early stage; 2 every 2 weeks as roots mature	Roots may split if crop is watered after soil has become too dry.
2 per week	Give 2 gallons before harvest for best crop.
2 per week	If conditions are very dry, water daily.
2 at important stages (left)	Cob size will be smaller if plants do not receive water when ears are forming.
1 per week	Water diligently when fruits form and throughout growth; give highest watering priority.
2 per week	Best crop will result with no water shortage.
1/2 to 1 per week if soil is very dry	Withhold water from bulb onions at later growth stages to improve storage qualities; water salad onions anytime soil is very dry.
1 per week in early stages	Water when dry to keep plants growing steadily. Too much water will encourage lush foliage and small roots.
2 per week	To reduce excess foliage and stem growth, do not water young seedlings unless wilting.
2 per week	In dry weather give 2 gallons throughout the growing season every 10 days. Swings from very dry to very wet produce oddly shaped and cracked tubers.
1 per week	Water diligently when fruits form and throughout their growth; give highest watering priority.
1 twice a week or more	Frequent watering may increase yield but adversely affect flavor.

stages of development. ■ **Does not need frequent watering.**

When Is a Good Time to Fertilize Your Vegetables?

Crop	Time of Application
Asparagus	Before growth starts in spring
Beans	After heavy blossom and set of pods
Broccoli	Three weeks after transplanting
Cabbage	Three weeks after transplanting
Cauliflower	Three weeks after transplanting
Corn	When eight to ten inches tall and again when silk first appears
Cucumber	One week after blossoming and again three weeks later
Eggplant	After first fruit-set
Kale	When plants are one-third grown
Lettuce, Head	Two to three weeks after transplanting
Muskmelon	One week after blossoming and again three weeks later
Onions	When bulbs begin to swell and again when plants are one foot tall
Peas	After heavy bloom and set of pods
Peppers	After first fruit-set
Potatoes	At blossom time or time of second hilling
Spinach	When plants are one-third grown
Squash	Just before vines start to run, when plants are about one foot tall
Tomatoes	One to two weeks before first picking and again two weeks after first picking
Watermelon	Just before vines start to run, when plants are about one foot tall

Manure Guide

Type of Manure	Water Content	Primary Nutrients (pounds per ton) Nitrogen	Phosphate	Potash
Cow, horse	60%-80%	12-14	5-9	9-12
Sheep, pig, goat	65%-75%	10-21	7	13-19
Chicken: Wet, sticky, and caked	75%	30	20	10
Moist, crumbly to sticky	50%	40	40	20
Crumbly	30%	60	55	30
Dry	15%	90	70	40
Ashed	none	none	135	100

Type of Garden	Best Type of Manure	Best Time to Apply
Flower	Cow, horse	Early spring
Vegetable	Chicken, cow, horse	Fall, spring
Potato or root crop	Cow, horse	Fall
Acid-loving plants (blueberries, azaleas, mountain laurels, rhododendrons)	Cow, horse	Early fall or not at all

General Rules for Pruning

What	When	How
Apple	Early spring	Prune moderately. Keep tree open with main branches well spaced. Avoid sharp V-shaped crotches.
Cherry	Early spring	Prune the most vigorous shoots moderately.
Clematis	Spring	Cut weak growth. Save as much old wood as possible.
Flowering dogwood	After flowering	Remove dead wood only.
Forsythia	After flowering	Remove old branches at ground. Trim new growth.
Lilac	After flowering	Remove diseased, scaly growth, flower heads, and suckers.
Peach	Early spring	Remove half of last year's growth. Keep tree headed low.
Plum	Early spring	Cut dead, diseased branches; trim rank growth moderately.
Rhododendron	After flowering	Prune judiciously. Snip branches from weak, leggy plants to induce growth from roots.
Roses (except climbers)	Spring, after frosts	Cut dead and weak growth; cut branches or canes to four or five eyes.
Roses, climbers	After flowering	Cut half of old growth; retain new shoots for next year.
Rose of Sharon	When buds begin	Cut all winter-killed wood to swell growth back to live wood.
Trumpet vine	Early spring	Prune side branches severely to main stem.
Virginia creeper	Spring	Clip young plants freely. Thin old plants and remove dead growth.
Wisteria	Spring, summer	Cut new growth to spurs at axils of leaves.

Symbolic Meanings of Herbs, Flowers, and Trees

Aloe . . . . Healing, protection, affection
Angelica . . . . Inspiration
Arbor vitae . . . . Unchanging friendship
Bachelor's button . . . . Single blessedness
Basil . . . . Good wishes, love
Bay . . . . Glory
Black-eyed Susan . . . . Justice
Carnation . . . . Alas for my poor heart
Chamomile . . . . Patience
Chives . . . . Usefulness
Clover, white . . . . Think of me
Coriander . . . . Hidden worth
Cumin . . . . Fidelity
Fennel . . . . Flattery
Fern . . . . Sincerity
Geranium, oak-leaved . . . . True friendship
Goldenrod . . . . Encouragement
Heliotrope . . . . Eternal love
Holly . . . . Hope
Hollyhock . . . . Ambition
Honeysuckle . . . . Bonds of love
Horehound . . . . Health
Hyssop . . . . Sacrifice, cleanliness
Ivy . . . . Friendship, continuity
Lady's-mantle . . . . Comforting
Lavender . . . . Devotion, virtue
Lemon balm . . . . Sympathy
Marjoram . . . . Joy, happiness
Mint . . . . Eternal refreshment
Morning glory . . . . Affectation
Nasturtium . . . . Patriotism
Oak . . . . Strength
Oregano . . . . Substance
Pansy . . . . Thoughts
Parsley . . . . Festivity

(continued on next page)

Pine . . . . . Humility
Poppy, red . . . . . Consolation
Rose . . . . . Love
Rosemary . . . . . Remembrance
Rue . . . . . Grace, clear vision
Sage . . . . . Wisdom, immortality
Salvia, blue . . . . . I think of you
Salvia, red . . . . . Forever mine
Savory . . . . . Spice, interest
Sorrel . . . . . Affection
Southernwood . . . . . Constancy, jest
Sweet pea . . . . . Pleasures
Sweet woodruff . . . . . Humility
Tansy . . . . . Hostile thoughts
Tarragon . . . . . Lasting interest
Thyme . . . . . Courage, strength
Valerian . . . . . Readiness
Violet . . . . . Loyalty, devotion
Violet, blue . . . . . Faithfulness
Violet, yellow . . . . . Rural happiness
Willow . . . . . Sadness
Zinnia . . . . . Thoughts of absent friends

Vegetable Gardening in Containers

Lack of yard space is no excuse for not gardening, since many vegetables can be readily grown in containers. In addition to providing five hours or more of full sun, attention must be given to choosing the proper container, using a good soil mix, planting and spacing requirements, fertilizing, watering, and variety selection.

VEGETABLE	TYPE OF CONTAINER	RECOMMENDED VARIETIES
Beans, snap	5-gallon window box	Bush 'Romano', Bush 'Blue Lake', 'Tender Crop'
Broccoli	1 plant/5-gallon pot 3 plants/15-gallon tub	'Green Comet', 'DeCicco'
Carrot	5-gallon window box at least 12 inches deep	'Short 'n Sweet', 'Danvers Half Long', 'Tiny Sweet'
Cucumber	1 plant/1-gallon pot	'Patio Pik', 'Spacemaster', 'Pot Luck'
Eggplant	5-gallon pot	'Slim Jim', 'Ichiban', 'Black Beauty'
Lettuce	5-gallon window box	'Salad Bowl', 'Ruby'
Onion	5-gallon window box	'White Sweet Spanish', 'Yellow Sweet Spanish'
Pepper	1 plant/2-gallon pot 5 plants/15-gallon tub	'Sweet Banana', 'Yolo', 'Wonder', 'Long Red', 'Cayenne'
Radish	5-gallon window box	'Cherry Belle', 'Icicle'
Tomatoes	Bushel basket	'Tiny Tim', 'Small Fry', 'Early Girl', 'Sweet 100', 'Patio'

Courtesy North Carolina Cooperative Extension Service

Fall Palette

Tree	Color
Sugar maple and sumac	Flame red and orange
Red maple, dogwood, sassafras, and scarlet oak	Dark red
Poplar, birch, tulip tree, willow	Yellow
Ash	Plum purple
Oak, beech, larch, elm, hickory, and sycamore	Tan or brown
Locust	Stays green (until leaves drop)
Black walnut and butternut	Drops leaves before turning color

Pan Sizes and Equivalents

In the midst of cooking but don't have the right pan? You can substitute one size for another, keeping in mind that when you change the pan size, you must sometimes change the cooking time. For example, if a recipe calls for using an 8-inch round cake pan and baking for 25 minutes, and you substitute a 9-inch pan, the cake may bake in only 20 minutes, since the batter forms a thinner layer in the larger pan. (Use a toothpick inserted into the center of the cake to test for doneness. If it comes out clean, the cake has finished baking.) Also, specialty pans such as tube and Bundt pans distribute heat differently; you may not get the same results if you substitute a regular cake pan for a specialty one, even if the volume is the same.

PAN SIZE	VOLUME	SUBSTITUTE
9-inch pie pan	4 cups	■ 8-inch round cake pan
8x4x2-1/2-inch loaf pan	6 cups	■ Three 5x2-inch loaf pans ■ Two 3x1-1/4-inch muffin tins ■ 12x8x2-inch cake pan
9x5x3-inch loaf pan	8 cups	■ 8-inch square cake pan ■ 9-inch round cake pan
15x10x1-inch jelly roll pan	10 cups	■ 9-inch square cake pan ■ Two 8-inch round cake pans ■ 8x3-inch springform pan
10x3-inch Bundt pan	12 cups	■ Two 8x4x2-1/2-inch loaf pans ■ 9x3-inch angel food cake pan ■ 9x3-inch springform pan
13x9x2-inch cake pan	14-15 cups	■ Two 9-inch round cake pans ■ Two 8-inch square cake pans

If you are cooking a casserole and don't have the correct size dish, here are some baking-pan substitutions. Again, think about the depth of the ingredients in the dish and lengthen or shorten the baking time accordingly.

CASSEROLE SIZE	BAKING-PAN SUBSTITUTE
1-1/2 quarts	9x5x3-inch loaf pan
2 quarts	8-inch square cake pan
2-1/2 quarts	9-inch square cake pan
3 quarts	13x9x2-inch cake pan
4 quarts	14x10x2-inch cake pan

When Is It Done?

■ When cooking meat and poultry, interior temperature is a critical factor, for safety and for flavor. Meat and poultry are cooked and juicy at certain temperatures but become dry and tough if cooked much longer. Traditionally, judging the doneness of a roast or a bird has meant visually checking the interior color of the meat while it is cooking — the redder the color, the rarer the meat. But this involves guesswork.

To be certain, we recommend using an *instant-read thermometer,* such as the ones made by Taylor Precision Products. Round-dial and digital instant-read thermometers are available from kitchen-supply stores and hardware stores, and cost from $12 to $20.

Instant-read thermometers give readings quickly, but they are not oven-safe and must not be left in the meat while cooking. Use the thermometer toward the end of the minimum cooking time, and allow it to remain in the meat for only 15 seconds at a depth of two inches or to the indicator mark on the thermometer's stem. Follow these guidelines for accurate readings:

■ **For roasts, steaks, and thick chops, insert the thermometer into the center at the thickest part, away from bone, fat, and gristle.**

■ **For whole poultry, insert the thermometer into the inner thigh area near the breast but not touching bone.**

■ **For ground meat (such as meat loaf), insert the thermometer into the thickest area.**

■ **For thin items such as chops and hamburger patties, insert the thermometer sideways.**

Internal Minimum Temperatures for Meat and Poultry

Adapted from *A Quick Consumer Guide to Safe Food Handling,* USDA/FSIS Bulletin No. 248, and from information on the USDA's Meat and Poultry Hot Line, 800-535-4555.

Product	Minimum Fahrenheit
Beef (roasts, steaks, and chops)	
Rare (some bacterial risk)	140°
Medium	160°
Well-done	170°
Casseroles	160°
Chicken	
Ground	170°
Whole	180°
Breasts, roasts	170°
Parts (thighs, wings)	Cook until juices run clear
Duck	180°
Goose	180°
Gravies, sauces, and soups	Bring to a boil
Ground beef, lamb, pork, and veal	160°
Ham	
Fresh (raw)	160°
Precooked (to reheat)	140°
Lamb (roasts, steaks, and chops)	
Medium-rare	145°
Medium	160°
Well-done	170°
Leftovers	165°
Pork, fresh	
Medium	160°
Well-done	170°
Stuffing (cooked alone or in bird)	165°
Turkey	
Ground	170°
Whole	180°
Breasts, roasts	170°
Parts (thighs, wings)	Cook until juices run clear
Veal (roasts, steaks, and chops)	
Medium-rare	145°
Medium	160°
Well-done	170°

**According to the National Cattlemen's Beef Association, beef roasts can be removed from the oven when the thermometer registers about 5° F below the desired doneness and allowed to stand for about 15 minutes. The outside layers will continue to transfer heat to the center of the roast until it reaches the desired doneness.*

– compiled by Randy Miller

The Party Planner

How much do you need when you're cooking for a crowd?

If you're planning a big meal, these estimates can help you determine how much food you should buy. They're based on "average" servings; adjust quantities upward for extra-big eaters and downward if children are included.

Food	To Serve 25	To Serve 50	To Serve 100
MEATS			
Chicken or turkey breast	12-1/2 pounds	25 pounds	50 pounds
Fish (fillets or steaks)	7-1/2 pounds	15 pounds	30 pounds
Hamburgers	8 to 9 pounds	15 to 18 pounds	30 to 36 pounds
Ham or roast beef	10 pounds	20 pounds	40 pounds
Hot dogs	6 pounds	12-1/2 pounds	25 pounds
Meat loaf	6 pounds	12 pounds	24 pounds
Oysters	1 gallon	2 gallons	4 gallons
Pork	10 pounds	20 pounds	40 pounds
MISCELLANEOUS			
Bread (loaves)	3	5	10
Butter	3/4 pound	1-1/2 pounds	3 pounds
Cheese	3/4 pound	1-1/2 pounds	3 pounds
Coffee	3/4 pound	1-1/2 pounds	3 pounds
Milk	1-1/2 gallons	3 gallons	6 gallons
Nuts	3/4 pound	1-1/2 pounds	3 pounds
Olives	1/2 pound	1 pound	2 pounds
Pickles	1/2 quart	1 quart	2 quarts
Rolls	50	100	200
Soup	5 quarts	2-1/2 gallons	5 gallons
SIDE DISHES			
Baked beans	5 quarts	2-1/2 gallons	5 gallons
Beets	7-1/2 pounds	15 pounds	30 pounds
Cabbage for cole slaw	5 pounds	10 pounds	20 pounds
Carrots	7-1/2 pounds	15 pounds	30 pounds
Lettuce for salad (heads)	5	10	20
Peas (fresh)	12 pounds	25 pounds	50 pounds
Potatoes	9 pounds	18 pounds	36 pounds
Potato salad	3 quarts	1-1/2 gallons	3 gallons
Salad dressing	3 cups	1-1/2 quarts	3 quarts
DESSERTS			
Cakes	2	4	8
Ice cream	1 gallon	2 gallons	4 gallons
Pies	4	9	18
Whipping cream	1 pint	2 pints	4 pints

Approximate Freezer Storage Life of Foods

Maintained at 0° Fahrenheit (-18° Celsius)

FOOD	MONTHS AT 0° F
BREAD	
Quick breads	2
Yeast breads	6
CAKES/COOKIES	4-6
DAIRY	
Butter	5
Cream*	2
Hard cheese	6
Milk*	1
Processed cheese	4
DOUGH	
Cookie dough	4
Unbaked pastry	2
Yeast dough	2 weeks
FISH/SEAFOOD	
Bluefish, mackerel, perch, salmon (fatty)	2-3
Cod, flounder, haddock, sole (lean)	6
Oysters, scallops, clams	3-4
Shrimp, uncooked	6-12
FRUITS/JUICES	
Citrus fruits and juices*	4-6
Sweetened fruits	12
Unsweetened fruits	8

FOOD	MONTHS AT 0° F
MEAT	
Beef cuts	6-9
Cured meats**	1
Ground beef, lamb, veal	2-3
Ground pork	1-2
Lamb cuts	3-4
Leftover cooked meat	2-3
Pork cuts	2-3
Veal cuts	3-4
PIES	
Fruit, baked	2-4
Fruit, unbaked	8
Pumpkin, chiffon	1
POULTRY	6
PRECOOKED FOODS	
Combination dishes (stews, casseroles, etc.)	3-6
Soups*	4-6
VEGETABLES	
Green peppers	6
Other vegetables	8-10
Unblanched corn on the cob	2

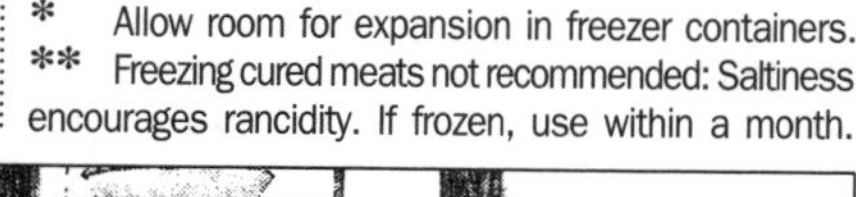
* Allow room for expansion in freezer containers.
** Freezing cured meats not recommended: Saltiness encourages rancidity. If frozen, use within a month.

Caffeine Content of Drinks and Chocolate

Item	Average Milligrams of Caffeine
Coffee (5-oz. cup)	
Brewed, drip	115
Brewed, percolator	80
Instant	65
Decaffeinated, brewed	3
Decaffeinated, instant	2
Tea (5-oz. cup)	
Brewed, major U.S. brands	40
Brewed, imported brands	60
Iced (12-oz. glass)	70
Soft Drinks (6-oz. serving)	
Cola	15-23
Diet cola	0.3
Root beer	0
Chocolate	
Cocoa beverage (5-oz. cup)	4
Milk chocolate (1-oz. piece)	6
Dark chocolate (1-oz. piece)	20
Baker's chocolate (1-oz. piece)	26

Best Baking and Cooking Apples in North America

Name	Introduced	Description
'Fuji'	1962	Sweet and juicy, firm, red skin
'Granny Smith'	1868	Moderately sweet, crisp flesh, green skin
'Jonathan'	1820s	Tart flesh, crisp, juicy, bright red on yellow skin
'McIntosh'	1870	Juicy, sweet, pinkish-white flesh, red skin
'Newton Pippin'	1700s	Sweet-tart flesh, crisp, greenish-yellow skin
'Rhode Island Greening'	1600s	Very tart, distinctively flavored, green skin
'Rome Beauty'	1820s	Mildly tart, crisp, greenish-white flesh, thick skin
'Winesap'	late 1700s	Firm, very juicy, sweet-sour flavor, red skin

1 pound of apples = 2 large, 3 medium, or 4 to 5 small apples
1 pound of apples = 3 cups peeled and sliced apples

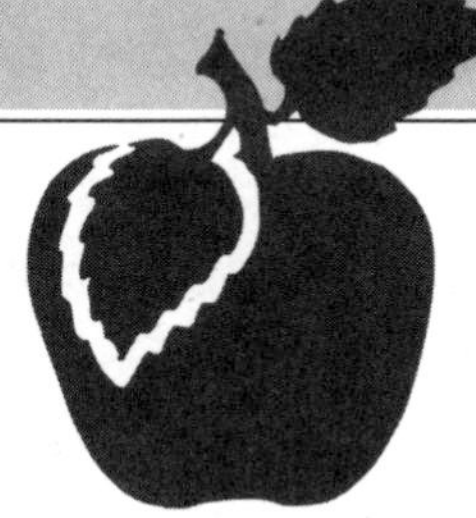

An average apple contains:

- 80 calories
- 5 g fiber
- ½ g fat
- 0 sodium
- 18 g carbohydrates
- 170 mg potassium
- 0 cholesterol

Basic Kitchen Equipment

FOOD PREPARATION

Measuring cups
- Dry measure: set of 4 cups
- Wet measure: 1-cup and 2-cup

Measuring spoons
Ruler
Thermometers
- Meat
- Candy/frying
- Freezer

Timer
Mixing bowls (3 sizes)
Chopping board
Knives
- Chef's knife
- Paring knife
- Bread knife (serrated edge)
- Carving knife

Knife sharpener
Kitchen shears
Vegetable parer
Openers
- Bottle opener
- Corkscrew
- Jar opener
- Can opener

Pepper grinder
Rotary eggbeater
Nutcracker
Funnel
Grater
Colander
Strainer
Juicer

COOKING

Pots, skillets, and pans
- Saucepans: 1- to 2-cup, 1-quart, 2-quart, and 8-quart
- Skillets/frying pans: 7-inch, 10-inch, and 12-inch
- Griddle
- Flameproof casserole or Dutch oven
- Casseroles and baking dishes
- Roasting pan (with rack)
- Double boiler
- Steamer

Kettle
Coffeepot
Wooden spoons
Rubber spatula
Metal utensils
- Metal spatula
- Slotted spoon
- Cooking fork
- Ladle
- Potato masher
- Tongs
- Whisk

Skewers
Bulb baster
Brush

BAKING

Pastry blender
Rolling pin
Sifter
Cake pans
- Pair of 8 (and/or 9) x1½-inch round
- 8- or 9-inch square
- 9x12-inch rectangular
- 10-inch tube

Loaf pans
Cookie sheets (at least 2)
Jelly-roll pan
Muffin tins
Pie pans
Custard cups
Cooling racks

Appetizing Amounts

Occasion	Number of bites per person
Hors d'oeuvres (with meal following)	**4**
Cocktail party	**10**
Grand affair, no dinner following (e.g., wedding reception)	**10-15**

Pass the Pasta

All pastas, when cooked, are not created equal. Four ounces of dry pasta, the usual serving size, yields different amounts depending on the pasta shape.

Type of pasta, 4 ounces uncooked	Cooked yield (in cups)
Spaghetti, vermicelli, capellini, linguine	2
Elbow macaroni, conchiglie (seashells), rotini, ruote (cartwheels), mostaccioli, ziti, penne	2½
Medium egg noodles, tagliatelle	3

What Counts as a Serving?

Bread Group
1 slice of bread
1 ounce of ready-to-eat cereal
½ cup of cooked cereal, rice, or pasta

Vegetable Group
1 cup of raw leafy vegetable
½ cup of other vegetable, cooked or chopped raw
¾ cup of vegetable juice

Fruit Group
1 medium apple, banana, or orange
½ cup of chopped, cooked, or canned fruit
¾ cup of fruit juice

Milk Group
1 cup of milk or yogurt
1½ ounces of natural cheese
2 ounces of processed cheese

Meat Group
2 to 3 ounces of cooked lean meat, poultry, or fish
½ cup of cooked dry beans, 1 egg, or 2 tablespoons of peanut butter count as 1 ounce of meat (about ⅓ serving)

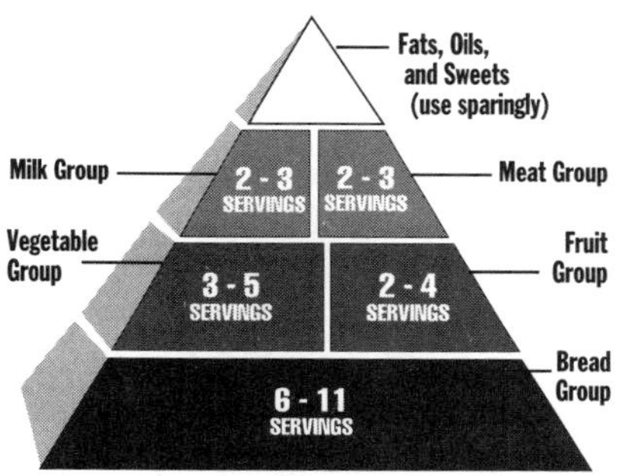

Suggested Daily Servings

Dietary Guidelines

The recommendations for a healthful diet from the USDA (United States Department of Agriculture) and HHS (Department of Health and Human Services) are:

- Eat a variety of foods
- Maintain a healthy weight
- Choose a diet low in fat, saturated fat, and cholesterol
- Choose a diet with plenty of vegetables, fruits, and grain products
- Use sugars only in moderation
- Use salt only in moderation
- If you drink alcoholic beverages, do so in moderation

Food for Thought

- ☞ Piece of pecan pie = 580 calories
- ☞ Grilled cheese sandwich = 440 calories
- ☞ Chocolate shake = 364 calories
- ☞ Bagel with cream cheese = 361 calories
- ☞ 20 potato chips = 228 calories
- ☞ 10 french fries = 214 calories
- ☞ Half a cantaloupe = 94 calories
- ☞ Corn on the cob = 70 calories (no butter)
- ☞ Carrot = 30 calories

Don't Freeze These

Bananas

Canned hams

Cooked eggs

Cooked potatoes

Cream fillings and puddings

Custards

Fried foods

Gelatin dishes

Mayonnaise

Raw vegetables, such as cabbage, celery, green onions, radishes, and salad greens

Soft cheeses, cottage cheese

Sour cream

Yogurt

Substitutions for Common Ingredients

ITEM	QUANTITY	SUBSTITUTION
Allspice	1 teaspoon	½ teaspoon cinnamon plus ⅛ teaspoon ground cloves
Arrowroot, as thickener	1½ teaspoons	1 tablespoon flour
Baking powder	1 teaspoon	¼ teaspoon baking soda plus ⅝ teaspoon cream of tartar
Bread crumbs, dry	¼ cup	1 slice bread
Bread crumbs, soft	½ cup	1 slice bread
Buttermilk	1 cup	1 cup plain yogurt
Chocolate, unsweetened	1 ounce	3 tablespoons cocoa plus 1 tablespoon butter or fat
Cracker crumbs	¾ cup	1 cup dry bread crumbs
Cream, heavy	1 cup	¾ cup milk plus ⅓ cup melted butter (this will not whip)
Cream, light	1 cup	⅞ cup milk plus 3 tablespoons melted butter
Cream, sour	1 cup	⅞ cup buttermilk or plain yogurt plus 3 tablespoons melted butter
Cream, whipping	1 cup	⅔ cup well-chilled evaporated milk, whipped; **or** 1 cup nonfat dry milk powder whipped with 1 cup ice water
Egg	1 whole	2 yolks
Flour, all-purpose	1 cup	1⅛ cups cake flour; **or** ⅝ cup potato flour; **or** 1¼ cups rye or coarsely ground whole grain flour; **or** 1 cup cornmeal
Flour, cake	1 cup	1 cup minus 2 tablespoons sifted all-purpose flour
Flour, self-rising	1 cup	1 cup all-purpose flour plus 1¼ teaspoons baking powder plus ¼ teaspoon salt
Garlic	1 small clove	⅛ teaspoon garlic powder; **or** ½ teaspoon instant minced garlic
Herbs, dried	½ to 1 teaspoon	1 tablespoon fresh, minced and packed
Honey	1 cup	1¼ cups sugar plus ½ cup liquid

Measuring Vegetables

Asparagus: 1 pound = 3 cups chopped
Beans (string): 1 pound = 4 cups chopped
Beets: 1 pound (5 medium) = 2-1/2 cups chopped
Broccoli: 1/2 pound = 6 cups chopped
Cabbage: 1 pound = 4-1/2 cups shredded
Carrots: 1 pound = 3-1/2 cups sliced or grated
Celery: 1 pound = 4 cups chopped
Cucumbers: 1 pound (2 medium) = 4 cups sliced
Eggplant: 1 pound = 4 cups chopped (6 cups raw, cubed = 3 cups cooked)
Garlic: 1 clove = 1 teaspoon chopped
Leeks: 1 pound = 4 cups chopped (2 cups cooked)
Mushrooms: 1 pound = 5 to 6 cups sliced = 2 cups cooked
Onions: 1 pound = 4 cups sliced = 2 cups cooked
Parsnips: 1 pound unpeeled = 1-1/2 cups cooked, pureed
Peas: 1 pound whole = 1 to 1-1/2 cups shelled
Potatoes: 1 pound (3 medium) sliced = 2 cups mashed
Pumpkin: 1 pound = 4 cups chopped = 2 cups cooked and drained
Spinach: 1 pound = 3/4 to 1 cup cooked

ITEM	QUANTITY	SUBSTITUTION
Lemon	1	1 to 3 tablespoons juice, 1 to 1½ teaspoons grated rind
Lemon juice	1 teaspoon	½ teaspoon vinegar
Lemon rind, grated	1 teaspoon	½ teaspoon lemon extract
Milk, skim	1 cup	⅓ cup instant nonfat dry milk plus about ¾ cup water
Milk, to sour	1 cup	Add 1 tablespoon vinegar or lemon juice to 1 cup milk minus 1 tablespoon. Stir and let stand 5 minutes.
Milk, whole	1 cup	½ cup evaporated milk plus ½ cup water; **or** 1 cup skim milk plus 2 teaspoons melted butter
Molasses	1 cup	1 cup honey
Mustard, prepared	1 tablespoon	1 teaspoon dry or powdered mustard
Onion, chopped	1 small	1 tablespoon instant minced onion; **or** 1 teaspoon onion powder; **or** ¼ cup frozen chopped onion
Sugar, granulated	1 cup	1 cup firmly packed brown sugar; **or** 1¾ cups confectioners' sugar (do not substitute in baking); **or** 2 cups corn syrup; **or** 1 cup superfine sugar
Tomatoes, canned	1 cup	½ cup tomato sauce plus ½ cup water; **or** 1⅓ cups chopped fresh tomatoes, simmered
Tomato juice	1 cup	½ cup tomato sauce plus ½ cup water plus dash each salt and sugar; **or** ¼ cup tomato paste plus ¾ cup water plus salt and sugar
Tomato ketchup	½ cup	½ cup tomato sauce plus 2 tablespoons sugar, 1 tablespoon vinegar, and ⅛ teaspoon ground cloves
Tomato puree	1 cup	½ cup tomato paste plus ½ cup water
Tomato soup	1 can (10¾ oz.)	1 cup tomato sauce plus ¼ cup water
Vanilla	1-inch bean	1 teaspoon vanilla extract
Yeast	1 cake (⅗ oz.)	1 package active dried yeast (1 scant tablespoon)
Yogurt, plain	1 cup	1 cup buttermilk

Squash (summer): 1 pound = 4 cups grated = 2 cups salted and drained

Squash (winter): 2 pounds = 2-1/2 cups cooked, pureed

Sweet Potatoes: 1 pound = 4 cups grated = 1 cup cooked, pureed

Swiss Chard: 1 pound = 5 to 6 cups packed leaves = 1 to 1-1/2 cups cooked

Tomatoes: 1 pound (3 or 4 medium) = 1-1/2 cups seeded pulp

Turnips: 1 pound = 4 cups chopped = 2 cups cooked, mashed

Measuring Fruits

Apples: 1 pound (3 or 4 medium) = 3 cups sliced

Bananas: 1 pound (3 or 4 medium) = 1-3/4 cups mashed

Berries: 1 quart = 3-1/2 cups

Dates: 1 pound = 2-1/2 cups pitted

Lemon: 1 whole = 1 to 3 tablespoons juice; 1 to 1-1/2 teaspoons grated rind

Lime: 1 whole = 1-1/2 to 2 tablespoons juice

Orange: 1 medium = 6 to 8 tablespoons juice; 2 to 3 tablespoons grated rind

Peaches: 1 pound (4 medium) = 3 cups sliced

Pears: 1 pound (4 medium) = 2 cups sliced

Rhubarb: 1 pound = 2 cups cooked

Strawberries: 1 quart = 4 cups sliced

What Do We Eat?

Our eating habits have changed dramatically since 1970. Here's a comparison between 1995 and 1970 food consumption from the USDA.

Food	Per Capita Annual Consumption 1995	1970
Going Down		
Eggs	237	309
Red meat (pounds)	110	132
Whole milk (gallons)	9	26
Going Up		
Cheese (pounds)	27	11
Fruits (pounds)	124	101
Grains (pounds)	189	135
Nonfat/1% milk (gallons)	6	2
Poultry (pounds)	63	34
Seafood (pounds)	15	12
Vegetables (pounds)	320	271
Yogurt (pounds)	4	1
Also Going Up		
Fats and oils (pounds)	67	55
Soft drinks (gallons)	52	24
Sugars (pounds)	150	123

The Healthiest Vegetables

These results come from adding up the percent of the USRDA for six nutrients (vitamin A, vitamin C, folate, iron, copper, calcium) plus fiber for each vegetable.

1 Sweet potato
2 Carrot
3 Spinach
4 Collard greens
5 Red pepper
6 Kale
7 Dandelion greens
8 Broccoli
9 Brussels sprouts
10 Potato

Daily Caloric Requirements

These hypothetical examples demonstrate changing caloric requirements at different times of life.

Age range	MALE Weight in pounds	MALE Calories needed	FEMALE Weight in pounds	FEMALE Calories needed
1	24	1,100	24	1,100
2-3	31	1,300	31	1,300
4-6	40	1,800	40	1,800
7-9	55	2,200	55	2,200
10-12	75	2,500	79	2,200
13-15	110	2,800	106	2,200
16-18	136	3,200	117	2,100
19-24	156	3,000	128	2,100
25-49	163	2,700	130	1,900
50-74	161	2,300	139	1,800

PLEASE NOTE: If pregnant or nursing, add 300 to 500 calories.

Are You Skinny, Just Right, or Overweight?

Here's an easy formula to figure your Body Mass Index (BMI), now thought to be a more accurate indicator of relative body size than the old insurance charts. **W** is your weight in pounds and **H** is your height in inches.

$$\text{BMI} = \frac{(W \times 705) \div H}{H}$$

- If the result is 25 or less, you are within a healthy weight range.
- If it's 19 or below, you are too skinny.
- Between 25 and 27, you are as much as 8 percent over your healthy weight.
- Between 27 and 30, you are at increased risk for health problems.
- Above 30, you are more than 20 percent over your healthy weight. It puts you at a dramatically increased risk for serious health problems.

There are a couple of exceptions to the above. Very muscular people with a high BMI generally have nothing to worry about, and extreme skinniness is generally a symptom of some other health problem, not the cause.

Here's another way to see if you are dangerously overweight. Measure your waistline. A waist measurement of 35 inches or more in women and 41 inches or more in men, regardless of height, suggests a serious risk of weight-related health problems.

Calorie Burning

If you hustle through your chores to get to the fitness center, relax. You're getting a great workout already. The left-hand column lists "chore" exercises, the middle column shows number of calories you burn per minute per pound of your body weight, the right-hand column lists comparable "recreational" exercises. For example, a 150-pound person forking straw bales burns 9.45 calories per minute, the same workout he/she would get playing basketball.

Chore	Calories	Recreational
Chopping with an ax, fast	0.135	Skiing, cross country, uphill
Climbing hills, with 44-pound load	0.066	Swimming, crawl, fast
Digging trenches	0.065	Skiing, cross country, steady walk
Forking straw bales	0.063	Basketball
Chopping down trees	0.060	Football
Climbing hills, with 9-pound load	0.058	Swimming, crawl, slow
Sawing by hand	0.055	Skiing, cross country, moderate
Mowing lawns	0.051	Horseback riding, trotting
Scrubbing floors	0.049	Tennis
Shoveling coal	0.049	Aerobic dance, medium
Hoeing	0.041	Weight training, circuit training
Stacking firewood	0.040	Weight lifting, free weights
Shoveling grain	0.038	Golf
Painting houses	0.035	Walking, normal pace, asphalt road
Weeding	0.033	Table tennis
Shopping for food	0.028	Cycling, 5.5 mph
Mopping floors	0.028	Fishing
Washing windows	0.026	Croquet
Raking	0.025	Dancing, ballroom
Driving a tractor	0.016	Drawing, standing position

Life Expectancy by Current Age

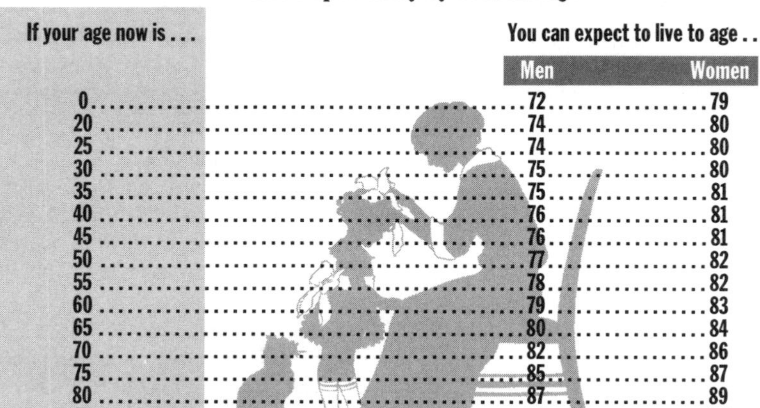

If your age now is . . .	You can expect to live to age . . . Men	Women
0	72	79
20	74	80
25	74	80
30	75	80
35	75	81
40	76	81
45	76	81
50	77	82
55	78	82
60	79	83
65	80	84
70	82	86
75	85	87
80	87	89
85	90	92

Source: U.S. Department of Health and Human Services, 1995

Is It a Cold or the Flu?

SYMPTOMS	FLU	COLD	ALLERGY	SINUSITIS
Headache	Always	Occasionally	Occasionally	Always
Muscle aches	Always	Usually	Rarely	Rarely
Fatigue, weakness	Always	Usually	Rarely	Rarely
Fever	Always	Occasionally	Never	Occasionally
Cough	Usually	Occasionally	Occasionally	Usually
Runny, stuffy nose	Occasionally	Usually	Usually	Always
Nasal discharge	Occasionally	Usually	Usually	Always
Sneezing	Rarely	Occasionally	Usually	Rarely
Sore throat	Rarely	Usually	Occasionally	Rarely
Itchy eyes, nose, throat	Rarely	Rarely	Usually	Never

How Long Trash Lasts

Glass bottles	1,000,000 years
Aluminum cans/tabs	80-100 years
Rubber boot soles	50-80 years
Leather	up to 50 years
Nylon fabric	30-40 years
Plastic film containers	20-30 years
Plastic bags	10-20 years
Plastic-coated papers	5 years
Cigarette butts	1-5 years
Wool socks	1-5 years
Orange/banana peels	2-5 weeks

– courtesy National Park Service

How Long Household Items Last

ITEMS	YEARS (Approx. averages)
Electric shavers	4
Personal computers	6
Lawn mowers	6
Automatic coffee makers	6
VCRs	6
Food processors	7
Electric can openers	7
CD players	7
Camcorders	7
Toasters	8
Stereo receivers	8
Color TV sets	8
Blenders	8
Room air conditioners	9
Vacuum cleaners	10
Microwave ovens	10
Dishwashers	11
Dehumidifiers	12
Washing machines	13
Electric dryers	13
Refrigerators	14
Gas dryers	14
Electric ranges	15
Gas ranges	18

The life span of a product depends not only on its actual durability but also on your desire for some new convenience found only on a new model.

– courtesy *Consumer Reports*

How Much Water Is Used?

The greatest water waste is in your bathroom. The numbers below show a typical distribution of household water use with standard fixtures:

	Percent
Dishwashers	3.1
Toilet leaks	5.5
Baths	8.9
Faucets	11.7
Showers	21.2
Washing machines	21.2
Toilets	28.4

	Gallons
To brush your teeth (water running)	1-2
To flush a toilet	5-7
To run a dishwasher	9-12
To shave (water running)	10-15
To wash dishes by hand	20
To take a shower	15-30
By an average person daily	123
In the average residence during a year	110,000

A Few Clues About Cords of Wood

- A cord of wood is a pile of logs 4 feet wide by 4 feet high by 8 feet long.
- A cord of wood may contain from 77 to 96 cubic feet of wood.
- The larger the unsplit logs, the larger the gaps, with fewer cubic feet of wood actually in the cord.

Hand Thermometer for Outdoor Cooking

Hold your palm close to where the food will be cooking: over the coals or in front of a reflector oven. Count "one-and-one, two-and-two," and so on, for as many seconds as you can hold your hand still.

Seconds Counted	Heat	Temperature
6-8	Slow	250-350° F
4-5	Moderate	350-400° F
2-3	Hot	400-450° F
1 or less	Very hot	450-500° F

Firewood Heat Values

High Heat Value

1 CORD = 200-250 GALLONS OF FUEL OIL

American beech
Apple
Ironwood
Red oak
Shagbark hickory
Sugar maple
White ash
White oak
Yellow birch

Medium Heat Value

1 CORD = 150-200 GALLONS OF FUEL OIL

American elm
Black cherry
Douglas fir
Red maple
Silver maple
Tamarack
White birch

Low Heat Value

1 CORD = 100-150 GALLONS OF FUEL OIL

Aspen
Cottonwood
Hemlock
Lodgepole pine
Red alder
Redwood
Sitka spruce
Western red cedar
White pine

How Many Trees in a Cord of Wood?

Diameter of Tree (breast high, in inches)	Number of Trees (per cord)
4	50
6	20
8	10
10	6
12	4
14	3

Heat Values of Fuels

(approximate)

Fuel	BTU	Unit of Measure
Oil	141,000	gallon
Coal	31,000	pound
Natural gas	1,000	cubic foot
Steam	1,000	cubic foot
Electricity	3,413	kilowatt-hour
Gasoline	124,000	gallon

How to Find the Number of Bricks in a Wall or Building

(or how to estimate how many bricks will be needed for a project)

RULE

■ Multiply the length of the wall in feet by its height in feet, and that by its thickness in feet, and then multiply that result by 20. The answer will be the number of bricks in the wall.

EXAMPLE

■ 30 feet (length) x 20 feet (height) x 1½ feet (thickness) = 900 x 20 = 18,000 bricks

Average Velocity Table

- A human walks 3 miles per hour, or 4 feet per second.
- A human on a bicycle can travel from 20 to 30 miles per hour.
- A horse trots 7 miles per hour, or 10 feet per second.
- A horse runs 20 miles per hour, or 29 feet per second.
- A snail travels 40 feet per hour.
- A sailing boat moves at 10 miles per hour, or 14 feet per second.
- Carrier pigeons fly 35 to 40 miles per hour.
- Slow rivers flow 3 miles per hour, or 4 feet per second.
- A typical raindrop in still air falls about 7 miles per hour, or 10 feet per second.
- A moderate wind blows at 7 miles per hour, or 10 feet per second.
- A storm moves at 36 miles per hour, or 52 feet per second.
- Sound travels at 760 miles per hour.
- Light travels at 186,282 miles per second.
- Electricity travels 1 foot per nanosecond (a billionth of a second).

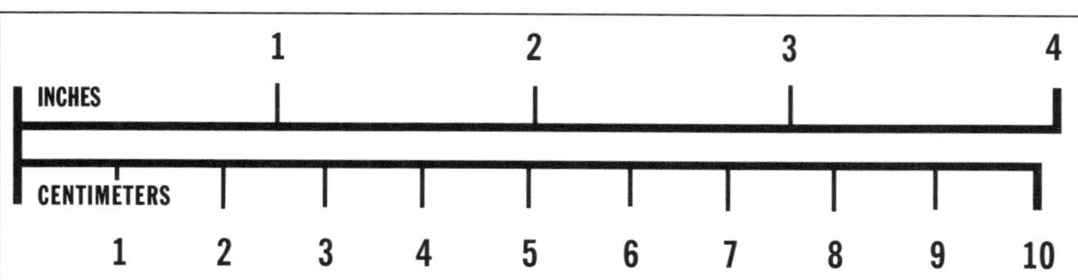

Makeshift Measurers

When you don't have a measuring stick or tape, use what is at hand. To this list, add any other items that you always (or nearly always) have handy.

Credit card: 3-3/8" x 2-1/8"
Business card (standard): 3-1/2" x 2"
Floor tile: 12" square
Dollar bill: 6-1/8" x 2-5/8"
Quarter (diameter): 1"
Penny (diameter): 3/4"
Sheet of paper: 8-1/2" x 11"
(legal size: 8-1/2" x 14")

Your foot/shoe: ______________
Your outstretched arms, fingertip to fingertip: ______________
Your shoelace: ______________
Your necktie: ______________
Your belt: ______________

Guide to Lumber and Nails

Lumber Width and Thickness in Inches

NOMINAL SIZE	ACTUAL SIZE Dry or Seasoned
1 x 3	¾ x 2½
1 x 4	¾ x 3½
1 x 6	¾ x 5½
1 x 8	¾ x 7¼
1 x 10	¾ x 9¼
1 x 12	¾ x 11¼
2 x 3	1½ x 2½
2 x 4	1½ x 3½
2 x 6	1½ x 5½
2 x 8	1½ x 7¼
2 x 10	1½ x 9¼
2 x 12	1½ x 11¼

Nail Sizes

The nail on the left is a 5d (penny) finish nail; on the right, 20d common. The numerals below the nail sizes indicate the approximate number of common nails per pound.

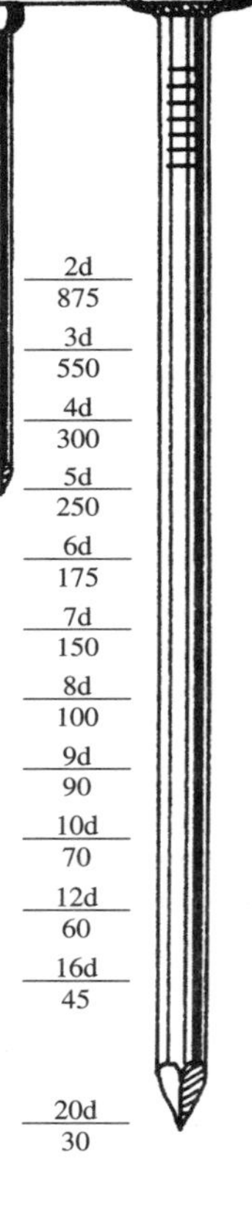

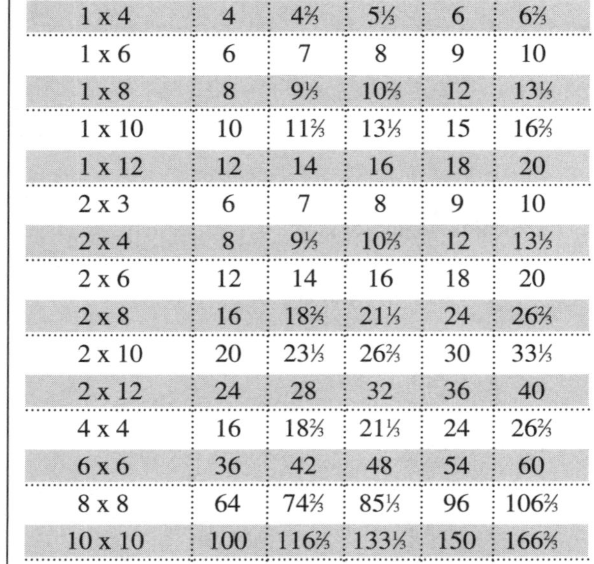

Lumber Measure in Board Feet

LENGTH Size in Inches	12 ft.	14 ft.	16 ft.	18 ft.	20 ft.
1 x 4	4	4⅔	5⅓	6	6⅔
1 x 6	6	7	8	9	10
1 x 8	8	9⅓	10⅔	12	13⅓
1 x 10	10	11⅔	13⅓	15	16⅔
1 x 12	12	14	16	18	20
2 x 3	6	7	8	9	10
2 x 4	8	9⅓	10⅔	12	13⅓
2 x 6	12	14	16	18	20
2 x 8	16	18⅔	21⅓	24	26⅔
2 x 10	20	23⅓	26⅔	30	33⅓
2 x 12	24	28	32	36	40
4 x 4	16	18⅔	21⅓	24	26⅔
6 x 6	36	42	48	54	60
8 x 8	64	74⅔	85⅓	96	106⅔
10 x 10	100	116⅔	133⅓	150	166⅔
12 x 12	144	168	192	216	240

Homeowner's Tool Kit

THE ESSENTIALS

Butt chisel
Putty knife
Adjustable wrench
Slip-joint pliers
Needle-nose pliers
Block plane
Four-in-one rasp
Hacksaw
Crosscut saw
Retractable steel ruler
Drain auger
C-clamp
Nail set
Curved-claw hammer
Push drill and drill point
3 standard screwdrivers (3 sizes)
2 Phillips screwdrivers (2 sizes)
Combination square
Level
Utility knife
Toilet plunger
Screws and nails

OTHER SUPPLIES

Machine oil
Penetrating lubricant
Pencils
Bolts and nuts, hollow-wall fasteners, etc.
Adhesives
Sandpaper and steel wool
Sharpening stone
Wire brush
Paintbrushes
Dustpan and brush
Lint-free rags or cheesecloth
Clip-on light
Grounded extension cord
Single-edge razor blades with holder
Scissors
Toolbox
Stepladder

Prescription-ese

Abbreviation	Latin	Meaning
ac	ante cibum	before meals
ad lib	ad libitum	at pleasure
bid	bis in die	twice a day
cum	cum	with
disp #50		pharmacist should dispense 50 pills
et	et	and
gtt	guttae	drops
hs	hora somni	at bedtime
npo	nihil per os	nothing by mouth
pc	post cibum	after meals
po	per os	by mouth
prn	pro re nata	as needed
qd	quaque die	every day
qh	quaque hora	every hour
qid	quater in die	four times a day
Rx	recipe	take
semis	semis	a half
Sig	signetur	let it be labeled
sine	sine	without
stat	statim	immediately
tid	ter in die	three times a day

How Much Paint Will You Need?

Estimate your room size and paint needs before you go to the store. Running out of a custom color halfway through the job could mean disaster. For the sake of the following exercise, assume you have a 10x15-foot room with an 8-foot ceiling. The room has two doors and two windows.

FOR WALLS

■ Measure the total distance (perimeter) around the room:

(10 ft. + 15 ft.) x 2 = 50 ft.

■ Multiply the perimeter by the ceiling height to get the total wall area:

50 ft. x 8 ft. = 400 sq. ft.

■ Doors are usually 21 square feet (there are two in this exercise):

21 sq. ft. x 2 = 42 sq. ft.

■ Windows average 15 square feet (there are two in this exercise):

15 sq. ft. x 2 = 30 sq. ft.

■ Take the total wall area and subtract the area for the doors and windows to get the wall surface to be painted:

400 sq. ft. (wall area)
– 42 sq. ft. (doors)
– 30 sq. ft. (windows)

328 sq. ft.

■ As a rule of thumb, one gallon of quality paint will usually cover 400 square feet. One quart will cover 100 square feet. Since you need to cover 328 square feet in this example, one gallon will be adequate to give one coat of paint to the walls. (Coverage will be affected by the porosity and texture of the surface. In addition, bright colors may require a minimum of two coats.)

FOR CEILINGS

■ Using the rule of thumb for coverage above, you can calculate the quantity of paint needed for the ceiling by multiplying the width by the length:

10 ft. x 15 ft. = 150 sq. ft.

This ceiling will require approximately two quarts of paint. (A flat finish is recommended to minimize surface imperfections.)

FOR DOORS, WINDOWS, AND TRIM

■ The area for the doors and windows has been calculated above. Determine the baseboard trim by taking the perimeter of the room, less 3 feet per door (3 ft. x 2 = 6 ft.), and multiplying this by the average trim width of your baseboard, which in this example is 6 inches (or 0.5 feet).

50 ft. (perimeter) - 6 ft. = 44 ft.
44 ft. x 0.5 ft. = 22 sq. ft.

■ Add the area for doors, windows, and baseboard trim.

42 sq. ft. (doors)
+30 sq. ft. (windows)
+22 sq. ft. (baseboard trim)

94 sq. ft.

One quart will probably be sufficient to cover the doors, windows, and trim in this example.

– courtesy M.A.B. Paints

United States Paper Currency

Currency	Portrait	Reverse
One-dollar bill	George Washington	Great Seal of the United States
Two-dollar bill	Thomas Jefferson	Declaration of Independence
Five-dollar bill	Abraham Lincoln	Lincoln Memorial
Ten-dollar bill	Alexander Hamilton	U.S. Treasury Building
Twenty-dollar bill	Andrew Jackson	White House
Fifty-dollar billl	Ulysses Grant	U.S. Capitol
One-hundred-dollar bill	Benjamin Franklin	Independence Hall
Five-hundred-dollar bill *	William McKinley	$500
One-thousand-dollar bill *	Grover Cleveland	ONE THOUSAND DOLLARS
Five-thousand-dollar bill *	James Madison	$5,000
Ten-thousand-dollar bill *	Salmon P. Chase	$10,000

* No longer printed and being withdrawn from circulation

Did you know that until 1929 our currency measured 7.42 x 3.13 inches? Since then, U.S. paper currency has measured 6.14 x 2.61 inches — an easier size to handle and store.

U.S. Department of the Treasury

Decibels

Decibels (dB) are used to measure the loudness or intensity of sounds. One decibel is the smallest difference between sounds detectable by the human ear. Intensity varies exponentially: A 20-dB sound is 10 times louder than a 10-dB sound; a 30-dB sound is 100 times louder than a 10-dB sound; a 40-dB sound is 1,000 times louder than a 10-dB sound; and so on. A 120-dB sound is painful.

DECIBELS	COMPARABLE SOUND
10	Light whisper
20	Quiet conversation
30	Normal conversation
40	Light traffic
50	Typewriter, loud conversation
60	Noisy office
70	Normal traffic, quiet train
80	Rock music, subway
90	Heavy traffic, thunder
100	Jet plane at takeoff

Dogs: Gentle, Fierce, Smart, Popular

GENTLEST BREEDS

Golden retriever
Labrador retriever
Shetland sheepdog
Old English sheepdog
Welsh terrier
Yorkshire terrier
Beagle
Dalmatian
Pointer

FIERCEST BREEDS

Pit bull
German shepherd
Husky
Malamute
Doberman pinscher
Rottweiler
Great Dane
Saint Bernard

SMARTEST BREEDS

Border collie
Poodle
German shepherd (Alsatian)
Golden retriever
Doberman pinscher
Shetland sheepdog
Labrador retriever
Papillon
Rottweiler
Australian cattle dog

MOST POPULAR BREEDS

Labrador retriever
Rottweiler
Cocker spaniel
German shepherd
Poodle
Golden retriever
Beagle
Dachshund
Shetland sheepdog
Chow chow

Don't Poison Your Pussycat!

Certain common houseplants are poisonous to cats. They should not be allowed to eat the following:

- ***Caladium*** **(elephant's ears)**
- ***Nerium oleander*** **(oleander)**
- ***Dieffenbachia*** **(dumb cane)**
- ***Philodendron*** **(philodendron)**
- ***Euphorbia pulcherrima*** **(poinsettia)**
- ***Prunus laurocerasus*** **(common or cherry laurel)**
- ***Hedera*** **(true ivy)**
- ***Rhododendron*** **(azalea)**
- ***Solanum capiscastrum*** **(winter or false Jerusalem cherry)**
- ***Ficus deltoidea*** **(mistletoe)**

How Old Is Your Dog?

Multiplying your dog's age by seven is easy, but it doesn't always hold true. The more carefully graded system below has the human equivalency years piled onto a dog's life more quickly during the dog's rapid growth to maturity, after which each year for a dog becomes the equivalent of four human years, and after age 13 it slows down to 2½ years.

Dog Age (years)	Equivalent Human Age (years)	Dog Age (years)	Equivalent Human Age (years)
½	10	15	73
1	15	16	75½
2	24	17	78
3	28	18	80½
4	32	19	83
5	36	20	85½
6	40	21	88
7	44	22	90½
8	48	23	93
9	52	24	95½
10	56	25	98
11	60	26	100½
12	64	27	103
13	68	28	105½
14	70½	29	108

Ten Most Intelligent Animals

(besides humans)

According to Edward O. Wilson, behavioral biologist, professor of zoology, Harvard University, they are:

1. **Chimpanzee (two species)**
2. **Gorilla**
3. **Orangutan**
4. **Baboon (seven species, including drill and mandrill)**
5. **Gibbon (seven species)**
6. **Monkey (many species, especially the macaques, the patas, and the Celebes black ape)**
7. **Smaller toothed whale (several species, especially killer whale)**
8. **Dolphin (many of the approximately 80 species)**
9. **Elephant (two species)**
10. **Pig**

For the Birds

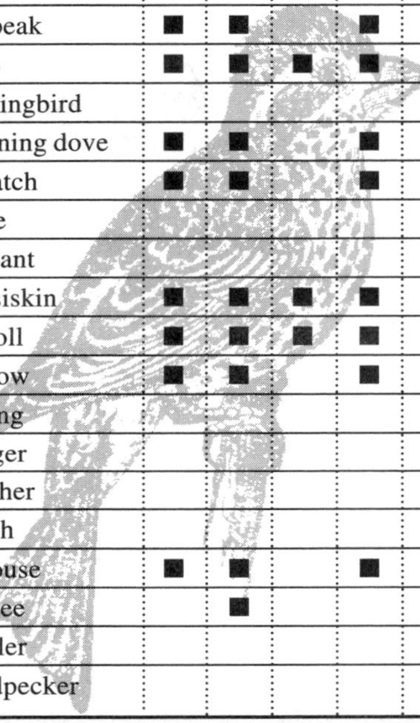

	Sunflower seeds	Millet (white proso)	Niger (thistle seeds)	Safflower seeds	Corn, cracked	Corn, whole	Peanuts	Peanut butter	Suet	Raisins	Apples	Oranges and grapefruit
Blue jay	■			■	■	■	■			■		
Bunting	■	■	■	■	■							
Cardinal	■	■		■	■					■	■	■
Catbird										■	■	■
Cedar waxwing											■	■
Chickadee	■	■		■	■		■	■	■			
Cowbird		■										
Crossbill	■	■		■				■				
Duck		■			■	■						
Finch	■	■	■	■	■		■	■				■
Flicker							■	■	■			
Goldfinch	■		■									
Goose					■	■						
Grackle	■											
Grosbeak	■	■		■			■			■	■	■
Junco	■	■	■	■	■							
Mockingbird										■	■	
Mourning dove	■	■		■	■	■	■					
Nuthatch	■	■		■			■	■	■			
Oriole												■
Pheasant					■							
Pine siskin	■	■	■	■			■			■		■
Redpoll	■	■	■	■								
Sparrow	■	■		■	■		■					
Starling					■							
Tanager												■
Thrasher					■		■			■	■	
Thrush										■	■	
Titmouse	■	■		■	■		■	■	■			
Towhee		■										
Warbler							■					■
Woodpecker							■	■	■			

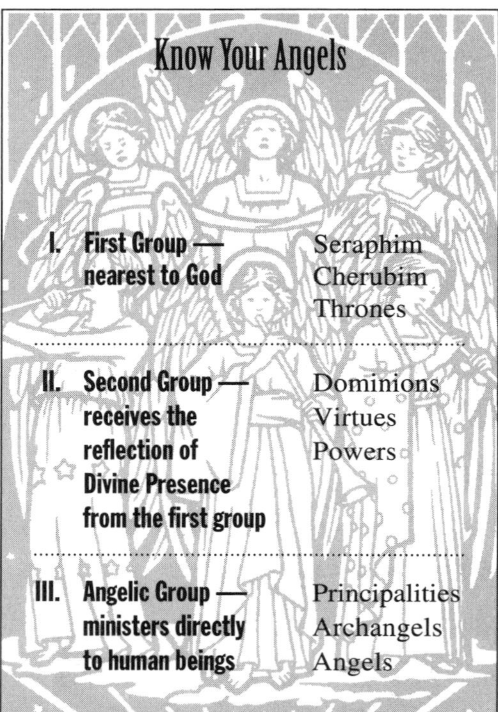

Know Your Angels

I.	**First Group — nearest to God**	Seraphim Cherubim Thrones
II.	**Second Group — receives the reflection of Divine Presence from the first group**	Dominions Virtues Powers
III.	**Angelic Group — ministers directly to human beings**	Principalities Archangels Angels

Animals in the Bible (KJV)

In addition to the following list of references to specific animals, there are numerous general references: beast (337), cattle (153), fowl (90), fish (56), bird (54), and serpent (53).

Animal	Old Testament	New Testament	Total
Sheep	155	45	200
Lamb	153	35	188
Ox	156	10	166
Ram	165	0	165
Lion	145	9	154
Horse	137	16	153
Bullock	152	0	152
Ass	142	9	151
Goat	127	7	134
Camel	56	6	62

The Golden Rule

(It's true in all faiths.)

BRAHMANISM:
This is the sum of duty: Do naught unto others which would cause you pain if done to you.
Mahabharata 5:1517

BUDDHISM:
Hurt not others in ways that you yourself would find hurtful.
Udana-Varga 5:18

CONFUCIANISM:
Surely it is the maxim of loving-kindness: Do not unto others what you would not have them do unto you. *Analects 15:23*

TAOISM:
Regard your neighbor's gain as your own gain and your neighbor's loss as your own loss.
T'ai Shang Kan Ying P'ien

ZOROASTRIANISM:
That nature alone is good which refrains from doing unto another whatsoever is not good for itself.
Dadistan-i-dinik 94:5

JUDAISM:
What is hateful to you, do not to your fellowman. That is the entire Law; all the rest is commentary.
Talmud, Shabbat 31a

CHRISTIANITY:
All things whatsoever ye would that men should do to you, do ye even so to them; for this is the law and the prophets.
Matthew 7:12

ISLAM:
No one of you is a believer until he desires for his brother that which he desires for himself.
Sunnah

– courtesy Elizabeth Pool